GOD'S
VERY
OWN
PEOPLE

D0817283

GOD'S VERY OWN PEOPLE

Keswick Ministry

Stuart Briscoe, Donald English, Philip Hacking, David Jackman, and others

Edited by
David Porter & Anthea Cousins

STL Books

PO Box 48, Bromley, Kent, England
PO Box 28, Waynesboro, Georgia, USA
PO Box 656, Bombay 1, India

Keswick Convention Council, England

STL Books are published by Send The Light (Operation Mobilisation), PO Box 48, Bromley, Kent, England.

ISBN 0 903843 93 5

Cover printed by Penderel Press Ltd, Croydon, Surrey.

Made and printed in Great Britain by
Hunt Barnard Printing Ltd, Aylesbury, Bucks.

CONTENTS

Introduction: Canon A S Neech   7

Editor's Introduction   9

The Bible Readings

A Warm Heart and Humble Mind (1 Peter)
Dr Donald English

1. Initiative and Response (1:1-2:3)   15
2. Grace and Integrity (2:4-3:7)   30
3. Goodness and Love (3:8-4:11)   45
4. Suffering and Glory (4:12-5:14)   60

God's Very Own People (Titus)
Rev Stuart Briscoe

1. Identifying and Overseeing (1:1-9)   77
2. Protecting and Training (1:10-2:10)   92
3. Purifying and Reminding (2:11-3:5)   106
4. Motivating and Warning (3:5-15)   121

The Addresses

Coming to Christ
Rev David Jackman   139

Drinking Is Believing
Rev Richard Bewes   148

Fullness of Life in Christ
Canon Keith Weston   157

The Helper from Heaven
Rev Gottfried Osei-Mensah   165

The Enabling Power of the Holy Spirit
Rev David Jackman   174

Holiness – Pitfalls and Errors
Rev Gervais Angel   183

Finished and Unfinished
Rev Philip Hacking   190

How To Avoid a Wasted Life
Rev Stuart Briscoe   200

A Commitment to the King
Rev Ian Barclay   209

Chosen, Called and Faithful
Dr Donald English   217

The Fruit of the Spirit Is Joy
Rev Stuart Briscoe   224

The Fruit of the Spirit Is Peace
Rev Stuart Briscoe   233

The Fruit of the Spirit Is Patience
Rev Stuart Briscoe   243

Keswick 1984 Tapes   251

Keswick 1985   252

INTRODUCTION

by Canon Alan S Neech
(Chairman of the Keswick Council)

The Conventions this year had a particular relevance to the church in Britain. Some were there who had recently found Christ at the great Mission England Billy Graham meetings. Anfield Stadium in Liverpool was crowded every night of Keswick's first week. The reports of those meetings given in the second week was one of the high points in a fortnight of mountain-top experiences.

Some of the addresses in this little book refer to what God has done in Britain in 1984 and convey something of the atmosphere of this year's meetings. There was a sense of thanksgiving for what had happened, an eager expectation of what could happen. Many had been involved in large-scale evangelism. Hundreds had recent experiences of answered prayer for the salvation of others. There was a renewed awareness of the power of the gospel. All of this brought people together with high hopes and a sense of urgency.

The continuing industrial disputes and the increasing social and moral problems of the country clamoured for attention. Only God could give lasting help. Perhaps this is one reason why there was more response at the evangelistic meetings in the open air than for several years.

As usual, both sets of Bible Readings were outstanding. It is right that the major part of the book is given to them. They alone make the book worth reading many times over. First Peter and Titus came alive for thousands at Keswick. They will for you too.

Space permits only a selection of the other addresses, and very abbreviated versions at that. But here too you will find biblical, relevant, helpful preaching. Give a copy of this book to someone else so that they too can discover what it means to be one of 'God's very own people' today.

EDITOR'S INTRODUCTION

The editors of the 1982 and 1983 Keswick reports have joined forces for this volume; the Bible Readings have been edited by David Porter and the Addresses by Anthea Cousins. As in previous years we are both extremely grateful for the opportunity to work on this material, and for the assistance we have had from the Keswick Council and the publishers.

One or two editorial matters should be mentioned. Firstly, the material in this book has found its way into print by way of tapes, transcribed by a small army of volunteer transcribers who did an excellent job against a very tight deadline; these transcripts were then used as the basis for producing this abridged and edited version which we believe includes all the meat of the speakers' comments. Readers should bear in mind that the speakers have all, as usual, graciously waived the right to inspect the edited versions of their contributions, in order to make it possible to publish as soon after the convention as possible. The book should be seen, therefore, as a carefully edited transcript of spoken addresses given at a particular convention. It should be added that the book is produced in close liaison with the Keswick Council and its representatives.

Secondly, we would repeat the customary advice that you should read this book with an open Bible on hand. In the Bible Readings, every Bible reference has been retained, but we have often been unable to quote them in their entirety for reasons of space. Often, just as the speakers did, we have merely provided the reference for you to look up. This has enabled us to include more of the teaching from the convention. (Perhaps I might add that I believe that actually looking up every reference – whether quoted in full or not – doubles the value of reading any book about the Bible.)

Thirdly, we have checked biblical references for accuracy where possible, but where a speaker has been paraphrasing to make a point we have not adjusted the text. As in previous years transliteration of Greek words is standardised according to Vine's *Expository Dictionary*, which is an editorial choice for convenience; references may have been in another form in the speakers' notes.

Fourthly, connoisseurs of Keswick humour and apt illustration will want to make use of the excellent tape library mentioned on p. 251 to explore all the good things that had to be edited out for reasons of space. From the same source you will be able to obtain a recording of any and every convention address apart from those included in this book.

This is the sixth Keswick report I have been involved in, and in each I have enjoyed the warm interest and support of Canon Alan Neech. As he relinquishes the demands of the Chairmanship of the Keswick Convention Council, the editorial team joins its good wishes with those of the rest of the Keswick movement. Our prayers will also be with the Rev Philip Hacking as he takes on this responsibility.

Finally, it should be an encouragement to all of us that in George Orwell's year of years 1984, the insistent theme of the convention was the massive evangelistic enterprises of this summer, to which even Big Brother the Media gave sympathetic hearing and an unprecedented amount of air time.

David Porter

THE BIBLE READINGS

A WARM HEART AND HUMBLE MIND

by Dr Donald English

1. Initiative and Response
(1 Peter 1:1-2:3)

I am very grateful indeed for your welcome. I do want us to feel that these studies are times when God is speaking to each of us directly, and I want you to be free to be led by God as He wishes to lead you, and to feel that you can take as much or as little of what I say as seems right for you.

Now I begin with 1 Peter 5:12, because there Peter says why he wrote this particular letter. I want to spend a moment or two on that verse because we need to understand what the purpose of his letter is.

The purpose of the letter

First of all, it is a letter of encouragement. The word Peter uses is *parakaleo* – encouragement 'from behind'. It means 'I am giving you reasons for going on – reasons for keeping on the Christian way.' And therefore the encouragement is given by way of *testimony* – 'This is the true grace of God.' This is the only time in the New Testament that this particular word is used, and in classical Greek you'll find it means 'to confirm a fact by evidence'.

I believe that this is something we need to ponder very carefully.

Testimony does not *make* the truth true; it confirms what *is* true. I underline that very seriously, because I believe we are reaching a stage in some branches of Christian thinking where a thing is held to be true 'because I experience it', and the more deeply I experience it the more true it is. The fact of the matter is that God is true whether I experience it or not; and there are all sorts of evil things that people experience, and the feeling of experience does not make them true.

All our experiences and all our testimonies need testing by the truth; and the truth is given in the objective Word of God. I fear a form of Christianity which is so experience-centred that it misses the truth. Peter is saying 'I write to encourage you to send you ahead by testifying to the truth.' And what is the truth? 'The true grace of God.' If it were not for that, there would be nothing to testify to.

Let us not mistake our experience for the grace of God; let us pray that our experience will *result* from the grace of God and testify to it. That is the aim of this letter; to encourage, by testifying to the true grace of God.

The origins of the letter

I believe that the apostle Peter wrote this letter, chiefly because of the relevance of what is written here to what is in Mark's Gospel, and I am sure that Peter stands behind Mark's Gospel. The content of 1 Peter is also closely related to the speeches of Peter in Acts. Many of the themes of the letter are true to the experience of Peter as we know him.

The scribe, I think, was probably Silvanus (sometimes known as Silas), and this would be the reason why the style is rather more polished than we might expect from Peter; the amenuensis, as he was called, had in New Testament times the freedom to present his text in a stylistically correct way.

I think the date is in the early '60s and that the persecution referred to is that leading up to Nero's persecution of the Roman Christians. It may well be that the note of urgency in 1 Peter 4:12 refers to the execution of the beloved Paul, and that Peter realised that he was writing to Christians who were literally going to pass through the fires.

I think that the recipients were in those areas of Asia Minor unevangelised by Paul. I owe this idea to Andrew Wall's very good commentary. Acts 16:6, 7 describes a particular moment when Paul was in Asia Minor, prevented from going to Bithynia. I believe that that may have been where Peter was ministering, and so the letter was written to those personally ministered to by Peter.

The sequence of place names in 1:1 simply reflects a journey – it follows a natural progress; and I think Peter wrote from Rome (5:13 refers to 'Babylon', which we know – from Revelation 14:8 and 17:5 – was the common name for the strength and threat which was Rome).

The greeting (1:1, 2)

Now let us turn to the text. You will know that it was typical in the first century to begin letters with a greeting. This is no ordinary greeting, however, and I want to draw your attention to one particular characteristic of it: there are actually two levels of description involved.

One level might be called the level of the newspaper report. That is, the description of things which would be obvious to everybody – names, places, well-known facts that anybody could see. But there is another level, which uses words like 'apostle', 'elect', 'for obedience', and then that lovely section which talks of the foreknowledge of God the Father. These are not so obvious, they are not the things that would appear in a newspaper account of what was going on in the early church. This is so typical of the way in which Peter himself operates. You can see this double level of factual statement and hidden truth working strikingly in that marvellous speech of Acts 2:22.

I underline this because I believe that the most significant thing about being a Christian is the ability to operate at these two levels. We begin when we look at the account of our Lord Jesus Christ; and by the gift of faith we perceive that He is the Son of God, that His life and death and resurrection and the hope of His coming are all the heart of new life for us. This only comes by perception of faith; and I believe that we Christians need to go an awfully long way down this line. This is why Jesus used parables. When He told them He touched ordinary things and they became the very windows of heaven. I believe that the gift of faith-perception of what is hidden (but more real than that which is evident) is the supreme gift of God to His people. As Christians, we need to exercise it in relation to world events, national events and the events of our own lives. There is much more to life than what is apparent, and the clue to it is what God has done in Jesus Christ. Peter is saying, 'My brothers and sisters, you are going to go through great persecution' – only don't be misled by what you see, see beneath it and above it and around it the grace of God which is operating. And the reason we have this knowledge is to be found in verse 2: the foreknowledge of God the Father, by the sanctifying work of the Spirit, obedience to Jesus Christ and sprinkling by His blood.

These are three great moments in our salvation – not always the three we choose when describing it. And the first moment in our salvation is the foreknowledge of God Himself. There is a line right back from every convert, to the foreknowledge of God. It is no coincidence. We do not become Christians by our own effort. We are set apart by the Spirit because God has foreknown us; and whom the Spirit is setting apart, the blood of Jesus sprinkles and cleanses. I think that Exodus 24:3-8 is in Peter's mind here. Do you remember the blood of the Covenant, God's promise of Himself? Maybe also behind this is Exodus 29:19-21 – the consecration of Aaron and his sons for a particular kind of service. When you came to Christ, says Peter, you started in the foreknowledge of God. You are an idea in the mind of God. His covenant with you, His promise to you, may never be forgotten; and whatever He calls you to do may constantly be reinforced and restated. What a marvellous thing! What we are, we are because of what God is. Therefore the greeting ends naturally, 'Grace and peace be yours in abundance.'

Grace is love in action. Peace comes from the Hebrew *shalom* – a state of well-being. Peter says, may they be yours in abundance.

The divine initiative (1:3-9)

The whole point of the encouragement being given is that God has done for Christians all that they need, even when they pass through the fires of persecution.

Verse 3 is the backward look, the look that says 'My word, look how far we have come already!' It begins with thanks because when you are dealing with God that's the first and most natural thing to do.

The Jews had two typical greetings which praised God;

one praised Him for being God, and the other praised Him for a particular gift. Peter takes that Jewish greeting but changes it dramatically. Christians are what they are because of Jesus Christ, and that is the only basis on which we can enter into discussion with any other group. If we are not Christocentric, we are nothing as Christians. Peter takes the Jewish greeting, he establishes the link with Israelite history; but he says 'Let's get it clear; the God of creation, of Israel, is to us the God and Father of our Lord Jesus Christ.'

As he looks back he wants to describe what God has done for us.

The backward look (1:3)
'By his great mercy' – repeatedly in the New Testament the word 'mercy' is used of God's reception of outsiders. It's the word that comes most naturally to the writers and speakers when describing God's going out to the unworthy. Thus shepherds hear the story of Jesus' birth, the Magi outsiders bring gifts, Jesus goes to publicans, Zacchaeus is picked from a tree, and mercy goes to those who are not accepted or respectable.

It's mercy. Peter says 'We too have experienced that mercy.' Look at Titus 3:5 – 'He saved us not because of righteous things we have done but because of his mercy' – and what have we received? 'New birth'. The word used describes any dramatic change in nature, history or experience, and here Peter says we are looking back to that dramatic change which our Lord called 'new birth'. We look back to that time (though we may not have perceived the exact moment) when God by His Holy Spirit caused us to be born again.

There is no alternative. You will remember that one day a lady asked George Whitefield at the end of one of his meetings: 'Mr Whitefield, why do you preach so much on "Ye must be born again"?'

'Because, Madam,' replied Whitefield, 'ye *must* be born again.'

As you look back, never forget that enormous gift, born 'into a living hope'. That is not the same sort of thing as the hope that it will be fine on your wedding day. It's more like the hope that the bride will come to your wedding day! In England there's no guarantee of the former, but all the evidence is there that the latter will be true. It is simply an unaccomplished fact which we all know will take place; and that's what hope is all about.

In the words of a South American theologian, Rubem Alves, Christians should be 'incorrigible dreamers'. The trouble, he says, is that our society lacks dreamers; it is controlled by the realists, the politicians, the soldiers, the economists who keep urging us to be 'realistic'. Like the short-legged dinosaur which perished because it couldn't move fast enough, our culture, says Alves, is slowing down; and it desperately needs dreamers who can keep saying 'Ah, yes; *but*, in the kingdom of heaven . . .' – that's what we were born again to, to be given the 'living hope'.

The purpose and the reason we talk like this is 'the resurrection of Jesus Christ from the dead'. Let me say first, that it is of course theologically and philosophically possible that what God was communicating to the world is that the most important thing to understand about Jesus is 'resurrection' – the concept. But this is not the way that the God of the Bible works, for He again and again does something in history and then explains it; the only reason we listen to the explanation is that He has done something in history. So it is, I believe with the resurrection of Jesus Christ from the dead. The God of the Bible would not declare 'resurrection' without declaring '*the* resurrection'.

How else do you get to an understanding of what God is like, unless He reveals Himself in history and then explains it to us? It is because we believe He rose bodily from the grave that we believe we will rise on the resurrection day, and it's that which gives us living hope when people say life is meaningless. The heart of God's Word into His world is the death and resurrection of Jesus Christ. I dare to hope for the future because God raised Jesus from the dead.

The great thing about the resurrection is that we are gathered into it, so that we experience it for ourselves. When I hear people talk about 'resurrection' and not 'the resurrection', I sometimes wonder whether they know *the* resurrection at all. To believe in the death and resurrection of Jesus is to be incorporated into it. The New Testament doesn't say 'Believe in the death of Jesus'; it says 'Carry your cross', it says 'Be buried with Him'. It doesn't say 'Believe in the resurrection', it says 'Be raised with Him'; and once you have experienced resurrection, it's not difficult to believe in it. As long as you are linked up. That's what we look back to.

The forward look (1:4)

What do we look forward to? An inheritance. The dominant theme of inheritance in the Bible is that of inheriting what you have not worked for yourself. It's given, it can't be taken away, and you and I in the midst of our trials and perplexities know that one day we will be in heaven with the Lord Jesus Christ. No more sorrowing, no more sighing, no more pain, no more inadequate perceptions, no more struggling through tears and difficulty and failure and sin. It is kept in heaven for us. Not even inflation can touch it! It's ready for us. My brothers and sisters, keep your hearts up, as you march towards glory.

The look around (1:5-9)

The first thing that Peter wants to assure those who will be going through all kinds of difficulties is, that they will be kept. They are guarded by power — the word means 'garrisoned'.

I sometimes wonder whether you and I worry too much about surviving. Perhaps we need to realise more that we will survive. God will keep us, and we don't have to worry about that. Maybe if we spent less time on worrying and more on serving, we would do better. There are too many Christians, I think, who are like my friend who owned a car; he spent more time under it than in it. He was too busy taking it to pieces and putting it back together again. My brothers and sisters, you will be guarded. You will be kept. Stop worrying; you are guarded by resurrection power — what more do you want? Trust it, launch out on it, serve the Lord in it and stop being so self-centred about your survival. If you keep on taking your radio to pieces, you will never hear any programmes at all.

Verse 6: 'Though now for a little while you may have had to suffer grief.' That's a very careful translation, for the word 'may' means something which makes an inevitability of it. Suffering is part of the Christian passage. We don't have to look for it, but it will happen to us, and I believe that what Peter is saying here is abundantly true for all of us. None of us want suffering or pain. But it remains true that it is in suffering that we discover more deeply what the gospel is about.

There is an irony in verse 7, because many of the people in this church were probably slaves. Imagine slaves, thinking of silver and gold — and Peter saying to them, 'Your faith is of greater worth.'

And then, verse 8, we come to the four guy-ropes of the tent of Christian experience (if I may be relevant to

Keswick!): love, believe, rejoice, receive. I believe Christians who hold up their tent on these won't go far wrong. Those of you who are campers will know that if you put too much tension on any one guy-rope, the whole tent begins to look a little lopsided. My brothers and sisters, pray that you will love more deeply, that you will believe more completely, that you will rejoice more whole-heartedly, and that you will receive everything that God has to offer.

They are the great key notes (to change the analogy) of the music of the gospel. Pray God to give you more of those.

The divine preparation (1:10-12)

We need not spend long here. I simply want to point out that the Christians in the New Testament constantly claimed that they were in a straight line with that which God had done in the Old Testament. It's a reminder of how carefully and patiently God makes His preparations. I sometimes wonder whether we are a little too impatient. How *long* God waited before the coming of Jesus! How those prophets searched and said, 'Lord, may it not come now?' And God was saying, 'No; we are not ready yet.' You can only wait. Even the prophets were content to play only a limited part – how many must have wanted to complete the whole work in their lifetime! But God kept saying, 'No – you have a part to play, but it's not all. Be patient.' How marvellous that He did it! The gospel is the climax of God's work in history. He worked so long for it. And the coming of Jesus is the turning-point of the Christian gospel. As Charles Wesley wrote:

> Emptied of His majesty,
> Of His dazzling glories shorn,
> Being's Source begins to be,
> And God Himself is born.

That's what God was working to through history until Jesus was born; and that's what He has been working from ever since. And you and I have the privilege of knowing that Jesus.

The appropriate response (1:13-2:3)

Peter has told us what God has done; now we come to 'therefore'. Whenever you come to 'therefore' in the Bible, look out! Whatever the translation you are using, the meaning is: 'I have told you what God has done; now I am going to tell you the appropriate response.' There is nothing more logical in the world than to be a Christian. If God through Jesus Christ has given Himself to us, what is more logical than to give our whole selves back to Him?

Now, the great truths of what God has done are meant to serve like marker buoys in a river. You need to know them, to understand them, in order that you might sail on the great ocean of God's love. If you ignore the marker buoys you will never reach the ocean. But don't spend your time going up and down the river making sure they are exactly in place, when the ocean of God's love is waiting for you.

In telling us what is involved, Peter sets out eight great principles.

Hard thinking (1:13)

If I may use my Anglican brethren as illustration, the picture here is of the robed Vicar riding a bicycle – he tucks up his cassock into his belt so he can ride. That's the exact meaning of what Peter's asking us to do with our minds. Or you could think of those posters you sometimes see displayed in offices – 'Don't operate mouth until mind is in gear.'

The great thing about the Christian faith, my brothers and sisters, is that it's true; and therefore you need your mind to understand the truth. I worry about forms of Christianity which depend on being bizarre and unlikely and unexpected; the more so, the more sanctity it's supposed to have; but I don't see a God like that in the Bible. I see a God who says, 'What I am is true; what I do is true; what I teach is true. Grasp it in your minds, and let your minds direct the rest. When you have grasped the truth, your faith and your feelings will follow. Neglect the truth at your peril.'

So even to this mixed congregation with many slaves in it, Peter says that the first response is to get your minds in action, think about the faith.

My brothers and sisters, there is a great neglect of Scripture even amongst evangelicals today. There is a great neglect of doctrine amongst us. We prefer the shallow, the exciting; we prefer tapes to books, we prefer something that keeps us on a 'high' all the time. I don't see that as a biblical picture. It's the truth of God that matters more than any other thing; I beg you to notice that. And how do you know who God is, unless you grapple with the truth? We have a great need of Christians who will think more.

Disciplined living (1:13)

The phrase 'be self-controlled' originally meant, 'abstain from wine'. It means to keep yourself under control, not to let yourself get out of hand so that you are an easy prey for the enemy. Christianity is only distinctive when those who understand the truth know how to discipline their lives accordingly. Discipline is an integral part of the Christian life.

Confident hope (1:13)

'Set your hope fully' is the 'aorist' tense – it means 'settle

it now, don't go fiddling on about it.' Sort it out once and
for all. That's the word used here.

Brothers and sisters, set your hope fully on the grace to be
given you when Jesus Christ is revealed. Say to yourself:
'Today my hope is fully built on Jesus Christ and nothing
else.' An old commentator asked a question which I think is
one of the most significant I have ever faced: 'If tomorrow
Jesus Christ were proved beyond shadow of a doubt to be
bankrupt, that His claims were false and that He was not at
all what He claimed to be – how different would your life
be?' I hope your answer is, 'It would be in ruins; because all
my life is fixed on Jesus Christ.' That's what Peter is saying
here.

Obedient living (1:14)

'Obedient children' really means, 'children of obedience'. I
wish that more of us as Christians would grasp this; that it's
one of the great family characteristics of Christians that
once you know what the Lord's will is, you do it. There is
only one question – 'What is the Lord's will?' There is no
second question – 'Shall I do it?'

That is what being a Christian means. But I think, if I
may say in passing, that those of us who are established in
our middle years maybe just need to ask ourselves how far
we are still being obedient to Jesus Christ Himself. I think in
social and political terms of how Jesus went out to the poor,
and showed enormous concern for the deprived and the
displaced. Is there not a need for more and more Christians
to ask whether obedience does not force us to reject the way
our nation is going? Obedient living is a mark of the
Christian, not conformity to present-day culture.

Being holy (1:15, 16)

The origin of the word 'holy' used here is 'cut', and

therefore 'set apart'. The holy, the sanctified people are those who recognise themselves as set apart for God. The reason there are negatives is that there have to be positives. The reason we don't do certain things is that we have been set free to do others.

And you and I have to learn, more deeply I think than many of us *have* learned, that we only pay attention to the negatives because the positives require it. It is easy to value the negatives for their own sake – particularly because of pressure on the group. We are sanctified. We are set apart in order to serve God.

'Aweful attitudes' (1:17-19)

Please note, there is an 'e' in the middle of 'awe-ful'. We are meant to be awed before God.

Slaves would have noticed the reference to judging each man's work in verse 17, and the word 'redeem' in verse 18. The latter was used freely in the Old Testament (for example Exodus 13:13; 21:8, 30; 30:12; Isaiah 40-66). In every case it means the payment of a price on behalf of someone else, to set them free from the implications of the condition they were in. Peter takes that marvellous picture of ransom, and says, 'You were ransomed with the price of the blood of Jesus Christ.' How awesome that is! We are in the area of mystery here.

Heartfelt loving (1:22-25)

That word 'having purified' is in another tense in the Greek. It has the meaning of 'something you do at one point which continues forever more'. It's the perfect tense. It begins at a certain point and goes on happening for ever. A reminder to us, that though there was a moment when we had to be purified, we need to go on being purified.

Spiritual feeding (2:1-3)

Children love food. So what Peter is saying is: 'You have seen children loving their food; you love the Word of the Lord.' But children can eat the wrong things too. Our first son when he was a baby in Nigeria once demolished half a comb! Therefore Peter says, 'Put all wrong things behind. Go for the Word of God which is living and abiding and unperishable, sustain yourself on the Word of God and you will see how God can keep you.' Why?

Because you have tasted that the Lord is good. That's a straight translation from Psalm 34. The interesting thing is that Peter takes an Old Testament text about God and applies it to Jesus. He says, 'You've tasted that the Lord is good – go on tasting.' Go on drinking at the fount, go on feeding from the Word; and whatever persecution comes, you will be kept by the power of God.

Please God that it may be so, for all of us.

2. Grace and Integrity
(1 Peter 2:4-3:7)

We turn today to ask ourselves how we can live at the kind of level we were thinking of in our last study, and we begin with the thought of a living building. In verse 4 the Greek allows either the translation 'As you come to Him' or 'When you come to Him', but the latter – a description – is, I think, more appropriate. As we learned in 1:17, they are coming to their father; you don't need to be instructed to come to your father. And as you do come, says Peter, you are being built into a living household.

However, the word translated 'come' is very interesting, because it's a word which in the Septuagint (the Greek version of the Old Testament) is almost always used in the context of sacrifice. It is most often used of priests coming to God. Peter is doing two things. Firstly he is picking up the Old Testament tradition, as he does again and again in this letter; but secondly, by his choice of language he is reminding us of the context of coming to God.

And that reminds me (as this letter often does) of Romans 12:1, 2, where almost all Paul's words there –

'present', 'holy', 'acceptable', 'sacrifice' – are taken from the environment of the sacrificial system too.

I believe that when New Testament writers address us in this way, what they are saying is something like this. We are no longer tied up in the Old Testament sacrificial system. Jesus Christ has set us free from all that, by offering Himself 'once for all', as the writer to the Hebrews says. He is the 'once for all' sacrifice for our sins; but would we wish to be less careful and precise in making our offering to God than our Old Testament brothers were? Would we not want, if anything, to be *more* so? After all, in the Old Testament you knew on every occasion what to offer, where to offer it, who was to offer it, the words to be used, in whose presence and with what result. There is precision, there is a prescription for every situation. And I believe that in their careful choice of vocabulary the New Testament writers are saying: 'Let's be at least as precise in our offering as our Old Testament forefathers are.'

So I ask, are we not sometimes a bit sloppy about our offering? Do we not often lack that awe, that reverence, that sense of being in a holy place for a holy occasion, when we come to God as Father? Are we as precise about our times for reading the Bible, saying our prayers, for self-examination? When you offer yourself, do you bring your mind and will and emotion and action? Sometimes when I have been sitting in a congregation I ask myself: which part of myself need I not have brought this morning? It's not a bad test for an act of worship.

The people of God (2:4-12)

Come to Him – 'As you come to Him, the living Stone'. In New Testament times there were clearly various collections of sayings in use by preachers and speakers. It's plain that there was such a collection centred on the word 'stone'. It's a good Old Testament picture too, but Peter isn't content to use it just in that sense – he wants it to be a 'living stone', which means that we are talking about Jesus Christ. And he says three things about this 'living stone' which are absolutely fascinating: *'rejected by men'*; *'chosen by God'*; and *'precious to Him'*. There are three great events in the life of our Lord. Rejected by men at the cross, chosen by God in the resurrection (Rom. 1:4), and precious to Him in the ascension, when the Father welcomes His Son back home after the expedition of salvation. Peter says that the living Stone to which you are coming is one who was crucified, rose and ascended.

Look back to Acts 2:22-24 and you will find exactly the same idea. Now this 'hidden perception' of which I have already talked doesn't always mean that what we say merely surprises our culture. Sometimes it directly opposes it. There are times when we simply have to stand up and say, 'You rejected the Son of God; but my Heavenly Father raised Him and took Him home again to Himself.'

A spiritual house (2:5)
So let's notice one or two things of importance in verse 5. First of all,

Believing is not just an academic, intellectual matter. I will never forget the letter which came from an ex-theological student, now in the ministry, which said: 'In college they taught me all about great men and women of prayer; but nobody taught me to pray. They taught me the theories of atonement and the evidence for the resurrection; but nobody taught me how to daily die and rise again with Christ.' What a tragic comment on his training; for the Christian faith is not mere academic, intellectual belief. It means to be gathered into all the experiences of the gospel. We are built into that which we believe.

Neither is it a static matter. We are being built into a living stone. That means growth. The church is an organism, not an organisation. I remember another letter, from a man whom I had been privileged to lead to Christ while he was an undergraduate. 'I would like to ask you – do you love Him as much now as you did when you led me to Him?' I took a while before I answered that letter. Then I wrote back, 'I love Him more.' How easy it is to lose the sense of a *growing* love – but to be gathered into a family means, to grow.

It is not a solitary experience. I have never seen a house built of just one stone. Maybe part of our experience as Christians is to discover that when we choose Him, we choose all the rest of them! Once you have taken Christ you have taken every other Christian. They come in all shapes and sizes. Read Romans 12:5 – 'So in Christ we who are many form one body, and each member belongs to all the others.' Don't assent to this, if what you mean is 'each evangelical member belongs to all the others'. Assent if you mean that each Roman Catholic Christian belongs to all the others, and each Pentecostal Christian, and each house-fellowship Christian – *every* Christian belongs to all the others. That means that they belong to me and I belong to them. I wish we would take that with greater seriousness!

A holy priesthood (2:5)

Now the metaphors are running riot, because the stones have become priests, and all the stones are priests.

The only times that the New Testament speaks of priests and priesthood are either when talking about the Old

Testament system which has passed away, or when it is talking about the priesthood of all believers. Now that doesn't mean that every man is his own priest. It means that there is one priesthood which is all the people of God.

What are our spiritual sacrifices? A life of obedience (Rom. 12:1); praise and thanksgiving (Heb. 13:15); a ministry to the practical needs of men (Heb. 13:16). These are all forms of the spiritual sacrifices which the whole priesthood offers. We can't all do everything, even though some of us feel that we are expected to. We all need one another.

And the test of all service is, are the sacrifices acceptable to God through Jesus Christ? It's a very serious question to ask. I note simply, that it has to do with the fact that since the *events* of Jesus, life has been totally different. The events of Jesus were a very short time in world history, but they have changed everything. 'Through Jesus Christ' means, 'Is what I am offering to God in harmony with what God did in Jesus?' I think it also means the *example* of Jesus – 'Is this consonant with the Spirit of Jesus?' – and the *experience* of Jesus; as we try to offer service sometimes we have an uneasy sense about it because it doesn't quite fit with Him. How important it is to ask these questions!

The living Stone – or a tripping-stone? (2:6-8)
Peter goes on to quote three passages of Scripture, and in each case the passage is about God's relationship with people. In quoting Isaiah 28:16 and Psalm 118:22, Peter is saying that what was said of Israel is now true of Jesus. In the third quotation (Isaiah 8:14), he is saying that what was true of God is now true of Jesus. And the real question raised for us in these quotations is whether Jesus is for us a cornerstone – or a tripping-stone.

What a crucial and decisive question that is! It is like the reply to John the Baptist in Luke 7:23. Do you remember John in prison, wondering why the Captain hasn't got his lieutenant out of prison? He sends a message – 'Are You He who is to come, or shall we look for another?' And Jesus says to the messengers, 'Go and tell John what you have seen and heard' – and then follows a recital of what is happening. At the very end is a 'PS': 'Blessed is he who takes no offence at Me' – Happy is the man who doesn't find Me to be a tripping-stone.

That's what sits at the bottom of all these questions here. Is Jesus foundation-, corner-, cap-stone for us (He is described as all three in Scripture) – or is He tripping-stone? If we are not willing to be the shape He wants us to be, He will be tripping-stone; but the aim of the New Testament faith is (2 Cor. 3:18) that as we fix our eyes on Him, we become like Him.

The mystery of salvation (2:8)
Now we come to one of the most difficult parts of the New Testament, in my opinion; the end of verse 8: 'They stumble because they disobey the message which is also what they were destined for.' My brothers and sisters, we are glimpsing into a divine mystery here. Does it mean that God from before the beginning of time chose those who are to be Christians and therefore by implication chose many that would not? Or does it mean that God's method of making known the gospel was designed so that those who respond are saved and those who do not are lost? Or is there a middle way that holds these two in tension, so that somehow in the experience of each of us is a moment when we hear 'Whoever comes to Me I will not turn away,' and we respond 'Yes, Lord, I come' – but when we go through that door and look on the other side

of it we read: 'You have not chosen Me; but I have chosen you'?

I simply desire, however you solve this question – and I'll come clean for myself in a moment – that you include as much of the biblical teaching as you can get into your conclusions. The real test of our theology is what is left over. We can quote all the texts that prove we've got it right – but it's what we've got down under the table that's the real test!

So I ask you: is it not possible to draw lines which look to your eye absolutely parallel but which will one day meet? Is it not possible that in the mystery of God's activity there is both a *necessity of our choosing*, which feels to us to be a free choice, and the *wonder of God's choosing*, which means that we have somehow chosen His will? Is there not an openness which makes the gospel available to all, and yet nevertheless says that all who choose, choose because God chose them?

That is what I believe. The two extremes are held in tension, as Charles Simeon said. There are times in Scripture when you have to say that both of two apparently opposing extremes must be stated equally clearly, and that, so far as you can see, the only way for truth is a tension between the poles. I worry about those whose knowledge is so clear that they seem to know the mysteries of God's nature better than He does! There is room for awe.

A privileged people (2:9, 10)
What a marvellous description this is! A privileged people, a chosen. Why were they chosen? I like William Barclay's suggestion that it was for privilege, obedience and service. If you are willing to sit in balance upon the three-legged stool of privilege, obedience and service you know what it

is to be the chosen people. If only Israel had grasped that!

'A royal priesthood' is a complicated phrase, because 'royal' can be either adjective or noun, but it certainly has something to do with authority connected with service. This is something to notice in these days when new types of Christian authority are being held up before us. True biblical authority is always authority that is attached to service. It's a poor leader who cannot stoop to wash his people's feet. If you have a form of authority that is not doing that, then I simply say look out, it is moving in the wrong direction. The royal priesthood is the priesthood of kings and servants in one. That's exactly what that of Jesus is (John 13).

'A holy nation' – that goes back to Exodus 19:6, and the 'chosen people' is Isaiah 43:20. A 'holy nation'; *hagios* (holy) means 'different'. And I come back once again to this idea not only of scriptural holiness but also of social righteousness.

Permit a Methodist to talk for a moment about John Wesley. It's a gross misunderstanding to think of him only as an evangelist. He also taught scriptural holiness – which is so important to this Convention – and he also taught social righteousness. He established orphanages and schools, he organised loans for people to start businesses, he wrote five dictionaries and a book on medicine (did you know that rubbing your head with onions cures baldness?); he risked his life in the snow collecting for the poor; his last letter was to Wilberforce, urging him to continue the fight against slavery.

My brothers and sisters, the evangelical tradition is free salvation, scriptural holiness and social righteousness; and if today evangelicals may be said to be misfiring on one cylinder that cylinder would be social righteousness. We are called to be a holy nation; but evils develop around us and we sit as if we hadn't noticed them.

'A people belonging to God' – that's Exodus 19:5. It's a lovely word which is translated in some older versions 'peculiar'. It's really a collection of prized objects. Don't you see? We are what He has gathered together as His precious possession. Isn't that marvellous? Isn't it lovely to be His possession?

Verse 9 – '. . . declare the praises of Him who called you'. To declare really means to advertise. It is God's 'free space', and what Peter is saying is that the gospel doesn't need better salesmen, it needs more free samples. '. . . But now you have received mercy.' Remember what it was like when you were not a Christian. Think what it now means to belong to the people of God. What grounds we have for being grateful! How easily we forget! And then in verse 12 Peter reminds us that the answer to criticism is a good life.

Putting the truth into practice (2:13-3:7)

So now we look at the various ways in which this can be worked out. In Scripture there is a distinction between principle and application. Not all the applications will be relevant to our present situation. I mean, we may not have many neighbours offering meat to idols! But we do have a lot of difficulty about dealing with other people's consciences; and that is what the principle is about. So let's bear this in mind as we come to these practical passages.

Citizens (2:13-17)

God's intention is that every person should honour and respect those in authority, because they are meant to be running the nation or group for the good of those over whom they rule. I must remind you, however, that that particular passage describes what the authorities *ought* to be doing – 'they are sent by him to punish those who do wrong and commend those who do right.' Romans 13 takes the same line. But in Revelation 13 you will find a very different view, because there the authority is clearly seen to be opposing the will of God.

So I think it is important when you read passages like this to remember that Peter is talking to a particular group of people at a particular time, when it seemed that the government to which they owed authority would act as it should. Later governments, however, acted contrary to the will of God. Let's not rush to stick a particular text on a particular situation until we are sure we have examined the whole of Scripture to see which biblical context matches our own. If we are not careful we may become simplistic.

The test of the citizen is also the test of the State, but what is clear is that goodness is meant to silence foolish talk, freedom always involves responsibility, and wherever we are we always have a duty to respect everyone, to love our brother and sister Christians, to fear God and honour the king.

Workers (2:18-25)

Sometimes we may wonder why Peter and Paul were not more outspoken against slavery. I simply offer one possible solution. To talk about even changing the government was not to talk of something which at that time would have made a tremendous change in the social structure of the time. To talk about freeing slaves in early gospel times would have almost certainly ensured that the gospel was seen as purely a political movement rather than a spiritual movement to declare the gospel of Jesus Christ. Martin Luther's attitude to the Church of Rome was very similar – he taught that though he opposed much of its teachings his followers must not rise against it. The

Peasant's Revolt happened as it were in a moment of relaxation of that teaching, and the Reformation suffered because of it.

I believe that Paul and Peter lit a slow-burning fuse under slavery which eventually destroyed it, and if they had tried to destroy it at once Christianity would have been totally misunderstood.

In verse 22 Peter uses an Old Testament verse to relate Jesus's experience to their own, and in verse 23 he says that Jesus didn't need to retaliate. When you are being unjustly treated the idea that God will eventually make all things right is a tremendous strength. The Lord has a way of vindicating, and if He doesn't vindicate now, He will vindicate then. Oh my brothers and sisters, don't let's retaliate, don't let's lash out! Always wait twenty-four hours before you write that letter. Give thanks if you are not good at thinking of quick retorts.

A theological footnote (2:21, 24)

Now right in the middle of a bit of practical advice on behaviour comes the most deep theology. Please notice, theology kept in church goes quickly stale and academic; but decisions about life outside the church which are not related to theology quickly become mere expediency. The aim of our theology should be to feed our lives. So Peter says, if you want a model when you are suffering or even when you have done good, go back to your theology.

Suddenly, after talking about 'you', Peter is saying 'our' — 'He himself bore our sins.' Isn't that a nice touch? He too is going to be included in the atonement which Jesus brought for him. The substitutionary element is unmistakable. Jesus bore on His body what we could not bear ourselves. It's a description of an actual event (and I say to myself: if the cross actually happened, why not the resurrection as well?).

He was not hounded to the cross. There is an idea here of willing movement. This is where the spiritual perception comes in. It *looks* as though the soldiers are pushing Him, lifting Him, nailing Him – no, says Peter; we know better than that. He went willingly.

It is not immoral that somebody else should bear for me what I cannot bear myself, because of what follows: 'so that we might die to sins and live for righteousness'. The word for 'to die' is very interesting. This is the only place it occurs in either the Septuagint or the Greek New Testament, and in classical Greek it means 'to be away from, to remove from, to depart'. In classical Greek it used to speak of the departed when talking of the dead. So Peter is saying, Jesus did all this so that we might depart from sin. We are the departed, where sin is concerned. We are dead to all that. Do you see? We have been gathered into what He did.

That's why we are baptised. That's why we take bread and wine into ourselves. We are saying 'Lord, gather me into what You did. I won't add anything. Everything You have died to, I want to be dead to. Let me die to everything that is contrary to Your Father's will, and let me rise to everything that is pleasing to the Father. Lord, let it be a daily death and resurrection.'

And, do you see, that's the clue to how you do your work.

'By his stripes you have been healed' – that's the word that would have been used of the marks on a slave's back after his master beat him. Sometimes you have to go the deep way to understand the great goodness of God. I talked to a man whose wife had died. He spoke of the gifts that had been given in her memory to finance medical work overseas. Thousands of people in India had had their cataracts removed because of the gifts given at his wife's funeral. As a special treat he had been invited to go to India to meet the patients. 'Do you know,' he said, 'they knelt to thank me.' He said, 'I hardly knew what to say.' And then he said, 'I wish she had been there, you know.'

I didn't say it, it would not have been appropriate. But if she *had* been there – it would not have happened. The deliverance of those people was through the death of his wife. I don't mean that that was why she died, but I mean that there is no short cut. So it is with our suffering and pain. If you are really hurting, ask 'What is the Lord trying to teach me deep down here?' Peter is leading his people the deep way.

Wives and husbands (3:1-7)

There is something ironic in the way that this passage is used so often to prove that Christianity is somehow about the subordination of women. Quite the opposite is the case. In Hebrew law, in Greek law and in Roman law women were simply possessions. They could be taken and disposed of at the whim of men.

So to be told to love your husband was to give you a great honour, because that was a choice you were not expected to have. Therefore these passages have, in my opinion, been totally misunderstood. Take verse 1. It is scandalous: women are being encouraged to make a spiritual commitment which their husbands have not yet made! In the first century that was not allowed; and therefore Christianity had already taken a step forward in encouraging women to be themselves and, if they wished, to commit themselves to Christ. But Peter goes on to counsel wives not to leave their husbands. Literally, 'that if the husbands do not believe *the* Word, they may be won over without *a* word'.

They were being encouraged to be different from contemporary women (verses 3, 4). He is not saying it is wrong to wear fine clothing or to look after your hair nicely to make the best of what you have. He is saying that if you rely upon these things, what a tragic woman you are; and that's how most of the women around you are. There is bankruptcy at the heart of their being. But, says Peter, you Christian women are meant to be developing your inner self, your character, you are meant to be becoming more and more whole people. In the first century he is encouraging them in this way!

He quotes from the Old Testament, and then writes what is I think the real give-away line – 'You are [Sarah's] daughters if you do what is right and do not give way to fear.' The better translation is, 'Do not be terrified.' You see, they were likely to be beaten by their husbands. 'Why can't you be like all the other women? Why can't you do what I tell you? Why do you have to go and get this religion thing?' My sisters, the New Testament started the liberation! And what Peter tells those first-century husbands is a greater surprise than that which many American men are experiencing just now at the prospect of a woman Vice-President of the USA! To be told to be considerate to your wife, to respect her, to see her as heir with you of everything – this was brand new teaching. These Christian men had to struggle to concede that a wife was different from a goat! No, she is a person, she must be treated with respect. This is where the liberation of women started, and if it were only carried out in this way, it would be a much lovelier, more peaceful experience.

And so I offer some judgements of my own. The beginning of the liberation of women was in the teaching of the Christian church. It was not more stridently taught because of the danger of misunderstanding Christianity.

When we try to treat men and women as the same we remove a great deal of richness from life. Christians who try to keep women subordinate are probably moving in the opposite direction to Scripture.

To put this into its proper context, I want to say with great seriousness (for I believe that great damage has been done to the gospel), that the reason why women should be treated by men as joint heirs is that all of us, male and female, have received the gracious gift of life.

I am so grateful for freedom, especially after recently experiencing the political tensions in Korea. And Peter says: 'Men and women, husbands and wives, stop arguing about rights. Start talking about giving privileges. If your relationships are right then your prayers are going to be right as well.'

What a marvellous way to end! We are all stewards of the good grace of God in life, and heirs together.

3. Goodness and Love
(1 Peter 3:8-4:11)

Now we turn to look at the kind of Christian Peter has in mind, and in verses 8 to 12 he gives a summary of Christian character. The last three of these verses are a quotation from Psalm 34.

I draw your attention first to the words '*all* of you'. In Greek it is one word, but I want you to notice the 'allness' of Christianity. Again and again when reading 1 Peter you will find yourself being reminded either of Acts or Romans, and here you will remember when in Acts 2 the gift of the Spirit was given. Luke says that they were all together; all spoke in tongues. The 'allness' of the Christian faith needs desperately to be regained today.

We evangelicals are very good at one of the three levels at which the New Testament speaks of salvation. We are very good at the *individual* level, and we glory in such verses as 2 Corinthians 5:17. And we are very good at developing the whole area of the individual's response to Christ, and that's quite central to the whole of the gospel. But there is a second dimension, to do with what is sometimes called the *cosmic* implications of the gospel:

that is, how the life, death, resurrection, ascension and second coming of Jesus relate to the whole area of the life of the world.

That is the kind of thing Paul was referring to in Colossians 1:19, where there is not only a question of what happens to each of us as individuals through the gospel of Jesus Christ but also the question of what it says to God's entire creation. Again and again in the New Testament this cosmic, universal element keeps breaking in, and we Christians do well to remember that there are the big issues of what is happening to the creation as well as the question of what is happening to us.

And between the two there is a third dimension of the gospel, which I would call the *corporate*. That is, the question of what happens to us not only as individuals but also as a church, the body of Christ. And here you have Peter saying what Luke was so clearly saying in Acts – the church is about 'allness'. All of us are loved by God, all are gifted by God, all have a responsibility in the life of the church and the world – all of us have a part to play. Indeed I am inclined to say that the test of a church is the degree to which every one of its members is able to operate freely and fully as a Christian.

That's what Peter is now leading them on to. 'All of you, live in harmony with one another.' It really means, 'be of one mind'. In this letter you are never far away from the admonition to operate your mind. Similar words are used elsewhere in the New Testament, for example in Jesus' rebuke to Peter in Mark 8:33, which I believe may be in Peter's mind as he writes this. Similarly the word 'attitude' in Philippians 2:5. The challenge of unity of thought is something we Christians need to take with absolute seriousness. We cannot simply go on thinking, 'Well, he's a Christian and he thinks differently from me – but I'll just let him go on like that.' That's pluralism and deadly to the life of the church. But neither can we go on thinking 'He thinks differently from me so I want nothing to do with him.' If God has accepted him, who am I to reject him?

John Wesley preached a sermon on 'The catholic spirit' based on a curious Old Testament text: 'Is thine heart right, as my heart is with thy heart? . . . If it be, give me thine hand' (2 Kgs. 10:15). The weight of the sermon is that if someone is in Christ, then I must begin by accepting him or her. Then the discussion of Christian truth takes place where it ought to take place, within the family and not on the battlefield.

Still in verse 8 we find the words 'be sympathetic', which really means 'suffer together with' (you will remember Romans 12:15 and 1 Corinthians 12:26). The New English Bible translates 'live in harmony' and 'be sympathetic' by the single apt phrase 'be one in thought and feeling'.

This for me is the ideal Christian fellowship; which when you enter in, has the capacity to discern exactly where you are, what your needs and strengths are, how you are best to be helped to grow and to be gathered into the fellowship – and then enables you to do it. The real test of Mission England and Mission to London is: what happens when the evangelists go home? What happens when the dear folk who haven't a clue about the Christian faith but have put their trust in Christ approach our congregations?

Peter has given us a picture of the Christian church. I long for it in every one of our fellowships.

Transformed love (3:8)

'Love as brothers' (verse 8). John 13:35 – 'All men will know that you are my disciples if you love one another.'

1 John 3:14 is even sharper: 'We know that we have passed from death to life, because we love our brothers. Anyone who does not love remains in death.' Think now of that brother or sister in the fellowship with whom you find it difficult to get on, or the person outside the fellowship to whom you would love to witness but with whom you find it difficult to get on. How much love is there?

We are to look at the whole world and treat them as precious; that is something I have been taught this week by Mr George Duncan. Oh, how we need that gift of love from the Spirit to fill our hearts towards those who are difficult to love! And this is where the theme of dying and rising comes in yet again. We die to our natural way of responding to such people, and we rise to the love which only God can give us.

After preaching on this theme at another convention I received a letter from a lady who had been criticised at church by somebody who took a constant delight in belittling her.

'I was deeply hurt. I went home and knelt at my bedside . . . There as I prayed I died to all the hurt and resentment and I rose to the love that was there. I want you to go on telling them wherever you go, to die and rise in Christ.'

So I'm telling you! It's God's gift by the Spirit to love like that, we can't generate it. We are expected to see everybody as precious in the sight of God. At least we can start, can we not, by loving one another? 'Be compassionate', says Peter. The Authorised Version used to translate this word as 'bowels and mercies', which was a good translation because the Greeks used this word to mean 'courage' – or, in our parlance, 'guts'. But the

Hebrews used the word to mean 'tender-heartedness', and we are being encouraged to be tender-hearted.

It's a fascinating word, because the verb derived from it is never used in the Gospels about somebody who felt like that naturally. It's used of the Good Samaritan to describe the way he felt, and it means to be so deeply disturbed inwardly that you have to do something for the person. The Gospels say that only Jesus is like that by nature. So if we are to be tender-hearted as we are called to be, how deeply we need to get near the Lord!

How easy it is in our age to see so many deaths and hear so much bad news on television – and to build a little film over our lives. Tender-heartedness is what we are looking for, says Peter. How easy it is to be fooled by propaganda which says, all these poor people are poor because they are lazy, all these hungry nations are hungry because they are feckless – how easy to fall for that! No, says Peter. We Christians have a pain to bear, and the pain is that we are going to be tender-hearted and look at the world as Jesus did, as He looked upon Jerusalem. How sad Jerusalem made Him! There is a place for such sadness in the Christian life, the sheer pain of feeling tender-hearted to those in need, some of whom won't even accept the solution you offer. But (verse 13) 'Who is going to harm you if you are eager to do good?'

Living as Christians (3:9-17)

How do you get to the position of verse 9 – to the benefits of living that way, described in Psalm 34 and quoted in verses 10-12 – isn't that very hard? In one sense Peter is saying that it is natural to live that way; and yet, in another way, we know it is not so natural.

The man who led me to Christ was a huge Geordie, Big

Bill Stoddart. He was a gracious man of God. One day he said to me, 'I had a hard time in Durham the other day.'

'Really?' I said.

'I heard an open-air Communist speaker denigrating the gospel. I closed my eyes and I said, "Lord, if you will just let me not be a Christian for five minutes . . ."!'

But he was not allowed, it was not granted. Do not repay evil with evil, insult with insult. There's no need, brothers and sisters! The Lord will look after His people, and as we take in love and with tender-heartedness all that is said, we will find that God gives us grace so to do.

Budgeting for Christ
Well, how do you do that? Look at verse 14. I think it is right to interpret places like this in the light of the Gospels, and I just remind you of what I think of as a kind of chorus hymn in Luke 14. It's where Luke says great crowds followed Him. Whenever you find that, look out, because it appears that the disciples gathered the crowds and Jesus dispersed them. Whenever the Gospels say 'great crowds followed Him' you can be sure that there are going to be some hard words.

Great crowds followed Him – and Jesus turned and said: 'If anyone comes to me and does not hate his father and mother, his wife and children, his brothers and sisters – yes, even his own life – [*chorus*] – he cannot be my disciple. And anyone who does not carry his cross and follow me – [*chorus*] – cannot be my disciple' (Luke 14:25-27). That is said in the context of Jesus' story of the two kings who went to war without counting their money and without counting the opposing armies. The point is that Jesus is talking about budgeting. He is saying not that He wants us to give Him everything we have now. He is saying that He wants us to budget for Him everything we will ever be. That is what discipleship is about, He is saying. It is making Christ Lord.

Sometimes we call that a hard saying. I have come to see it as a most liberating offer; for what Jesus is saying is that when you have budgeted everything, you don't have to worry any more. When you have handed it all over and decided that the claim of Jesus is the one absolute claim on your life, and all else is relative – then you've got your priorities right. After that, how will they persecute you? What will they attack? What will they take away that you haven't already handed over? And, as it happens, everything that you hand over becomes sweet and precious and fresh, once it's been through the hands of the Lord.

My brothers and sisters, we fear the hard sayings, not realising that they are God's most gracious gifts. When you have said, 'Lord, I have budgeted everything, and, as far as I understand it, I give it all into Your hands' – oh, the freedom that that brings! The establishing of priorities becomes possible – you have a central point to relate to.

Peter knows these people are being persecuted and that they are going to be persecuted more and more. 'In your hearts, set apart Christ as Lord' – I am almost sure that Peter had Luke 14 in mind here – 'Always be prepared to give an answer to everyone who asks you to give the reason for the hope that you have' (verse 15). In verse 16 Peter adds, 'Do this with gentleness and respect . . .'

The call to apologetics (3:15)
The word here for 'giving an answer' is *apologia*. Theologians talk about 'apologetic'. It's a word taken from the courtroom, and means making a detailed answer to accusations. I have come to think that the task of apologetic, of answering questions and dealing with criticisms, has become extremely important in our world

today. There is a growing attitude outside the church that Christianity is mentally bankrupt. I believe we need people who can really think within the church to identify the real questions which are being put by those who mould opinions. Those questions need answering in the light of the gospel. I believe that it is a very heavy responsibility.

I was with a group of soldiers recently in Gibraltar, and I was there as a visiting Bible teacher; and many of the soldiers openly described the Bible as fairy tales to be discarded when you grew up. Where did they get that from? From the fact that we do very little apologetic. We do very little listening to the questions and answering them face to face. You who are school teachers – did you know that recent research suggests that children begin to be agnostic and then atheistic between the ages of 8 and 13? That's when it starts to come down the grapevine that Christianity isn't intelligible or worth following. How important the task of apologetic is among schoolchildren!

And I believe that every one of us has the task of explaining to our neighbours, as humbly as we can, why we continue to be Christians. We can only do that if we think about it ourselves. Why, in view of the news every day, are you still a Christian? Those of you with teenage children – how do you keep going as Christians in that situation? And how important are Peter's words in verses 16 and 17, that however we are criticised there will be no fault in our behaviour.

The theology of Christian living (3:18-22)

And now, suddenly, we are off into deep theology again. Peter is in the middle of practical matters regarding relationships, and then we drop into this deep theological teaching.

I think this passage may be what Bishop Jack Dain had in mind, when he said I was a brave chap to be talking about 1 Peter! Well, let's start with the theology of it, and incidentally, it's often said that a congregation should be more exposed to what the theologians are teaching. But I feel it may be more important for the theologians to be exposed to what the congregation is thinking and doing, and that anybody who made that more possible would be doing us a lot of good. Theology is not an academic activity to be conducted behind closed walls. It's the task of the whole church, it relates to the Christian life, and that is why Peter again and again drops into quite deep theology while he's in the middle of giving us practical advice.

'Christ died for sins once for all' (verse 18). 'Once for all' is a single Greek word – a marvellous word! In Hebrews 9:26 and 28 you can almost hear the writer's sigh of relief. He reminds them of the blood of bulls and goats, the endless sacrifices, the annual day of atonement, all the paraphernalia of the High Priests – and then he says 'now Christ appeared once for all'. How marvellous! 'You remember,' he says, 'all those sacrificial birds and animals, and how we had to go on and on, offering and offering – well, Christ has died once for all – we're finished with that. We simply trust our Lord!'

Why can we trust our Lord? Because He died for our sin. He was doing for us what we could not do. Why? Because it was the righteous for the unrighteous. Jesus was right, He did right, He made us right. But was it so that we might for the rest of time stand back as spectators at the cross, and say: How wonderful, I put my vote for that? No. It was to bring us to God, though we had no part in it. We can add nothing to it. We are gathered into it. When you begin to understand that Christ bore your sins on His body on the tree, that He died for your sins, then as your heart is opened by the Lord you can no longer stand back, because He died to bring us to God. Bit by bit we are gathered into His dying and His rising again until it becomes the rhythm of our lives, a dynamic not a static thing. It is not what C. K. Barrett calls 'the manipulation of theological counters'. It's not a theologians' game; it's the life in which you become involved.

I'm sure that when he says 'He was put to death in the body but made alive by the Spirit' (verse 18) Peter has in mind the kind of idea Paul has in Romans 1:4, where you have that lovely picture of the dynamic interaction within the Trinity. Be careful about your doctrine. God isn't static. He is alive and well, a dynamic interaction. And Peter here gives a lovely picture of the movement within the Trinity which, I fancy, is meant to be a picture of the unity of each and every church — willing submission to each other in the interests of an over-riding task.

Two further implications
It's nice to see that even the New Testament writers get carried away sometimes. Peter could actually have stopped there. 'Made alive in the Spirit' would have been an excellent stopping point. But he wrote more. Now, who are the spirits mentioned in verse 19? It would take a long time to discuss all the possibilities. I believe that the time referred to when this preaching occurred is between our Lord's death and resurrection. I don't think that this verse refers to the souls of the departed, or that they were given a second chance. 'Rebellious spirits' is a regular New Testament term for 'evil spirits', those who rebelled against God and are now imprisoned.

The word being used for 'preaching' does not mean evangelising, but heralding. It may be that this means that during the interval between His death and His resurrection, Jesus actually went to the rebellious (angelic) spirits to declare His victory over them. This would seem to lead us to the conclusion that there may have been a chance of salvation for them then. I have a feeling that the Lord would always have wanted to enable them to see now what it was really all about.

But the passage is not about second chances for those who have departed this life. I think that is pretty clear.

And now Peter gets carried away again; having referred to the disobedience long ago in the days of Noah he just can't resist going on a little further. Now the ark becomes a picture of baptism.

Let us try to carefully unravel this. The waters destroyed some, but were the vehicle by which others were being saved. The water kept the ark up and the people safe; the water didn't save them, being in the ark saved them. But the water helped the ark to save them. So the water is now transposed in Peter's mind to the waters of baptism. But lest people think that going through those waters meant that they were saved by the washing of their bodies (verse 21), he points out that baptism is 'the pledge of a good conscience towards God'. Therefore the significant thing of which baptism is the symbol is, getting into the ark. It is based, says Peter, on nothing we can do, but on the resurrection of Jesus Christ.

So the ark stands for the community of the faithful, and in every baptism, there should be the community of the faithful. Baptism represents not just the washing of a body but a response of faith. The three elements – the faithful community, the understanding of the need for individual faith, and the basis in what God has done in Jesus Christ – are inalienable elements of the sacrament.

There is discussion between Christians about whether

the reality must always precede the symbol. That's worth discussing – but not here, for all of us here believe that the basis of our baptism is the resurrection of Jesus Christ from the dead. We all believe that it is necessary to be gathered into the community. We all believe that it is necessary individually to believe in Jesus Christ.

Christ's authority to save is in no doubt so far as Peter is concerned (verse 22). He is saying, 'You can name as many authorities and angels as you like, it doesn't matter; whoever they are, they are subject to our Lord Jesus Christ.' My brothers and sisters, the important thing is that Jesus takes the highest place. He is our Saviour.

The Christian's conduct (4:1-11)

So what is appropriate behaviour in the light of that? Well, I don't believe that verse 1 means that if you are to be done with sin, you have to suffer in your body. I think that it is a reference to what we have been hearing about all through this letter; that Christ died once for all, that we are gathered into that dying and rising experience, and that therefore, if we suffer in the body we know where our association is. It is with what He did for us.

> Jesus, Thy blood and righteousness
> My beauty are, my glorious dress;
> Midst flaming worlds in these arrayed
> With joy shall I lift up my head.

Christ suffered in the body. If we suffer in the body we shall be gathered into His suffering, but we don't have to so suffer to gain the benefits of what He has done. That is why (verses 2 and 3) we do not live for evil desires; we have spent enough time in the past doing what the pagans do.

Then there follows a great account of what the pagans do (4:3-5).

From this passage, let me pick out three things.

Firstly, *He who has suffered in his body is done with sin* (verse 1). The point being made is that God counts us as done with sin. Why did Jesus die? To deal the death-blow to sin. What is our attitude to the death of Jesus? We are dead to sin. God counts us so, that's why He accepts us in Jesus Christ. But then you have got to go on. So, 'he does not live the rest of his life for evil desires but rather for the will of God.'

Secondly, *We have to count ourselves dead to sin*. God counts us thus so we count ourselves thus. As far as we are concerned, whenever sin touches us it is an alien presence in our lives. I believe that that is what the Keswick Convention is all about. It is about recognising that it is one thing to be saved by Jesus Christ – thank God for that! – but that it is another to recognise the extent of the implication. The extent is, that Jesus died to say to sin 'We don't want anything more to do with you at all' – and that's meant to be a recognition of a moment, if you can get to it and settle it in your mind for evermore.

But the third point has to do with the difficult bit at the end of the passage – verse 6. *For this is the reason the gospel was preached even to those who are now dead . . .*

Now, whoever are they? It seems to me that they could be one of at least three groups of people.

One is *the spiritually dead* – people who are walking around, but are spiritually dead. Or it could mean the *dead who never heard the gospel* – some kind of second chance? Or it could mean *Christians now dead who heard the gospel when alive*. The last seems to me to be the likeliest, for this reason. The question being asked is this: why is it that we who gave our lives to Jesus now see that we are

suffering and those who do not believe are not suffering –
and are leading profligate lives? What's worse, some of
our fellow-Christians who we thought might be here when
Jesus returned are dead, and that doesn't seem fair!

Peter says, Let's get it straight. They pity you now – but
wait till the day of judgement. Wait till they face the Lord.
They'll be sorry. So don't worry about whether or not they
are getting the best end of it. Sadly, they are not, for the
day of judgement will come.

And, says Peter, don't worry about those who believed
and are now dead. That's why they heard the gospel
preached, so that they might be safe in the arms of Jesus.
So don't give up recognising that God counts you dead to
sin, that you must count yourself dead to sin, that those
who have died in Christ are safe and that those who sin
without remission will die without remission. How
important to get the message to them as quickly and as
wholly as we can!

The perspective of love
What then is the appropriate behaviour for the Christian
who understands these things? 'The end of all things is
near' (verse 7) – I just want to comment that it always has
been, since Jesus came. 'Therefore be clear-minded' –
there it is again, the need to think clearly and be disciplined
– 'so that you can pray'. And then in verse 8, 'Love each
other deeply, for love covers a multitude of sins.' It
doesn't quite sound what we would say, does it? I think
there are two possibilities here.

One is that in a community where there is love, forgiveness becomes easier. But I think that there may be more to
it than that. It may be that Peter is saying, 'You may spend
so much time on worrying about sin that you forget to
love. And if you could only learn to love, then you might

recognise that if you love, it doesn't matter so much if you don't always get it right.'

Now I know how dangerous this teaching is, but it may be what Peter is saying here; that some of us are so pains-taking about the quality of our lives that we have lost the art of loving, which is what the gospel is really about. Love covers a multitude of sins, if you see it like that. I'll forgive people a lot if they love the Lord and if they love me. If out of love they make mistakes, I can meet them more than halfway to forgive them. Maybe Peter is saying, concen-trate on loving.

And then (verses 8-11) he spells it out. I wish I had time to expound the deep and meaningful details of these verses. But what Peter is saying is, I think, this: there is an appropriate way to do the work of God, and when you do the work of God appropriately, people become aware that God is actually there.

My brothers and sisters, it isn't always enough to have the right intentions. There is a way to preach, to use gifts, to administer the church, which makes people aware of the presence of God; and there's a way which doesn't. The aim of our church life is that people might be able to say 'They not only do these things; they do them in the power and strength of Jesus Christ.'

And that's the way it ends. 'So that in all things God may be praised through Jesus Christ. To him be the glory and the power for ever and ever.' Everything we do for the praise and glory of God through Jesus Christ; and we won't go far wrong.

4. Suffering and Glory
(1 Peter 4:12-5:14)

It may be that a new note of urgency enters in at this point; it may even be that there has been some significant event which has caused Peter to realise that the persecution for which he has been preparing them is now actually beginning; or, that persecution which had been sporadic is now becoming the regular experience of Christians. It may even be, as Andrew Walls has suggested, that the apostle Paul himself had been put to death, and that therefore we now begin to sense a greater urgency, a greater certainty that suffering is going to come.

I do not believe that the earlier part of the letter is a baptismal sermon or liturgy, as it is sometimes thought to be. But I do believe that at this point Peter begins to drive home something which he now realises is not just likely, but actual.

Suffering (4:12-19)

He addresses his readers as 'Dear friends', as he is turning to another subject, as he did in 2:11. 'Do not be surprised' really means, 'do not be surprised by the novelty of something'. It can mean 'astonished'. What Peter is saying is 'Don't be astonished unpleasantly because of the painful experience through which you go.' And I can't move on without reflecting that for most of us it would be an astonishing thing to be persecuted, for really, we have a very easy situation here.

I simply make two comments. One is that in other parts of the world Christians have also felt secure, and then things have changed very rapidly. Pastor Wurmbrand told me that one afternoon in Romania he went out to do his visiting, and they had a king and a government and a system that he knew and was familiar with. But by the time he had finished his pastoral visits it was all gone. In one afternoon the political situation was totally changed. So let us not feel that we will never be persecuted. Let us ask what kind of Christians we need to be, if we have to bear persecution.

The second comment I would like to make relates to one of the levels of salvation we talked of in our last study. At the individual level, I am not being persecuted – well, not very much; but at the corporate level, if you think about the church, we are being persecuted. We are being persecuted because our brothers and sisters are being persecuted. We ought not, must not think of the Christian faith as though there were no persecution about. *We* are being persecuted, because our brothers and sisters are being persecuted for their faith. Let us feel for them and gather them into our love and prayers.

The persecution that refines (4:12)
'Painful trial' could be translated 'fiery trial'. It's tempting to think that Peter has the pyromaniac Nero in mind, but I think he's thinking of fire as a biblical picture of suffering

which refines and makes us better people. The word used
for trial is *peirasmon*, which is the word translated
'temptation' in the Lord's prayer. When it means 'trial' it
can either mean a trial to trip you up, or a trial to build you
up. It's quite clear here that Peter means that these fiery
trials and persecutions are meant to refine us, to make us
better people. And I reflect that the decline in numbers in
our churches in this country may not be the worst thing
that could have happened to us. Maybe we've lost the
camp followers. Maybe the rest of us have had to realise
that it's a matter of great seriousness to be a Christian. It
may be that God, having refined us and slimmed us down,
is now ready to build us up again with a church that has
been refined through the fires.

What the circumstances do to you is not determined by
the nature of the circumstances. Persecution does not
refine you. It's the attitude of mind you bring to the
persecution. And Peter says (and here we are back at the
'hidden level' of perception again) that when persecution
hits you everybody says 'I'm so sorry'; but the perception
of faith says, 'I wonder what the Lord wants to give me
today? I wonder how I'm going to be refined today?'

The privilege of suffering (4:13)
Verse 13: 'Rejoice that you participate in Christ's
sufferings.' We don't add anything to the sufferings of
Christ, but the marvellous thing is that when we suffer we
are actually privileged to have our suffering put at the
same level as His. It's as though you were to do some little
painting, and suddenly find it on exhibition in London
alongside the great masters. You wouldn't say, 'Didn't I
add to that occasion!' You would say, 'Why did they lift
me up and put me there?' But my word, you might just let
it drop from time to time that you were exhibited with the

masters. And you might look at your painting in a different way, too.

Peter says 'When you suffer, make no mistake; your suffering goes into the same Hall of Fame as the suffering of Jesus.' Don't just put up with it, he says – rejoice in it! That's a bit harder. I have come to believe that it is possible to rejoice with tears in your eyes; when your heart is broken; when you actually feel so numb that you wonder whether you will ever feel again – but you know that it's going to be all right because, in God's hands, it *is* all right.

So you can rejoice through the tears and the pain, and that is precisely what Peter is commending to us here: 'So that you may be overjoyed when his glory is revealed'. You see, the Christian is in effect putting all his eggs in one basket. He says 'If that isn't true, I'm sunk.' And the other side of that is, that when it is proved to be true we'll be overjoyed.

Faith's perception (4:13b)
This is where this 'faith-perception' comes in again, because we are constantly looking forward. 'When his glory is revealed' – it means 'uncovered'; it's like the unveiling of a statue or a picture. Some people know what's under the cover. The guest pulls the cord, and everybody says 'Ooh!', but there are some people who are thinking, 'I knew it was like that.' How do we know? Because we have faith's perception. And every time we perceive something, we say 'How marvellous!'

Why do empires come and go, and the kingdom of God goes on for ever? Why was it that Voltaire wrote, in that lovely house in Paris, 'When my writings have gone once round the world, the Bible will be a forgotten book' – and in that very house they established a distributing centre for the British and Foreign Bible Society? Voltaire is just

about forgotten except by students. Again and again we
perceive how God just moves in and does His work, and
He is lifting the corner of the cloth for us, you see; He's
saying, 'Mmm! See!'

When they put in flood-lighting at Newcastle United's
football ground some of us who were supporters went
along to the first evening game that season, and when the
flood-lights came on we all automatically applauded; it
was wonderful. What we didn't know was that there were
four more lots of lights still to come on. And it got
brighter, and brighter, and brighter, until people just
stopped applauding because they were speechless at this
tremendous sea of light. Even those of us who thought we
knew what to expect were speechless. And that's the other
side of it; Peter says 'I keep lifting the corner for you.'
God keeps saying, 'How about that? Isn't that going to be
something?' But when it happens, when Jesus is revealed
in all His glory, we won't be sitting saying 'I could have
told you that long ago.' We'll be saying 'Lord, I couldn't
have imagined it would be as wonderful as that!'

Thank God! And every bit of suffering leads us to say
'There's going to be a day when I'll join in the glad song of
praise to the glory of the Lord.' Meanwhile I simply say to
you: if you know what it's going to be like, are you helping
people who don't know, so that on that day they may not
be surprised?

Suffering for Jesus (4:14-19)
In verse 14 I can't believe that Peter has not got in mind
passages like Acts 3:16. The name of Jesus is the revealed
presence, and when it was revealed, they were insulted for
the name; as soon as they had had that marvellous healing,
Peter with his companion was whipped off to prison. Then
they were told, 'You can go free – but you mustn't talk

about Him.' And you remember what Peter said: 'We cannot but speak of the things we have seen and heard.'

And when Peter says 'If you are insulted because of the name of Christ, you are blessed,' I'm sure he also had in mind what we know as Matthew 5:11, 12. Persecution, pain and suffering are not only *not* a sign that God has left us, they are quite the opposite. They are an invitation to discover more deeply that He is actually with us.

The next bit is really quite remarkable. This version says, 'The Spirit of glory and of God rests on you.' The Greek says 'The "of the glory" and Spirit of God rests upon you.' Now, it may be that there is an error in the text as it has come down to us. But I have a feeling that the 'of the glory' means the Shekinah. I think Peter is saying to those who can see, 'You remember how the Shekinah, the cloud of God's presence, was there when they stopped and worshipped, and when they moved forward? When you're suffering,' he says, 'the Shekinah silently rests over you.' It's a beautiful picture. Only those who perceive with the eyes of faith will be aware that the glory of God has come to dwell upon them.

So verses 15 and 16. Don't give grounds for suffering, and particularly, don't do so by criminal activities; but isn't it lovely that at the end of verse 15, he adds 'or even as a meddler' – a busy-body; I wonder whether he had someone in mind? He lifts meddling to the level of a criminal offence, and says 'Don't do it.' My brothers and sisters – don't do it!

The word 'Christian' (verse 16) only occurs three times in the New Testament; in Acts 11:26, Acts 26:28, and here. The New Testament writers are more inclined to talk of 'In-Christ-people' or 'Christ-in-you-people'. But what a proud name it is to hold!

Why should we exercise care? Because (verses 17-19) it is

time for judgement to begin. Some scholars believe that
this means that Peter thought the second coming was very
close, but I don't believe that myself. I think that the early
Christians believed it to be imminent, as it is today. But I
believe Peter is suggesting that the suffering we experience
is a kind of judgement. Not that each of us goes through
suffering in proportion to his sin – nothing could be
further from the truth. But rather, that it often takes
suffering to release us from the imprisonment of earthly,
material ties. If judgement begins with God's people, says
Peter, whatever is going to happen to the rest? The idea of
judgement beginning with God's people is an Old
Testament idea, for example in Malachi 3:1-5, Jeremiah
25:29, and Ezekiel 9:6. But oh, what a terrible thing; if it's
hard for us to be saved – what about the others (verse 18,
which is a quotation from Psalm 34)?

Suffering's true perspective (4:19)
So then verse 19, and that word 'commit', which Jesus
used on the cross: 'Into Your hands I commit – commend
– My spirit' (Luke 23:46). Peter takes the very same verb
and says, 'If you are going through suffering, do what the
Lord did; commit yourself to God.' The suffering we go
through is joined to the suffering of Christ Himself. Jesus
said 'I commit my spirit' (*pneuma*). Here we are told to
commit our souls (*psuche*). 'Soul' means the totality of
ourselves. In the case of Jesus we understand what was
happening to spirit and body and risen body; here Peter is
talking about people who have got to go on living, so he
says 'Commit all that you are and have.' Jesus gave all to
us; logically, give all to Him.

So I remind you again; the nature of Christian commitment is not determined by the degree of my commitment to
Christ, but by that of Christ to me. Though, when I came

to Christ, what I thought was total commitment was in fact only partial commitment, God accepted me through the total commitment of Christ to me. So the level of commitment I have now to Christ won't do for next year, because, please God, I will know more then, I'll understand more; and, by His grace, I'll move nearer towards that total commitment with which He has blessed me. And that's what's being said here.

'. . . Commit themselves to their faithful Creator' — this is the only place in the New Testament where God is called the Creator in this sense, and I think that here Peter is inviting us to step back yet again. We've looked at the individual in this passage, we've looked at the corporate — the church — and now we look at the greatest level of all of our salvation; the cosmic, the whole of the universe. And Peter is really saying, 'When you suffer, commit yourself to Him who has the whole world in His hands.'

Then two things happen. Firstly your suffering is put into perspective. When you bring your suffering to the feet of the Creator you realise how much suffering there is, how many suffer without knowledge of Christ. But secondly you suddenly realise that the great Creator is actually interested in *your* suffering! He doesn't say, 'Go away, I'm trying to keep earthquakes out of San Francisco.' He says, 'Your suffering matters infinitely to me. I was counting the hairs of your head again only this morning.' He Himself will deal with it.

When we suffer, when the way is difficult, when we wonder whether we're going to come through it at all, God the Creator says, 'Yes, I've got time for that, my dear; I've got time for that; as long as you realise that you're not the only one who is suffering today.'

Glory (5:1-11)

The Greek text of chapter 5 actually begins with the word 'therefore'. I think Peter addresses the elders thus because he's been talking about very serious matters of suffering and of doctrine, and it's natural to turn to those who are the leaders.

The Greek word for elders here is *presbuteros*, from which we derive the word 'presbyter'. Elsewhere they are called *episkopos*, or 'bishops', or they are called *poimenas* – 'shepherds', or 'pastors'. It seems clear that in the New Testament 'elder', 'shepherd', 'bishop' and 'pastor' are all used interchangeably (Alan Stibbs has pointed out that 'elder' describes their status, and the other terms describe their functions).

I want to warn against what I feel has been a great bane of the church, and that is the way that different denominations have felt that they have found a particular, permanent, detailed shape of ministry in the New Testament which must be universally applied. I don't believe that for one minute. I think that the *principles* of pastoral care are set out, and even in the New Testament there is great variety in how they were put into practice. I'm sorry to see how we have hardened certain patterns instead of shaping them according to situation and place. I hope that some ecumenical spirit will teach each of us that no system of ministry is perfect, none is eternal, and what we ought to be asking is not 'What is my received tradition?' but 'What does God want us to do in the world today?'

Peter – God's choice (5:1)

It's lovely to see that Peter doesn't say, 'As an apostle I order you,' but 'As a fellow elder, I appeal to you.' You may notice a change in dear old Peter. He was the one who had actually rebuked Jesus; he lectured our Lord on the kingdom; and now here he is with this very mixed church, most of them slaves. How easily he could have drawn himself up to his full height and said, 'As an apostle, I command you' – and nobody would have batted an eyelid. But he doesn't, and I think that's a lovely lesson in humility.

When he says 'as a witness of Christ's sufferings', I don't think that he means he was an actual spectator at the crucifixion. If that were so I think we would have more evidence. 'Witness' can mean 'bear testimony to', as he did in Acts 2. He preaches the death of Jesus. It could mean more than that; some suggest that the sufferings of Christ are continued in those of the church, so Peter is a witness in that he shares in those sufferings. I think that that is stretching it a little bit. I fancy that it means something like this: 1 Peter is a document of reminiscence, and I think he is saying here, 'All the way from Caesarea Philippi I remember it; right through to Jerusalem, I remember the sufferings of Christ.' If that is so he is talking of the transfiguration, of the agony in Gethsemane, of the trial, and of the crucifixion, about which he would of course have heard from the women.

If that is true then it highlights what is present but not immediately apparent right through this letter; that it was at Caesarea Philippi that Jesus said to Peter, 'You are Peter, [*Petros, petra*, a rock] and on this rock I will build my church, and the gates of Hades shall not prevail against it' (Matt. 16:18). Now it's not the most popular Protestant text around, because it has been used to establish a doctrine of papacy by the Roman Catholic Church. But Jesus isn't talking about a system; He's talking about Peter, not those who will come after him. And I'm not

happy with the typical Protestant response, which says
that it is Peter's *faith* which is the rock, because if that is
so then Jesus is using a pun very badly. It's quite clear to
me that what Jesus is saying is, 'Peter, you are the one on
whom I will build the church.'

And, if you remember Acts, that's exactly what
happened. Acts 1, Peter takes the initiative. Acts 2, Peter
preaches the sermon. Acts 3, Peter heals. Acts 4, Peter
refuses to be quieted. Acts 5, in that awful story of
Ananias and Sapphira, it's Peter who says, 'You lied
against the Holy Spirit.' The fact is that in the early days
the Lord did build His church around this man. But the
wonderful thing is, that the promise was given before
Peter's boast (Mark 14:29), his falling asleep on guard
(Mark 14:37), and his denial of Jesus (Mark 14:66-72). It
was to that man that Jesus said, 'I'm going to build my
church on you, Peter.'

That is far from infallibility, it is far from establishing
a tradition. But it is also very far from saying, 'It's your
faith, really, Peter.' He is saying, 'Peter, it is you; I am
going to build them up around you; and Peter, what a
fallible person you are! How easily you go astray!' And
that is why He says 'Satan is after you, Peter, but I am
going to be praying for you.'

My brothers and sisters, Jesus builds His church on
people like us. He doesn't do a market research project to
find the most brilliant, the most noble, the strongest, the
most knowledgeable, the most eloquent. Paul writes to
the Corinthians: 'Well, look at you! Where is there
anyone noble amongst you? A brilliant person? A strong
person? Not one!' Why? Because Jesus doesn't build His
church according to human strength. He takes ordinary
people who tremble at the thought of doing what He calls
them to do, and He turns them into saints. He takes

people who tremble and He says, 'If you lean on Me, I'll do it.'

And here is Peter saying, 'I am asking you as a fellow elder, as a witness of his sufferings.' Oh, how many things were going through Peter's mind as he wrote that, because he'd been through it with our Lord! What a marvellous thing, that Jesus offers us His yoke. Treasure in earthen vessels – well, Peter's was in a cracked jam jar, really; there was so little promise in it. But what a marvellous thing God did through him!

Instructions to the shepherds (5:2-4)
Notice, it's God's flock. We ministers tend to speak of 'my congregation' – we should watch that; they are God's people. Paul had to recognise that on the Damascus Road. 'I've never persecuted You in my life; I'm just persecuting the Christians.' To which Jesus would have said, 'Precisely! Touch Ebenezer, Wigan, and you touch Me; touch the tin tabernacle on the corner, and you touch Me; touch those four widows who worship every week in those scruffy little premises and you touch Me; criticise them, and you are criticising Me.' My brothers and sisters; be careful how you criticise the church of Jesus Christ.

Peter gives three contrasts in verses 2 and 3. Serve as overseers – *not because you must, but because you are willing*. I wonder whether there was a shortage of candidates for the ministry when it was known they would be persecuted? Was it better to be in the pew than the pulpit when the authorities came round? So that they were dragooning people into being leaders – Peter says, we don't want any of that. Then, *not greedy for money, but eager to serve*. You don't have to be paid a lot of money to be greedy for it. You lay people, if you think that by not paying us much you preserve us from greed, I've got news for you! And finally, *not lording it over those entrusted to you, but being examples to the flock*. What a lovely picture. Maybe the words of Jesus are running through his mind in Mark 10:45 – 'Even the Son of Man did not come to be served . . .'; maybe he has in mind also Jesus washing the disciples' feet. The point is that Jesus is the pattern for the minister's ministry.

Jesus is the Chief Shepherd (verse 4); we are His shepherds. There is a great temptation for the minister to preach one thing and do another. I don't mean, to live immorally. I mean, to preach grace and put yourself under law, to offer forgiveness to others but never forgive yourself – it's so easy for us ministers to do that. We put ourselves into an entirely different system, preaching faith and testing ourselves by works. We have got to ask ourselves again: 'Am I not only preaching the gospel, but living it as well?'

Advice to the young (5:5)

This is a lovely bit! I wonder whether Peter is remembering his own young days? Do you remember John 21:18 – 'When you were younger you dressed yourself and went where you wanted'? Can't you imagine the answer that the young buck, Peter, would have had for anybody who wanted to tell him what to do? And now he is saying: 'That's not real strength, as I had to discover. There's something about older people worth listening to.'

Advice to everybody (5:5-11)

Quickly, lest he seem to be getting at the young, he turns to address everybody. 'Clothe' means 'put on'. That's the model; each day, says Peter, as you get up, just clothe yourself with humility again. Isn't that beautiful! Isn't that a lovely picture for us!

He doesn't say, 'Are you willing to be humbled?' Most of us settle for that: 'I'm willing to be humbled, Lord, for Your sake.' But Jesus says, 'I didn't say that; I said, humble yourselves, under the mighty hand of God.' Verse 7: in Scripture the mighty hand of God is used to mean the way God guides circumstances to guide our lives. You know, a lot of our complaining about society, about churches, about circumstances and about the country is actually complaining about God, but we don't like to say it. We ministers must learn to take a lot of the flak that is really aimed at God. When our parishioners and members get up and say, 'When's this meeting going to finish? It seems to be going on for ever' – they're really saying, 'I'm angry with God.'

No. 'Humble yourselves, therefore, under God's mighty hand,' says Peter, 'that he may lift you up in due time.' Dying is rising; slavery is freedom; weakness is strength; emptying is filling; humbling is exalting; and in Philippians 2 there is the pattern of Jesus again, in that great parabola from glory down to death and from death to glory. That's the rhythm of the Christian life.

Cast your anxiety on Him (verse 7) – that's the aorist tense; decide once for all that Jesus can bear your anxiety. He cares for you! And then in verses 8 and 9 comes a warning about the battle we're engaged in. 'Enemy' and 'devil' are two different words. 'Enemy' means 'adversary', 'devil' means 'liar'. Is Peter imagining the circus arena, or is he, I wonder, using Old Testament language about the way evil comes upon us? Whatever the picture is, he is telling us to be very careful and self-controlled.

And then in verses 10 and 11 that lovely promise appears again which we've studied again and again.

Conclusion

I'm not going to talk about the last two verses, as I covered them when we began these studies. I want now to simply offer you a summary, in the form of six words (and I've got a rash of alliteration!) which I think sum up this epistle.

The broadest possible basis of salvation is there for us in 1 Peter 1:3-5. Peter says, *explore* it more and more; explore the basis of your salvation.

What God has done for us as the basis of our salvation invites a total response from our innermost being; so, alongside your exploration, *experience* what you explore. Die and rise with Christ daily.

And if you explore and experience, it will show in your lives, in humility, in service, in apologetic, in witness, in the quality of your life. So what you experience, you will want to *express*.

As you go through this experience of expressing more and more what you are learning, in head and heart, you will need to learn to *endure*, because not everyone is going to treat you like a long-lost friend.

You will suffer and you will need to endure, but as you do so, keep your eyes ahead. There is a great glory-day coming, when Jesus is unveiled. What you know now to be true in part, you will see to be true in full—so *expect* that great glory-day, and keep walking towards it.

And in the midst of exploring, experiencing, expressing, enduring and expecting—*enjoy* it! It's meant to be good to be a Christian. There's nothing wrong with smiling about being born again.

So we pick the letter up; explore the depths; experience their meaning; express it in life; endure the hard moments, expect the great day of glory when Jesus is shown to be the Lord of all the world; and day by day, enjoy being a Christian, for that is to the glory of God. Amen.

GOD'S VERY OWN PEOPLE

by Rev Stuart Briscoe

1. Identifying and Overseeing God's People (Titus 1:1-9)

I want to thank you for the superlatively kind way I have been introduced to you. Let's now read together the first four verses of Paul's letter to Titus.

Introduction (1:1-4)

Notice how Paul describes himself. In verse 1 he is very humble—a 'servant of God'. But then immediately he calls himself an 'apostle of Jesus Christ'—a title of unique authority in the church. Paul had a remarkable ability to combine humility with a deep sense of responsibility. Have you noticed the kind of people who are so very, very, humble . . . that you don't take them seriously? Or the other kind, who have a great sense of leadership ability but little sense of humility, so that you're rather turned off by them? Like so many aspects of spiritual life there is a tension between the two. Paul holds them in tension. He insists on his apostleship, he requires that people regard him as an apostle; yet at the same time, he proves the reality of his apostleship—not by domineering, but by desiring to serve the people to whom God has sent him.

You'll notice that in verse 4 he calls Titus 'my son'. He regards himself as his spiritual father. But immediately he says, 'But we share a common faith.' So on the one hand he's suggesting that there is a father-son relationship, but on the other hand there's a very intimate brother-brother relationship. Once again, a lovely example of the apostle Paul holding two aspects of a spiritual truth in tension.

We can mention just one or two things about Titus. He is referred to in Galatians 2. Paul came to Jerusalem to discuss with the church leadership the issue of what part Judaism ought to play in the experience of new believers. He took Barnabas with him, who was already deeply respected in the Jerusalem church. Somewhat surprisingly, he took Titus with him as well. Titus was going to be the test case. The big issue was whether Gentiles should be circumcised. Titus was a Gentile, he was uncircumcised, and so he was being marched up to Jerusalem and he was going to be the one at the centre of the whole issue. In a sense, he was the worm on the hook! However, he left from Jerusalem without being circumcised.

There's something else special about Titus. If you check Paul's second letter to the Corinthians you'll find that Paul needed a trouble-shooter to go and deal with some of the problems he was having with the Corinthian church. Titus, who'd been a worm on the hook in Jerusalem, was sent to Corinth as a trouble-shooter. Paul waited very anxiously for news of his progress. When he arrived in Troas he had no rest in his spirit because Titus had not arrived. But then a little later on he found him, and was absolutely overjoyed to hear of the good things happening at Corinth partly as a result, no doubt, of the ministry of Titus.

So Titus is one of those members of Paul's team about whom we don't know a lot, but what we do know about him gives us a lovely picture of Paul's approach to ministry: building up his team, identifying different people's gifts, using them in various ways. It comes as no surprise to find in verse 5 that Paul has left Titus in Crete in order to 'straighten out what was left unfinished and appoint elders in every town'. Now he's functioning as a straightener-out! I rather like Titus. He seems to have been a very special kind of person.

The purpose of the letter

As we have seen, Paul and Titus have been engaging in evangelism on Crete. Paul has moved on – we don't know precisely when this happened. Titus now presumably has what we would call a 'church-planting ministry'. In every town there were to be communities of believers overseen by appointed elders.

In an interesting phrase in Titus 2:14 it says that Christ 'gave himself for us to redeem us from all wickedness and to purify for himself a people that are his very own, eager to do good'. In other words Titus is involved at the practical level in a similar work to that in which, if you like, Christ is spiritually involved: drawing out a people that are His very own and then purifying them. Titus is helping to form these local fellowships. He's helping to straighten things out, to appoint elders, to establish discernible groups of the people of God.

It's from this phrase that I have taken the title for our studies: 'God's very own people'. What a privilege to recognise that we are members of a people belonging peculiarly, and in a very precious sense, to God Himself.

Identifying the people of God (1:1-4)

The calling of the people of God

In the first verse of the first chapter it says that Paul is an apostle of Jesus Christ 'for the faith of God's elect'. He calls the elect people of God, those whom God has, for reasons known only to Himself, chosen for a specific purpose.

Clearly this idea is rooted in the Old Testament. Let me refer you briefly to Deuteronomy 4:32, where Moses' theme is very clear. He is reminding the people of Israel that God has done a unique thing in their experience. He has chosen them to be His people. He has never done it before, but now He has chosen a nation out of the nations, a people out of the people; the express purpose of God is that He wants to have a very special, very precious people for Himself.

We might ask: why does God want a very special people for Himself? I think there are various answers. One is, to demonstrate in this people's experience His own sovereignty, which He clearly did in the exodus – moving into Egypt, dramatically demonstrating His mighty power in a miraculour way, bringing them out of Egypt – thereby letting all the surrounding people know of the magnificent sovereignty of the Lord in the experience of this people. In the wilderness they grumbled about their diet, and the Lord sent them manna. In the gift of the manna He was demonstrating His sufficiency. Why did He call out this people? To demonstrate His sovereignty in the exodus. And the surrounding peoples could see a wonderful demonstration of who God really is, by His work among this people.

In the Minor Prophets we discover that God speaks to this people, and speaks in no uncertain terms. He reminds them that they are His people. They're going to have to shape up and behave like His people, and if they will not, they will come under His judgement. Amos, for example, speaks very powerfully about this in chapter 3.

Let me digress for a moment. In the beginning, God created man. A single, male man. And after an unspecified period of time God decided that man was not doing very well on his own, and He revealed His marvellous idea, which of course was woman. Now – when God created man, he created an individual. But as soon as He created woman he had created society.

Along came the fall. What happened? Well, individuals fell. But a second thing happened. Society began to fracture and fragment. It came apart at the seams. The first generation on the earth produced two brothers, one a murderer, the other his victim. We need to look no further to see that already, society is fracturing and fragmenting.

Now then – if you go to the average evangelical believer and ask whether God is concerned for fallen individuals, he or she will answer emphatically, 'Yes'. If you ask, 'How do you know?', the answer will be: 'Because He gave Christ to die on the cross to redeem fallen individuals.' But if you ask that same person whether God is concerned about fragmented society you probably won't get such a quick or positive answer. In my experience evangelicals tend to be somewhat individualised in their approach to spiritual experience. We have so emphasised the need for a personal relationship with Christ that we sometimes don't worry too much about the societal or community aspects.

I believe that God *is* concerned for fractured society. And if we ask that average evangelical what God's antidote is, we may have to wait a little while for the answer, but I assure you that the answer is an alternative society, a new community. Why are Israel God's elect people? It is in order that He might demonstrate to fractured, fragmented nations – to societies coming apart at the seams – what it means to be a people, a community operating under divine principle.

So what do we see as we study Israel, the elect people of God in the Old Testament? We see clearly ordained principles of behaviour for society. We see specific approaches to economics, for instance, and to political structures; all kinds of things of which communities and societies need to be aware. And we see this only as we see God calling out a people for Himself.

Now then: what is the application of this as far as we're concerned?

In writing to Titus, Paul takes this idea of an elect people of Israel and applies it to a different group of people; the 'Israel of God', the church of Jesus Christ. And we see something that is very important. God has not only chosen a people *Israel* to be an alternative, unique society, but He has chosen people *in Christ*, who will also be His people, His elect, alternative society. Is this important? Yes, it is. For I firmly believe that in our day and our generation, as it was in the days of Israel, society is fracturing and fragmenting. Our secular society needs a model of how society and community is supposed to function under God. What is this living illustration? I believe that it is the people of God, the church of Jesus Christ.

That is one reason why it is so important that in all our evangelism we not only bring people to Christ on an individual basis, but we also bring these regenerate individuals into a corporate whole – so that they can begin to function as the people of God. I submit to you that any believer who wants to operate on an individualistic basis is robbing society of something society can reasonably expect to have from believers. And that is, a model of community, of society, of the local church. Surely this is part of Paul's burden as he writes to Titus. 'Please, Titus,' he is saying in effect, 'make sure that all over Crete there are discernible groups of people, functioning as the chosen people of God.'

Of course they are not just to sit in holy huddles. They are to have an impact on society. In Titus 1:8 Paul says that the elder must be one 'who loves what is good'. In 1:16 some people are criticised for being 'unfit for doing anything good'. In 2:7 Titus is urged to set an example 'by doing what is good'. In 2:14 Paul says that God is purifying a people 'eager to do what is good'. Chapter 3:1 – 'Remind the people . . . to be ready to do whatever is good.' In verse 8 he insists that the people take care to devote themselves to 'doing what is good'. And (just in case they haven't yet got the message!) in 3:14 he says, 'Our people must learn to devote themselves to doing what is good.'

You don't have to be a great theologian to find out what he's talking about, do you? What is his theme? It is that the people of God should understand why they are called to function as a community within a fragmenting society, and by the sheer goodness of their corporate and individual lives be giving secular society a magnificent model of what life can be when life is lived under the principles of God.

The characteristics of the people of God
There are three things that we note in this introduction concerning the characteristics of the people of God. First of all, they are people of faith. This is mentioned in both the first and the second verses. Secondly, they have (verse 2) a faith and knowledge, resting on the hope of eternal life.

And this gives us the third characteristic – they are people of hope. But underneath the faith and the knowledge and the hope is – what? God 'who does not lie', who has 'promised before the beginning of time' and, 'at his appointed season . . . has brought his word to light.'

The people of God are related to the living God, and the nature of their relationship is one of faith and knowledge and hope. Christians are different from unbelievers, and that is why.

There are two theories as to how people can get right with God. One is that you do the best you can and hope, when you die, that it was good enough. People call that 'justification by works'. Then there's another theory, which is the biblical theory: that it doesn't matter how hard you've tried, you won't be good enough – therefore admit it. Repent, come to God and ask for mercy, trusting Him for Christ's sake to forgive you. This, of course, is called 'justification by faith'.

The people of God know that this is the only way you can be justified. But they know also that when you've *been* justified, you don't put your faith on the shelf. The Bible says that we are saved by faith – but it also says, we live by faith. It goes further. We don't walk by sight, but by faith. As we read Scripture we see that the Christian life in every aspect is a life of dependence – faith, trust and dependence on the living God.

Perhaps it's hardly necessary to say this, but I'm going to anyway. The important thing about faith is the object of faith, not its volume. There are some people who have tremendous amounts of faith in objects that do not warrant it. For instance, some at the start of the skating season are so impatient that, exhibiting phenomenal faith, they leap onto thin ice and are drowned by faith. On the other hand, some timid souls wait until the temperature has been below zero for six weeks, and then very timorously they lower themselves onto the ice and are utterly secure. A lot of faith in thin ice will drown you; a little faith in thick ice will save you.

Now, notice what Paul is saying. These special people are people of faith – but it is faith in God, 'who does not lie'. I submit to you that one of the healthy correctives to our secularised society, with its phenomenal faith (for no apparent reason) in humanity, would be for us to produce men and women who have phenomenal faith and trust in our living God and demonstrate it in their lifestyle.

Then, the people of God know the truth. Now, you cannot know the truth without learning the truth! Let me emphasise the imperative necessity for teaching. I find increasingly that people want to be Christians without bothering themselves too much. They want experience without taking time to learn that which God has revealed to us.

When my sons were younger they weren't interested in study (they were their father's sons!). I tried all kinds of ways to get them to read, and finally in desperation I rubbed their text books furiously on top of their heads to see if that would do any good!

It didn't help at all. And there are some Christians who won't study the Word, who won't listen to teachers, who won't associate with others who could lead them deeper into the truth. They would like someone just to rub the book on their heads once in a while. They'd like to use it as a substitute leg for the piano, or have it sitting under the aspidistra. They have Bibles with ribbons in them, and pressed cornflowers, and details of when they were born and when Grandma died, and they have pictures of old girlfriends in them – and they assume that all this will do them some good.

It won't. Christians are people of knowledge of the truth, and knowledge of the truth comes from taking time out to learn the truth. There is no short cut.

But notice something important. The word Paul uses for knowledge so carefully in verses 1 and 2 does not just mean an academic assimilation of data. It does not only mean that they have an intellectual assent to the truth, it means that they are prepared to acknowledge it, to fully appreciate the truth that they know. That is what Paul is talking about here. *Epignosis*, 'full knowledge' of the truth – 'I've got the information, I acknowledge it to be the truth, and I am carefully and assiduously applying it to my life.'

Let me read to you Isaiah 66:2: 'This is the one I esteem: he who is humble and contrite in spirit, and trembles at my word.' That's what I believe Paul means by these people being people of faith and people of knowledge. Have you noticed how it is with the truth sometimes? That sometimes we have a very inadequate grasp of it, and it has an even less adequate grasp of us? And very, very rarely in our lives – we have to admit with sorrow – does it really get a grip on us, so that it is clear that we're not only people of faith, but people of knowledge.

You have probably met people who talk of hope but have no confidence. Their voice rises hopefully as they say the words, but there is no real hope. The people of God, however, do not lack confidence. It is not confidence in self, but confidence in God 'who does not lie', who has given us eternal life; who 'at his appointed season' has revealed truth to us. We know who He is, what He said, what He's done, what He's promised, what He is going to do; and accordingly we are brimming with confidence.

Now think of your own town. Think of your own little fellowship of believers, the people of God, the called people of God; placed there to be a unique people of God, showing fragmented society what it means to be a people, what it means to be a community, what it means to be knit together under divine principle.

Think what you can demonstrate to that fractured and fragmented society, in faith and knowledge and hope.

The care of the people of God
In verse 4, Paul uses the common greeting: 'Grace and peace from God the Father and Christ Jesus our Saviour'. In a dramatic way he invested these common greetings with deep spiritual significance. The idea of *grace* is that of the sufficiency of God made available to His people. The idea of *peace* is that our lives are in order, in tune, in step with the God who orders all things. How are God's people cared for? They are cared for by God the Father through Christ Jesus our Saviour as He makes grace and peace abound towards us.

That's why the people of God are so special in the midst of a fragmented society; for in a society that is running hither and thither looking for answers, there is a peculiar sense of sufficiency, a fullness, about the people of God. There's a great sense of order, of knowing who we are and what we're about and where we're going. It's attractive. It's winsome. It's powerful. It's compelling. The people of God! And we are cared for by the grace and peace that comes from God the Father and Christ Jesus our Saviour.

But not only that. We're cared for by the ministry that God has ordained for these fellowships. We've already pointed out servants and apostles. In verse 3 there's a hint about preachers. In verse 5 there are some like Titus who are sent to 'straighten things out', and a little bit further on we're going to read about elders. You see, God has got the thing beautifully together. He makes available spiritual resources for the care of His people, and then He puts people – gifted people – among His people. Some are delightful *servants* – though of course all must learn to serve. Some have *preaching gifts*. And notice what preachers do – they bring the Word to light! There are preachers who give you the impression that they've studied very, very hard to make things difficult. That's not the objective! We should try to take the deep things of God and make them readily understandable.

God has given us some delightful *straighteners-out*. Have you got any trouble-shooters in your church, some of those people who have the remarkable capability of moving in on a situation, shedding light on it, taking the heat out of it, letting harmony rule? They are an absolute gift to the church of Jesus Christ. And there are also of course the *elders*.

Overseeing the people of God (1:5-9)

We turn in closing to talk about overseeing God's people. Notice two words in this passage concerning the oversight or leadership of this Christian community, these Christians established in Crete. In verses 5 and 6 we have 'elder', and in verse 7 'overseer'. Now clearly these mean the same people, but they are two different Greek words. The word translated 'elder' is *presbuteros*, and that translated 'overseer' is *episkopos*.

The word *presbuteros* originally meant 'an old man' or 'a bearded one', the idea being that if you could grow a beard with grey hairs there was some semblance of dignity. The word was used in the Septuagint (the Greek translation of the Old Testament) to describe some of the leaders in the wilderness. It was also used to describe some governors of cities. In addition, it was used to describe the Sadducean members of the Sanhedrin and the governors of the Synagogue. So it's really no surprise that the word was taken over into these Christian fellowships to describe those mature people who had leadership capabilities – spiritual maturity. Of course it wasn't because they had grey hair! It was because they had these spiritual capabilities of which we'll talk a little more in a moment.

The word *episkopos* was applied in Greek mythology to the god who watched over a particular country, in much the same way that certain nations have patron saints like England's St George. He was the *episkopos*, and the word simply means to oversee or to watch over. However, in political usage, the word was applied to the administrators of the states that Greece had taken over. In Nehemiah 11:9 in the Septuagint it is the word used for the chief officer in restored Jerusalem. So it is again no surprise that the word is used in the Christian church to describe one who watches or oversees the Christian community. We can use the words in tandem, the one speaking more of the office, the other speaking more of the operation.

In the Christian church we need good oversight and care. This is what Paul is speaking about. And now he lists some general qualifications for these people.

Qualifications for overseers
First of all *they require moral integrity*. Overseers must be blameless. That does not mean that they must be perfect, without fault. If it did, it would be very hard to find elders! One of the encouraging things about the church of God is that it is made up exclusively of sinners, and all elders fall into that category as well. It does not mean that they should be perfect. It means that there should be moral integrity that is clearly recognisable both inside and outside the church.

Secondly *an overseer should be 'the husband of but one*

wife'. This is difficult to understand and even more so to interpret. One interesting thing is that the Greeks had only one word for 'man' and 'husband', and only one word for 'woman' and 'wife'. In fact in the New Testament the Greek word is translated 'man' 156 times and 'husband' only 50; and the other is translated 'woman' 129 times and 'wife' 92 times. A good case could be made out that here the correct translation is 'a one woman man'. And there the connotation would be, 'somebody known for sexual purity'.

Thirdly – *'a man whose children believe and are not open to the charge of being wild and disobedient'*. We need leadership that is characterised by domestic authority. As Paul says elsewhere – 'If a man can't run his own household, how on earth can he look after the church of God?'

Then (verse 7) *the overseer must be 'blameless'*. This is repeating the same thing, but Paul goes on to expand it. I suggest that Paul is saying: keep away from those who tend to extremes. There are some people who do not have personalities suitable for being leaders. They can't handle it.

In verse 8 Paul mentions *spiritual quality*. The overseer must be given to hospitality, must love what is good, be self-controlled, upright, holy and disciplined.

Sixthly there must be *doctrinal stability*. He must 'hold firmly to the trustworthy message as it has been taught'.

And seventhly, there must be *biblical capability*. He must be able to take the Word of God so that he can 'encourage others by sound doctrine' positively, and, negatively, refute people who have gone off the rails or are teaching heresy.

We should pray for the leadership of our home churches, because leadership is crucial. If you find a church that is moving and doing anything, you'll almost invariably find that there is godly and capable leadership. Surely one of our great concerns should be that this should be our experience.

Obligations of overseers

Those are the general qualifications. Now what should these elders be doing?

I suggest three things. They should be *stewards* who love God's church. They should be *students* who love God's Word. They should be *shepherds* who love God's people.

So, firstly they see that the church is *well-fed*. They spend a lot of time teaching and training – we'll talk more about this later. Secondly, they see that the church is *well-led*. They develop a clear sense of leadership, leading by example and encouraging 'followship'. Getting people to follow is an art. One of the reasons that a lot of churches aren't going anywhere is that the leadership doesn't know where to go. If it does it doesn't know how to communicate how to get there, and if it could communicate how to get there they don't know how to get there themselves. So nobody can follow them.

Seeing that the church is well-fed – seeing that it is well-led – and then seeing that it is *well-bred*, which means protecting that community of believers from heretical influences and preserving it from moral and spiritual decline and disintegration. This is what we need in our fellowships.

2. Protecting and Training God's People (Titus 1:10-2:10)

Protecting God's people (1:10-16)

The sound doctrine of the apostles

Firstly notice that in these verses there is a great emphasis in Paul's use of the word 'sound'. Repeatedly you will find him talking about 'sound doctrine' and 'sound lifestyle'. It's a rather interesting word in Greek. It's the word from which we get our English word 'hygiene'. It means, literally, 'healthy' or 'health-giving'.

What Paul is saying is this: 'Titus, if you're going to finish off what needs finishing off and straighten out what needs straightening out in the local fellowship, if you're going to be part of God's purifying His people, you're going to have to make absolutely certain that you're giving them a good solid diet of healthy food. Because without that they can't produce a healthy body. And without a healthy body, how can they live a healthy church life?' Repeatedly in this brief epistle we find an emphasis on hygienic, healthy teaching, doctrine or lifestyle.

Would you say that the church from which you come is

healthy? Would you say that it is robust, that it glows with spiritual vitality? It ought to be! But the key is plenty of healthy food.

Now remember that in his ministry Paul claims that the sound teaching he propagates was not dreamed up by him. In Galatians he insists that his sound teaching is not man-made: it is God-given. He is saying that he has become the recipient of revealed truth. This is one of the most exciting things that human beings can ever discover.

There are two ways of developing a lifestyle. One way is to ask speculative questions like 'Who am I?', 'Why am I here?' or 'Where am I going?' We ask these philosophical questions and then guess at the answers – 'I think I am this' . . . 'I think I am going here' . . . 'I think I am supposed to be doing this, or that, or the other'. You will notice that speculative philosophical questions produce speculative philosophical answers. Our world is full of speculative philosophies. They are man's best attempts to answer man's best questions – but they are limited by man's capability. Some people build their lives on them, and then run into difficulties because somebody speculates on the initial speculation. So they have to start all over again. New questions, new answers; they sort the whole thing out again and – guess what? Somebody else speculates on the speculations based on the initial speculations! If you wonder why our society is changing so dramatically and so rapidly, it is, I believe, because people's lifestyles are built on philosophies that never produce any degree of certainty whatsoever.

There is, praise God, an alternative to speculative philosophy. It is called revealed theology. The difference is this. Speculative philosophy is man's best attempt at answering his best questions. Revealed theology is God leaning out of heaven and saying: 'If you will kindly give me your attention, I will *tell* you who you are. I will *tell* you where you came from. I will *tell* you where you are going. But I will tell you something far more important. I will tell you who *I* am. Because it is only when you discover who I am that you really know the answers to those questions.' The wonderful thing about revealed truth is that it is God-made and God-revealed. It does not change with every brand of speculation. It is settled in heaven. God has spoken.

Personally I can think of nothing more exciting than to be a person who – to use Paul's language in writing to Titus – having received sound, healthy teaching should now devote myself to propagating sound, healthy teaching; so that in a society characterised by uncertainty and turmoil, change and disintegration, I might be part and parcel of building up a group of people – God's very own people. A people who demonstrate security in the midst of insecurity, direction in the midst of confusion, and who know what it is to know who they are and what they're doing.

This is what I believe Paul is conveying to Titus: the absolute necessity of concentrating on sound, healthy doctrine. Again I ask you, is there such a concentration in your local fellowship so that there is a robust, healthy fellowship of people who stand out in the midst of an unhealthy society, and thereby bring glory to God and challenge to humanity? That's our objective. God is purifying for Himself a people that are His very own, and He calls us to be involved as we seek to straighten out what is twisted, finish what has been left unfinished, and see God work.

The spurious teaching of those who oppose the gospel
Now Paul begins to deal with what is opposing Titus in his task. There are people in the fellowship, in the environment

in which Titus is ministering, who are reacting against the apostles' teaching. In verse 14 he speaks of 'those who reject the truth'. There are some people in the community of the believers whom he describes (verse 10) as 'rebellious people'. Notice that he talks about their motives and says in effect that they are utterly reprehensible. They are engaging in all kinds of teaching that is contrary to apostolic truth – that is, to all that God would have taught. It is singularly unhealthy.

Their motivation (verse 11) is that they seek 'dishonest gain'. And in verse 16 he says that these people are 'detestable, disobedient and unfit for doing anything good'. Paul is here talking very seriously and powerfully. 'The elders, the leaders of the church, have not only got to be so firmly rooted in the word of God themselves that they can encourage the believers as they disseminate it, but they have also got to be strong men in the Spirit and in the Word so that they can deal with those who come into the community of believers and introduce germs into an otherwise healthy body.'

It may be that some of us are saying, 'Well, we only get good solid teaching in our church. Everybody who's doing it has been doing it for donkey's years and, between you and me, they're still teaching the same old thing – so there's no danger of anything wrong creeping in. We all know what they're going to say before they even get up to say it!'

Of course there is that tendency and, yes, it's obvious that you don't have a problem with spurious teaching. But let me suggest something to you. There has in recent months been a wonderful period of evangelism in Britain. How exciting it is! And if it is doing what it is supposed to be doing, it will result in people being introduced into the life and death of Jesus Christ. So all kinds of people will

shortly be brought into our fellowships who will bring the
weirdest ideas. And there's a real possibility that if they are
given the opportunity to share in the fellowship of the
Lord Jesus Christ, they will start sharing some of those
ideas, and you may find yourselves with a real problem on
your hands. And what a delightful problem it is!

I believe that many of our churches have become
defence-orientated. I've got a feeling that this evangelism
that's been going on may have moved the church into the
offensive by introducing all kinds of new things into our
fellowships. That's good. But we'd better face up to it – we
may find ourselves vulnerable at the back.

It means we're going to have to be careful in our
fellowships as new people come in with new ideas. It means
that we're going to have to have leadership that knows
what it believes and why, and is strong enough to be able to
handle apostolic teaching and counter-attack the spurious
teaching of those who come in. That's part of the
responsibility of the leadership of the church.

The Elitists. The spurious teaching which Titus had to
encounter, was *related to Judaism*. We're familiar with the
Judaizers who came after Paul's ministry insisting that for
people to be really born again, really in Christ, they must
adhere to all the niceties of Judaism. They are called in
verse 10 'the circumcision group'.

In all probability there was another important emphasis,
and that was *the emphasis of Gnosticism*. Gnostics were
people who believed in *gnosis* – knowledge. They believed
that matter was evil and that spirit was essentially good.
Therefore spirit and matter could have no contact
whatsoever; and if God was spirit He couldn't get His
hands dirty creating matter. They overcame this problem
by suggesting that between God (who was spirit) and

matter (which was evil) there were all sorts of intermediary stages called 'emanations'.

The important thing about these emanations was that only those with special *gnosis*, special revelation, could understand the concept. So the Gnostics became proud, and they looked down upon others because those lesser mortals hadn't arrived at the spiritual position that *they* had. They had a spiritual superiority complex – the very worst kind – and they were coming in and lording it over other people.

In addition they applied their belief that matter was evil, in two ways. Some became very ascetic in their approach and would have nothing to do with anything physical. Nothing sexual, nothing like that at all. It was taboo. They became like monks. Others on the other hand said that as matter was evil there was nothing you could do about it, so you may as well ignore it and let it have its own way. And so they engaged in all kinds of licentiousness.

Now, if we gather all this together, we see some of the important influences in these infant churches. A supercilious spiritual elite coming into the church claiming to have had a very special revelation that lesser mortals had not. Doesn't that pose problems in the church? In my experience you come across such people quite often. We had such a spiritual elite in our church. They were good and godly people. It was just that they had such a high opinion of their knowledge. They would sit with pained faces in the pews. Periodically you would see them leap into an attitude of prayer in the middle of the sermon. Whenever they had something to say they would preface it with 'The Lord has told me . . .'

It is very difficult in the church of Jesus Christ when you come up against people who will not subject themselves to others' input, who will not be subject to other people's

ideas nor recognise the possibility that they may not have
learned everything that there is to learn. Titus is going to
be up against it with these people.

The Syncretists. There's another thing he is going to have a
problem with as well. There are people in these churches
who have got a little bit of Christianity, a little bit of
Judaism and a little bit of Gnosticism. And they are having
the most marvellous time juggling the three in the air, and
they're finishing up with the most remarkable syncretic
religion. Now of course, that doesn't happen in England
. . . or does it? It sometimes happens in Africa – we've
taken the gospel and the Africans have brought in tribal
thinking and now they're juggling their tribal beliefs and
the Christian gospel. And it happens in Latin America,
where they've had Marxist infiltration and they have come
up with liberation theology which is now mixed up with the
truth as it is in Jesus – but it will never happen in our
churches – will it?

Well, sometimes I wonder. I wonder whether we've got
people in our churches who can identify what is going on in
people's lives to such an extent that they can say, 'Listen,
you really are messed up, friend, because what you are
calling spiritual truth is simply secular truth with a very
thin spiritual veneer.' That's the kind of leadership we
need. That's the kind of church community we've got to
produce, where there's a kind of relationship, a kind of
insight, a kind of discernment that will allow us to address
all these things.

The Genealogists. In addition these were people *who loved
endless genealogies.* Paul talks about 'myths and endless
genealogies' in 1 Timothy 1:4, where there's a similar
situation: Timothy was sent to Ephesus to 'straighten

things out', and of course here Titus is sent to Crete.

These 'endless genealogies' are fascinating. The rabbis had decided that the Bible was somewhat deficient, that there were things missing in the genealogies. So they had filled in the details. It was unbelievable, ludicrous nonsense that would be hilarious were it not that people were taking it seriously as God's Word. And let's face it, there's an awful lot of speculative nonsense today that people try to 'fit in', and if you're not careful it will become as important as God's Word in people's thinking – in some cases, more important.

The Sensualists. There was something else: all kinds of *sensual behaviour.* In verse 16 Paul talks about those who claim to know God but deny Him by their actions. They are giving themselves up to all kinds of corruption. Why? Because (verse 15) both their consciences and their minds have become corrupted. Paul quotes a very interesting statement here: 'To the pure, all things are pure.' He may have been referring to our Lord Jesus' statement in Mark 7:15, that it isn't what goes into man that corrupts him but what comes out of him. If your mind is warped in its understanding then everything that comes your way will be warped by it. But if you've got an open heart and an open mind and a clear conscience to the Lord, then whatever comes your way will pass through that pure filter of God's Word.

The problem with many people in the church was that they hadn't got round to purifying their minds and their consciences and keeping them pure by the constant administering of the Word of God.

Let's say this frankly: it is a problem in our churches. It really is. You know the old principle of computers – 'Garbage in – garbage out'. A computer doesn't think for itself. It thinks your thoughts after you. What you put in is what you're going to get out. If people are coming into the churches with corrupt minds because they are putting all kinds of garbage in, then whatever comes their way will be corrupted and twisted and warped. They will spew out all kinds of garbage in the Christian community. We need to be protected against this.

So, if we're going to take seriously this whole business of seeing God's people as a Christian community built up and nurtured in healthy fashion, what have we got to do? We have got to counteract all the spurious teaching, all the wrong attitudes, all the warped thinking. We've got to counteract it all, with a clear, consistent, relevant, powerful dissemination of healthy teaching. Is that what *your* church is doing?

Notice how Paul points out the serious responsibility of the elders in this regard. First of all, in regard to the opposition. In verse 13 he says 'rebuke them sharply'. In verse 11 he says 'They must be silenced.' Be careful before you silence too abruptly, even though the machinery exists in the churches to do that. The word used for 'silence' strictly means 'muzzle'. 'Rebuke' means not just 'tell them what's wrong', but also 'help them see what's right'. The important thing he points out in verse 13 is this: 'Rebuke them sharply, *so that they will become sound in the faith.*' The job of the leadership is to deal with what is coming in that is contrary to apostolic teaching and will produce unhealthiness in the healthy body. We are to rebuke and correct those who so teach, and to correct them; but notice that the objective is not to kick them out. It is to win them over, so that they might become profitable, healthy members of the church of Jesus Christ.

Isn't it interesting to notice that he quotes – with apparent approval – one of the Cretan prophets (verse 12)?

He adds his little word — 'This testimony is true.' The lovely thing about it is this: he knows the reputation of the Cretans! In those days there was a fashionable word 'cretanising', which you used about those who were really reprehensible and really corrupt. But mark Paul's emphasis. When he talks about Cretans he says, 'They're liars and gluttons and brutes and rascals — they've got everything wrong — now, rebuke them, correct them, silence them . . . and win them. Win them over; that's the job.'

Training God's people (2:1-10)

Now we talk about training God's people. I want to outline to you the intent, the extent, and the content of this training.

The intent of the training

Here we find the idea continued in verse 1: 'You must teach what is in accord with sound doctrine.' Literally, the order in Greek is: 'But you speak things which become healthy teaching'. 'But *you*' — in other words, in marked contrast to the spurious teachers who are spewing out all the garbage, you, Titus, stand firm with sound teaching.

But notice something else important here. We are not just to disseminate healthy teaching, we are to teach *what is in accord with* healthy teaching. That means 'that which is becoming'. It's a lovely old word. My understanding of it is this. You know that you have to be careful what you wear, depending on what shape you are. If you are rather large, you are not supposed to wear horizontal stripes. They are not 'becoming' to you. Some things are suitable and some are not suitable, not 'becoming'.

Now then, in the training of the church of Jesus Christ

we get all these new believers coming in. They've gone forward at an evangelistic crusade, perhaps. They come into our churches; and they haven't a clue. They've only been Christians for a short time. They know hardly anything of biblical Christianity. They'll come in with all kinds of weird ideas they had before they became Christians. They're going to propagate utter heresy; their lifestyles will be abominable.

So what are we going to do? Kick them out on their ears? No! We're going to lead them into healthy teaching, and then we're going to show them that which is in accord with healthy teaching. We're going to show them what is suitable behaviour for healthy teaching.

One of the most exciting mornings that my wife Jill and I ever had in our lives was after one of the first coffee-bar crusades ever held in this country — in fact I think it was the first. We decided we would take some of our converts to church. It wasn't a very big church — we took along with us about as many people who were in the congregation already.

We all marched down to the front — being an evangelical church all the back seats were already taken! Our long-haired friends had never been in church before. The only thing remotely like it that they knew was the cinema. So they went in as if it were a cinema; they put their feet on the chairs in front of them, produced combs and combed their long locks, and chatted in normal voices — nobody had told them about 'holy hushes'! The minister got up and said 'Shall we sing together hymn number 34?' — and seeing that they'd been asked they said 'Why not?'. Then the offering came, without any explanation, and suddenly to their untold delight a plate appeared covered in money, so they helped themselves and then discussed how much they'd got . . . then the sermon, full of rhetorical questions – 'As I confronted this angry man, I asked, what should I do? And friends, what would you do?' – well, he shouldn't have asked!

A question: when these pagans, these lovely pagans just converted, come into your right little, tight little fellowships – who is going to give them sound teaching? Who is going to get alongside them to show them what is suitable behaviour on the part of those who believe sound teaching? It's such an immense job that has to be done. There's got to be a training programme. There have got to be trainers.

But there's something else important here. In verse 10 the original language used for 'make the teaching . . . attractive' is that used to describe putting a jewel in a setting that will show it off to best advantage. Isn't that delightful? You have a diamond that just looks like a dirty piece of glass. Then it gets into the hands of an expert. He knows how to cut it and he knows how to polish it and soon it sparkles in your hand. And then, you can give it to a jeweller who will put it in exactly the right setting and it will be shown off to its best advantage.

The intent of training in the church of Jesus Christ is: number one, get sound doctrine across to its members; number two, show them suitable behaviour as it applies to that sound doctrine; number three, teach them that they themselves have a unique opportunity in their own situations to show off the truth of God, like a jewel in the proper setting.

A good friend of mine who came to Christ recently came to see me. 'I'm leaving my job,' he said. 'It's impossible to be a Christian and to manage a used car showroom.' I replied, 'I don't believe that.' So we read Titus together and we came to the conclusion that his used car showroom could be the setting in which the jewel of his Christianity could be seen to its fullest advantage.

The wife of one of our elders was dying in hospital. I spent a lot of time with her. We spent that time finding out how her hospital bed could be the ideal setting in which the jewel of sound teaching and suitable behaviour could be displayed. A constant stream of people passing through that hospital ward were being exposed to a radiant testimony that came from sound teaching, suitable behaviour, properly set off in that situation.

But people need training to know how to do it. Occasional sermons aren't enough. It's not enough to once in a while tell people to read their Bibles. In my experience most people don't listen very carefully to sermons. Don't let's kid ourselves! If we are to take seriously this question of training God's people it's going to take some creative training. It's going to take some people who know what they're doing — and will do it.

Now, I ask you; is your church doing that?

The extent of the training
Here I'll just give you my outline, and you can follow it through if you want to.

First of all, *we've got to manage the people*. Notice what Paul says in verse 2 — 'we've got some older men'. Then in verse 3 — 'older women'. In verse 4 — 'younger women'; in verse 5, 'young men'. Notice especially that he is saying that old men need one thing, old women another, young women another and young men another. He goes on to say 'We've got some slaves around here, and some masters. Slaves need one thing, masters another' (verses 9, 10).

My experience in the ministry is that if we're going to even half-way seriously attempt to train God's people to mature in the Word, we've got to manage them, get them into different groups where we can address things that are relevant to them. If we just lump everybody together all the time, I think we're not going to get very far.

Secondly, *we've got to mobilise the team*. We've got to mobilise the elders by appointing them – finding out who they are – showing them what to do and how to do it. We've got to mobilise the older women, the younger women, the older men, the younger men.

And then *we've got to model the truth*. Verse 7: '. . . set them an example by doing what is good.' Don't just tell them – show them. Not only that; as you model the truth yourself, make sure that your teaching comes across with integrity, seriousness and soundness of speech, so much so that even your opponents are hard put to find anything to criticse about you. It's a tall order – but that's what he tells us to do.

Then he said, 'If you're going to train these people, you're going to have to *maintain the pressure*.' Verse 15: 'These, then, are the things you should teach' – but notice how you teach them. By encouraging, by rebuking 'with all authority' and by refusing to let anybody put you down. You get on with it. That's the extent of the training.

The content of the training

Well, this you can study for yourself. Find out what we've got to teach the older men, the older women, the younger women, the younger men. Find out what we've got to teach the disadvantaged. Then ask yourself a question. What exactly are *we* doing in *our* church to produce a healthy, radiant, robust body, as we carefully protect from that which would hinder and spoil, as we positively teach and train and equip the people?

3. Purifying and Reminding God's People (Titus 2:11-3:5)

We have been endeavouring to identify the double theme that runs through Paul's letter to Titus: on one hand, we are taught that God is drawing out for Himself and (2:14) purifying for Himself a people that is His very own. On the other hand, we see that this people of God is to be found in a visible and tangible dimension, in local fellowships dotted throughout the world.

We've been thinking, therefore, of what it means to be a believer in terms of our individual relationship to the Lord Jesus Christ, and also in terms of our corporate relationship not only to Him but to His people. Sometimes people say 'I'm a member of the church – I'm a member of that invisible, mystical, universal body, the church.' That's great. But the New Testament talks about the church not only in that sense but in the sense of churches in little towns and big centres all over Crete, and in Rome, and Corinth, and Ephesus. Therefore we've got to recognise that it's not enough to say that my spiritual experience is found in that mystical, invisible, universal body. It has also to be evidenced in a highly visible, highly tangible, highly geographical body of Christ called the local church.

Purifying God's people (2:11-15)

Now I want to try to explain this beautiful passage of Scripture by means of an illustration. San Francisco is, without doubt, the most beautiful city in the United States. It has many things to commend it. One of them is the magnificent Golden Gate Bridge. The object of this bridge is to make it possible for people to get from one side of the deep harbour channel to the other.

Now, I want to suggest that first of all, this passage shows *where people are*. It speaks of people who have all kinds of problems with ungodliness and worldly passions – they're filled with wickedness. But the passage shows that God's intent is to get people to *where He wants them to be* – to the position of being a people that are His very own, purified for Himself.

The question is, how does He get them from one side to the other? Well, He's built something rather like the Golden Gate Bridge. I want to show you what I mean as we go along.

Where people are

First of all let's look in a little more detail at where people are. First of all, Paul says we're a people active in ungodliness. Verse 12 – we are taught by the grace of God 'to say "No" to ungodliness'. And secondly, we're very much attracted to worldly passions. Ungodliness means simply to live as if God is irrelevant. Some have taken a great step of faith and decided that He does not exist. Unfortunately, while you don't need to know everything in order to know that God exists, you *do* have to know everything to know whether He doesn't. But of course nobody does know everything! Yet there are people who have taken this illogical position and have built their lives on it, and live ungodly lives.

Not all ungodly people are atheists. A lot of them go to church, and simply keep God delightfully isolated from the realities of their lives. They visit Him once a week. They relate to Him like a sick relative in hospital – they grudgingly give Him an hour a week, but fundamentally they're living in ungodliness, where God is irrelevant and esteemed as less than God.

In addition, people who are actively living as though God is irrelevant are automatically attracted to worldly passions. Now we get into a lot of problems with these. Often standards of worldliness vary from one national culture to another, and if we're not very careful we can get ourselves hooked into issues which may be secondary – while at the same time avoiding the primary issues. So what does 'worldly passions' mean here?

John gives us the answer in 1 John 2, where he says that they are: the lusts of the flesh, the lusts of the eyes, and the pride of life. I would suggest to you that the lust of the flesh means wanting total freedom to give reign to one's own passions; that the lust of the eyes means wanting total freedom to amass my own possessions; and that the pride of life means wanting total freedom to establish my own position. Our secular society is comprised of people who are defending their own patch of turf, who are amassing their own material things and are reserving the right to do exactly what they wish. That's worldliness as I understand it.

We must be very careful. If we live in a society that simply regards God as irrelevant and has filled the gap by allowing itself to be governed by attitudes of self-interest, then we'll begin to see that our society has the seeds of its own destruction already sown.

But Paul points out where people are, and where they are is rooted 'in this present age' (verse 12). He teaches us to say 'No' to unrighteousness and worldly passions, and to live self-controlled, upright and godly lives in this present age. In Scripture 'this present age' is constantly set in contradistinction to the age to come, in which God's glory will be seen, the age wherein dwells righteousness. In marked contrast to that, there is a present age that is ungodly, governed by intrinsic selfishness; the result is that there is a great sense of wickedness. And Paul refers to this in verse 14, where he says that Jesus Christ 'gave himself for us to redeem us from all wickedness' (the word literally means, 'lawlessness'). Now put all that together and – if we can put it this way – you'll see the problem confronting God.

This is where people are. Don't let's kid ourselves. This is where people live.

Building the bridge

God sees them on one side of that deep channel, and He says, 'Now I want to get them from that place into the position of being My special, purified people.'

It is one of the great challenges, one of the exciting things that confront the church of Jesus Christ. The world in which we live is characterised by those things of which Paul speaks. We could say 'That's how the world is. We'll ignore it. We'll isolate ourselves, insulate ourselves from it.' But that hardly fits into God's plan, for His plan is that from this group He will draw out a people that are His special possession, purified for Himself. And surely we have to be involved in that!

The question is, how does He do it? Let's look at His project. When the bridge-builders in San Francisco built, the first thing they did was to build two towers; then from those towers they suspended two cables to carry a road upon which people could move from where they were to where they wanted to be. God's project is not dissimilar.

First, the towers. I draw your attention to the word 'appear' that occurs in verse 11 and in verse 13. The Greek word is the one from which we get the word 'epiphany', which still has a place in the Church of England calendar. It means, literally, 'an appearing'. I suggest to you that God has determined to get people from where they are to where He wants them to be by building two towers in space and time. Those two towers are the two appearings, the epiphanies. The first is *the epiphany of grace*: it has happened. The second is *the epiphany of glory*: it is our glorious hope, it is yet to come.

The epiphany of grace. It's very important that we understand that God's purpose in getting people to where He wants them to be is based on specific, verifiable facts in terms of time and history. The great God, our Saviour, really did come. He really was born, lived, died and rose again. Many people would prefer to treat the Christian religion as a set of fables and fairy tales. But God did not send us fairy tales. He sent His Son into time and space, to earth; and He has built His tower deeply-rooted in our world. The epiphany of grace has happened. Equally certainly, the epiphany of glory will happen. It is something still shrouded in the mists of the future, but as surely as He has come, He will come.

See the beautiful things Paul says about this first epiphany, this first tower on which God is building the road to take people from where they are to where He wants them to be. He calls it 'the epiphany of grace, that brings salvation'.

'Grace' is a delightful term, isn't it? The way I like to

think of grace is that it is set in contrast to justice and mercy. Justice gives me what I deserve. Mercy refrains from giving me all I deserve. Grace gives me what I do not deserve. When I punish my son for a misdemeanour by spanking him, that's justice. When I let him off with eight spanks when he deserves ten, that's mercy. When I buy him an ice-cream afterwards, that's grace – I am giving him what he doesn't deserve.

The marvellous thing is that God, who has freely chosen to deal with us on the basis of justice (as He must, to be consistent with His own nature as the Righteous Judge), has also freely chosen to mingle mercy and grace with His justice, to give us what we do not deserve. He freely chose to give us His Son. He has appeared, in time and space, and as surely as that great tower of the Golden Gate Bridge stands tall and true, the epiphany of grace has happened.

Notice the sheer greatness of what He has done. In verse 13 He is called 'our great God and Saviour'. How is greatness demonstrated? In a variety of ways, but surely the greatness of God in terms of our salvation is demonstrated in the fact that He laid His greatness aside and accepted the humble role. That takes real greatness. God humbled Himself when He had all sorts of options to do otherwise, and therein lies His greatness. And so the tower stands tall and true and strong. In grace Christ has appeared. In greatness God has invaded our planet. Without comment, the text simply says, 'He gave himself'. The greatness of that gift!

The epiphany of glory. In verse 13 Paul says, 'We wait for the blessed hope – the glorious appearing of our great God and Saviour, Jesus Christ.' He is of course referring to the fact that we await another historical event, which will be as much an invasion of time and space and human history as

the initial epiphany. Scripture talks of it in two different
ways. Here and in Acts 2 it is referred to as the *glorious*
day of the Lord; but sometimes it is referred to as the
dreadful day of the Lord. The Jewish people often spoke
of the 'Day of the Lord'. They felt that though they had
been oppressed through much of their history, they were
still God's people and that they were doing things properly
and that one day, in the consummation of all things, God
would vindicate them. One way in which He would
vindicate them would be by pouring out His holy
indignation upon their enemies. That idea is picked up in
the New Testament, and we are shown the day of the Lord
as a day of dreadful judgement for those who are not
God's people and a day of glorious vindication for those
who are His people. And that is something we keenly
anticipate.

The cable of redemption. Suspended on those two
historical events we find two great theological truths,
suspended like cables. In verse 14 Paul talks about God
giving Himself 'to redeem us from all wickedness'. But
also in verse 14 he says it was 'to purify for himself a
people that are his very own'. The two theological 'cables'
suspended from the two historical facts are the truth of
redemption and the truth of sanctification – for that is the
key meaning of the word here for 'purify'.

You can't build a suspension bridge with only one
tower, ladies and gentlemen. Neither can you build a
suspension bridge with only one cable. You need two –
otherwise the whole thing will collapse! Let's make certain
that in our presentation of the gospel we understand the
two epiphanies, but equally that we hold in tension the two
cables. It's not enough just to tell people how to be saved.
It is imperative that the cable alongside the message of

redemption is the cable of the message of sanctification.

The idea of redemption has its roots in the slave market, where somebody would come into the market, be concerned for the slaves, pay the price, remove their chains, take them by the hand and lead them from the market. It's a rather nice illustration. However, it doesn't really make an awful lot of sense to us today. A more modern illustration of what redemption is might be the story I heard recently of a helicopter pilot who flew, at terrible risk to himself, into a blazing oilfire and was winched into the smoke and flames to rescue a man who was trapped. As I thought about what he did at considerable risk to himself, I couldn't help thinking of the glorious truth of redemption. For the two epiphanies have, suspended upon them, the truth that our Lord Jesus came into the clouds and the oily smoke and the flames, was lowered down right alongside us, put His arms around us, gave the signal and has raised us up into newness of life with Him. That's how He does it.

The cable of sanctification. But that's only half the story. The other half is the story of sanctification. We recognise a very simple truth; if the Lord Jesus Christ has redeemed us it is in order that we might become His possession. We belong to Him. In a special way we are His, and, as we have been mentioning already in the course of these studies, we have been set apart for Him.

It's important that we stress this, for one very simple reason. It is not uncommon to find people who know that Christ *has* come, but do not live in terms of the fact that He *will* come. Equally, it is not uncommon to come across people who rejoice in the fact that they have been redeemed, but have absolutely no sense of being set apart or sanctified or purified or peculiarly belonging to Him.

It is important that we understand these things and keep them in tension.

Crossing the bridge

Now, having built His towers and suspended His cables, God walks across His bridge to where we are active in ungodliness, worldly passions and so forth, and invites us – on the basis of the epiphany, on the basis of the theological truths of redemption and sanctification – to become His people. And we begin the journey, from where we are to where He wants us to finish up, specially purified – His people.

A question. Are you on the bridge? Are you progressing, across the bridge?

Let's see where we go from here in this purifying process. Let's look again at this passage of Scripture, and we will see that there are three factors that are involved.

Firstly, in verse 12 Paul tells us that the epiphany of grace teaches us something. This is important. There is an *educational factor* here. The epiphany of grace teaches us – what? It teaches us to say 'No' to ungodliness and worldly passions and 'Yes' to a self-controlled, upright and godly life.

The extent to which the grace of God has taught us to do this tells us how we're doing in terms of belonging to an increasingly set-apart, purified, sanctified people. And if we are being saved from ungodliness and worldly passions and the encroachment of this present age, then we have to accept the fact that whilst we still live in this present age we have got to learn to disassociate ourselves from much of the attitudes, aspirations and activities of the secular society in which we're a part. But be careful! This is not a call to a hermitage. We are called to live this self-denying life *in this present age*. We're still here, we're still in the midst of it – for what? To be salt and light. So the educational process is that as I understand the grace of God, the epiphany of grace and the epiphany of glory, so I'm going to understand salvation and redemption. I'm going to understand sanctification. I'm going to see how so much of what was normative in my life before is incompatible with my new relationship with Christ. And carefully, I'm going to learn to say 'No'.

It's a growth process. I don't know any short cuts. When I was at the Lausanne Convention a number of years ago I signed the 'Lausanne Covenant'. One part of signing that was that we thereby committed ourselves to a simple lifestyle. I wasn't sure what that was, exactly, but I certainly committed myself to a *simpler* lifestyle. You wouldn't believe what a struggle it was. Do you know, people have certain expectations of you? The way you dress, the kind of home you live in, the kind of car you drive, the kind of schools your children go to – one member of my church came up to me and said, 'Stuart, why are you wearing that suit? You make it look as if we don't pay you round here!'

It's difficult. You know it's difficult to say 'No' to worldly attitudes. It's difficult to say 'No' – and it's difficult to say 'Yes'. Yes to what? To discipline. To righteousness. To a godly reverence in the whole of life. That, of course, is what in verse 12 Paul says we should say 'Yes' to. We are to say 'Yes' to a disciplined life. Are you disciplined in your life? In the way you eat? In sleep, in study, in exercise? Or are you just sort of flopping around the place?

So in the purifying process we're crossing the bridge, and the educational factor is important.

Secondly, verse 13: *the expectation factor*. There are some who are not looking for Christ's return, who do not

long for His appearing. They're too selfish. They're
bound up in their materialism, and for Christ to come
back again – quite frankly, it would spoil everything for
them. They're in no hurry. They're like the wealthy
Californian Christian of whom her friend said, 'When she
dies and gets to heaven, she's going to long for the good
old days.'

Of course, some people *are* looking for the return of the
Lord Jesus Christ – for the same selfish reasons. 'I blew
it!' they say. 'Oh Lord, come quickly and rescue me,
before I live with the consequences of my own stupidity!'
They seem to have no concern whatsoever for the fact that
the gospel of the kingdom has first to be preached in all
nations – then the end will come. Let's get this glorious
return of Jesus Christ out of the realm of the selfish and
into the realm of understanding that when He does come
in great glory it will be the consummation of all things.
We are going to be ushered into something totally beyond
our expectations. But what a terrible day of judgement it
will be for those who are not ready.

Now we live in the light of His coming. That affects
you. The grace of God educates you; the expectation of
the return of Christ educates you too, and begins to affect
the way you say 'No' and the way you say 'Yes'.

Thirdly, *the enthusiasm factor*. It's an interesting word,
related to the Greek word *entheosmania*, which described
the idea that the gods get into you, and when they do they
liven things up a bit! In the same way, if you get into God
because God gets into you, it produces a kind of mania.
It's called enthusiasm.

Notice the enthusiasm that is talked about here.
Because of the epiphany, because of the theological
structure, because of where we were, because of where we
can be and what God is doing and what we expect God to

do – we get all enthusiastic; and do you know how we show it? By being (verse 14) eager to do what is good.

Do you belong to a fellowship of God's very own people? Are they on tip-toe, eager to do what needs to be done? We're going to be talking about motivation shortly. The best way to get people motivated is to go up to them and say, 'Isn't God good? Isn't it exciting to serve Him?' Then they say 'Yes', and then you say 'Right – this is what we want you to do!' It's amazing how they can then start demonstrating their love for God and desire to do good works.

Reminding God's people (3:1-5)

You will notice that the tense with which this section begins is '*Go on* reminding.' Not just 'Remind them once and for all', but go on doing so.

My memory is something I use to forget things with. Do you have that problem? Dr Johnson is said to have remarked that 'men more often need to be reminded than instructed.' Let's remind God's people constantly! Let's go on reminding them constantly of three things; how they used to live, how they were saved, and how they ought to behave. Those are the three things Paul speaks of here.

Remind them how they used to live in relation to God
Verse 3: they were foolish and disobedient. Foolish means having their understanding darkened. It's possible to hear something without understanding it. There are people at Keswick today who lived for years hearing God's words but not understanding what they were hearing. It didn't register.

The first time I went to a cricket match I asked the reason for a sudden burst of applause. 'He just bowled a maiden over,' I was told. 'They ought not to encourage him!' I replied. My understanding was darkened.

Let's be sensitive to where people are. Let's go on reminding ourselves of where we were, because if you go on reminding yourself where you were, it's much easier to know where they are.

In relation to ourselves, he goes on to say, still in verse 3, 'deceived and enslaved by all kinds of passions'. Deceived by mis-information. 'In times of war,' remarked Churchill, 'the truth is so precious she must always be attended by a bodyguard of lies.' I want to suggest to you that the devil has the same philosophy. In times of war he specialises in surrounding everybody with a bodyguard of lies – and we're suckers for it, we're deceived. And the basic deception is that God is irrelevant and we are all-important.

That's where we used to be. And it helps you to understand the people out there who are not interested in your church nor in your Jesus. You see, they've been sold a bill of goods. So we've got to go on reminding God's people how they used to live, in relation to God and to themselves and to others.

People are so interested in getting their relationships right! But they don't realise that before they can do that they have to get their act together with God. If we're out of sync with Him, we're out of touch with ourselves and out of favour with others. That's why Paul puts it so beautifully here. 'We were foolish and disobedient' – Godward; 'deceived and enslaved' – as far as we ourselves are concerned; 'malice, envy, being hated and hating one another' – the result in relation to others. That's how we used to live. We've got to go on reminding.

Remind them how they were saved
Three things here; I'll just outline them for you. Firstly,

salvation is an act. God acts, as Saviour. Think of all the capacities in which He could have acted! But He chooses to act in the capacity of Saviour. He acts, in loving kindness, in mercy. The result is renewal and rebirth. Go on reminding the people of the act of God in their lives, of the initiative He took.

Secondly, *salvation is a fact*. It is readily verifiable by the epiphany, as we have said already; by the dramatic intervention by God in time and space, into human affairs.

And *it is a pact*. God has said it, offered it, sealed it with His blood.

Remind them how they should behave

Here we find Paul emphasising behaviour in verses 1 and 2. God's people should behave well in terms of authority, in terms of charity – 'eager to do what is good'.

God's people are to be kind. You'll find the word 'kindness' relating to God all over the place in Titus, and you'll also find it all over the place relating to God's people. We've got to go on reminding people what it means to have a spirit of helpfulness, to have an eagerness to do what's good and to be just old-fashioned kind.

Behaviour in terms of authority – in terms of charity, kindness – and also in terms of integrity. Don't slander people. Say what is true, speak what is necessary. Also behaviour in terms of dignity; be peaceable (don't get into fights), be considerate, show true humility towards all people. I take that to mean the dignity of handling relationships with deep concern, of treating people with care, of doing things with courtesy. The church of Jesus Christ breeds more than its fair share of rude, inconsiderate, pig-headed, hard-nosed believers, who by no stretch of the imagination give you the impression that they've got far across the bridge. Those same kind of people do absolutely nothing to make the gospel of our Lord Jesus attractive. That's why we've got to go on reminding people. Where they were. How they were saved. How they should behave. So there's lots to do, isn't there, as we get back to our churches? We are part of straightening out what's crooked and finishing off what's unfinished – all in order that God might purify for Himself a people that are His very own.

4. Motivating and Warning God's People (Titus 3:5-15)

Now we go back to the passage we were looking at in our previous study. Let us read together verses 5-8.

I want to draw your attention to what Paul tells Titus in verse 8. After some marvellous passages describing Christian theology – the gospel – he says, 'I want you to *stress* these things.' Again the emphasis is on the absolute necessity of teaching the Word of God. But notice the objective in all his teaching: 'so that those who have trusted in God may be careful to devote themselves to doing what is good'. In other words, it's not a matter of accumulating theological information for its own sake, but so that it might become the fuel of our endeavours. There are all sorts of people who want to get into all kinds of endeavours without fuel. On the other hand there are people who want to be filling their tanks with fuel all the time, but don't want to switch on the ignition! They don't want to start their wheels roaring down the freeway to achieve something for the glory of God. And we have to ensure not only that people are getting the fuel of the teaching of God, but that they know how to put all this tremendous power into gear, so that there is powerful motivation and powerful mobilisation.

So I would suggest to you that the great climax of these beautiful passages concerning our redemption and sanctification is to show that all these things are intended to become a powerful motivating factor in our lives.

Motivating God's people (3:5-9)

Those of us who are in the ministry know that motivating people is one of our prime tasks, and, not infrequently, one of our less encouraging ones. I have listened to various preachers trying to motivate their congregations. Some adopt the pleading approach ('Who among you will help me in this task?'). Some use the challenging approach ('I challenge you to help me . . .'). Some try the threatening approach ('With great sorrow I have to announce that unless there is a dramatic change I must tender my resignation at the end of the month . . .')!

Well, don't let's laugh too hard at them, because we're probably laughing at ourselves. But what *can* we do to motivate people?

I believe that what Paul is telling Titus is something that we have very often overlooked in our ministry, and it is this. The most powerful, most enduring motivating factor in the church of Jesus Christ is to ensure that people are taught the truth; then to ensure that they know how to apply the truth; and to teach the truth in such a way that they become excited about the truth.

We can teach the Word of God, we can get it across to people. We can make absolutely certain that they've got it all right. But let's face it, they may still end up deserving the same verdict as the competitor at the singing contest who had rehearsed until he knew the piece perfectly but was still adjudged to 'lack passion'.

Somehow or other we can fail to motivate the people of God. Somehow or other, if we're not careful in our ministry, we may not be doing what Paul tells Titus to do in the church of Crete. 'Stress those things' – so that the end product will be that God's people are devoting themselves to doing what is good.

There are several factors involved in motivating the people of God. We'll look at them in turn. Firstly, it involves,

Underscoring what is important
Note that Paul outlines three very, very important things here. First of all,

Where salvation originates. Salvation originates with the grace of God. Verse 7: salvation becomes real in the appearing of Jesus Christ. Verse 6: salvation becomes actual in our lives through the outpouring of the Holy Spirit in our lives. It's important to remember that real motivation in spiritual life and witness and service comes from underscoring what is important. And the most important thing we can underscore is that our salvation in which we rejoice originates in the grace of God, comes to us through the appearing of the Lord Jesus, and is actualised in our lives through the outpouring of the Holy Spirit.

What salvation incorporates. What is involved? First of all in verse 5: *the washing of rebirth.* The cleansing from past defilement, the opportunity of a fresh beginning, the application of the blood of Christ, the invasion of our lives, the cleansing power of the Word of God, and the experience of baptism – which clearly demonstrates what it really means to be cleansed in clean, fresh water and have all the junk and filth washed away and become excited about the fact that I'm washed and I'm *clean*.

It's hard for some people to experience this, to get excited about it. You've heard their rather apologetic testimonies, where they describe their conversion in a Christian home at a very early age. That's a perfectly valid testimony, but the problem is that they are having to think very, very hard to remember what all those bad things are from which they have been cleansed. On the other hand there are some people who've got a rip-roaring testimony, and one gets the impression that the more times they give it the more it rips and the more it roars. Exaggeration can be a problem!

I sympathise with people who, in a sense, don't have a dramatic testimony so they can talk about all the junk and garbage that has been washed away; but on the other hand, even if we were very young when we came to the Lord Jesus, we've got to remember this. There was an attitude of rebellion, there was a state of alienation, there was a life that was not directed to the glory of God; and that is the heinousness of sin, and that did need to be cleansed.

All of us, however early we came to know Christ, have got to rejoice in what it means to be cleansed in the blood of Christ.

The second thing that salvation incorporates is *renewal by the Holy Spirit*. Paul speaks of this also in verse 5. What a beautiful thing it is to know that I have been renewed! I have a new mind. How wonderful to know that I do not need to lose heart, for while my outward body is collapsing, my inward mind is being constantly renewed. This something God is doing in my life. It's a simple fact. How grateful I am for the washing of rebirth! How grateful I am for renewal by the Holy Spirit!

The third thing that salvation incorporates is *justification by grace*. This is mentioned in verse 7. God is righteous. When we put ourselves alongside the righteousness of His character, we see our own intrinsic unrighteousness. But then we see the divine initiative, which has reached out from heaven and brought us to the point of making us right with God. Then we know that the evidence has been presented, the Judge has found us guilty, but He has then stepped down from the bench, removed His robes and His wig, and, having passed the penalty, has paid it Himself and totally acquitted us. We have been justified freely by His grace. And now we are in right standing before Him. Stress these things!

The fourth thing is also mentioned in verse 7. *We have become heirs of eternal life*. We are rich beyond our wildest dreams. I can at the present time know eternal life in some measure, but I look forward to that time when in its full actualisation I will enjoy all that eternal life means, both in terms of quality and quantity. To this I look forward. It is my hope.

Stress these things. Get people excited about being heirs of God and joint-heirs with Christ. Get people excited about heaven. Give people that high sense of privilege! I believe that this is the undergirding factor in motivating God's people.

Do you have a problem in getting people motivated? Is that the problem in your church? Well, let me encourage you to make absolutely certain that the people really understand what is important in terms of what God has done.

How salvation relates. The third thing to underscore is how salvation relates, and in verse 8 we are reminded that it becomes real to us, it relates to our experience, as we trust God. The grace of God makes it available to us. Faith appropriates these things, and they become real in our experience. These are the things that we must go on underscoring.

I sometimes wonder whether we're producing anaemic believers, because when you look at the nourishment they're taking in from the Scriptures they seem somewhat undernourished, somewhat underfed. Am I talking to somebody now, who would have to say: 'Quite frankly, if I had to give a talk on the washing of rebirth, or the renewal of the Holy Spirit, or justification by grace, or what it means to be an heir of eternal life – I couldn't do it. Yet I've been in church for twenty years.'?

I wonder why that is? I think perhaps it's because we don't understand that truly motivated people are those who have had the truth of God properly stressed in their lives and applied.

Understanding what is significant
Now secondly, motivating includes understanding what is significant. There's a very simple thing I want to draw out which I find constantly encouraging. It is this. Christian theology is based on the doctrine of grace; but *Christian ethics are based on the doctrine of gratitude.*

Let me explain what I mean. I have always regretted failing Latin at school. If you want to understand the English language a knowledge of Latin is tremendously helpful; and if you want to read some of the Reformers and their theology, a little Latin goes a long way. Now, one of the things that the Reformers used to say was 'Sola gratia' – 'grace alone'. Let me show you the point of this so far as my limited Latin is concerned, and it's simply this; 'gratia' is the Latin word for 'grace', but it's also the word from which we get our English word 'gratitude'. In other words, if you've got a good dose of 'gratia', then you demonstrate it by a good dose of 'gratitude'.

Paul explains this in 1 Corinthians 15:10, where you'll remember he says first of all that he is the least of all the apostles, that Christ appeared to him out of due time; and then he says: His grace was not wasted on me, for 'I worked harder than all of them.' What is he saying? That his experience of the grace of God resulted in a lifetime of work to the point of exhaustion – that's the Greek word he uses.

Gratitude towards the Lord

Possibly the most delightful motivating factor in the church of Jesus Christ is that people do things out of gratitude to God. 'Lord,' they say, 'how can I express my gratitude?' Sometimes they go off in very extravagant ways. We get the idea, you see, that we could really demonstrate how grateful we are to God by dreaming up the most extravagant, extreme thing imaginable. But that isn't what He wants us to do. He wants us to demonstrate our gratitude to Him for His 'gratia' in our lives by being willingly committed to the point of exhaustion to doing what He wants us to do. What a lovely thing it would be if those who sit in their churches and those who preach and teach would stress these things, so thoroughly that they light a fire of gratitude in people's hearts! So that the people look around and say, 'If I don't find a way of expressing my gratitude, I'll burst!'

Then those in the leadership must say, 'Well, before you burst, may I suggest you do this . . . that you do that . . . that you do the other?' Here is a great burden on the leadership of the church. Mobilising the motivated!

If you look at an average church and work out what it's really doing, and then take pen and paper and calculate

how many man-hours that requires in the week, you'll find
that the average church only requires ten per cent of its
people to be doing anything at all. That's a wasted
resource, and it suggests to me that what the leadership
probably needs to be doing constantly is so to stress the
truth that people begin to get a kindling gratitude. Then
the leadership should be looking for new avenues, new
areas of outreach, new involvements where people can
begin to do things they've never done before out of the
sheer exuberance of doing it unto the Lord, out of
gratitude. I have to say that one of the most challenging
things in my ministry is to be constantly looking for
opportunities for people to channel their burgeoning
gratitude. It's important!

Gratitude for what I have received
Understanding the truth of the gospel not only produces
gratitude in me towards the Lord, it also produces
gratitude in me for what I have received in contrast to
other people. When I begin to understand the grace of God
I remember where I used to be. And the lovely thing about
that is that it helps me to recognise where people are.

Some of us have been in church, surrounded by
Christian people, for so long that we've forgotten how
unbelievers really feel. We don't know how to relate to
them any more – and that's sad. If we stress the message of
the gospel and all the riches that are ours in Christ, it will
of course only help us to remember what *we* have. But
when we remember what we have, it helps us to remember
what people need. However, sometimes we're so picky
about what we have and what we don't have, that we have
lost sight of what it is that people need. But as I soak up
the truth and it reminds me of what I have, it's supposed to
go on reminding me of what people *need*. I must stress

these things, so that people will become eager; eager to do
the things that need doing.

Undertaking what is necessary

One final point about motivation; it includes undertaking
what is necessary. Notice 3:8 – it's delightful: 'These things
are excellent and profitable for everyone.' What things?
Devoting themselves to doing what is good. There are three
expressions here. Motivation: I am prepared to undertake
what is necessary (which is first and foremost a devotion to
what is good). Desire: desire for what is excellent. And
thirdly, willingness: a willingness to do what is profitable
in eternal currency.

Now would you ask yourselves a question? Ask yourself:
'Can I see the expression of "gratia" in my life, in terms of
gratitude; and is my gratitude being expressed in a lifestyle
of utter devotion to what's good? A desire for that which is
excellent in God's service, and a thorough involvement in
doing things that are profitable for eternity?

Warning God's people (3:9-15)

Now I want to pick out another aspect of church life that is
obviously on the apostle's heart and, I think, needs to be
on our hearts too; and that is the whole matter of warning
God's people.

Read with me from verse 9 of chapter 3, and notice that
though the concluding verses of the letter contain mostly
personal greetings, in verse 14 Paul returns to the theme
that has been prevalent right through, a very dominant,
powerful theme: 'Our people must learn to devote themselves to doing what is good, in order that they may
provide for daily necessities and not live unproductive
lives.'

Undoubtedly, the church of Christ in the apostolic era was subjected to all kinds of threatening outside influences. But it is equally without doubt that as it began to grow it began to have influences bearing upon it inside, too. The great concern that the apostle Paul has is that there is a very real possibility of division from within the Christian fellowship, producing disintegration; and the result will be splits in the body of believers. He warns about what will happen if the people become divisive.

I want to identify two warnings here. Firstly, *division in the church cannot be accepted*. Secondly, *discipline in the church must not be avoided*. Very often the Christian church gets them the wrong way round.

Division in the church

There's a kind of build-up in verses 9 and 10. You start off with 'foolish controversies' – the raising of an issue. But then you find that the raising of the issue produces different reactions in people; now all kinds of argument develops. And if they are not handled properly they degenerate into quarrels. The word translated 'quarrels' in verse 9 means 'fights'. We've all seen it, unfortunately. It begins with the raising of a church issue, and before we know it we finish up with a church fight. And the only way it is 'resolved' (though nothing is resolved thereby) is that the believers split.

Paul says that we have got to be aware of this, we have got to be on our toes and on our knees. So let's spend a little time on what I would like to call, an analysis of a division in the church.

Let me first suggest to you, that differences are inevitable. Why? Because of *the nature of people* and *the nature of the church*.

The nature of people is simply this; that when you get a

community of believers, you get differences between those people. For example, you get *differences in scriptural knowledge*. Now we're all well aware of that. If you have a man who's read theology at Oxford or Cambridge in your fellowship, and you also get some dear old souls who, like the preacher I once knew, get confused between 'Mary Magdalene' and 'Mary Mandoline' – well, you've got some obvious differences. But they all belong in the fellowship equally. So differences will be there.

There are *differences in spiritual experience*. One of the delightful things about the church of Jesus Christ is that it's a family; and families have grandmas and grandpas, and occasionally great-grandmas and great-grandpas; and mums and dads, and kids. You don't expect them all to know the same, and you don't expect them all to behave in the same way. You let the kids be kids, the mums be mums, the grandpas be grandpas. It's normal. In the church of Christ people have differences in spiritual experience. Hopefully, we're all growing, and some have grown a little bit more than others, for the very simple reason that they've been at it longer.

There are *differences in social graces*. Have you noticed that? You've come across some people in the church of Jesus Christ who will tell you very proudly, 'Well, I call a spade a spade.' But then you've met other people who are absolutely sweet, they're marvellous; they come to you and beam at you and they say, 'Er . . . I wonder whether . . .?' They don't call a spade a spade – but they get there in the end. It takes longer, but you feel better about the whole thing when they're through! We've got differences there, and finally we've got *differences in psychological make-up*. Have you noticed, some people seem to have very short fuses? Some seem to have no fuses at all!

Differences in the church of Christ are inevitable also

because of the nature of the church. One of the most marvellous things we can read about the church of Jesus Christ is found in 1 Corinthians 12:4. There really are different spiritual gifts. There really are different ministries. There really are different ways of doing things. Did you know the Bible said that? Why don't we allow for it? God ordained differences! But before you get too excited about that, notice that he says that there are different gifts but the same Spirit; different kinds of service but the same Lord; and different kinds of work, but the same God.

The nature of the church is that God has built into it a unity that allows for all kinds of diversity. In fact, I submit to you, when God makes anything, that's how He does it. I recall demonstrating this with a group of missionaries in Japan, when we set out to count how many different kinds of the colour green there were in the countryside around us in Hokkaido. We discovered that no green was 'just' green. No two shades of green were identical. Neither did any two clash with each other. We discovered delightful unity and we discovered the most glorious diversity. That's how God makes things!

Differences in the church of Christ are inevitable because of the nature of people and because of the very nature of the church. God wants it that way. The unity He wants is not the unity of uniformity – everybody humming one note. He wants the unity of harmony – all kinds of different notes that fit in beautifully with each other and enrich each other.

Because differences are inevitable, differences are probable. But given the differences, along come the difficulties. Why? Sometimes, it's because of the position we have taken.

There's a marvellous story of Fraser of Lisuland, who,

after translating portions of the New Testament into the Lisu language left a young man with the people to teach them to read. Six months later he went back to see how they were getting on. He discovered something very fascinating. The three who were learning to read sat around a little table. The Scriptures were opened up on the table before them. The man on the left read them sideways. The man at the top read them upside down. The man on the right read them the other way up, and the man sitting in front of the book read the Scriptures the right way up. They'd learned to read like that. They each thought that was the way the language was written. The reason was that they had always sat in the same chairs and always read from the same positions.

I know people in the churches who've always sat the same way on every issue. And that's why you'll find all sorts of difficulties in the Christian church. People take up their positions and nobody ever changes chairs. Nobody ever discovers how somebody else sees it. Not only that. When your preconceptions become totally rigid, then your perceptions become clouded. You'll look at those who disagree with you with suspicion. It simply won't dawn on you that there may be validity in both sides.

Then as you begin to take up a position you promote a spokesman for your particular point of view, a personality who can put it better than you can. So what happens? The other side promotes a spokesman as well. Personality is set against personality, and in no time at all you've got party strife in the church, as happened at Corinth.

So you start with differences, which are delightful. You end up with some difficulties, which, if they're not handled properly, are very nasty indeed.

In such a situation, divisions are very possible. If differences have degenerated into difficulties and those difficulties are not being handled graciously and carefully, then there is a high probability that division in the church will be the result. It's a shame. Usually, it happens because diversity is valued more than unity, or individual pride is allowed to take precedence over the well-being of the corporate whole. That's how we get division.

The anathema of a division is this. The body of Christ suffers amputation, the cause of Christ suffers misrepresentation, and the disciples of Christ almost invariably suffer humiliation. And some of us are involved in it; and it won't do.

Discipline in the church

Now what does Paul say to Titus about this? Well, I'll just point it out to you. He says that when this sort of thing is happening, discipline is necessary.

When is discipline necessary? When people are disrupting the unity of the body. Why is Titus in Crete? He's there to straighten out what was left unfinished and appoint elders in every town – he is there to be instrumental in God purifying for Himself a people that are His very own.

When is discipline necessary? When the practices of part of the body corrupt the life of the whole. When there is inconsistency between professed belief and evident behaviour. When problems become so severe that they interrupt the ministry of the body of Christ.

How is discipline to be administered? Verse 10 tells us that those concerned are to be approached with a word of warning. There is to be an attempt at instruction, at speaking the truth in love. It's a fine balance. Some people are so loving, they'll lie to you. They'll say 'That was a marvellous sermon' – and it really wasn't; on the other hand, some people are *so* truthful – but are harsh and unloving. The prayers of the fellowship must be behind those who confront people, so that they will do it properly.

What happens if that doesn't work? Verse 10: they are to be warned a second time. And then? If they still don't take any notice, the people concerned have to be disciplined. They are to have nothing to do with the divisive person. Paul's language is very strong here.

I don't know of anything that conveys to me more powerfully how seriously God takes His church, than the Scriptures' statements about disciplining those who are divisive. And I think that one of the reasons we are not being what we need to be, nor doing what we ought to do, is that we're not motivating God's people or we're not warning them seriously enough of what it means to be a member of the body of Christ.

It's a down-note to finish on, isn't it? But perhaps that's what some of us need to look at seriously. We may be the divisive person. Or we may be leaders who have been missing out on the duties of leadership. It may be that our church has become corrupted. It may be that the ministry has become corrupted. It may be that because we're not doing what Paul told us to do, the name of Christ is not being uplifted and demonstrated as it ought to be.

My prayer is that we might get on with the work, straightening out what's left unfinished and being involved in seeing God prepare the people for Himself.

THE ADDRESSES

COMING TO CHRIST

by Rev David Jackman

Matthew 11:28-30

All over the country people have been coming to Christ in recent months during Mission England. We have rejoiced in that and prayed for those great meetings. Some of us will never forget the sound of all those feet going down the steps and walking out to come to Christ. But there is a very real sense in which we never stop coming; and these words remind us that to Christian people, as well as to those who come for the first time, He says, 'Come to Me.'

Now, it's hardly surprising that these words are described in the *Book of Common Prayer* as 'comfortable words', and yet even that could be misleading. For the call of the Lord Jesus is not a call to a nice warm drink by a cosy fireside with our slippered feet up on the spiritual mantelpiece. He calls us to take a yoke, and the yoke is a picture of obedience. He calls us not to repose but to activity, and as He does that, He calls us to fulfilment and freedom in the place of frustration and bondage. The comfort which Christ offers re-equips and strengthens us to live for Him in His world.

The background to the call

This invitation comes as the climax to a chapter full of questions and disappointments and denunciations. For John the Baptist, with whom the chapter opens, there was the burden of doubt that gave rise to his question from prison. When John heard what Christ was doing he sent his disciples to ask Him, 'Are You the one who was to come, or should we expect someone else?' John had portrayed the Christ as the one who would purge and cleanse, burning up the chaff with unquenchable fire, and that, says our Lord, in verses 20-24, will indeed be His work on the day of judgement. But His answer to John in verse 5 is that He has come in these days so that the blind may receive their sight, the lame walk, those that have leprosy be cured, the deaf hear, the dead be raised and the good news be preached to the poor. So our Lord says to John with his burden of doubt: 'My function is to reveal the Father's heart of love and mercy in compassion, in healing, yes, in resurrection and supremely in proclaiming the good news of the kingdom of God; and "Blessed is the man who does not fall away on account of me"' (verse 6). To recognise who Jesus really is, to submit to His wisdom and His authority is the way to fulfilment and blessing. That is the answer to the burdens of doubt and disappointment.

But then the chapter also shows us those who were scandalised by Christ and offended by His mission. He describes them in verse 16 as 'this generation'. Many of them were religious people, but they had their own opinions and ideas. They were quite ready to sit in judgement on God or on anybody else and our Lord said of them that they were like children sitting in the market place and calling out to others, 'We played the flute for you, and you did not dance; we sang a dirge, and you did not mourn.' Nothing was ever right for them. John the Baptist came as an ascetic and that, they said, was too extreme. 'He has a demon' (verse 18). 'The Son of Man came eating and drinking, and they say, "Here is a glutton and a drunkard, a friend of tax collectors and 'sinners' " ' (verse 19).

Jesus speaks then to those who carry the burden of their own right judgement, who think that they know better than He does. There are Christians like that, aren't there? And He says, 'Is that wisdom? Look at its fruits.'

But then there were others who had deliberately rejected the evidence of Christ's Lordship (verse 20). Jesus began to denounce the cities in which most of His miracles had been performed, because they did not repent. Although these people had approved and applauded what Jesus did, although they had been benefited and even blessed by Him, yet the Lord says in verse 20 that they will be judged because there is only one authentic response to the claims of Christ, and that is repentance. That is the touchstone by which our Christian reality is ultimately judged. So the towns of Galilee carried their burden of guilt.

That is the background against which this beautiful and gracious invitation is issued.

Two commands, two results and two incentives

There are in these verses two parallel commands, with two results and two incentives. That's always the pattern of Scripture, isn't it? There are no commands without our being taught the resources that are available for us to follow them. The commands are at the beginning of verses 28 and 29: 'Come to me' and 'Take my yoke'. The result of coming is, the Lord Jesus says at the end of verse 28, 'I will give you rest', or better, as the New English Bible puts it, 'relief'. The result of taking His yoke is that we become His learners or His disciples.

The incentives are that our teacher is gentle and humble in heart, that His yoke is easy and His burden is light. To distil these wonderful words into their absolute essence: the Lord Jesus is saying that what He wants from us is our trust and obedience, and that this is the way to rest.

Now many of us know that this is true. Yet, if we are honest before God, our souls are weary and burdened and restless, because, you see, it's not the knowing that brings relief but the trusting. What will make the difference is if we take seriously the invitation of the Lord to come to Him personally, to know Him and to experience Him more deeply than ever before. As we come to Christ, the burden bearer, He will refresh us.

The results of obeying the invitation

Three very wonderful things happen when we act on that very gracious invitation. Firstly, *when we come to Christ there will be a revelation of who He is*. Everything in this invitation focuses on Him. 'Come to me,' he says, 'Take my yoke. Learn of me.' And yet, on the other hand, He speaks of Himself as meek and lowly, gentle and humble. There is here that characteristic gospel blend of authority and meekness, of total sufficiency and humility, of Lordship and servanthood. So, although the invitation is to rest, it is the One who invites us who dominates the scene rather than the gift that He offers. That is the thrust of the verses that immediately precede the ones we are looking at. Verses 25-27 are a little record of the prayer that Jesus prayed to His Father, and as such they are one of those marvellous windows into the character of the

Lord Jesus that the Gospels occasionally open for us. It has been truly said that what a man is before God, that he is and no more. Here the Son is revealed to us in His relationship with the Father and it is a relationship of trust and obedience. As He calls us to trust and obey, so in His prayer He demonstrates that trust and obedience that was characteristic of His whole earthly life.

In verse 25 Jesus said, 'I praise you, Father, Lord of heaven and earth, because you have hidden these things from the wise and learned, and revealed them to little children.' To know who Christ is depends not on being well versed in the rabbinic traditions or endowed with special abilities or intellectual power. Knowledge of the Lord Jesus is given to those who have hearts like little children, who are teachable and trusting. Are you going to let Him teach you? The quality revealed in verse 26 is what He looks for in us. Whatever the Father's will was shown to be during the earthly ministry of the Lord Jesus, it was His joy to accept it and delight in it.

So Jesus the Son is perfectly qualified to be the channel by which the Father is revealed. As you come to Jesus you understand more deeply than ever before – and nowhere else can you understand it – the nature of God Himself. No one knows the Father except the Son and those to whom the Son chooses to reveal Him. Only the Son can know the depths of the Father's heart of love, for only He fully understands the Father's will, and only He can fulfil that will in His perfect human life, and in His atoning death on the cross; and only He can pass on that knowledge of God.

Do you want to know God? Come to the Lord Jesus. For verse 27 says that all things have been committed to Christ and as we come to Him we come to the full revelation of the Godhead. But I want you to notice that as we come, we discover that He is gentle and humble in heart. The scholars tell us that the Aramaic roots for rest and gentleness are the same. So in the Syriac version of the New Testament it reads like this: 'Come to me and I will rest you, for I am restful and you will find rest.' There can be no rest apart from His presence; there can be no coming, unless we grasp that He is the sovereign Lord who became a servant for us and for our salvation.

Secondly, *when we come to Christ there will be refreshment for our souls*. Just as we can never discover what God has not revealed, so we can never find unless Christ gives. Only Christ gives relief and refreshment, because only Christ has this character of gentleness and peace. We don't have that sort of rest naturally because of the heavy burdens we carry.

Now I have little doubt that in its original context the Lord Jesus was thinking especially of the burdens of false religion that are mentioned earlier in the chapter. His reference to His own burden being light is contrasted later in the Gospel with the heavy burdens which the Scribes and the Pharisees tied on men's shoulders. Speaking about the teachers of the law in Matthew 23:4 Jesus says, 'They tie up heavy loads and put them on men's shoulders, but they themselves are not willing to lift a finger to move them.' He sets that in the context of their teaching of the law. They 'sit in Moses' seat. So you must obey them and do everything they tell you. But do not do what they do, for they do not practise what they preach' (verses 2, 3). It was not that Jesus took a lighter view of the law of Moses to which the Scribes demanded meticulous obedience. What He is attacking here is the fact that the teachers of the law added to the law of God their own traditions of men, and elevated them to the status of the law and that made their religion such an intolerable burden. It was all external; it was done for effect.

'Everything they do is done for men to see: they make
their phylacteries wide and the tassels of their prayer shawls
long; they love the place of honour at banquets and the most
important seats in the synagogues; they love to be greeted in
the market places and to have men call them "Rabbi"
[which literally means "my great one"]' (verse 5). Those are
the heavy burdens from which Christ delivers us.

I believe that some of us need that sort of deliverance,
from the heavy burden of human tradition, from the
bondage of a Christian sub-culture which is the word of
men and not of Scripture. We need to be liberated from the
burdens of a religion that has become a duty which is never
adequately performed, of an attitude that has forgotten
the meaning of grace and become imprisoned in a treadmill
of activity, desperately being good enough, or trying to be
good enough for God to bless us. That's Pharisaism, the
burden of doing it for men to see. How easy it is for
twentieth-century Christians to fall into that trap. We go
to the right places. We read the right books. We know the
right people. We make the right noises. But inwardly
before God we may be empty and restless.

May God deliver us from the burden of always having to
be successful! So many Christians are seeking for status
and position and fulfilment through their Christianity. It is
so easy for our service for the Lord to become an idol that
we subtly worship, instead of coming to Him and submitting to His love and His Lordship. The Lord Jesus wants
you for yourself, not for what you do for Him. He says to
you, 'Come, if you are weary and heavy laden, and you
have been carrying a load of man-made religion and heavy
duty and drudgery. Come, and I will give you rest.'

Thirdly, *when we come to Christ there will be a
replacement of the yoke*. Isn't Matthew 11:30 a wonderful
promise with which to end? 'For my yoke is easy and my

burden is light.' The Pharisees often spoke about the law as a yoke and the Lord Jesus doesn't dismiss this concept. He doesn't say, 'If you come to Me there won't be a yoke.' He redefines the concept. We know that the purpose of the yoke was to enable a carrier to bear a load more comfortably and efficiently. For that to happen two things are necessary. Firstly the yoke has to be easy. It has to fit smoothly and comfortably so that it is a help and not a hindrance. Secondly the load has to be not too heavy.

This is what the Lord Jesus is assuring us as He invites us to come to Him. He is saying, 'If you trust Me, if you become a learner of Me, if you seek in your life to follow Me, gentle and humble in heart, you will find that the yoke perfectly fits you and you will not find that it is a heavy burden any more than wings are a burden to a bird.' When we trust Him and obey Him, when we really put Him first in our lives before what we may do for Him, when we stop trying to 'make it' with God, and let His grace restore us and His Spirit empower us – then we discover our delight, our fulfilment, our joy, our peace. We are set free to serve the Lord from our hearts. Why is that so? Because we are not keeping an external system of rules and regulations any more. We are loving a person. And the mark of those who really love the Lord Jesus is that they keep His commandments. But it's the love that comes first, and it is as we love Him and trust Him that we find His yoke is easy and His burden is light. So as we come to Christ and put ourselves, as it were, into His nail-pierced hands, He begins to work so graciously and so gently, taking away the strain and the stress, the weariness and the drudgery. He begins to plant His love in our hearts instead, so that our greatest desire is to wear that easy yoke and carry that light load, because above everything else, we want to be like Jesus.

And what is He looking for in His disciples? It's there in verse 29. He is looking for gentleness and heart-humility. That is the lightness of His burden. His demands are far more penetrating than anything the Scribes or Pharisees had imagined. They uncover our weaknesses and our failures. They make us face up to what we are, and our utter dependence on Christ. But they are far easier to bear than any of the burdens we lay on ourselves. What is your soul like before God? Is it restless? What is your Christianity like? Have you been pushing yourself? Do you feel guilty, discouraged? Maybe you are full of doubts and anxieties. What the Lord wants to do for all of us is to put within us His gentleness and His humility and His rest. He wants to deliver us from our own impossible efforts to make ourselves right with God. He wants to take from us our weariness and our self-imposed burdens and our restlessness; and He says to us —

'Come to Me, take My yoke, learn of Me and you will find rest for your souls. For My yoke is still easy and My burden still light.'

DRINKING IS BELIEVING

by Rev Richard Bewes

Isaiah 55

Here we have a pen picture of what life with God is like. 'Ho, everyone who thirsts, come to the waters; and he who has no money, come, buy and eat! Come, buy wine and milk without money and without price' (verse 1).

In a London subway, one August, a jewel thief was cornered and arrested. The police removed him from Farringdon Underground Station, and picked up what they thought was the bag of missing gems. In fact it was a similar bag belonging to the train driver. When he reached the end of the line, feeling a little peckish, he opened his lunch bag, only to recoil with amazement at the sight of thousands of pounds worth of jewellery. Miles away, the police opened up their bag. They were equally dumbfounded to be confronted by a flask of tea and three cheese sandwiches!

So, appearances can deceive. Apply that to the concept of life with God. Is it possible that we are deceived at times by the externals of Christianity and the church; the structures, the trappings, the antiquity of it all, even to the extent that some people pick up the wrong bag altogether in their search for satisfaction? Let us see what it is in this chapter that makes life with God equivalent to the jewel-haul of a lifetime! Not that the imagery is of gems. It is more basic and yet it's more than basic. There is wine and milk as well, without money, without price.

This is God's great invitation. It follows hard on the heels of the prophet's description of the Jerusalem that is to be, with renewed foundations, towers and walls, a city of security, a refuge of peace. In this chapter we are in the atmosphere of appeal. Is there a chapter like it in either the Old or New Testament? Evangelists love to preach from it, and we can see why. True, it's written with the Jewish exiles in Babylon in mind when, for example, it gives the assurance, 'For you shall go out in joy, and be led forth in peace' (verse 12). Yet the appeal of this chapter is to every man and woman.

It is collective, and yet it is also individual. In verse 1 the invitation is to 'every one who thirsts', and yet verse 2 says, 'Delight yourselves in fatness'. The appeal is universal because thirst is a great equaliser.

In our church in central London we encounter seekers after satisfaction from all walks of life. I'll never forget baptising a journalist from a Marxist background. We baptised him on May Day! He said, 'All this time my energies have been set on a socialist Utopian ideal. Now I have a new vision, the Kingdom of God.' Another time we baptised a Muslim. Despite his limited English he was equally enthusiastic. In his own style he said, 'It was very nice. I liked it!' But where did the appeal lie in this great invitation from the one true God to us all? Let's identify it. First,

There is satisfaction in it

'Why do you spend your money for that which is not bread, and your labour for that which does not satisfy? Hearken diligently to me, and eat what is good, and delight yourself in fatness' (verse 2). Here the prophet is using language that everyone would understand. It's that of the bargain-hunter at the sales, the vocabulary of the street vendor, the barrow man. The Jewish people became desperate for satisfaction in the degradation of their Babylonian exile. But they were looking for it in the wrong place. Here is the challenge. 'Don't you realise that you are spending your ever-dwindling resources on junk foods? You have picked up the wrong bag.'

Ah, but we all do that. 'What then are men looking for today?' wrote Professor Hans Rookmaaker of Amsterdam. 'What is the force that drives them on, always searching, never satisfied, always up and away again without a moment's peace?' He goes on, 'The answer is the fact that the answers are no answers.'

One of the greatest of the English Romantic poets, Lord Byron, described his own experience vividly. 'Drank every cup of joy, drank early, deeply drank, drank draughts which common millions might have drunk, then died of thirst because there was no more to drink.'

It was a Galilean, the son of a carpenter, an itinerant preacher who said, 'Every one who drinks of this water will thirst again, but whoever drinks of the water that I shall give him will never thirst; the water that I shall give him will become in him a spring of water welling up to eternal life' (John 4:13). We have to believe that the divine offer of Isaiah 55, of satisfaction to everyone who comes, is an authentic offer to be accepted by faith. In the terminology of our passage, faith is coming; faith is buying; faith is drinking.

D. L. Moody knew a period in his own life as a Christian when his own soul was dried up in the desert of an over-busy life that lacked integration and direction. But he emerged from that period and rediscovered the freshness of walking in fellowship with God every day. We read in his biography, 'The dead dry days were gone. I was all the time tugging and carrying water, but now I have a river carrying me.'

When as a pastor I meet with fellow-Christians who have got stuck – and it happens to all of us – I tend to ask them about their habits of Bible-reading and worship. That's where the sticking point so often occurs. Either they're not reading the Bible, or they're not attending a regular place of worship, or both. 'Ah!' somebody says. 'The Bible is such a long book. Can't cope.' Now listen. The whole Bible is smaller than many university text books. Try it! Get up in the morning; give yourself a cup of tea. Make yourself comfortable and then be a reader. Keep up the pattern for seven days. Take a little of what you read out into the day with you. When you get to the end of the seven days, look back and review how you are as a person, then start a second period of seven days. It is not impossible. Each day as you wake up, commit that day to God and resolve, "This is going to be a day of friendship, of adventure with my unseen companion Jesus Christ, through the Holy Spirit.'

Now this isn't simply a matter of complacent immobility that we are talking about. We're not just sitting in our own little spiritual igloos all around Europe singing choruses to each other as the twilight gathers. Not at all. There's a progression in these sentences. The movement is from poverty, thirst and hunger to abundant satisfaction and service. Mission is to the fore.

'Incline your ear, and come to me; hear, that your soul may live; and I will make with you an everlasting covenant, my steadfast, sure love for David. Behold, I made him a witness to the peoples, a leader and commander for the peoples. Behold, you shall call nations that you know not, and nations that knew you not shall run to you, because of the Lord your God' (verses 3-5). The reference in verse 3 to David, the former king, was to remind the prophet's listeners that a new age was to dawn. What was once David's role was from now on to be the privilege of God's people as a whole. Of course, we cannot be deeply satisfied by God and remain quarantined within our own tight little fellowships.

When Bishop Festo Kivengere, as a young man, was awakened in the days of the Ugandan revival, he cried out to God in his little room, 'O God, give me just seven more days to live for you, and I will tell everybody in sight about this.' And he rushed out of his little room and saw a lady two hundred yards away. 'Stop! Stop!' said Festo. 'Jesus came my way today.' The woman tossed her head. She thought he was drunk. In a way he was. When we've accepted again the great Bible invitation, 'Come to the waters', we must overflow to others with the same appeal.

There is restoration in it

'Seek the Lord while he may be found, call upon him while he is near; let the wicked forsake his way, and the unrighteous man his thoughts; let him return to the Lord, that he may have mercy upon him, and to our God, for he will abundantly pardon' (verses 6, 7). Derek Kidner has made the observation, 'If man is hungry and needs satisfying, he is also wicked and needs salvation.'

The question has already been posing itself this week for us all: have I abandoned my first love? Do I love Christ more or less, since first I encountered Him? Has my discipleship become a routine, fossilised thing, almost without my knowing it?

The great scientist Charles Darwin evidently had some kind of Christian orientation in his earlier days. It seems that these bonds weakened as time went by, so that on 17 June 1868 he wrote to a friend of his, 'I am glad you were at "The Messiah". It is the one thing I would like to hear again. But I dare say I should find my soul too dried up to appreciate it as in olden days, for it is a horrid bore to feel as I constantly do, that I am a withered leaf for everything except science.' That speaks of the very opposite of satisfaction.

God's people of old knew this dryness in the days of Isaiah when they were in exile, seemingly cut off, abandoned, useless, discarded. Salvation seemed a long way away. Does it to you? I have no telepathic abilities to say that in row 53 there is a person who is very nearly spiritually dead, or that at the bookstall end of the tent there is a man up to his ears in unpaid debts. I don't know whether, out of sight, someone listening, a Christian leader maybe, is having an affair, entangled in a world of fantasy. God knows what we are like. But these things happen, and at times a sort of helpless hopelessness can take hold of us, and we say, 'God and His power to restore are a long way away.' But they aren't really. They are very near. God simply says, 'Stop it! Come off the road you are on. And I will abundantly pardon.'

A new Christian once said to me, 'God has forgiven all my sins.' What did he expect? Did he think that God would say, 'I will forgive that and that, but I'm afraid not *that*'? No, when God forgives, He forgives abundantly. The cross is the secret. At the foot of the cross God says, 'I will *abundantly* pardon.' Very likely someone here has got tired of the fight for purity and for God. Let the ministry of God lift you. Let the cross speak to you once again of abundance, so that tonight, you can say with gratitude and humble resolve, 'I am back in the fight.' Can you say that?

All we need is the assurance once more that God's way is indeed the right way, and that for the truth's sake, however uncomfortable it may be, we are on the road of return. Is His the right way? Am I holding the right bag? Accept from this passage that you are. Verses 8 and 9 say it.

'My thoughts are not your thoughts, neither are your ways my ways, says the Lord.' This is speaking of God's plan. God's standard is the right one and He invites us to accept it. Therein lies the way of satisfaction and restoration.

There is culmination in it

'For, as the rain and the snow come down from heaven and return not thither but water the earth, making it bring forth and sprout, giving seed to the sower and bread to the eater, so shall my word be that goes forth from my mouth. It shall not return to me empty, but it shall accomplish that which I purpose, and prosper in the thing for which I sent it' (verses 10, 11). This is really the epilogue to chapters 40-55. In chapter 40:8, we had the words, 'The grass withers, the flower fades; but the word of our God will stand for ever.' The principle is restated here. God's purpose has been at work throughout the career of God's people. His word of prophecy will always be fulfilled. The whole of His saving work is built upon it. It's steady like the sun and rain referred to here. It's effective for it won't return to Him empty. It's beneficial because it brings bread to the eater and it prospers.

Of course, it's not magic. It's not an automatic word. But for the person who receives this prophetic word, submits to it and absorbs it, it is a creative word. There's direction and purpose and culmination in God's great invitation. It's not just an optional extra tacked on to our lives. It's going to shape everything, our attitude to finance and politics and employment and love and marriage. Once take God's disclosures in His spoken revelation seriously, and it creates in us an internal dynamo of creativity.

There is rejuvenation in it

The closing words of our chapter portray the journey home of the once exiled people. 'For you shall go out in joy, and be led forth in peace, the mountains and hills before you shall break forth into singing, and all the trees of the field shall clap their hands' (verse 12). Here's a picture of the transformation of nature, a sort of reversal of the judgement pronounced upon the fallen Adam when God told him, 'Cursed is the ground because of you; thorns and thistles it shall bring forth to you' (Genesis 3:18). It's different here. 'Instead of the thorns shall come up the cypress; instead of the briar shall come up the myrtle' (verse 13). There is fruitfulness and productivity here. This is basic. Arm yourself with this great biblical principle. In a day when the bankruptcy of western civilisation issues us all with a threadbare currency of negative pessimism, we need not succumb to that.

When in Carthage in 410 AD Augustine heard the stunning news that Alaric, the leader of the barbarian Visigoths, had accomplished the sack of Rome, it seemed that civilisation itself had ended. But then Augustine rallied, compared Rome's destruction with that of Sodom, and encouraged his Christian friends with these words, 'There will be an end to every earthly kingdom. You are surprised that the world is losing its grip and is full of pressing tribulations. Do not hold on to the world. Do not refuse to regain your youth in Christ. He says to you, ''The world is passing away. The world is short of breath. Do not fear. Thy youth shall be renewed as an eagle.'' ' And Augustine's great work, *The City of God* became a source of inspiration and hope for Christians living in a changing world.

Yes, we may be witnessing the death of Europe at the present time, but there is a growing generation in England who refuse to succumb to the kiss of death. We go God's way. We accept God's invitation which beckons us away from the transient sideshows that masquerade as the vendors of freedom. So, when we've seen the cross and the resurrection, when we've recaptured the vision of Christ once crucified and now raised to the right hand of power; when we have comprehended God's offer of things that money cannot buy, we recognise that other world as an empty balloon-ride, as a vain excursion to the funfair. We rediscover our youth and vitality in Christ, the only Messiah and Shepherd we could ever look for.

So let us absorb into ourselves the message of this chapter, and allow God's great invitation to thunder its way across the centuries to us. There is satisfaction in it. There is restoration in it. There is culmination and purpose in it. There is rejuvenation in it. Be assured that in Christ and in His way, you have not picked up the wrong bag. Isaiah 55 tells us that believing is drinking, and that when we drink at God's beckoning, we shall not be disappointed.

FULLNESS OF LIFE IN CHRIST

by Canon Keith Weston

Romans 7:1-4

Paul has a wonderful statement in Colossians 2:10 which in the AV reads, 'Ye are complete in him.' The RSV translates it, 'You have come to fullness of life in him.' In Romans 7:4 we read, 'You belong to another' and, belonging to Him, you have everything. My purpose is simply to say to you that in Christ you have everything. I would suggest to you that if you want a title for these chapters in Romans, spreading either side of the verses we read, you could not go far wrong in choosing that verse from Colossians, 'Fullness of life in Him'.

For instance, in chapter 5, Paul says, 'Therefore, since we have been justified through faith, we have peace with God through our Lord Jesus Christ, through whom we have gained access by faith into this grace in which we now stand, and we rejoice in our hope of sharing the glory of God' (verses 1, 2). That is to say, we have peace with the past as the past is all blotted out, forgiven and forgotten. Hallelujah! We have access into grace for every moment of every day in the here and now. So the past is covered and the present is covered, and we look on into the future and with great joy we say that we look forward to that day when we shall share the glory of God. So the future is covered. We are complete in Christ.

But how do you get that across to Christians? I admire preachers like Richard Bewes who can illustrate their talks. Where did he get that story about the bag in the Underground? I didn't see that in the paper! Well, here we have a set of illustrations which the apostle Paul uses to bring home to his readers the truth that you have everything in the Lord Jesus Christ. (If you would like a bit of homework see if you can work out those illustrations from chapter 6 right through to where we are in chapter 7. There are four of them but we have time to look at only the fourth.) It all starts in verse 1 of chapter 6. 'What shall we say then? Are we to continue in sin that grace may abound?' Are we to be the sort of people who say, 'Well, if we are complete in Christ it doesn't matter how we live. We can sin here, there and everywhere because grace will come and meet us, will always clean us up again.' Paul is horrified at the thought that you and I should think so trivially about sin. He says, 'By no means' – literally, his words mean 'Let that thought never have existed.' How *dare* you think like that? You are complete in Christ. What are you doing wandering back into the old paths of sin? What are you doing saying that it doesn't matter how you live? What are you doing saying that besetting sins really are meaningless and you can enjoy them as you like?

'Does it really matter', you are saying, 'if I don't pray as I ought to? If I am not reading the Scriptures day by day? If I fail to share my faith with others?' 'How dare you talk like that?' says the apostle Paul. 'If we continue in sin then grace will cope.' Is that the level you live on? I believe there are many Christians who may not articulate like that but actually do try to live like that, and their lives are full of the sins of the past which they still hanker after and relish from time to time; yet they are Christians and they are saying that it doesn't matter. Grace will abound and I can continue in sin. Paul is concerned to show in vivid illustrations that that is an impossible way of thinking and he does it by showing the overwhelming wonder of the completeness that is ours in Jesus Christ.

You will immediately recognise the illustration from our passage. In verse 1 of chapter 7 he says that the law holds a person under its authority all the days of his life. Only after his death does the long arm of the law lose interest in him. So, if I rob a bank and then flee the country with my ill-gotten gains to live in exile in South America, the law will still hold me to the crime I have committed. Only if I die are the files closed and, we must add at this stage, only then so far as this life is concerned. The moment the police files are closed God opens up His files in heaven; and we shall all appear before the judgement seat of Christ. But Paul is saying here that the law holds a man under its authority all the days of his life, and when he dies there is an end of it. This principle is familiar to us all in the sphere of marriage. So he says that a married woman is bound to her husband as long as he lives. The principle underlying marriage to this very day is, 'till death do us part'. So, if she lives with another man while her husband is alive (verse 3), she is an adulteress; and it is only if he dies that she is discharged from her marriage vows and thus able to marry another without the stigma of adultery. May I just add here that Paul is not primarily trying to teach us here about marriage; he does that, of course, in other epistles, on other occasions. He gives us the bare bones here; he is using a well-known marriage principle to make his point about a believer's life in Christ. So let us see how he applies it.

The unbeliever is in bondage, rather like a woman who is married to a cruel husband and is in bondage to him as long as she lives, though she may long to get rid of him. How tragic this can be in everyday life! I met such a woman here at Keswick one year and tried my hardest to counsel her. Perhaps many of us know of desperately unhappy people with cruel partners in the misery of a marriage that is as it never should have been. There are wives with husbands who have a drink problem. They come home every night to bring untold misery and cruelty into the home. There are husbands who are compulsive gamblers. They waste all the family's money on their crazy pleasure and leave the family in penury. We all know such people and pray for them and plead that they may be converted.

Paul is using a very poignant illustration here – a woman who longs to be free from bondage. Look at the expressions he has used. He's talked about 'being enslaved' (6:6), about 'sin reigning in your mortal bodies to make you obey their passions' (6:12), or 'sin having dominion over you' (6:14). In this present chapter Paul says that while living in the flesh 'our sinful passions, aroused by the law, were at work in our members to bear fruit for death' (verse 5). As a result we were 'held captive' (verse 6). If only I could be free!

Now that was the state of each one of us before we came to know the Lord Jesus Christ. He heard our cries. 'Is there no way out from this intolerable situation?' And the answer, of course, comes gloriously through the gospel; that there is a way out to liberty, joy and peace in believing. But now, notice how Paul brings it home to us. Using his illustration, he says that if the husband dies the woman is free from that law; and if she marries another man she is not an adulteress (verse 3). It is indeed till death parts us. Now listen to how Paul expresses it: 'Do you not realise that death has parted you from Satan's dominion?' That is how you are free to marry another, to belong to Christ. You have been freed by death, but you ask, 'How can that be? As far as my experience goes, Satan seems to be very much alive and well, and he comes after me day by day. Far from being dead, he seems more active than ever in my Christian life. I am battling away with Satan and you say he is dead.'

No, I did not say he is dead; neither did Paul. He is very careful how he applies his illustration. 'Accordingly, she will be called an adulteress if she lives with another man while her husband is alive. But if her husband dies she is free from that law . . . Likewise, my brethren, [look who has died!] you have died to the law through the body of Christ, so that you might belong to another [to Christ]' (verses 3, 4). It is you who have died and it is true that Satan is still around and still tries to claim authority over you but you died, and sin has no more dominion over you.

What does Paul mean, and how does he get there? Let's backtrack a little. In the previous verses Paul has spoken of the death of Christ in two distinct ways. He has taught us first that Christ died for our sins. 'Jesus our Lord, who was put to death for our trespasses' (4:25). That little preposition is vitally important. It means 'in our place'. This is the first and major way in which Paul speaks of the death of the Lord Jesus Christ. He died, not for His own sins, but for our sins, and that is a basic truth in the gospel which I trust is precious to every one of you. It became very precious to me when I was a boy of eleven. I hope it is precious to you. It speaks truly of the substitutionary death of Jesus. The Lord took our transgressions and laid them on Him. It says in the Scriptures, 'The wages of sin is death', and He died that I might not die. The load of my sins was lifted off me and laid on Him, and that load crushed Him to death on the cross. The judgement had to fall because of the righteous character of God, but in the marvellous goodness of God the sinless Son of God stood in the way and the judgement fell on Him. Forgiveness can be proclaimed to penitent sinners, for Christ died.

Now that is the first way in which Paul speaks of the Lord's death. But secondly he speaks of it in another way which is relevant now to the continuing of our Christian life and our enjoyment of abundant life in Christ. It is as though Paul is saying that on the way to the cross at Calvary, the Lord invited us to join Him, and be, as Paul puts it here, united with Him in a death like His (6:5), to be incorporated in the death of Jesus Christ in a real way. He is saying that there is something in each of us that needs to die. It is called the old self (verse 6), the sinful body; and Paul sees the believer as handing that old self to Christ; it goes with Him to the cross, and as Jesus dies on the cross we are united with Him in that death. So the old self that had the liaison with Satan dies. The old past is not only forgiven, it is finished. It has been put to death on the cross, incorporated in Christ, so that you died with Him.

This is the theme of the whole of chapter 6 and you can see now how he can write in chapter 7 of death parting us from sin and Satan, as a wife is parted from her old husband through death. Jesus died, therefore, not only as your substitute but as your representative. 'Consider yourselves as dead to sin' (6:11). You have died in Christ so reckon yourself dead to sin. Not only that, but just as Jesus died and was raised to newness of life, so also you who died with Him have been raised to newness of life in Him, so there is a new person, which is you following your life in Christ.

'For if we have been united with him in a death like his,

we shall certainly be united with him in a resurrection like his' (6:5). I believe that the apostle here is not speaking of the future glory of the resurrection which will come in the last day when Jesus comes again; he is speaking of newness of life in the here and now, in the same sense in which he writes to those Corinthian Christians, 'You are a new creation (2 Cor. 5:17).

So, you went to the cross with Jesus and that old person was put to death with Him. Now, says the apostle, 'Reckon yourself to be dead, indeed, unto sin but alive to God through Jesus Christ our Lord.' You are gloriously free to belong to Another, and surely 'Another' should have a capital 'A' because it is the Lord Jesus who is spoken of there. You have been set free from that marriage bond to Satan so that you may be married to Christ. The church is the bride of Christ, and Christ is the bridegroom of the church.

I have said that you died and rose again in Christ that you may belong to Him in perfect loyalty. But what has happened to Satan? He has not died and, of course, he is still around and he is furious with you! Of course you have discovered that he is much more lively than before. Previously he had you in his grasp. He didn't have to bother with you, but now he has seen you move away from him finally and for ever. You now belong to another and he is furious. Of course he will be after you, he will shout at you and say, 'You belong to me! You are mine! Come back to me!' and you have to reply in the words of Romans 6:14, 'Sin has no dominion over me.' The word means authority. 'Satan, you have no authority to say that to me; it is a lie and you know it. I belong to another and you have no authority over me at all.'

Satan will come subtly one way or another to try to claim you back to himself and to make you his again, to cause you to walk in those old sinful paths and to relish those old besetting sins again; but it is all lies. Satan is the deceiver. He will deceive the very elect if he can, for he wants you to believe that he has dominion over you; and he can tell you what you ought to be doing and put ideas into your heart. But you have got to learn to live wholly with that One to whom you belong.

I have a feeling that what we need to do when Satan comes with his wretched insinuations, is not actually to answer him, not even to shout at him through the letter box – so to speak – because if you don't watch it he will suck you through the letter box. No, you want to go and shut yourself away with Christ; run into that inner sanctum where Christ is, who is your Saviour and your wonderful Husband. It is a scriptural principle to flee youthful lusts, but you do not flee just anywhere, you flee to the arms of the One to whom you belong. Let Him go to the door and deal with Satan, for Satan cannot cope with that. But he will be back again and you will constantly have to flee to Christ.

Complete in Christ – it's a beautiful title, isn't it? We are severed from that old relationship which is finished for ever. Recognise the truth, reckon yourself dead to sin, but alive to God through Jesus, and come to that life in Him that is joy and peace in believing.

THE HELPER FROM HEAVEN

by Rev Gottfried Osei-Mensah

John 16:7-15

In the words of our reading we have the mission and the purpose of the Holy Spirit summed up for us by the Lord Jesus Christ Himself. The four words, 'He shall glorify me', summarise the entire mission of the Holy Spirit as conceived by the Lord Jesus Christ. And the way He would carry out this work of glorifying the Lord Jesus Christ was also clearly spelt out: He takes what belongs to Christ and He discloses it to those who belong to Christ. He reveals things to God's people; He makes the truth, the reality of the Lord Jesus Christ known to His people. He takes of the unsearchable riches of Christ and discloses them to us, so that we may enter into what the Lord has freely purposed for us. He is described as the Spirit of revelation and wisdom in the knowledge of God, for He takes the things of Christ and makes them known to us, so that we may know the mind of Christ. And of course, we know the mind of Christ in order that we may live according to the purpose of Christ. He comes to glorify the Lord Jesus Christ in us.

This is what happened as soon as He came on the day of

Pentecost. He opened the eyes of the disciples and showed them things from the Old Testament Scriptures that they had not known. That is why Peter could stand up and preach spontaneously, quoting from the prophets and from the Psalms and from Moses, establishing that this is the Christ, the Son of the living God. Until that time he didn't know that the Psalms were referring to the Lord Jesus Christ. But the Spirit of wisdom and revelation in the knowledge of Jesus Christ came to the apostles, and He opened their inner eyes to see and understand things concerning the Lord Jesus.

The Holy Spirit comes to Christ's people as His coronation gift. It is because He is risen and enthroned at the right hand of the Majesty on high and crowned King of kings and Lord of lords, that He has received this gift from His Father, and poured Him forth, as Peter says, upon His disciples.

Now there are three realms where Jesus Christ is to be glorified by His people, as the Holy Spirit comes upon them.

In the world (verses 8-11)

The world is the sphere where men and women who are not Christians organise and live their lives without reference to God. The Lord Jesus was sent into the world to do a work for mankind, that men and women might be saved. Yet the world still carries on as though God had not sent His Son into the world, as though Christ had not died on Calvary, as though atonement had not been made for the sin of the world.

Now of course, we have a responsibility here. Nearly half of the men and women in our world today are not Christians, not because they have rejected Christ, but because they haven't heard of Him. They don't know there is such a Saviour as Jesus Christ. That may be very difficult for some of us to believe, but it is true. These people have not been given the opportunity to receive or reject Him. And that, of course, is our responsibility, because we have had a commission for nearly two thousand years now.

But the Lord was referring to those who hear the gospel, yet still do not believe in Him. They dishonour His claims and treat Him as though He were an impostor. The ultimate reason why the Lord Jesus Christ was condemned to die was that He claimed to be what, in fact, He was. At the trial before the High Priest they tried in every way to bring witnesses to testify against Him. When they didn't succeed, the High Priest stood up and almost desperately said, 'I place you under oath to tell us plainly if you are the Christ, the Son of the living God.' And the Lord Jesus, who had kept quiet up to that point, said, 'Precisely; you've said it. And I tell you, from now on, you will see the Son of Man sitting at the right hand of power, and coming on the clouds of heaven.' Then the High Priest tore his mantle and said, 'You've heard his blasphemy. What do you think?' And everybody gave their vote against Him and said, 'He's deserving of death.' He claimed to be what He was, the Son of God, who had come to do a work that no other could do, in order that we may have salvation through Him, and He was condemned to death.

Now when the Spirit comes upon His people they are able to establish with convicting and convincing power that Jesus is the Christ, the Son of the living God. And the world is convicted of sin because they do not believe on Him. Again, this is what happened on the day of Pentecost, and as the word came with convicting power, the cry of those who were there was, 'Men and brethren,

what shall we do?' And there were many who went their
way that day, through repentance and faith, to new life in
the Lord Jesus Christ. The Holy Spirit comes upon His
people and enables us to proclaim the Lord Jesus Christ,
not just in words, but in power and with conviction.

He also convicts the world of judgement. For it is the
prince of this world who blinds the minds of unbelievers,
and prevents them from seeing the light of the glory of
God in the face of Jesus Christ. The unbeliever is not only
in darkness, he is spiritually blind, so that however brightly
the light shines, he cannot see it. Unless the Holy Spirit
comes and does this work of giving inward light, men and
women hear the good news and never really receive it with
faith. But He does come, and one of the things He does is
to tell the unbelievers that the prince of lies, whose lies they
have swallowed whole, and therefore dishonour the Lord
Jesus Christ and will not believe in Him, that prince has
been judged on the cross, and those who continue to
follow his lies will share his condemnation.

That is the power that is at work in the gospel. The Holy
Spirit comes to do this work of glorifying the Lord Jesus
Christ in the world. He does so, as He convicts people of
sin and leads them to faith in the Lord Jesus that they, too,
may receive the gift of the Holy Spirit.

In the believer

The Holy Spirit comes, secondly, to work and to glorify
the Lord Jesus Christ in the believer. For, you see, the new
birth is the beginning of the Holy Spirit's personal dealings
with a Christian; and this work is not finished until He
makes us reflect, in our own personalities, the likeness of
the Lord Jesus Christ. The work of sanctification must go
on, and it is the Holy Spirit who is the Sanctifier. He is

called the Holy Spirit, not just because He himself is holy, but also because of what He does to the people of God. He makes us holy, He sanctifies us, He makes us Christ-like. And again, He takes the things of Christ and applies them to us. The truth of Christ, in the hands of the Spirit of Christ, makes the people of God reflect the likeness of their Master, Christ. That is His work. By opening our inner eyes to see the Lord Jesus Christ, He captivates not only our minds but our hearts, and we long to be like Him. He creates in us a desire for the Lord Jesus Christ.

Now of course, that has tremendous consequences. It means that we should give Him time to do this work in us. If He uses the Word of God to renew our minds, and to create in us a desire for Him, then we need to give Him time to teach us. He's the Spirit of truth who takes the truth of Christ and applies it to us. The apostle says in 2 Corinthians 3:18, 'We all with an unveiled face, as we behold, as in a glass, the glory of the Lord Jesus Christ, are being changed into his likeness, from one degree of glory to another; by his Spirit who is the Lord.' 'Beholding' means that we are looking at Him through the mirror He has given us – His Word. That is where we see Christ. Through the written word we come to see the living Word, and as we behold Him in study and meditation, in giving our minds to Him, we are being transformed into His likeness. The Word will rebuke us for our faults. It will correct our errors. It will instruct us in righteousness. And by one degree upon another, we are beginning to reflect in our personalities, the likeness of the Lord Jesus Christ.

So, we are given commandments concerning the Holy Spirit. We are not to grieve Him by sin. If He has shown us quite clearly what is the will of the Lord, and we do contrary to that, we grieve Him, and we are commanded not to do so, because He has been sent to seal us for the day of our salvation. He is sensitive. Be careful that you don't grieve Him as He reveals to you things that ought not to be there.

We are also not to quench Him. When He's wooing us along, trying to lead us into new ways, we are not to say, 'No' to our Master. That's a contradiction in terms. We are to obey Him, to let Him lead us, for that is why He has been sent.

We are not to grieve Him or to quench Him. Instead we are to be filled, day by day, with Him. We are to cause ourselves to be filled by Him on an ongoing basis. We are to give ourselves to Him so that He may come and control every department of our lives with the authority of Christ, for that is what He wants us to do.

Then we are to walk with Him. We are to keep in step with Him. He leads us in the paths of righteousness and obedience and service to the Master.

If we take care to do these things, He will bring to us many and tremendous experiences. Often, as a pastor, I rejoice in the experiences that people share with me, when I know they are seeking to walk with the Holy Spirit. But I always say, 'Don't follow Him just for the experiences. You follow Him as your teacher.' When the experiences come, they are like icing on a cake. Now, if you try to live on icing all the time, you will have trouble with your health. If you take care to feed yourself properly on a balanced diet, occasionally there will be the icing on the cake. It is He who determines. And that's why I also counsel people, 'Don't go speaking of your experiences as though they were the norm for everyone. Why do you expect me to have the same experiences and become a carbon copy of you, when it is the Holy Spirit who leads me? If I am walking in step with Him, He will grant me experiences which are peculiarly for me. So teach the doctrines that are common to us but don't teach your experiences as if they were doctrines. That will divide us. Let us emphasise the doctrines that unite us. Then we can share our experiences in testimony, to encourage one another to walk in obedience to Him.'

In the church

The third area that I want to mention is in the church. We are not redeemed as individuals floating about in space. We are brought into a family, the family of God. We've been given the Holy Spirit to drink. We have been baptised into the body of Christ and we are the body of the Lord Jesus Christ. He is the Head and the church of Jesus Christ is very important to Him. The Holy Spirit exalts the Lord Jesus Christ as the supreme head of His redeemed people by helping us to recognise the organic unity of the body.

Now we, and particularly those of us who are evangelicals, have allowed others to rob us of this sense of corporate unity, because there have been those who have made this their speciality, and so we shy away from talk about unity. But unity is that into which the Holy Spirit brings us, and we are not to be afraid of unity among Christians. I am not talking about uniformity but about an organic unity. This is, after all, why the Lord Jesus prayed in His high-priestly prayer, that we might be one. He poured out His heart before His Father that He would make us one in Him; and blessed consequences flow from this, when we are away of our unity and take care to keep and maintain it. Yes, we are to maintain it, because the Holy Spirit is the author. In Ephesians 4:3 and 1 Corinthians 12:13, and elsewhere in Romans we are told that it is the Holy Spirit who has brought about the unity, and it is up to us to maintain it. We have to keep the unity of the Spirit in the bonds of love.

Now the reason why we have been brought together in this way is that, in His sovereignty, the Holy Spirit has given to us different gifts so that no Christian is able to go it alone. I have something given to me by the Holy Spirit that you need, and you have something that I need. And in the body of the Lord Jesus Christ there is not an appendix! There is not a redundant member. However humble you may think you are, you have something that the Lord has given to you which the rest of the body needs, and you are not to deprive them of what He has given to them through you. You and I have been made stewards by the Holy Spirit to the rest of the body. So we are to operate, submitting ourselves to His leadership, to build up the body of Christ, contributing the gifts He has given to us in whatever local expression of the body we find ourselves.

The evangelistic potential of this obedience is tremendous. It is that the world may know and believe. The Lord said that if we are one in this way, the world will take note. A world that experiences all kinds of disunity and division suddenly begins to see people from such diverse backgrounds living as though they are one family, and they begin to ask, 'What is the secret of that?' They may try to explain it in many ways, but they will not succeed until they begin to see it as the work of the Spirit of Christ. That is the new thing that the world must see, that the Lord makes us one.

What have a Briton and a Ghanaian in common? What have a Canadian and an Australian in common? What have an Indian and a Papua New Guinean in common? And you can go on and on. And I tell you, what they have in common is not the United Nations Charter. If any of you have ever visited the United Nations, they all sit there in one room, but they sit there as islands, every one of them out for what they can get for their own nation. They are not one.

It is only in a body like this that we sit here, not just for what we can get for ourselves, or for our own particular point of interest, but our eyes together focused on the One seated on the throne, on the Lamb of God. Our eyes are together on Him. He makes us one. As we look at Him together so we are one in Him, and that is the new thing that the world must see so that the world may take note.

Now the Holy Spirit does other things as well. Occasionally, when it pleases Him – and He is sovereign – He comes upon the church in mighty power, in revival, in renewal, and things that have been burdens upon the church are suddenly lifted, and the church enters into a new experience, and sinners are converted as they see a new phenomenon in the church of Jesus Christ. He doesn't tell us when He's going to do this, but we know that He does it. And it is our task to discern when our need is great and to pray that He may come upon us, not just for our own personal benefit, but that we may be better equipped for the tremendous task that has been given to us. And surely, if there was ever a time when Christians ought to be on their knees praying for revival in the church of Jesus Christ, surely that time is now.

We have a great King. Let us now begin to go to Him with large petitions and see what He is able to do. Pray that day by day you will be able to take the opportunities He gives you for the glory of the Lord Jesus Christ. Pray that in the problems you experience He will manifest Himself in His word and by His Spirit in you, so that you are equal to the challenges you face day by day. Pray that He may descend upon the church as a whole also, and grant us to manifest our unity as part of our testimony. But pray above everything that, in these difficult days, He will visit us in many new ways, and that the church of Jesus Christ may be revived.

THE ENABLING POWER OF THE HOLY SPIRIT

by Rev David Jackman

Galatians 5:16-18, 22, 23

When I was a schoolboy I used to be very keen on cricket, so keen that I used to dream great dreams about at least a test match career as a batsman. But I knew that you had to practise, and one year I had a book for my birthday which was a book on how to be a complete batsman. It showed you exactly where your feet had to be and how you had to play each particular stroke. It advised you to use a long wardrobe mirror and to practise these strokes in front of the mirror. That I duly did, until, according to the book, I was really expert. The one slight problem was, that to be a real batsman, you have to face real bowling. When I got on to the cricket pitch, it never seemed quite to match up. The lack of ability was fairly obvious.

I wonder if that's true of many of us, as Christians. The lack of ability is really rather obvious. We know all about how to play the strokes from the 'text book'. We've been learning that, perhaps for many years, as we've studied the Bible. We're really quite good at going through the motions in front of a mirror, as it were, but when we face the bowling, we tend to go to pieces. We don't have the ability.

Now one of the great New Testament words to describe the activity of the Holy Spirit is the word *dunamis*, which is usually translated 'power', but which might perhaps more accurately and helpfully be translated, 'the ability to get the job done'. Jesus promised that He would send us His Spirit as our ability, and He is the power. That is why Paul says, 'The law of the Spirit of life in Christ Jesus has set me free from the law of sin and death' (Rom. 8:2). But what is the job that God wants to be done in our lives? Over this week we have heard so many times from God's word that His greatest desire is that we should be like the Lord Jesus. That's what holiness is. He wants to restore His image in us. He wants us to be fruitful Christians who produce the life of Jesus.

I want us to consider two questions. First, how do we know that the Holy Spirit is working in us? Secondly, how are we to experience that working in all its fullness so that we may be fruitful Christians?

Notice firstly that the Holy Spirit is not the preserve of a few special Christians. When the Holy Spirit came on the day of Pentecost, the disciples were all together, a rushing mighty wind filled the whole house, tongues of fire came on each of them, and they were all filled with the Holy Spirit. God was saying, 'This is to be the norm for my Church.' The church is a living body, energised by the life of God. In the same way Paul says, 'If anybody does not have the Spirit of Christ, he does not belong to Christ' (Rom. 8:9). In other words he says, 'You cannot be a Christian without having the Holy Spirit.'

Nor is the Holy Spirit simply given for our private enjoyment. As you study the New Testament letters, you find that over and over again the word 'you' is in the plural, because the perspective is continually a corporate one. The Holy Spirit is the author of unity among

Christians through the truth which He teaches. And just as our individual bodies are the temple of the Holy Spirit, so the church is the holy temple of the Lord, in which God dwells by His Spirit. So as you study the New Testament, you find that you cannot be personally brought into salvation without the work of the Holy Spirit, and you cannot enjoy fellowship with other Christians apart from the work of the Holy Spirit. He does not produce spiritual lone rangers.

Nor is the Holy Spirit confined to special experiences. Paul clearly sets that out before us three times: *Live by the Spirit* (Gal. 5:16); *Be led by the Spirit* (verse 18); *Keep in step with the Spirit* (verse 25). All these expressions refer to the continuous outworking of what the Holy Spirit is doing within the Christian. The initiative is all His. He provides the resources, so we are to live on those resources by the power of the Spirit. He sets the direction, so we are to be led by the Spirit. He controls the pace so we are to keep in step with the Spirit.

So Paul says, 'The potential for you to be like Jesus Christ is all there in God's provision of His Spirit' – but as with all potential, it has to be appropriated in order for it to be enjoyed. The verbs in Galatians 5 are verbs of progress and development and growth. It is as though Paul were saying, 'Really spiritual Christians are people who are always moving forward.' They want to be moving out into the adventure of life in the Spirit. Ultimately they want to be Christians who bear fruit, not Christians who vegetate.

God has so ordained this world that all life will bear fruit after its kind. So it is with the life of the Spirit and the fruit of the Spirit. In a very real sense, it is the most natural thing in the world, that *all* Christians who are being filled with the Spirit should be fruitful Christians – not just a few special Christians. Neither is fruit-bearing an optional extra. Within the natural world we know that fruit-bearing is the major purpose of the tree's life cycle. And it doesn't bear fruit for itself, does it? We enjoy the fruit. Again, fruit-bearing does not happen suddenly. It isn't just a matter of sudden crisis experiences. If you have a garden and you watch your fruit trees, you can see the fruit growing and developing, and the quiet hidden movement of the sap within the tree is revealed more and more as the fruit comes to maturity. As someone has put it, 'When God ripens apples, He isn't in a hurry, and He doesn't make a noise.' So bearing fruit is a natural spiritual process.

Now of course, the amount of fruit depends on the health of the tree, the conditions of the soil, the climate and so on. And it is because Paul is so concerned that we Christians are living in a hostile environment that he says, 'You must live by the Spirit, if you are not to gratify the desires of the sinful nature. For the sinful nature desires what is contrary to the Spirit, and the Spirit what is contrary to the sinful nature' (verses 16, 17). That's why we must live by the Spirit. Someone who does that is not hard to recognise. Someone who is responding to the life of God within them, is able to demonstrate the character of the Lord Jesus, and you know people like that by their fruit.

So what is God looking for in our lives? He is looking for the fruit of His own life, His Spirit within us (verses 22, 23). You will, perhaps, be very familiar with these verses. But I want us to look very briefly at these nine examples, and as we look at them, consciously in the presence of God, to seek to put our lives alongside this pen-picture of the Lord Jesus. We know that we shall fall short of what we ought to be, but as we do it, let's ask Him to show us those particular areas in which He's wanting, by His Spirit, to produce fruit in us. Holiness is seen here in very down-to-earth terms. It is often pointed out that the word for fruit is singular, as though it is one fruit. I believe that means holiness. It means being like the Lord Jesus, and there are nine expressions of it. That saves us from regarding the fruit of the Spirit a bit like some of those exam papers where you went into the exam room and found the optimistic exhortation at the top of the exam paper, 'Attempt any four questions.' But God is not saying, 'Choose three or four of these and opt for them.' You don't add them one by one. They are all to be growing in our lives.

It has often been pointed out that Paul is thinking about three dimensions here. The first three – love, joy and peace – refer especially to our relationship with the Lord. The second three – patience, kindness and goodness – refer to our relationship with other people. The last three – faithfulness, gentleness or meekness, and self-control – refer to our relationship with ourselves. They can be described as the upward, the outward and the inward dimensions.

Love, joy and peace are the initial demonstration of the Holy Spirit in a new Christian's life. They are the signs of the new birth. But they are never superseded. We never grow out of them. Rather, we grow more and more into them. I find it very helpful to think about love, joy and peace, not as abstract virtues, but as evidence of Jesus Christ living out His life, by His Spirit in us, because they all come from Christ and they come only from Christ. If you look back to John 15 you'll find there, that as the Lord talks about Himself as the true Vine and us as the branches grafted into Him, He makes it very clear that this love and joy and peace that He wants to see in our lives are what He first gives us. 'As the Father has loved me, so have I loved you. Now remain in my love' (15:9). 'I told you this so that my joy might be in you, and your joy may be complete' (15:11). 'Peace I leave with you. My peace I give you. I do not give to you as the world gives' (14:27). Jesus speaks of 'My love', 'My joy', 'My peace'. They can come only from the Lord, Himself. And He imparts them to His people by His Spirit.

When we come to think about the fullness of the Spirit in terms of fruit-bearing, the Lord is surely teaching us that this fruit may be produced abundantly in our lives. As you follow these themes through the New Testament, you find that the fullness of the Spirit means just this, that each of the characteristics of the Lord Jesus is to be experienced to an increasing, even to a superlative degree, by His people. So Paul prays that we may know this love of Christ which surpasses knowledge, that we may be filled with all the fullness of God (Eph. 3:19). Peter writes, 'You love the Lord Jesus, and you believe in him and are filled with an inexpressible and glorious joy' (1 Pet. 1:8). So there's a love that passes knowledge, and a joy that passes description, and your minds may already have gone to Philippians 4:7, where Paul talks about the peace of God which passes all understanding guarding our hearts and our minds in Christ Jesus. That is the purpose of the fullness of the Spirit, that we might know the love that passes knowledge, the joy that passes description, and the peace that passes understanding. Now every new born Christian knows something of that. But the Christian who is being filled with the Spirit is increasing in each of these areas.

How do you know that Christ's love is in you? Jesus says, 'Remain in my love' (John 15:9). Then He goes on, 'If you obey my command you will remain in my love' (verse 10). How do you stay joyful when life brings its difficulties and its problems and sometimes its overwhelming trials?

'I told you this so that my joy may be in you.' What has He told us? He has told us to obey His commands. How do you keep untroubled and unafraid? How do you know the peace of God in the midst of all the turmoils of life? Jesus said, 'If anyone loves me, he will obey my teaching. My Father will come to him, will love him, and we will come to him and make our home with him' (John 14:23). See what the Lord is saying. As you obey the Scriptures you are responding to the Holy Spirit who uses the Word of God to produce fruit in the children of God. And as you open your life fully to Christ, He will produce in abundance in your character His characteristics of love, joy and peace.

People get very concerned about what it means to be filled with the Spirit, and rightly so, because it's a very clear New Testament command. The New English Bible translates Ephesians 5:18 as, 'Let the Holy Spirit fill you.' It is the present imperative. It means, 'Be being filled with the Spirit.' The emphasis in the New Testament is not on a once for all filling, but on a continuous, renewed filling. Clearly, Paul does not see being filled with the Spirit as an unusual experience for the few. He sees it as the norm for every Christian. If I am to live the Christian life at all, I can do so only in the power of the Holy Spirit. And I need the fullness of that resource. So being filled with the Spirit is the fresh inflow of God's life into every part of my life, constantly being repeated, so that every area of my life is permeated and controlled by Him. It is not that I bring my little cup, as it were, and try to get it filled once, and then carry it ever so carefully so that none of it spills out. But I bring my little cup to the 'Niagara Falls' and the fullness of God's water of life flows into my cup and out from it, and produces the fruit of the Spirit in my character.

When people talk about the crisis experiences which they have had, usually what has happened is that God has removed barriers which we have erected to the free flow of His life within us. For being filled with the Holy Spirit doesn't mean that we somehow get more of Him as though you could receive Him in instalments. The Holy Spirit is a person and you can't have a person in instalments. You can't say, 'This coming week sixty per cent of my mother is coming to stay with me.' That's an absolute impossibility. Either she is coming to stay with you, or she isn't. And if you are a Christian, you have the Holy Spirit. But does the Holy Spirit have access to every part of you? If the Spirit is not in every part of our lives, then we are not being filled with His fullness. And that's the only power by which I can live as a Christian, and it results in love and joy and peace.

It also results in patience, kindness and goodness. We don't have time to look at these in any detail, but just stop and think about your own life, and ask God to give you a sober estimate of yourself. Longsuffering, patience: someone has defined it as 'being in a hostile world and feeling no hostility to it'. Kindness or graciousness, goodness; the Lord Jesus went about doing good. In a sense He couldn't help it. That was His nature. That's what's so attractive about the work of the Spirit. It doesn't produce the busy do-gooder that everybody resents. It produces the overflowing life of Christ, that doesn't miss an opportunity to help, or to encourage, or to bear a burden, or to give. That's where you see the power of the Spirit in His fullness. And if we are allowing Him to fill us, people will notice. It will make a difference in your church. I remember a dear old lady in our own church who used to love to say, 'Well, I can't really hold much, but I guess I can overflow lots.' That's what He wants us to do. He wants us to be overflowing Christians in terms of patience,

kindness and goodness. We don't have that in ourselves.
It's only as the Spirit fills us that He gets the job done, that
He makes us like Christ.

Lastly, with regard to ourselves, there is faithfulness,
meekness or gentleness (perhaps a better word would be
teachability) and self-control. Notice that the Spirit
changes us from inside out. He did that with the disciples.
They weren't faithful. Do you remember how they ran
away in the Garden of Gethsemane? But look at their
boldness in the Acts of the Apostles. What's the
difference? The Holy Spirit has come into their lives and is
producing His fruit of faithfulness. They weren't gentle
and meek, were they? In the Gospels they were always
arguing about status and power, and who'd be the
greatest. You don't find that in the Acts of the Apostles.
Why? Because the Holy Spirit has come into their lives.
And strong Christians are not all bluster and noise, forcing
other people to go their way. Strong Christians are meek
and lowly in heart. They follow a servant Lord. They have
no room for pride. You don't find that in the Gospels.
Think of the 'sons of thunder'. Think of Peter's impetu-
osity. What changed them? It was the Holy Spirit coming
into their lives. So, as every area of life came under His
control, they exemplified that fruit of His Spirit which is
self-control. And the horrifying list of sins in verses 19-21
is full of failure of self-control. But the Christian is
controlled by the Holy Spirit.

'Those who belong to Christ Jesus have crucified the
sinful nature with its passions and desires. Since we live by
the Spirit, let us keep in step with the Spirit' (verses 24, 25).
All the resources are available. The question is, 'Do you
really want to be like Jesus?'

HOLINESS – PITFALLS AND ERRORS

by Rev Gervais Angel

Ephesians 4:22

'Another Pentecost' – that's the way that two Scots described the work that God did through Paul the apostle in Ephesus. Luke, in his account said this: 'All they who dwelt in Asia heard the word of the Lord, both Jews and Greeks'. Was he exaggerating? Consider the curiosity of the Asiatics to hear something new. Consider the massive population drawn to the temple of Artemis with its sex cult at Ephesus. Consider, if you like, that Ephesus was the London of Asia, and I find it quite easy to believe that indeed many people passed through that place at one time or another in those three years when Paul was ministering there, and they heard the word of God.

But if you want a particular indication of the tremendous work that was done there, think about the bonfire! Many of the converts of Paul were asked to bring their books on the occult and their instruments to deal with magic, to put them together and have them burnt; and the value of all those books came to half a million pounds in today's money. Take any one of the regions of Mission England; if all the people who were converted there were to put their pornographic books in one big bonfire and the value of those books came to half a million pounds, then I think we could start talking about a revival on our hands. And then consider how hard it was for Paul; there were indeed 300,000 people living at Ephesus, less than in Bristol, but of course there were people passing through.

But how hard it was to break the ground there! He told the elders at Ephesus, 'When I preached to you, I tell you, remember that for three years I never failed day nor night to warn you, even with tears in my eyes.' That fruit came through weeping. Think of the odds stacked against him; that big temple of Artemis, twice as long as any of the football pitches that Billy Graham has been preaching from and almost three times as wide; manned by over a thousand male and female prostitutes; and the act of worship was, in fact, to go to bed with one of those prostitutes.

Think of the massive lust that those Christians would have to give up for Jesus' sake. And what about the greed? When Paul preached at Ephesus he nearly put the jewellers out of business. They used to build little silver statues of the goddess and sell them to the tourists who came to the temple. But Paul began to preach and people found Christ and they didn't want the souvenirs any more, there was a drop in sales and the jewellers got anxious. They said, 'We're going to be bankrupt. Let's get hold of Paul and his companions', and they hauled them into the theatre in front of between 25,000 and 50,000 people. And there in front of the crowd these jewellers tried to discredit Paul because they wanted their business back again. The profit motive! What Paul calls in Ephesians 5:5, 'idolatry'. Lust, greed; these were two engrained features, among many others, in the sinners at Ephesus which through the mercy of God were swept away and there was this tremendous crusade.

Now what was the message? 'Repentance to God and faith in our Lord Jesus Christ' (Acts 20:21). That's what he preached. And when later he wrote his great letter to the Ephesians he reflected on the meaning of that, in the text that we have before us (4:20-25).

I've chosen the AV because it leaves open two variant interpretations of this text. The RSV translation gives us Paul commanding the Christians at Ephesus to put off the old nature which belongs to 'your former manner of life', as if they had not done so already. They were converted, they were seated with Christ in the heavenlies, but, according to the RSV, or the way it is written, they still had to put off the old nature.

Now John Stott finds difficulty with this translation, and therefore I have to attend to what he says. In his commentary on Ephesians he finds difficulty with the idea that people who are already converted should be asked to renounce their old nature. And this challenge to the RSV translation is fully supported by J. B. Phillips, the NEB and the NIV which make the call to put off the old nature a description of what they've been taught already. Now maybe you don't agree completely with John Stott, but you're not going to argue with Paul when he says in Romans 6:6, 'We know that our old self was crucified with him.' In the face of this kind of authority it is very difficult indeed to escape the conclusion that Paul is here talking about the meaning of repentance and faith which he had preached at Ephesus with such powerful effect.

Now, if that's so, why do you sit there in rows with memories of your sins? Why do you sit there with fantasies of evil intentions? Why is it that you can have your conscience pricked at the sound of a single sermon? Why do you feel guilty, upset, embarrassed, tense, with memories of your sins like stinking birds around your

necks? Of course, not everybody in the church is like that.
There are some who, whilst they are not conscious of their
own sins, are conscious of the sins of others. 'Ah, those
South Africans with their apartheid policy', and detestable
it is! Or again, 'Did you see what was in the paper?
Terrible! Fraud, theft, rape, murder!' While all the time
they don't spare a thought for their partners in marriage to
whom they are being unfaithful in thought if not in deed.
They don't spare a thought about using the firm's facilities
without permission, for their private needs. They don't
spare a thought as they wrangle with their accountant
about tax evasion and tax avoidance. They don't want to
pay the tax on their massive income and they leave it to the
Chancellor of the Exchequer to bleed the difference out of
people who are on lower incomes and haven't got a chance
to fill in an assessment form. Why is it, if our old man was
crucified with Christ, there is still sin in the life of the
believer? Why have I a guilty conscience, when I believe
that my old nature was killed on Christ's cross? Paul
doesn't tell us why; but he does tell us what to do about it.

Now this platform is notorious for answers to this
question. Robert Pearsall Smith, a man who never spoke
in Keswick but whose ministry in England led to the
earliest Keswick Conventions, argued that the answer to
this particular problem was that real sin is only the sin I'm
aware of, and every time I recognise a new sin then I must
put off the old nature. This was taught also by Evan
Hopkins, for many years the iron hand behind the Keswick
Chair. Now it's pretty obvious that if you are aware of sin
you must try to put it behind you. But it is not so obvious
that that is what Paul means here. The Greek tense for
'putting away' cannot refer to something continuous; it
must refer to a decisive act.

It is true that later Evan Hopkins did speak of a single,

decisive act of breaking with sin. He wrote, 'The believer does not get disentangled from sin gradually. He breaks with it in Christ once for all. He is placed by a decisive act of will in the sphere of perfect holiness and it is within it that the gradual renewing of the personal life goes forward.' Now Hopkins was correct to point to a decisive break with sin. But the suggestion that so often ran at those early Convention meetings was that the decisive act must be made by the believer after he has become a believer, and that is wrong. We have seen already here that Paul is explaining the repentance of the Ephesians. They had learned when they first came to believe that they were turning from sin to righteousness, from man to God, from self and Adam to Christ.

That this is Paul's meaning here is more obvious in the letter to the Colossians; a church which had similar problems to those of the Ephesians. There he writes (and again I use the AV) 'Lie not one to another, seeing that ye *have* put off the old man with his deeds' (Col. 3:9). Notice that the Colossians are not to lie now because some time before they put off the old nature. If this wasn't proof enough look at Romans chapter 6. We are told there that as we identify with the death of Christ there is a break with sin. As we identify with the resurrection of Christ so we become alive to God. But at what time does it happen? Paul says, 'baptism', which for the New Testament Christians carried the same meaning as conversion by repentance and faith. Scripture is not calling sinful believers to turn to Christ a second time. It is calling us to the position in which our initial repentance put us when we received the Saviour. What were we doing? This is how the NIV puts it: 'Surely you heard of him and were taught in him in accordance with the truth that is in Jesus. You were taught, with regard to your former way of life, to put off your old self.'

That one decisive act was carried out then. Then why do you still go on sinning? Paul doesn't tell us why but he tells us what to do. 'Stop it!' Stop what? Lying (verse 25), persistent anger (verse 26), theft (verse 28), foul language (verse 29), bitterness, temper, rage, brawling, blasphemy, evil (verse 31), sexual irregularity, which for Paul included adultery; filth, avarice or the profit motive (5:3), obscenity, foolish talk, coarse joking (verse 4) and so on. 'Just stop it!' That's the answer. Because people who practise this kind of thing do not belong to the Kingdom of God and of Christ (Eph. 5:5). Now this always requires a super-human effort. Paul teaches that it is the power of God which makes us break with sin as we apply ourselves to the task. To the Roman Christians he wrote on this point: 'If by the Spirit you put to death the misdeeds of the body, you will live' (Rom. 8:13).

And there is the key. Our discipline with our prayer; the two go together. When we do all we can by way of self-control, self-denial, persistent application to healthy pursuits, we can at the same time do nothing other than throw ourselves like weaklings on the merciful power of God. The Spirit helps us in our weaknesses; we do not know how to pray as we ought. Sometimes we do not even want to pray as we ought. Paul could do anything through Christ who strengthened him. Where do you and I go from here? We know perfectly well that our sins disqualify us from our inheritance in the Kingdom of God. So what are we going to do?

We must remember that He died for us. Remember that our sinful nature hung as it were upon that cross, and bled and died and was buried with Him. He broke the power of sin over our lives and the embarrassment we now suffer is punishment for forgetting what He has done for us already. But let's not get carried away with sentiment.

Let's be practical. What are we going to do? There are two things to do. First, as we recognise that when we first turned to Christ our sins were taken by Jesus, we are now going to face up to the particular sins of which we are now aware and we are going to stop doing them. Secondly, and more importantly, as we live day by day, we are going to drop on our knees and ask the Spirit of God, the resurrecting Spirit of God to make that break in us good and firm! Very often other people are involved in our wrongdoing. No doubt we will be embarrassed that other people should know that we've changed. Perhaps we may even hurt other people in the process. That doesn't matter. Christ is more important than anybody else. We've got to do what our Saviour wants, to break with our sins and pray the power of Heaven to make that decision good and firm.

FINISHED AND UNFINISHED
by Rev Philip Hacking

Hebrews 10:11-25

You may not be surprised that a preacher from South Yorkshire wants to speak about revolution, for that's always in the air in South Yorkshire and I believe as Christians we ought to be ready for it. When I was walking this afternoon and looking at the hills that never change, when I was meditating upon the beauty of Keswick, it seemed all out of place to talk about revolution in Keswick, but I've said it more than once and I say it again (and I don't claim to be particularly prophetic) that I do not believe the question is whether there will be revolution in our land. The only two questions are when and what kind. About the first I have nothing to say – God is sovereign.

But I do have something to say about the second, for I believe that there could come the greatest revolution of all, which is what I call a revolution of love – the Christian revolution. It's terribly easy in Keswick to assume that Christianity is a kind of gentle, beautiful, flowing, unchanging thing and to forget the sheer dynamic of it. The 'Magnificat' is infinitely more revolutionary than the

'Red Flag', the message of Jesus is in itself a most revolutionary thing. All that there is in Christian truth has within it the note of revolution. The church as we are looking at it here in Keswick is the most revolutionary body upon earth with its message, 'All One in Christ Jesus'. God's great new creation has turned the world upside down.

Now most of us don't expect revolution. I recollect years ago in the church in which I was nurtured, there was to be a meeting to do with crime and the church. It was one of those rather dull meetings that only the faithful went to, but the printer made a slight error which made it sound much more exciting. Instead of 'Crime and the Church' he printed, 'Crime in the Church'. Now that really was worth coming to – the thoughts of revelations about bishops and all the rest of it made us flock along – unfortunately we were much disappointed. And my guess is that we might almost as much expect to find crime in the church as revolution in the church.

But as we dare to look at what happened when Jesus Christ finished His work upon the cross, I suggest to you that the revolution of the cross is the greatest revolution of all time. The danger is that we pay lip service to it and rejoice in the truth of the atonement, but our lives are not revolutionised. Stephen got the message and he was martyred for his pains and the church began to grow; Paul who held the coats while they martyred Stephen got the message; whoever wrote the letter to the Hebrews got the message. In these verses we're reminded by that writer of what happened when Jesus died on the cross and cried, 'Finished!'

Now the danger for the people to whom he was writing was that they could be content just to live as a sect of Judaism, just to take on board the Christian message and the Christian ethic and some Christian dogmas, but not to dare to carry through the implications. If we get the message it will take us where this writer wanted these Christians to be, outside the camp. It will take us out of the easy respectability which is so often our kind of Christianity, out of the ease and comfort into revolution; the only kind that we pray for in our nation and our world.

Can I remind you first what the apostle Paul dared to say about the revolution of the cross. 'For the love of Christ controls us, because we are convinced that one has died for all; therefore all have died. And he died for all, that those who live might live no longer for themselves but for him who for their sake died and was raised' (2 Cor. 5:14, 15). Once we let the message of the cross permeate to every part of our being, what we do with our money, what we do with our time, what we do with our future, what we do with our wills – then the revolution's happened.

There are two thoughts here. It's all about the finished work and the unfinished work.

The finished work of the Saviour

The great note of the letter to the Hebrews is the once-for-allness of the death of Jesus. There are three things in it.

First, there's *a sacrifice completed*. 'When Christ had offered for all time a single sacrifice for sins, he sat down at the right hand of God' (10:12). Only once is He seen standing, and that's when Stephen, the first martyr, sees Him welcoming him to heaven; but He's normally seated. What a contrast that is with verse 11. There the old ritual was going on. The priest was standing every day offering the same sacrifice with no power. Jesus, having once for all offered His own life, is seated. And when He cried from the cross, 'Finished!' – that tremendous word – that was the revolution.

Now you can look on to verse 20 where it talks about His going through the curtain, that is, the flesh. And we remember how the veil of the Temple was rent in two. I've often wondered what it must have been like to have been in the Temple at that moment when, on the first Good Friday, with no human hand, the veil was rent in two from top to bottom and a whole era was ended. You could see now into the symbolic presence of God into which only one man, once a year, covered with blood, had ever gone. Do remember how marvellous that is! There is no more sacrifice, no more trying to earn my salvation. A sacrifice has been complete and because He's there I have access and I can pray.

Even today, if I want to meet the Queen I am not expected just to knock at the door of the palace and say, 'I've come.' I need somebody to introduce me. I need somebody who has got one foot in the royal household to say, 'This man's worthy of entrance. Can he come?' And the glory of the gospel's revolution that we take for granted is that I've got a friend in high places; I've got the risen Son of God, my Saviour, at the right hand of God and I can come, not just when I die but always, through Him because of a sacrifice that's completed.

Secondly, the finished work of the Saviour is *a victory enjoyed*. There in verse 13, He's waiting for the day when victory's finally accomplished, but it is already accomplished. Have you ever realised the joy of Ascensiontide? The Ascension looks back and forwards. When Jesus went back into heaven, into the presence of God, it was the end and it was the beginning. The fifth chapter of Revelation is, if you like, watching the Ascension from the other end, seeing Jesus come home.

It's a marvellous chapter and it begins with a message: the Lion of Judah has conquered. And John says, 'I searched to find the Lion and behold a Lamb as it had been slain.' He was looking for the conquering Lion and he saw the gentle sacrificial Lamb, and the note of victory was there. He's conquered and we are more than conquerors. Victory is ours to live in now and then one day in all the final glory of His return and the glory of heaven. It's a victory enjoyed.

On Sunday I was sharing with one of the churches about that D-Day forty years ago. I can just remember it, and I thought then that it was marvellous, exciting stuff; and only this year, watching on television something of the drama of D-Day, did I realise that it wasn't exciting. It was terribly ugly; it was very heroic; it was almost certainly necessary, but it wasn't just exciting. It had to be, that there might be victory, and as I come to the cross of Jesus, and the Lamb upon the throne, it isn't just exciting. Young people sing the songs of Zion. Let's enjoy them. We need more of them. We need to tell the world that the revolution's on and we're singing for it. But let's remember that the cross was not just exciting. It meant the self-giving of the Son of God that we might enjoy victory. There would be no V-Day without D-Day.

When I was pondering on this passage my mind was taken over to some words in 1 Corinthians 15 where Paul says that one day even death itself will be destroyed. That great Greek verb 'to destroy' is a word which speaks of somebody taking the sting out of death, somebody defusing the bomb. It's a word we've learnt something of in our world. I met one day the widow of a man who defused a bomb in Northern Ireland and lost his life. Yes, that's the picture. By death He destroyed death so that we can enter into victory.

Thirdly, 'By *a single offering* He has perfected for all time those who are being sanctified' (verse 14). We are told in verse 10 that we have been sanctified, set apart. We belong to Him and we were set apart at the cross. But verse 14 says that He has perfected those who are being sanctified. We are being made like Jesus; and that is what thrills me. To be sanctified, to be made holy, is to become like Jesus. And the Jesus I want with all my heart to become like, is the Jesus who went to the cross. By His offering on the cross He has made it possible, because now the Holy Spirit has been released to come into our hearts, and it's possible for me to become like Jesus. Does your view of holiness take you to the cross? It ought to. In a sense we ought to stop at the finished work of the Saviour and say, 'Hallelujah!' The revolution has come. Do you know, I think the worst thing we've done to the Christian faith is to make it dull. It seems to me that whatever else Christianity is, it's not dull, it's not a soporific thing. It should make some people excited, some people overjoyed, some people angry, because it knocks from under your feet the kind of foundation that you've been living on. But God forgive us that we've made it boring.

The unfinished work of the church

Now I want to point out in verses 19-25 three exhortations of this writer to the Hebrews. Because of the finished work of the Saviour, because of what He's done, let the cross shed its influence over your lives in three ways.

Firstly, in *our worship*. We think we revolutionise our worship when we tinker with the mechanics. I mean, everything's possible in worship nowadays. In some churches some people hug each other, some people dance down the aisle. We have bands and orchestras. Great stuff!

All these things can happen in our churches and sometimes
we kid ourselves that because we've made everything very
exciting and modern, the revolution has come. No, the
revolution in worship of which this writer speaks is very
different.

'Let us draw near' (verse 22). Because of all that our
Lord has done, let us draw near, and let us draw near with
boldness. Can I ask you, 'How bold are you in your
worship and in your praying?' He's made the way and
He's made it at great cost. Do we draw near? When I read
some of the great Old Testament prayers I say to myself,
'How could a man like Abraham pray like Abraham
prayed in Genesis 18? How dare he be so bold with God?'
And then I think of my praying, with all its timidity and
lack of faith, and there's old Abraham way before the
revelation of Jesus, way before the revolution of the cross,
praying like that. Couldn't it begin, this revolution of love,
when we start – because of the cross – praying with
boldness? Let us draw near. Let us do what the priest did
once a year, but we can do always. So we do it with
boldness and yet at the same time with reverence, and
you'll note that we can draw near only if our hearts are
right with God, if our faith is being fully exercised and if
we are truly cleansed.

Are these things true of you? Let's draw near, let's make
this Convention the beginning of some real awakening as
we begin to pray. Isn't to live as if it never happened the
worst thing we can do to what Jesus did for us? I think you
may have heard me say before that I am not one of those
people who find prayer easy. So I speak to you not as some
preacher who's found all the answers, but as one who
battles with the problem. But I know that Jesus died to
make it possible.

Do you remember the Old Testament story of David and

his friends? When David happened to say, 'I wish I could have some water from the well at the gate of Bethlehem,' they fought their way through the enemies' ranks, they got the water from the well at Bethlehem, and they carried it back to David. And I've always felt he shouldn't have done it. David didn't drink it – he poured it out – and I feel like saying, 'Oh, David, that really was a bit rough. These poor men have risked their lives to give you a drink and you pour it out.' Oh, I know what the experts say. It was an offering, a libation, but I still wish he'd drunk it. And I find the Lord saying to me, 'Think how deep were the waters crossed. Think how dark was the night that I went through for you. What difference has it made? Have you poured out the water or have you drunk it?' Has the revolution happened? Of course, revival is according to God's sovereign purpose, but we know what could begin to happen if we as the people of God took seriously our worship and our prayer.

Secondly, there is *our witness*. 'Hold fast to the confession of our hope without wavering, for he who promised is faithful' (verse 23). If He was a faithful witness to death, hold on to it. I want to say to all of us who name the name of Jesus, that God needs people who will not be ashamed of the message of Christ crucified and all that goes with it. There's no message of Christ crucified if He is not the eternal Son of God, and there is no message of Christ crucified, if He is not risen and triumphant. So what the writer is saying is, 'Hold on to the faith once delivered to the saints, and don't be ashamed of the message of the faith of Christ crucified.' And I trust that all of us will go on with that unfinished work of witnessing faithfully; that whatever it may cost, we will hold on to the truth.

Thirdly, there is *our fellowship*. Let's 'encourage one

another' (verse 25). You see, we meet as part of a family born at the cross. Think sometimes of that family created at the cross, think of the odd people who became associated there – a Roman centurion, Joseph of Arimathea, the mother of Jesus, John – all these people who were drawn to the cross as a new kind of family. Paul in Ephesians points out that not only has Jesus made peace with God at the cross, but peace with one another. I see here this tremendous possibility of a revolutionary fellowship at the foot of the cross. I see it as I saw it a few weeks ago when a released IRA prisoner and a released Loyalist prisoner were holding the same big Bible in the tent at Port Stewart, Northern Ireland and reading the word together – that's the revolution. Nobody else and nothing else could have done it. And when I look at my church – and I want you to look at your church – I want you to ask the question, 'Is it true, are the barriers broken down? Is ours a fellowship where we encourage each other, where we meet together, where we provoke to love and good works because we are the kind of family that only God could have made?' Every church fellowship should be an act of God, so that everybody can say about that group, that fellowship, that family, that church around the cross, that only God could have done it.

I've had to write an article about our church recently so I addressed myself to this awful sentence, 'The Church of England is basically elderly, female and middle class.' Well now, I love older people, and I'm very fond of the female of the species, and there's nothing wrong with being middle-class, but if it's true that that's what the church is, the church is not what it's meant to be. I long that we at Keswick, as one aspect of that family at the foot of the cross, might become even more than we are, an act of God. I long that nobody could ever leave Keswick without knowing that Jesus who died reigns, the Lamb upon the throne. He is Lord on the throne in heaven. He was Lord on that strange throne of the cross. I wonder, in all honesty, does that same Lord who cried, 'Finished!', who won our salvation, does He reign as Lord on the throne of your life? Is there the unmistakable mark of the Lord Jesus – self on the cross and Christ upon the throne?

The other night I was watching what for English people is a very strange thing, the Democratic nomination that takes place in the United States. But I also happened to listen to a bit of oratory – there isn't much left in our world today – and as the Reverend Jesse Jackson, who represents black people, preached, I found myself getting warm, worked-up in front of the 'telly', almost rising to my feet. Do you remember how it all ended? Jesse Jackson cried, 'Our time has come!' and you felt the whole place move. Seriously, very seriously, it bothers me that that can happen in just an election – it's an important one, of course, but it's very much in the secular world. Oh, for the passion, that we could go out and say with the living Lord who died for us, 'Our time has come!' No! 'His time has come!' And when we put Him on the throne that may be true. The finished work of the Saviour – praise God! The unfinished work of the servant church – pray that that may be accomplished to His glory.

HOW TO AVOID A WASTED LIFE

by Rev Stuart Briscoe

Matthew 6:25-34

Some years ago there was a very beautiful musical that was made into a movie called 'Fiddler on the Roof'. It was a lovely story of a Russian Jew with a very faithful wife and a lot of beautiful daughters. As his daughters are busy getting married, he and his wife have a little discussion in the form of a gorgeous duet, and he turns to his old wife and says, 'Do you love me?' and she is totally taken aback. But her response in the duet goes something like this: 'Do I love you? Well, I wash your shirts, and I darn your socks, and I've borne your children and I've raised your daughters. If that's loving you, I suppose I do.' And this couple who have been married for many, many years suddenly come to realise that what is going on in their lives is a very deep, abiding love. The problem was, that they didn't know that was what you called it.

Sometimes we use expressions and we are not absolutely certain what they mean right down at grass-roots level. We talk about being totally committed to the Lord. The problem that people sometimes experience is this – they use the expression but they are not really altogether quite sure what it means. Now, if loving is washing shirts, and darning socks, and bearing children, and raising families and putting food on the table, I wonder if it's possible for us to discover in our spiritual lives some very down-to-earth evidences of total commitment to the Lord. It seems to me that we might be able to discover some.

I want you to notice that little expression in Matthew 6:33, where the Lord Jesus says to these people gathered round Him, 'Seek ye first the kingdom of God and his righteousness.' Some time ago a reporter came to see me, asked a whole lot of questions, and when he was leaving, he whirled round and said, 'What's your biggest problem?'. He was trying to catch me off guard, which he did, and I simply blurted out the first thing which came into my mind. He didn't look very impressed and he left. He obviously wasn't impressed – he never wrote the article. But after he left I thought to myself, 'What is my biggest problem?', and I decided that it has to be that of establishing priorities.

Now I happen to be pastor of a large church, which means that I have a lot of people who are totally committed to helping me decide what my priorities are – and they all have different ideas about it. But when I came to read Matthew 6 it told me something very helpful and very important. 'Seek ye first the kingdom of God and his righteousness' (6:33) – and all the other things will fit into place. And so I began to think about that and I came to a conclusion. If I determine in my heart that the top priority of my life is to be the kingdom of God, then God will look after all the other things.

Now this is the way it works, as I understand it. If I can look at the grass-root realities of my life, I discover that there are a whole set of priorities. And the reality of my commitment to the Lord can very often be identified by my priorities. Now that's pretty simple. The Lord Jesus in this particular passage points out to these people that they already have their priorities set. He talks about all the things they are worrying about. What are they worrying about? What they are going to eat? Food! What they are going to wear? Fashion! What they are going to do with their money? Finance! Can they add one hour to their life? Fitness!

Things haven't changed very much, have they? The anxieties were food and fashion and fitness and family and finance. All these things were gripping their minds. I want you to notice something so elementary. If you have an anxiety, you have a priority. If there's something you are worrying about, it's because it's important, and if it's so worrisome to you that you are perpetually and continually anxious, guess what – you've found your priority. So, if you ever wonder what your priorities *really* are, I'll make it easy for you. Identify your anxieties.

Then the Lord Jesus goes on to talk about activities. He says, 'The pagans are going round doing this and that and the other.' You know what I've discovered? I can always find time to do what I really want to do. Have you discovered that? So, if I want to identify my priorities (and I must), then the easy way to do it is to identify my anxieties, and then to identify my activities. And when I've got a list of them I say to myself, 'Well, I never did. These are my priorities.'

Then identify your ambitions. The Lord Jesus said, 'You seek after this and you seek after that'. The word 'seeking' here is more than just casually looking. It is close to being obsessed. It is the word for ambition. Now some people have no ambition. Shame on them! You were created by God to be something unique. If you are not ambitious to be what you were uniquely created to be, shame on you. But unfortunately we can get our ambitions warped and twisted, and can get ourselves in the most awful mess. But everybody has got some kind of inclination, something deep down they would really like to do or be. Well, dig it out folks, write it down on a piece of paper and say, 'Well, I never did. There's an ambition. Those are my activities, there are my anxieties, and those must be my priorities.'

Then the Lord Jesus, having told these people to identify their existing priorities, points out to them that it is absolutely essential that they evaluate their priorities. If you're going to evaluate them, however, you need something against which to measure them. That's where our text comes in: 'Seek ye first the kingdom.' Measure your priorities against whether the kingdom of God is always first. Now, we can have a marvellous time talking about the kingdom of God. We could talk about it for a week, and there's a high probability that we wouldn't always agree. But I think there's one thing we would agree on. The thing that makes a kingdom is a king. And the realm in which the king operates, and the people over whom the king rules, constitute the kingdom.

Some people would talk about the kingdom having come, and some would say it is yet to come. Some would say it is individual, some would say it is corporate. Some would say it is eschatalogical. They would all say all kinds of different things about the kingdom of God, but let's keep it at the very simplest level just now. Let's think in terms of the kingdom of God being that area of human experience in which it is abundantly clear that God's the boss. The Lord Jesus says that has got to be the top priority. Now then, some people began to examine their sandals. They began to shuffle their feet in the dust because some of them knew that their food and their fashion, their fitness and their finances were far more important than God being boss. And some of those people realised that they had been rushing hither and thither and yonder and they had never even got round to stopping and finding out who God was in their lives. It's very easy to do that.

The Lord Jesus put it very clearly to Nicodemus. He said, 'Sir, I want you to understand something. You will neither enter the kingdom nor understand the kingdom until you are born again.' So if the top priority is the kingdom of God, it is abundantly clear that the top priority of the top priority is to make sure you have experienced the kingdom of God, which means simply, that you've been born again. But being born again means a whole lot of different things to different people. We had a rash of 'born agains' in America not long ago. Jimmy Carter announced he was born again, and suddenly everyone and his auntie was born again. We had 'born again' everything. The term became totally devalued. It simply meant making a new start. But that isn't what the Bible means. It means literally 'born from above' and to be born from above means that the King who died for you and rose again for you comes to live in you and be your boss.

Now there are some people here who have been so busy with food and fashion and fitness and family that they have never got round to making sure that the risen Christ is their boss. They have never been born again. And if you never get round to being born again, you won't ever enter the kingdom. In fact, between you and me, Jesus said that you won't even understand it. What a sad thing it is to begin to evaluate your priorities and say to yourself, 'I've been living fifty years, and now I sit down and discover that the top priority of the top priority is that I might experience the King in my life as His kingdom, and I never got round to it.'

You notice that the Lord Jesus, however, does not just say, 'Seek ye first the kingdom' but He talks of seeking the kingdom of God and His righteousness. The kingdom of God must not only be experienced – it must be expressed. To put it another way, if the King takes up residence in your life as boss, it will show. The top priority of your life is not how you dress or how you are fed or how your investments are doing. The top priority in your life is, whether having experienced the kingdom, it shows in your life. That takes discipline; it takes growth; it takes being interested. Some people don't really care too much. They sing in choirs like angels, then go home and live like devils. Some people have one set of rules for Sunday and an entirely different set of rules for the week. Some people have an ecclesiastical ethic which they bring out and take to church on Sundays, and then they have what they call a business ethic for the rest of the week. You know what the problem is? They didn't get their priorities right.

People like things that are popular. If you could choose between being popular and being unpopular, you'd probably prefer to be popular. People like things that are profitable. If you can choose between things being unprofitable and profitable, you probably prefer them to be profitable. People like to be comfortable. If you can choose between being comfortable and uncomfortable, you will probably go for being comfortable. That's easy. Unfortunately, it's not that simple, because the kingdom of God stands for things like that which is true and good and right. You say, 'I'm all in favour of what is true and good and right, and popular and profitable and comfortable.' I don't have any problems with that either. But the problems come when the two sets of three begin to collide.

For instance, you could get yourself into a situation where you are required to say something that is not true in business, and you have to decide whether you are going to say what is not true and be very popular with the people for whom you are covering, or whether you are going to take a stand and say, 'I'm terribly sorry. I sound like an awful bore and an awful prig but I'm really more concerned with expressing the kingdom', and they'll ask you what you mean and you can explain. That hurts and is tough but you have a commitment to the kingdom being expressed, and kingdom expression demands truth, and you have to trade popularity for truth. That's the kingdom. That's the King in charge.

Do you love me? Well, I darn your socks and I wash your shirts. Are you totally committed to the Lord? Well, I guess I do have a commitment to truth even when it clashes head on with popularity.

Not long ago I preached up a real storm in my church. I really took off on abortion. One of my colleagues came up to me afterwards. He said, 'I gather you're against abortion.' I said, 'I most emphatically am.' Then he asked, 'What are you for?' And he went on to point out that there would have been maybe three or four pregnant girls in my congregation. What were they to do if they daren't go home and I'd closed the door of abortion on them? He pointed out that what they needed was a home. I felt rebuked. The problem is this: we know the right thing to do, but isn't it uncomfortable to bring a pregnant girl into your home? But that's the kingdom.

There's another thing about the kingdom that's got to be a top priority. The Lord Jesus, on one occasion said, 'This gospel of the kingdom must first be preached to all nations. Then comes the end.' A lot of Christians get very excited about the end and what is going to happen then. A lady came to see me recently. She asked me, 'Will the church go through the tribulation?' I asked, 'Which church and which tribulation?' Quite frankly, I've been in a lot of countries recently, and if you ask that question they'll feel it's totally academic because they can only be killed once and a lot of their people are being killed. It seems suspiciously like tribulation to them. I felt that lady was asking a question a lot of people ask when they get into prophecy. What they really want to know is, 'Will it be all right for us?'

Now you can work out your own systems here. I'm just going to apply one thing. According to what Jesus said, the end is going to come when the gospel has been preached to all nations. And it seems to me there's a fair way to go. So if the kingdom of God is a priority it seems to me that the priority in my life will be its extension. How on earth can I say that I'm in favour of the King and committed to the kingdom if I'm not in favour of following the King's commands, and in seeing that His kingdom extends from shore to shore?

Are you totally committed to the Lordship of Christ? Well, I spend an awful lot of time worrying about the kingdom. I'm busy in all kinds of activities but I have an over-riding desire to see the kingdom expressed in my activities. I am careful what I eat and about my fitness, and I do watch my finances, I am concerned about fashion and what's suitable and what isn't, for the sake of the kingdom. I think I'm beginning to understand. Jesus was saying that if I put Him first and His kingdom first, in terms of experiencing it myself, and expressing it in everyday situations, and in having a lifestyle that is realistically involved in the extension of the kingdom, it will begin to pervade all the other aspects of my life.

May I suggest that one of the best ways to find out your

commitment to the Lord Jesus is to find out what your priorities are? When you've found out what they are, may I suggest that you put them against that measuring rod, 'Seek ye first the kingdom'? And if you find yourself slipping or wanting at that point, say, 'Lord Jesus, I think that I need a dose of Lordship. I have got very lax in expressing the kingdom because, quite frankly, I've been more interested in what was popular than what was right. I got involved in what was profitable rather than in what was good, and I've really been into this comfortable stuff and I've ignored what is true. And Lord Jesus, I've got to admit something else. I hate to tell you this, but I have turned a totally blind eye to the extension of Your kingdom. I really haven't lifted an evangelical finger for a long, long time. So, I have come to a conclusion. If you ask me, do I acknowledge the Lordship of Christ, I guess, when it comes to the grass-roots of the thing, the answer is, "No" and I'd like to put it right.'

A COMMITMENT TO THE KING

by Rev Ian Barclay

2 Samuel 15:10-21

I want us to think about the whole subject of commitment to the Lord Jesus Christ. He is our Lord. In the language of the New Testament, He is *despotes*, the Lord of the universe. And that commands every bit of loyalty and commitment and unswerving allegiance from us.

We are going to look particularly at 2 Samuel 15:21. In the NIV (the Now Indispensable Version!) it's just a little clearer. 'But Ittai replied to the king, "As surely as the Lord [Jehovah] lives, and as my lord [David] the king lives, wherever my lord the king may be, whether it means life or death, there will your servant be." ' And, of course, Ittai was quite right. The soldier's commitment to the king is similar to the vows that a husband and wife make in marriage. It has to be for better or for worse, for richer, for poorer, in sickness and in health. It has to be total commitment.

Of course you are familiar with the story behind this chapter, of how David's extremely handsome and equally rebellious son Absalom planned and effected a coup d'état, and David had to flee with his family and the majority of his concubines and his bodyguard. The problem was for David, which direction should he flee in? He certainly couldn't have gone in a southerly direction, because Hebron is just twenty miles away in that direction. He couldn't have gone in a westerly direction because that would have meant going down through the foothills into the coastal plain, and David was a hill fighter; he wasn't too good on the plains. He couldn't go in a northerly direction because he couldn't trust the loyalty of the people in that direction. So he went east, down into the rift valley across the Jordan, up on the other side and then began to head north-easterly to Gilead, to Manahaim in particular.

You can see from the verses we are looking at, that it was a rushed and hurried escape. Everyone seems to have left in the clothes they were standing up in. If David was the sort of king who wore a crown and royal clothes then presumably he changed into something more comfortable and practical for escaping from Jerusalem. Then of course, once David was free of Jerusalem he had to slim down his party. It was a question of food. They weren't carrying enough to feed everybody. It was a question of pay as far as those professional soldiers, those mercenaries were concerned. That is why David told the Gittites that they might dismiss. And of course, Ittai was right. He had to say to the king, 'I can't go because my commitment is to you whether you pay me or not.' And our commitment to the King is on similar terms.

First of all we can notice that *Ittai recognised the king without a crown*. David was not standing on ceremony and yet Ittai recognised him. David had experienced a coup d'état and yet Ittai recognised him. Jesus is not standing on ceremony, but we have to recognise Him. Jesus has experienced a coup d'état and we still have to recognise Him. By that coup d'état the evil one has temporarily usurped the rightful place of Jesus. It's for a short time only because he has been mortally wounded. But the evil one is still temporarily prince of this world. We have to recognise the king without a crown. Of course there are things and there are people who would hinder our recognition of Jesus. Some of them may be theologians. Their doubt is their problem. Our fundamental need is to recognise the king.

Let me just list one or two things we need to say about Jesus. First of all He is an historical figure. Time and time again the Gospel writers tie Jesus to history; for example, Luke 1:5, Luke 2:2, and Luke 23:1. King Herod, Caesar Augustus, Publius Quirinius and Pontius Pilate — they tie Jesus to history. You may not want what Jesus has to offer. You may not like what Jesus has to say. But you cannot say that Jesus did not live and make statements and make demands on those who follow Him.

Jesus is a divine figure. There was a miraculous conception. A virgin did give birth, and what a child! He became the worker of miracles. He healed men. He raised the dead. He forgave their sins. He was an historical figure, a human figure and a divine figure. That's what really stumped the Jews. In the words of George MacDonald,

> They all were looking for a king
> To slay their foes and lift them high.
> Thou came'st, a little baby thing
> That made a woman cry.

The other thing about the Gospels is that Jesus is so relevant. If a man comes and needs healing, Jesus heals. If it's a question of forgiveness, Jesus forgives. When an enormous crowd needs bread and fish, Jesus supplies bread and fish. He's relevant. Would you believe it? There was a wedding reception once and the father of the bride hadn't ordered enough wine for the toasts. And once again

Jesus is relevant. He doesn't speak to them about not drinking wine. He doesn't give them a tract or a portion of Scripture. What they need He supplies. He is relevant. Ittai recognises the king without a crown, and we have to do that.

Then *Ittai serves the king without a country*. The coup d'état of Absalom had temporarily removed David from his land. And the evil one has temporarily removed Jesus from His land. That is why the Bible speaks about the evil one being the prince of this world (John 16:11). That's why Paul can speak about the evil one being the god of this world (2 Cor. 4:4). Do you remember that phrase in Ephesians 2 – 'The prince of the power of the air'? That's a marvellous phrase. In the original it means 'the dingy air', 'the dark air', 'the air without light', the air that surrounds what Paul is going to call later in the Epistle, 'this dark world' (6:12). Do you have problems, wondering how God can be on the throne of the universe while tragedies are happening down here; accidents and wars and tragedies that affect us all? It's because, temporarily, this is the dark world of the evil one and we have to live here. We are like agents, if you like, in an occupied territory. There's a war on. There are difficulties. There are privations. How could it be otherwise? We are waiting for a spiritual D-day when Jesus returns to establish His sovereignty in a fallen world. But we have to learn to live by the principles that agents have always lived by in occupied territory. Let me list some of these.

First of all we have to *harass the enemy*. That's important. We must not let the evil one get away with his standards of morality. We have to harass him and we have to say, 'That's not good enough.' And then we have to *encourage other agents*. What a marvellous missionary meeting we had this morning! But I suspect that if we were to question these missionaries, they would speak about difficulties and loneliness, because that's something that happens to the servants of Jesus, to the agent who has to work in an occupied country. Let me read you the words of an agent like that, a missionary, David Brainerd. He was the first great missionary to the Red Indians in North America and he wrote, 'I've got no fellow Christians to whom I might unburden myself or lay open my spiritual sorrows. Most of my diet consists of boiled corn and pastry. I lodge in a bundle of straw. My labour is hard and extremely difficult and I have no appearance of success to comfort me.' That's really the pattern for the majority of the people that have lived to serve Jesus. You can't really say that we're promised success. I suppose you can say that we're promised difficulty.

Then of course, one of the other things that we have to do as agents in occupied territory, is to *make sure that supplies are getting through*. I love to look at that in terms of the Word of God. I love that phrase in Ecclesiastes 8:4, 'Where the word of the king is, there is power.' Thank God, that's been demonstrated afresh in our land by God's good servants, Billy Graham and Luis Palau. It shouldn't have needed to be demonstrated but they've done it.

And a further point is that as agents in occupied territory, we have to *make sure that the channels of communication are open between us as agents and the headquarters*. That's very important. In difficult times, in wartime there's nothing so important as communications. Yet our prayerlessness makes us helpless. We know exactly what John Donne meant when he said, 'I throw myself down in my room, and I invite God and His angels thither; and when they come there, I neglect God for the noise of a fly, the rattle of a coach and the whining of a door.' Everything distracts us from prayer, and yet it's so important.

Then *Ittai follows the king without conditions*. I've seen
some Roman coins that have an ox on them and the ox is
standing between a plough and an altar and underneath is
the phrase, 'Ready for either'. That is what we have to be
as we serve King Jesus. We have to be ready for life or
death. That is what Ittai is saying.

I believe this raises one of the most difficult problems in
following Jesus. That is the question of matching our
revelation of God with our circumstances. Do you find
that difficult? In Luke 7:18-21 we read, 'The disciples of
John told him of all these things. And John, calling to him
two of his disciples, sent them to the Lord, saying, "Are
you he who is to come, or shall we look for another?"
And when the men had come to Jesus they said, "John the
Baptist has sent us to you, saying, 'Are you he who is to
come or shall we look for another?'" In that hour he
cured many of diseases and plagues and evil spirits, and on
many that were blind he bestowed sight.' And he answered
these two men who had come from John the Baptist, 'Go
and tell John what you have seen and heard: the blind
receive their sight, the lame walk, lepers are cleansed, and
the deaf hear, the dead are raised up, and the poor have
good news preached to them.'

Can you see what the revelation to John the Baptist is?
Yes, John, this is the Messiah. He heals people, He raises
the dead, He gives sight to the blind. He is the King of the
universe. The trouble for John, and it's often a similar
trouble for us, is matching revelation with circumstance.
Because as you know, John is still in prison; and yet the
revelation of the Mighty God is still the revelation of the
Mighty God to him. In one sense he is not going to stay in
prison, because his head is going to be required, and yet
God is still the Mighty God. And it is the same for us.
Quite often we will not be able to match revelation and

circumstance. He is the Mighty God, but He may not choose at the moment to take away our cancer. He is the Mighty God, and yet He may not choose to deal with the fact that we haven't got a job at the moment. He's God and none other. Yet we may have to strive with the problems of our children when we try to bring them up in the nurture and admonition of the Lord and we see them going slowly away from the Lord. We have to do exactly what John the Baptist did. We have to do what Ittai did. We have to follow the King without conditions.

While the Bishop from Africa was speaking this morning my mind went across to the things I used to do when I was a merchant banker in London dealing with coffee, and I thought about the spot where the Kampala martyrs died in previous years. They were young page boys at the court of a homosexual king, but when they found Christ they had to repel the advances of the king and so he had them all executed. As they were going to be killed one said to the rest, 'A few moments and then you'll be with the Lord. We are allowed to do this because we follow Him who carried a cross.' I wonder how many Christians have been saying that to each other during the last few years in Uganda. Oh, how easy it is here to follow the King without conditions, and how much more difficult it must be in a place like Uganda!

Of course, from our own country, there have been people like Catherine Booth, the wife of the founder of the Salvation Army. She had spinal trouble at the age of fourteen, infected lungs at seventeen, yet she produced eight children for her husband. She was temperamentally timid, intellectually self-taught, and yet she helped her husband for twenty-five years. Then, at the age of sixty, cancer was diagnosed, and just before she died she sent a final message to the Salvation Army: 'The waters are rising, but so am I. I am not going under. I am going over.'

What a glorious affirmation of commitment! We don't know what conditions are going to be like in our country in the next few years. All we can do is to make our affirmation to the King: recognise the King without a crown; serve the King without a country; follow the King without conditions.

CHOSEN, CALLED AND FAITHFUL

by Dr Donald English

Mark 3:13

Mark says that Jesus went up into the hills and called to Him those He wanted, and they came to Him. You will know as well as I do, the significance of the mountain or hill. You think immediately of Abraham and Isaac, of Moses and the giving of the law, of Elijah and the still small voice, of the mount of Transfiguration, of Calvary. The hill is the place in the Bible of drawing apart to get a better view, of getting closer to God, of having a sense of inspiration about what we should be doing for Him. It seems to me that Mark 3:13 might have been written for Keswick. Where better can we draw apart than here, where better than the quiet elevated place to stop and reflect about His world?

But Mark says that the people who went up that hill were chosen. I wonder why you are at Keswick? Some of us are here because a convention has to have speakers. Some of you are here because you come every year. Some of you are here because friends invited you. Some of you are here reluctantly, some expectantly, some maybe resignedly. Some of you were just passing through and noticed that the Keswick Convention was on. I believe that every one of you is here because Jesus called you. John Wesley, whom I mention from time to time, spoke of prevenient grace, grace which goes ahead. By that he meant not simply that when the gospel was preached, then grace was at work, helping people to respond to the gospel; but that in all the challenges of life, whatever the decisions are, when there is a choice between good and evil, prevenient grace is operating so that there is no choice for good, made anywhere in the world, which is not aided by the Spirit of God. I believe therefore, that some of the simplest choices we make are actually inspired by the Holy Spirit. This call is never a casual one.

As the people in Luke 9 discovered they were called to a very uncertain future. 'Foxes have holes and birds have nests but I don't have anywhere to lay my head', said Jesus to a man who said he would follow Him. When another man made a very reasonable request about burying his father, though there was some suspicion that his father was still alive – he wanted to wait until the event – Jesus said, 'There's no time for that.' And another person said, 'Well, at least let me go home and say cheerio and have a farewell party.' 'No', said Jesus, 'Sorry. When you put your hand to the plough there's no turning back.' When Jesus calls us, He does not call us casually, He calls us seriously and with intent. He called them, says Mark, to be with Him.

I cannot think of anywhere in the world where you have a greater sense of the presence of God than here at Keswick. How close to the Lord you can be here! But Mark says that He called them to be with Him that He might send them out. Have you ever had a day or two just breathing in? Commend that to some of the friends you don't care for! This week I will breathe in, next week I will breathe out. Of course, it's ridiculous. You live by breathing in and then breathing out. But I suspect that the Christian church today is suffering from inflation, not money inflation, but the inflation of breathing in and in and in until we are almost floating to heaven because we are not breathing out. Jesus intended that what is taken in should go out. He wanted to send them out to preach and to have authority to cast out demons. They were to redeem souls and to redeem bodies, to preach the Word and to apply its healing. They were to take God's love to the whole of a person.

Now each of us needs individually to live like that. We know that if we keep on taking in and giving nothing out, we become stale and dry and dull, and the very things we study become stale and dry and dull. But the Body of Christ, the church also needs to take in and give out, as a Body, and that means that as a body we have responsibilities which not each of us can personally carry. Many of you can't go overseas, but what about prayer? What about giving? What about helping others who *can* go, and enabling them to go? The point I am trying to make is this, that the Body of Christ has a responsibility as the Body of Christ, for the world, and if there are some of us who cannot go, there is an enormous responsibility on those of us who can. I wonder if you have asked yourself what it might mean to you – young person, youngish person, middle-aged person – if God were to take you and send you overseas. It's not a question of missionaries being better than the rest. It is a case of each one of us finding the very best place in God's purposes for us. And for many of us, God's very best place is probably in some form of full-time service.

I don't know if you are aware of the facts and figures, but did you know that there are an estimated three billion non-Christians in the world? If you work out on a basis not of nations, but of people groups (that is, groups who feel a cultural relationship to each other), two billion of those don't even have any Christians living among them. I can't imagine two billion, but I do know that it's an awful lot. It's not just that those two billion haven't heard the gospel, but they have no Christians living among them. Now what was Jesus doing when He wanted to send them out? I think that He called them to be with Him so that they might reflect with Him on what His mission was about, and His mission was to show them the Father's love. He told them the Father's messages, He gave them the Father's healing, He reached out, as His Father wished Him to, to the poor and the needy and the outcast. That's what the whole story of Jesus is about. He told them of a heavenly Father's love who noticed every sparrow falling, who counted the hair of every head, and He lived that out for them. How else could God have shown them, except through Jesus? Now Jesus gathers them to Him, so that they may understand this more fully; and then Jesus says, 'As the Father sent me, so I send you.' Just as He had embodied what His Father was, He now calls them to embody what He is.

Therefore, the question we are facing is simply this. Can it be right, that nearly two thousand years after the coming of Jesus, two billion people should not only not have heard the gospel, but actually have no Christians living among them? I mean, does Jesus not want that two billion and if He does want them, how is He going to get them? We know what the answer is. Jesus will reach that two billion people only if people like us are ready to go.

Every denomination I know of is needing ordained ministers. This is a time when the Christian church in our land is beginning to pick up again. There is a new willingness to reach out. Billy Graham and Luis Palau have been God's gifts to us. We must take up the ball and run with it and there are churches all over the place saying, 'Yes, we want to be more involved in evangelism now', but who will pastor them? Who will look after them, if the churches are short of people who are willing to give their lives to this work? There are many places in most of our churches for lay people, who will work full-time in the life of the church. Part of my job is to make sure that inner city churches have ministers and full-time helpers, that in rural areas there are people to serve full-time. But God seems to call people to better places than these. The call to the inner cities doesn't seem to be heard all that clearly. But Jesus calls us and He says to us, 'Look at the world. Look at the harvest field.' And He goes on to ask us, 'Dare you look on the world as I and my heavenly Father look on it?'

When I came back from working in Nigeria, the Biafran war broke out. Everybody around us was saying, 'Isn't all that bombing awful?' But it wasn't as awful for them as it was for me. I knew the buildings being blown up; I knew the people being killed; some of them were my friends. It felt very different to 'know'. Jesus says, 'My brothers and sisters, dare you look from where I am looking? Dare you look at every one of them with a character and a right as God's child, to live a fully human life?' And by that, I mean a Christian life. Dare you look like that? Can you bear the pain? For that's the challenge that Jesus offers today. You young people, with all your life before you, dare you look with the eyes of God at the world I'm talking about?

Do you remember Amy Carmichael's dream of the blind people going over the edge of the cliff? There were one or two sighted people standing there, turning them back. Then as she watched, she looked back and there was a group of people sitting under a tree, singing hymns, reading their Bibles and making daisy chains. Every now and again cries from the cliff edge would be heard and someone would get up to go, and people would say, 'Oh, no, we need you in the fellowship here.' Then Amy Carmichael saw a young girl brought away from the cliff edge where she had been saving people because her mother was dying. In her dream she said, 'God, why aren't there more people there?' and God answered, 'Amy, what about you?'

Dare you look, with God's eyes, down upon His world and name the people and say, 'I can't do anything about it'? 'But, doesn't it cost?' you say to me. Yes it does. But we need to view costs the right way round. Paul says that any man in Christ is a new creature (2 Cor. 5:17). We are to be counted as dead to sin and alive to Jesus Christ. Christians who came into faith with a career, have you ever stopped and asked, 'I wonder whether I need to die to that and rise to something new'? Christians who came into faith with an ambition and are now fulfilling it or on the way to fulfilling it, have you ever stopped and said, 'Does being a new creature mean that I am on a different tack?'? Dying and rising with Christ is a costly thing. It's meant to apply to our whole lives, or there's no new creation, just bits and pieces. That's why Jesus says, 'You may not have a place to lay your head if you follow me. There's no time to bury your father when he dies. We haven't even time to say farewell. It's too urgent for that.' That's why He talked about taking up our cross and following.

So I ask every one of us, are you really wholeheartedly committed to the mission of Christ? I mean, is it hurting you to look upon the world as Jesus looks and to take the obvious steps? For those of you who can't go overseas, but have got gifts to offer, have you honestly asked whether

God might not be calling you to full-time ordained ministry or full-time service in His church somewhere? I'm not saying that that's better than being an architect. It would be stupid to say so. I'm simply saying that the arithmetic doesn't add up. With two billion people without a Christian there must be something wrong in the accounting somewhere. Therefore every one of us has to say again, 'Lord, am I exactly where I should be?' And those of you who have got ahead of you the possibility of overseas service, doesn't dying and rising with Christ say to you, 'Lord, I'm hanging on to something I should have given up long ago. I should have seen, quite clearly, that the call is to overseas service.' If you do see it like that, why don't you go and do what He calls you to do?

Yes, it's costly. But it's the kind of cost that brings you the deepest joy you could have, for first class service is the only way to be happy. He called them to Himself, that He might send them out, to preach, to cast out demons; to heal souls and bodies; to redeem whole people. Let us every one, ask, 'Am I in the place I ought to be?' If I'm not, why don't I say today, 'Lord, I'll go wherever you want me to be.' That is the place of happiness.

THE FRUIT OF THE SPIRIT IS JOY

by Rev Stuart Briscoe

Romans 5:1-5, 11

Some Christians like to impress upon us what a solemn thing Christianity is. They say that God is high and holy and separate from sin, that He is awesome and we should come before Him with reverence. And, of course, they are right. Other people point out that being a Christian is a very serious thing indeed. The only reason you became a Christian is that you discovered that you were a sinner and that Christ died for your sin. Christians are very serious people as well, because they recognise that there are a lot of people in the world who don't know Christ. Christians, of course, are people who have got a terrible concern for such things as famine and abortion and the threat of nuclear war. Christians should take all these things seriously. You can't just go round rejoicing and clapping your hands and kicking up your heels when there are problems like famine and abortion and nuclear war, can you?

There is a difficulty here, because on the one hand, it is perfectly clear that Christians are to have a tremendous sense of awe and reverence before God. They have got to have a tremendous sense of the cost of their redemption. They have got to have an overwhelming burden for those who don't know Christ and they have to face all the horrendous problems that confront our society. Yet the Scriptures make it very clear that we are intended to be a joyful people. Now I think, as we put these two things together, we will see immediately that when the Bible is talking about us being joyful, it is not talking about being silly or irresponsible. But equally, it is pointing out to us that there is nothing particularly holy in being miserable and depressed. We are to be responsibly joyful. We are to have a quality of joy that never ignores the realities of the harsh world of which we are a part, but at the same time, we are never to be so overwhelmed by the immensity of things around us that we are incapable of rejoicing in the midst of them.

I want you to ask yourself a question. 'Would I say that my life is characterised by joy?' Let's spend a little time trying to answer that.

The first thing that I want you to notice is that the Old Testament uses all kinds of different words to describe joy. So many statements are there about joy, that it is necessary to use a whole cluster of different Hebrew words. I'm just going to point out one or two. In 1 Samuel 18:6 the word literally means 'bright and shining'; in Psalm 48:2 it means 'leaping and jumping'; in Psalm 126:6 it means 'shouting'; and in Psalm 13:5 it means 'running round in circles'. Now put all those words together and you get a very remarkable picture of God's people all bright and shining, leaping and jumping, shouting, rushing around in circles to express their joy. What a beautiful picture this is. Just like the Keswick Convention! I think it is important that we realise this. Sometimes we have an emphasis in the other direction that ignores this tremendous theme of joy in the Old Testament.

Now, when we look into the New Testament there is something which I find very attractive. You are probably familiar with the fact that the Greek word for grace is *charis*. It means literally 'delightful'. It is a beautiful word. Related to this word *charis* is another word *chara*. You don't need to know a lot of Greek to realise that these two words are 'first cousins'. The lovely thing about it is this. *Chara* is the Greek word for joy. To put it in very simple terms, if you have been saved by grace (*charis*), one would reasonably expect to see a whole lot of joy (*chara*), for *charis* and *chara* get along very well together.

If you look into the New Testament you will find the theme of joy very obvious. When the angels announced the incarnation they said that they had come with good tidings of great joy. When the Lord Jesus was here on earth it was said of Him that He was a man of sorrows and acquainted with grief. But a lot of people don't seem to know that it also says that at one time Jesus, full of joy through the Holy Spirit said, 'I praise you Father, Lord of heaven and earth, because you have hidden these things from the wise and learned and revealed them to little children.' The message of the incarnation was good news of great joy. The demeanour of our Lord Jesus, serious as He was, was a demeanour that was full of joy through the Holy Spirit.

The early church that came into being through the proclamation of the message of the once crucified, risen Lord Jesus, was a fellowship of joy. Repeatedly in the Acts of the Apostles we hear of the Christians being joyful. It did not mean, of course, that they were exempt from problems. In fact they went through deep persecution. But we read that in the midst of their problems and persecutions they were joyful. They went in for all kinds of evangelistic enterprises. At the end of these we read that the people who were converted went on their way rejoicing.

You remember that in the days of the gospel and of the early church the result of the preaching of the gospel was that sinners repented. What is the result in heaven of sinners repenting on earth? There was joy in the presence of the angels.

So, it is perfectly legitimate, indeed it is mandatory for Christians to live lives characterised by joy. But how does this work?

One of the things which is intriguing to me is that a lot of people who aren't Christians seem to have resources of joy. They derive it from somewhere other than their spiritual experience. This leads me to believe that God has built into our world tremendous resources of joy for people who are not even believers. This would rather tie in with something we read in Paul's letter to Timothy. He said, 'God has given us all things richly to enjoy.' Has it ever dawned upon you, that God in His grace and in His big heart has filled this great big world of ours with innumerable things that are so interesting, so fascinating and so exciting that we can derive infinite pleasure from them? He has been so good to us. One of the sad things, however, about Christians is that sometimes they don't seem to realise how full of exciting things this world is. They don't seem to understand how many glorious things God has put into this world for our enjoyment. As a result we sometimes become somewhat cramped and crabbed in our experience. Are you interested in this glorious world that God has filled with all things for us to enjoy? That doesn't mean you have got to be interested in everything, but it does mean that you have got to go around with your eyes wide open, your nostrils dilated and your ears wide open and to be healthily interested in God's great and glorious creation of which He made you a part.

May I say this very gently to you? Sometimes Christians

are a bit of a bore. May I say to you very gently that sometimes we don't see any new believers coming to our fellowships because, quite frankly, the people outside our fellowships look at us and say, 'All those people are interested in is a very narrow list of things'? If we could begin to show them that we honestly, genuinely believe that God has given us all things richly to enjoy, and give the impression that we *are* enjoying them, then, maybe, some of those people would enjoy what we are enjoying, and we would come together to glorify God, and in that way they would discover Christ.

Well, you say, 'What has that got to do with the Holy Spirit?' It has a lot to do with the Holy Spirit. If I move round my world and see that it is my Father's world, it takes the Holy Spirit to impress that on me. And then He will interpret that world to me, helping me to see things with new eyes, smell things with a new nose and hear with new ears.

But now let's look at Romans 5 and see a lot more things that we have been given richly to enjoy. First Paul is telling believers that *they should rejoice in their spiritual position*. He talks about being justified through faith, about having peace with God and about having gained the position where they stand in grace. Let me just give you some little ideas about these things.

One aspect of justification is that righteousness has been reckoned to us. The Greek word is a book-keeping term. God has taken the totality of the terrible things He has got against my name in His ledger and He has transferred it to the account of the Lord Jesus Christ. Then He has added the sum totality of the righteousness of the Lord Jesus and He has transferred that to my account. So He transferred all the bad stuff on my account to Christ and He transferred all the good stuff out of Christ's account to mine and that is only one aspect of being justified. Now Paul says that when you are justified it is perfectly legitimate to rejoice. When did you last come across somebody who got so excited about being justified that they started getting all bright and shining, leaping and jumping, shouting and hollering, rushing round in circles and giving you the impression that they were thoroughly enjoying being justified?

I have been justified by faith. I have peace with God — but I am going to talk about that tomorrow! We stand in grace. I travel quite a lot and one problem is that I don't always remember where I am. One thing I have discovered, however, is that wherever I am at a particular moment, I am surrounded by the characteristics of where I am. I am in England now, and I am totally surrounded by England. The week before last I was in Bermuda, and I was totally surrounded by Bermuda. But while all these things change, one thing doesn't change. I stand in grace. So when I stand in England or Bermuda or America one thing never changes. Underneath me is grace, above me is grace, to the left and to the right hand, behind me and before me is grace and that is God's unmerited favour totally enveloping me at any given moment under any given set of circumstances. When I know this, I rejoice. I am even allowed to let rip a very gentle little 'Hallelujah' once in a while because I rejoice in my position.

But now Paul talks about *rejoicing in their future prospects*. 'We rejoice in the hope of the glory of God' (verse 2). There are two kinds of hope. There is hope where nothing works but we just hope, and there is another hope that is overwhelming confidence. New Testament hope is overwhelming confidence. It is the hope that in the future when all the mess has been finally sorted out by God in His good time, when the whole thing has gone up in smoke, when He has made a new heaven and a new earth wherein is righteousness, I know exactly where I'll be. I'll be with Him in glory. Of that I am totally confident.

We rejoice in our spiritual position. We rejoice in our future prospects. Have you ever noticed, however, that there is a little time that has to elapse between our spiritual position being sorted out and our future prospects being realised? Sometimes our spiritual position is like an old bedstead. It is rock-firm both ends but it does sag in the middle. Your spiritual position is in great shape. Your future prospects are in great shape. The trouble is the bit in between where there are all sorts of problems. What has Paul to say about these? 'We also rejoice in our sufferings, because we know that suffering produces perseverance; perseverance, character; and character, hope. And hope does not disappoint us, because God has poured out his love into our hearts by the Holy Spirit, whom he has given us' (verses 3-5). It's comparatively easy for us to ignore the immediate difficulties. But the Bible doesn't do that. It tells us to learn to rejoice in them. Paul says that we can rejoice in them because of what we know. Well, what do we know? We know that suffering produces perseverance. The word for suffering here means 'pressure' or 'stress'. The word for perseverance means literally 'abiding under'. It's one thing to abide in Christ when everything is going great. It is entirely different to abide in Christ when everything is getting difficult. God allows things to get difficult so that we can abide in Christ through the difficulties. The Korean Christians say we are like nails — the harder you hit us, the deeper you drive us. Then Paul goes on to say that perseverance produces character. This word means the evidence of being approved, of being tested. As we abide in Christ under pressure a certain stamp of His approval begins to appear on our lives. Now when you know this your attitude towards your pressure changes. If you want that badge of approval, if you want to deepen in Christ, the prerequisite is pressure.

Not only that, but character produces hope or confidence. Why? Well, if you have gone through one test and proved Christ adequate, that changes the attitude with which you approach the next test. You came through one tremendous testing time, you found Him faithful, there is evidence of His power in a new way in your life, so you march into the new testing in an entirely different way.

When you know all this, your attitude to your pressures changes dramatically. You know what God is allowing and you know why He is doing it. And all the time the Holy Spirit is shedding the love of God in your heart. He is saying to you, 'I love you so much that I want you to have a little more pressure, so that I can drive you deeper into Christ, so that you can grow up and reflect His glory.' This is how Christians get round to saying, 'All right. I accept it. I don't understand it. I don't appreciate it. But I will rejoice in You in it, because I trust You and what You are going to accomplish through it.'

Finally *we rejoice in God's person* (verse 11). Have you noticed that so rarely do we come to God and say, 'I love You, God, I like You, God, You're great'? We don't tend to rejoice in Him. We rejoice in His blessing. 'What did You bring me God? Please God, give me . . .' What He wants us to do is to rejoice in our spiritual position and in our future prospects and in our present problems and in God's person. That's a whole lot of rejoicing, and on top of that He's given us all things richly to enjoy!

So your homework is to go and work hard on being miserable! See if you can make it in the light of all that the Spirit of God would impress upon your hearts. How is this going to work? You've just got to stand there and the

Spirit will produce it? No, the Bible says, 'Rejoice in the Lord always.' You say, 'I don't feel like rejoicing.' He says, 'I didn't ask you if you felt like it.' You say, 'I can't.' He says, 'I know you can't. That's why the Spirit of God will work in your heart.' In dependence on Him and in obedience to Him, concentrate today on seeing that the fruit of the Spirit is joy. It will be so nice to have you around. People will enjoy you very much indeed.

THE FRUIT OF THE SPIRIT IS PEACE

by Rev Stuart Briscoe

Isaiah 48:17, 18

I wonder what sort of a definition you would give of peace? My observation has been that most people define it in negative terms; for instance, the end of hostilities or the absence of tension. That, of course, is a perfectly understandable approach, but I want to suggest that there is a fatal flaw in defining peace in those terms. If, as we all do, we would like to have peace in our lives, then, if we regard peace in negative terms, we will probably spend all our time trying to eradicate what we see as opponents of peace. Now I submit to you that that is not the way to go, because when we look into the Scriptures to see what they have to say about peace, we find that it is not described as the end of hostilities, nor as that state of affairs when all tension ends.

The Hebrew word for peace is *shalom*. If you were to go to Israel today you would probably be greeted by a very tanned Israeli who would welcome you with the word, *Shalom*. The fact that he was carrying an automatic rifle would not seem incongruous to him. Funnily enough, if you went over into one of the Arab countries, you would find some equally tanned people, and they would wish you, *Shalam*. I don't need to know much Arabic and Hebrew to realise that *shalom* and *shalam* are close relatives. The fact that when they wished you *Shalam* they were sitting on top of a Russian tank would not seem incongruous to them either.

Now, I cannot build a theological theory on an illustration like that. So I need to dig a little deeper. Do you remember the occasion when Gideon was doing a most remarkable thing, threshing wheat in a winepress, and the Lord, with good humour, came up behind him and said, 'Hail, thou mighty man of valour.' Now we know that he was not a mighty man of valour, because he was trying to thresh wheat in a wine press. Why was he trying to do this? He was afraid that the Midianites would come to take all his crops. So the Lord with good humour says to him, 'Hail, mighty man of valour!' Gideon turns round, somewhat surprised. Then the Lord told him to do all kinds of interesting things like – 'Go and knock down your father's altar; kill your father's prize bull; build another altar to the Lord, sacrifice his bull on it, chop down the Ashtaroth pole and declare war on the Midianites.' And the Lord, of course, gave him lots of lovely signs and proved that He, the Lord, would be with him, and Gideon was convinced and built an altar to the Lord and called it Jehovah Shalom, of all things.

Now, he was not getting rid of tension; he was introducing some. He was not ending a war. He was going to start one. But he was saying that he understood what peace was and that it was related to God, and that the peace which he experienced had nothing to do with the end of war or with the absence of tension. 'Gideon, are you ready to tackle this job?' 'Yes, I am.' 'Why?' 'Because You are Jehovah Shalom, the God of order, and it is going to be total chaos as far as I am concerned, but evidently You know what You are doing and so, confident of the fact that You are the God of order, dependent upon You, I will move into tension. I will move into stress. I will move into hostilities. And I will enjoy peace.'

It is very important that we see it this way, because many people fondly imagine that they will enjoy peace when they can get rid of hostilities and tension and pressure. The simple fact of the matter is this; in this world of ours you will never get rid of them. Therefore, if that is where peace lies, forget it. You will never have it. Praise God, it does not lie there. It lies in Jehovah Shalom. Now let me just remind you of the reading from Isaiah. What the Lord says there is very simple. 'I am the Lord your God, who teaches you what is best for you, who directs you in the way you should go. If only you had paid attention to my commands, your peace would have been like a river' (Isa. 48:17, 18).

Of course it would. For if peace is a sense of order, and God is a God of order, and He teaches me what is best and directs me in the right way, and I pay attention to His commands, what do I do? I order my life according to the orders of the God of order. And what is the result? A sense of order, which is what the Old Testament calls peace. The bishop of Hippo, St Augustine, has a wonderful definition of peace. He calls it 'the tranquillity of order'.

If we move into the New Testament we find something very similar. The Lord Jesus had a marvellous approach to His disciples. He didn't say, 'Now folks, if you would like to follow me, everything will be absolutely superb. You will have a most marvellous time.' He said things like, 'Behold I send you forth as sheep in the midst of wolves.' He also said, 'In the world you will have trouble.' But He says something else as well. 'Don't worry about it, because you will have peace.' For peace isn't the end of hostilities, or the absence of tension. Peace is the deep-rooted sense of order that comes in the midst of tension and stress and hostilities, when you know that you are ordering your life according to the orders of the God of order.

There are three particular areas where this becomes very practical in our lives. The Bible talks about peace with God. It also talks about the peace *of* God, and it talks about peace on earth. Three very simple little expressions. But what profound, powerful expressions they are! I want to suggest to you that peace with God means a sense of spiritual order, that the peace of God means a sense of psychological order, and that peace on earth means a sense of sociological or relational order.

First of all this idea of *spiritual order*. Let's look at it this way. There is something sadly wrong with the human race. There appears to be a sense of foreboding, a sense of dismay. When I first went to America a little over twenty years ago, it was a very exciting, invigorating place. The statement you heard all the time was, 'No problem. We will fix it.' They had lots of initiative and drive, and I thought, 'How exciting!' Now, however, all kinds of things are happening in America and people there are coming to the conclusion that maybe they can't fix it; maybe saying 'No problem' isn't the answer at all. There is a deep sense of dismay in America at the present time. I have come to the conclusion that this dismay comes out of a sense of disorder, that things are getting out of hand. But if the dismay is the produce of disorder, where does the disorder come from? It comes from disobedience. This gets me right back into Isaiah 48. The Lord said that there is no sense of tranquillity or order for the wicked. Why not? Because they won't go His way and they won't do what He says, and they will not follow His leading. Put it round another way. If we choose to be disobedient we will produce all kinds of disorder in our individual lives, in our relationships and ultimately in our world. Disobedience will produce disorder. But I want to tell you something exciting. I cannot think of anything more exciting than to live in a world characterised by disobedience, disorder and dismay, and to have a message of what to do about it.

I spend my life with people whose lives are in a dreadful state of disorder. I take them back to God's word and show them that the root cause is disobedience, and they say, 'What can I do?' Then I tell them, 'You can repent and ask for forgiveness for Christ's sake. You can then, on the basis of that forgiveness, make a commitment to order your life according to the orders of the God of order; and if you do that, then the tranquillity of order will take place in your life; and the Bible calls it peace with God.' Not a week goes by without stories about total chaos being brought into order, utter dismay being banished, and disobedient people being brought to repentance, faith, cleansing and the willingness to order their lives according to the orders of the God of order.

A couple in our church not long ago heard of two people who were doing very well in business; then the wife started running round with somebody else, and the husband lost his job, and the kids got hooked on drugs. Just your normal suburban family! But the Christian family got to them, befriended them, showed them something else, and one by one the whole family brought their lives into order and the transformation was palpable. On the anniversary of their conversion they asked if they could give their testimony. It was recorded in our church. A policeman who had been involved in the same sort of problems as this family took the tape to the police station and played it, and the next Sunday we had other policemen coming to church to hear how they could get their lives put into order. It's just never-ending.

Now let's talk about a sense of *psychological order*. Let's look at Philippians 4. 'Rejoice in the Lord always. I will say it again: Rejoice! Let your gentleness be evident to all. The Lord is near. Do not be anxious about anything, but in everything, by prayer and petition, with thanksgiving, present your requests to God. And the peace of God, which transcends all understanding, will guard your hearts and your minds in Christ Jesus' (verses 4-7). The peace of God – a sense of psychological order. Let's start with the human condition again. What is the human condition? What is the state of affairs in our world? I submit to you that it is a nasty world. I think that a lot of Christians have tended to overlook that, because they have mistaken the biblical doctrine of separation for the unbiblical doctrine of isolation. They have got themselves out of touch. On the other hand, there are Christians who are deeply aware of what is going on, and they know it is a nasty world.

There was a wedding recently at our church. While I was waiting to sign the register, I saw two of our congregation crying. I asked if there was something wrong, and at first they wouldn't talk about it. But then the lady said, 'My husband walked out on me and divorced me and there's not a thing I can do about it.' Then she told me how unhelpful the judge had been; and he had been sitting in front of her at the wedding. The other person was a young fellow. He was a doctor who had been called out to an emergency with his brother, who was in the same medical team. They suddenly realised that they were being called to the home of their parents. There they found one of their brothers sitting with a revolver in his hand and the fourth brother lying dead at his feet. That's our world, folks.

But, as we look at this nasty world of ours, some of us feel that we can't handle it. So what do we do? We do what the ostrich does. We stick our heads in the sand and because we can't see it we presume that it went away. And it didn't. It is there. Do you notice how we handle the problem of death? We say, 'If you die'. It isn't an 'if'; it's a 'when'. We talk about illness and assume that just about everybody else could get sick, but it just couln't happen to me. Of course it could! The big problem is, what do we do with it?

Do you know what we do? We take a good, long, hard look at what the Bible says. 'We know that all things work together for the good of those who love God, to those who are called according to his purpose' (Rom. 8:28).

Do you know what we tell people? It is a harsh world. It's a fallen world, populated by a fallen society, created by fallen people. Sin and Satan run riot and all hell is let loose. But of one thing you can be absolutely sure. God is working in these things, and He is totally committed to bringing you to the ultimate good. And the ultimate good is locked up in glory and is locked up in eternity, and that's where you are heading. You can bring all your hurt and your heartache and disappointment and frustration to Him with thanksgiving, not for all the nasty things that are happening, but with thanksgiving for who He is and the fact that He is working everything to the good. And God promises you something. When you do that, the peace of God will be built like a garrison around your heart.

Blessed are the peacemakers! What a lovely thing it is to go to people whose lives are utterly paralysed by fear and say, 'I've got great news for you. All things are working together for the good and the God to whom you are committed is committed to you, and He is committed to working things out gloriously and magnificently in glory. Trust Him, and you may not see it now, and it may not make sense now, but trust Him.' It is a delightful thing to see a sense of psychological order coming into people's lives.

Finally, there is a sense of *relational*, a sense of *sociological order*. Don't you love that expression – 'Peace on earth to men of goodwill'? We bring it out at Christmas, don't we? Aren't you amazed at what we can do at Christmas? My mother had a favourite saying at Christmas. 'Isn't it nice for us all to be together?' It is – for a short while. Even at Christmas there's a bit of tension about being all together, isn't there? And that is when we specialise on peace on earth. I heard a marvellous story from an elderly German gentleman. He was in the trenches in the first world war. On Christmas Eve they had a truce. The German trenches and the English trenches were very close to each other and suddenly from one of the English trenches a light tenor voice started singing in the cool, crisp air, 'The Lord is my Shepherd'. The old German said it was the most beautiful thing he had ever heard until he heard from the German trench a deep baritone voice joining in with, '*Der Herr ist mein Herter*'. That is, 'The Lord is my Shepherd' in German. The tenor and the bass were singing in glorious harmony. They had been killing each other, and then there was a truce, and they sang the same hymn together. The next day it was Christmas Day and the truce continued. The British soldiers got out a football and began to play between the trenches. The Germans climbed out and they played England. The sad thing was, that the next day the truce was over and they went back to killing each other. That is about the best peace on earth we can imagine.

But in Ephesians 2 there is something very challenging indeed. Christ is our peace (verse 14). This does not mean peace with God. Paul is saying that Christ has brought a sense of order into the lives and relationships of two groups of people who had nothing to do with each other, the Jews and the Gentiles. He did it by becoming the Saviour on the cross for both of them.

This is how it works. An old Gentile hears the gospel and comes to the cross in repentance and is delivered from his sins and is utterly forgiven. While that is going on, an old Jew hears the gospel, comes to repentance, kneels at the foot of the cross, is forgiven and is made a new creature. The Gentile opens his eyes, just happens to look to his right and cannot believe what he sees. There is an old Jew! The old Jew opens his eyes, turns to his left and can't believe what he sees. There is a Gentile! Now, the Jews and the Gentiles have no dealings with each other. But Paul says to the Ephesians that in Christ they do; for He has broken down the middle wall of partition and Christ is our peace.

I love to hear about warring factions stopping warring by coming to the cross, being united in Christ, and then beginning to build peace. It is happening in the north of Ireland. It is happening in the south of Ireland. Blessed are the peacemakers who begin to understand what it means to order their relationships according to the God of order. Put simply, if you come to repentance and somebody else has come to repentance, there are absolutely no grounds for antagonism between you. What a message for Christians who have got bad marriages! Christ is your peace in your marriage. What a message for parents and children who are at loggerheads! Christ is your peace if it's a Christian family. What a message for Christian churches where people sit around the Lord's table and share the bread and wine, but have deep-rooted resentments! Christ is your peace, which means that you order your relationships according to the orders of the God of order, and the fruit of the Spirit is peace.

How does it work? It works when obedience to the word of God and dependence upon the Spirit of God have an explosive mix in our lives and begin to create a new dynamic.

This is what the Scripture says: Seek peace and pursue it (1 Pet. 3:11); Make every effort to keep the bond of peace (Eph. 4:3); Do what leads to peace (Rom. 14:19). But it also tells me that the Spirit of God is there to enable me to do what He calls me to do. The fruit of the Spirit is peace.

THE FRUIT OF THE SPIRIT IS PATIENCE

by Rev Stuart Briscoe

Matthew 18:21-35

Let's talk about patience. The Greek word translated patience is *makrothumia*. This incorporates two Greek words, *makro* meaning 'long and slow' and *thumia* which means 'anger'. When God revealed His character to Moses, one of the things He said was that He was a God who was slow to anger, and the Greek translation of the Old Testament uses that word *makrothumia*. When we put together the ideas of 'slow' and 'anger' we get the clue to the meaning of patience.

You see, anger is a basic part of our lives. Evangelical Christians particularly have a problem with this subject of anger, because somewhere along the line we got the idea that it is always wrong. How on earth we got that idea I don't know, because it was certainly not from reading our Bibles. The Bible tells us that the Lord Jesus, on one occasion, went into the Temple, looked around Him with anger and did all kinds of exciting things. We believe that He was without sin; but if we believe that He looked round in anger and that anger is sin, then we can't believe that He was without sin. But very often we do not think about this.

We just have this deep-rooted idea that anger is sin. The Bible also says, 'Be angry but do not sin.' So it ought to be obvious to us that anger is a fact of life and not necessarily sin. In fact, we can go as far as to say this, that sometimes to be angry is sinful, but equally, sometimes *not* to be angry is sinful. When gross, scandalous things happen in our society, if we simply shrug our shoulders, it is a sin not to be angry. Where then does *makrothumia* come in? If anger is an indignant reaction that is justified, patience is expressing that justified indignation slowly.

The Bible tells us that the fruit of the Spirit is patience. In order to get this into proper perspective, let me just remind you of something that is terribly important. Our understanding of what the fruit of the Spirit is all about comes only as we look at the character of God. If we really want to see slowness to anger properly demonstrated, we need to look into the revelation of God's character.

The wrath of God or the anger of God is an integral part of His character. Unfortunately a lot of people do not want to hear that, but it seems to me that those people are not thinking very hard. God's anger is absolutely necessary if God is going to be just. God's anger is absolutely necessary if God is to be a God of love. If God is a just God who stands for what is right, then He will demonstrate how firmly He stands for what is right by how indignantly He reacts against what is wrong. You cannot have the justice of God without anger. In the same way, if we want to see a picture of the love of God, sometimes we see it reflected in the anger of God.

However, we must be very clear about one thing. When we think in terms of the anger of God we mustn't start thinking in terms of human anger and then work back from there, because human anger can be very unfair. Now my children are grown up and have the great freedom to tell me exactly what they think, they have pointed out to me that at times I was wrong or unjust, and they have pointed out what a terrible person I was. They are very loving, and it was very helpful of them to point this out. But God's anger is part of His holiness and righteousness. Having said all that, God reveals that He is a God of patience, slow to anger.

Why is that? The Scripture gives a number of answers, but here is just one, in Peter's second epistle. A lot of the Christians had been getting it in the neck from the sceptics who were saying to them, 'Where is the coming that you promised us? Every since the beginning of creation everything continues as it always did.' They were getting very cynical about the second coming of Christ. Peter answers them, 'Don't be too cocky, for He will come. God will intervene, but He is not intervening yet. Why? Because He is longsuffering.' This is the same word — *makrothumia*. He is not willing that any should perish. So the anger of God is holy, it is just, it is loving; but it is expressed slowly, in order that there might be time for repentance.

Now we come to the story we have read. Peter comes to the Lord Jesus and says, 'Lord, how many times should I forgive my brother? I've had it with my brother! Have I really got to forgive him seven times?' And the Lord Jesus answers, 'Not seven times, but seventy-seven times.' Indeed, it may be not seventy-seven but seventy *times* seven, which is four hundred and ninety. Whichever way you look at it, the Lord is certainly ballooning way past anything Peter is interested in.

Then He tells a lovely story. A king wanted to settle accounts with his servants. A man came in who owed him 10,000 talents. He was not able to pay, so the king was going to take possession of all his property, including his wife and family. But the man fell on his knees and cried,

'Be patient with me!' And the king was nice and let him off. Then the person who had been let off because of the king's patience rushed outside, and met one of his fellow-servants who owed him one 600,000th part of what he himself had been forgiven. So, if he has been forgiven £600,000, and his friend owes him £1, it is obvious what he will do, isn't it? He will say to his friend, 'You owe me a pound. Forget it. In fact I'll buy you a coffee. Let's go out.' This is not what he did. He turned to his fellow-servant and began to insist that he paid up the pound. He even grabbed him and began to choke him. 'Pay me', he said. And the king looked at him and said, 'You wicked servant.'

The moral of the story is simply this: if God has been patient with us, that in itself is motivation enough for the fruit of the Spirit which is patience, to be demonstrated in us. It is excruciatingly simple, and it is inescapable. God has manifested His untold patience to us; He expects to see the same from us. In very basic terms, what does that mean? It means that we have got to make sure that we are handling our indignant reaction to people and circumstances properly.

When is slowness to anger necessary? I would suggest, first of all, when we find ourselves in relationships that get very frustrating. Relationships tend to produce frustrating circumstances. Some people feel that they can be something, can do something, can achieve something — but the relationship they've got into thwarts them. If my mother told me once, she told me a thousand times, 'When I was a girl I wanted to be a nurse, but my father said a woman's place was in the home.' She wasn't a rebel, but she felt frustrated because in this particular area she had been thwarted.

I often counsel people, and one question I ask is this: 'If

you could really be what you want to be, and do what you really want to do, what would it be?' It's amazing how often people won't even begin to think about this and they recite all the things in their lives which will hinder them from being what they would really love to be, or doing what they would really love to do. And very often, under the surface, there's a considerable degree of frustration; or just call it what it is – anger. Sometimes we find ourselves in situations where in our relationships we aren't appreciated. Two of our dearest friends in England are Harry and Dorothy Green. Harry was doing his share of grumbling on one occasion and Dorothy, in characteristic fashion, simply responded as follows – 'Harry Green, you had all the world to choose from and you chose me. Now shut up and be satisfied.' Certainly there are more than a few people who feel they are not appreciated in their marriages.

I come across a lot of people in the ministry who are thoroughly frustrated. There are many things they feel need to be done. There are many things they feel that they could do, but their hands are tied. When I ask why they say it is because they have a board or a parochial church council who work under that old text – 'As it was in the beginning, is now and ever shall be, world without end, Amen.'

And there are frustrated kids in families. Isn't it interesting that Paul, writing to the Ephesians, gives this advice to parents, 'Parents, don't frustrate your children'? He doesn't say much else. 'Bring them up in the nurture and admonition of the Lord, and don't drive them up the wall!' Have you noticed how often good, sound evangelical Christian families are super in church – but not so good in the car coming to church? Have you noticed how we put on the right face and the right smile and hold the Bible at the right angle, but it's been a ding-dong battle all the way to church? After the church service we simply get back into our cars and resume the battle where we left off. Why is it? Often it's because there is a lot of frustration and anger.

Now, how can we handle this anger? There are at least four ways of doing it. The technical word for the first is *repression*. That means a refusal to admit that there is anger. Sometimes Christians jump up in a church meeting and the first thing they say is, 'Now brothers and sisters, I don't want you to think I'm angry.' But they are the ones who put the thought of anger into everyone's head because it was already in theirs. Now that is not particularly helpful to anyone!

Then there is *suppression*. That means that I hide the anger from everyone else, even though I'm prepared to admit it's there to myself. That's another good way that Christians fool themselves and think they're being spiritual. They get up in church business meetings and are very cool and calm, and make it abundantly clear that they are not going to make a fuss, but if they don't get their own way they will go on being cool and calm and will walk out and never speak to you again. But they're terribly spiritual about it because they didn't get angry. Don't kid yourself! They are so mad that they are simply suppressing their anger.

There's a third way of handling your anger. It is called *expression*. Now expression may be all right for the person who is expressing it, but the problem is that people express it indiscriminately and do terrible damage.

There's another way. It's called *confession*. First of all we confess it to the Lord. 'Lord, I'm hurt, I'm upset, I'm frustrated.' What a healthy thing it is to admit it to the Lord, and how very often this is not done. We say that we don't want to bother Him or we feel that we ought not to feel the way we feel, and if we don't mention it, He'll never notice. But this isn't good enough. Confession is absolutely imperative. But then comes the hard part. That is, talking to the person concerned and confessing it to him, but doing it slowly. Why? To give opportunity for hasty words to be recalled, to give opportunity for wrong attitudes to be rectified, to give opportunity for people to come and apologise, to give opportunity for damage that has been done to be healed.

If there's something about someone close to you that irritates you because it's wrong, is the loving thing to be angry about it and deny being angry about it? Or is the loving thing to confess your indignation to the Lord and eventually, when the time is right, confess it to the person who irritates you, and help to put it right? Speaking the truth in love requires loving confrontation, in order that those things that are wrong, that make us angry, might be handled – but slowly.

Let me just point out to you one verse in 1 Thessalonians 5:14. 'We urge you, brothers, warn those who are idle, encourage the timid, help the weak, be patient with everyone.' My nature is to be impatient. It says here, 'Be patient with everyone', and that includes the idle. I react against people I think are idle. Shortly after I went to be a pastor in the USA somebody came up to me and asked, 'Will you stop telling everyone how uncommitted they are?' I said, 'But they're not doing anything. They're idle.' Then he sat down and pointed out to me that I had just assumed they were idle; he pointed out to me that the reason that people were not doing the things I wanted them to was not that they were idle, it was just that some of them didn't know how to do them. So a much more sensible thing would have been to take them by the hand and show them how. So I tried it, and it was amazing. The only thing was, it took patience, and I had to do and tell them I was sorry, and I had to give them time to learn and to grow, and express my frustration slowly.

It's amazing what happens if we start being patient. But how do you do it? Well, some people say that it's just the fruit of the Spirit. All you have to say is, 'I'm impatient. The Spirit is patient. He'll have to be patient through me.' Somebody else will ask, 'Then why does Paul tell *you* to be patient?' And here again we come to that delightful blend of having to rely upon the Spirit for His resources, yet of being obedient to the commands of Scripture. The fruit of the Spirit is patience.

KESWICK 1984 TAPES

Here is a list of tape numbers for all the messages in this book. The numbers follow the sequence of the contents.

Bible Readings
Dr Donald English: 881, 882, 883, 884

Rev Stuart Briscoe: 911, 912, 913, 914

Addresses

Rev David Jackman	880
Rev Richard Bewes	900
Canon Keith Weston	901
Rev Gottfried Osei-Mensah	923
Rev David Jackman	904
Rev Gervais Angel	917
Rev Philip Hacking	919
Rev Stuart Briscoe	903
Rev Ian Barclay	902
Dr Donald English	892
Rev Stuart Briscoe	895/6/7

These tapes can be obtained, together with a full list of Keswick tapes, from:

The Keswick Convention Tape Library
13 Lismore Road
Eastbourne
East Sussex
BN21 3BA

KESWICK 1985

The annual Keswick Convention takes place each July at the heart of England's beautiful Lake District. The two separate weeks of the Convention offer an unparalleled opportunity for listening to gifted Bible exposition, experiencing Christian fellowship with believers from all over the world, and enjoying something of the unspoilt grandeur of God's creation.

Each of the two weeks has a series of four morning Bible Readings, followed by other messages throughout the rest of the day. The programme in the second week is a little less intensive, and it is often referred to as 'Holiday Week'. There are also regular meetings throughout the fortnight for young people, and in the second week for children.

The dates for the 1985 Keswick Convention are 13-20 July and 20-27 July. The Bible Reading speakers for the two weeks are Rev Eric Alexander (Glasgow) and Bishop Michael Baughen (Chester). Other speakers during the fortnight include Mr Alan Nute, Dr Stephen Olford, and the Revs Ken Prior, Michael Wilcock, Gordon Bridger and Hugh Palmer.

Further details may be obtained from:

> The Keswick Convention Secretary
> 25 Camden Road
> London
> NW1 9LN

Chapter 2 - Protecting Bald Eagle Nests
1975 - 1984

In 1975, I had little interest in flying airplanes and did not expect to become a pilot. If someone told me then that I would eventually be flying airplanes into Russia, I would have labeled their statement as nonsensical fiction.

Early that spring, I was close to finishing my Masters Degree program in statistics at Oregon State University. I received a phone call from the U.S. Fish and Wildlife Service in Juneau, Alaska. The leader of the bald eagle project, Fred Robards, was asking me if I would be interested in applying for a position as his assistant. I couldn't think of any job I would rather have. I would be working on the coastal waters of Alaska, driving boats, studying bald eagles, and protecting old growth forest. Fred had gotten to know me during three previous summers while I was working out of the same office as a temporary fisheries technician.

Bald eagles in Alaska were placed on the "most wanted" list by the territorial government in 1917. They were considered vile – they ate salmon, a cash crop and rich food source for the local communities. Any citizen who obtained two eagle talons could turn them in to the government and receive $.50 in return. The government also paid a bounty on seals and Dolly Varden fish. By 1953, when the bounty ended, 127,000 sets of talons had been exchanged for reimbursement. The eagle population was probably lowered by 75 percent from this persecution, and the birds had become wary of humans.

Our mother ship, M/V *SURFBIRD.*

17

Six years after the end of the bounty, when Alaska became a state in 1959, killing of an eagle suddenly became illegal. The bald eagles in Alaska were, at statehood, given full protection under the Bald and Golden Eagle Protection Act of 1940. It also became illegal to destroy or even disturb a bald eagle nest. This created a problem for the large scale logging industry in Southeast Alaska. They were clear-cutting thousands of acres each year. The easiest and most accessible timber was along the beaches, the preferred location for eagles to build their nests.

Fred Robards was a Wildlife Protection Agent for the U.S. Fish and Wildlife Service at the time. He had a reputation for effectively enforcing the law. To him, it didn't make sense to wait in the woods for a logger to cut down an eagle nest and then arrest him. It also was unrealistic to arrest the U.S. Forest Service employee that laid out the timber sale area for the logging company to buy the rights to cut the trees. Yet the law needed to be enforced.

Fortunately, the regional biologist for the U.S. Forest Service was a good bureaucrat. Sigurd Olson, son of the famous Minnesotan environmentalist with the same name, worked collaboratively with Fred, and the two forged an agreement between both federal agencies. The U.S. Forest Service would provide maps to the U.S. Fish and Wildlife Service each year, showing the hundreds of miles of shoreline habitat which were being considered for logging or road-building operations. The U.S. Fish and Wildlife Service staff would use its boats to find the eagle nests in the proposed areas. They would mark the nest trees with signs, identify the nest locations on maps and provide this data to the U.S. Forest Service. The U.S. Forest Service would protect the marked nests within their sale areas and prevent any tree cutting within a 330-foot-radius buffer zone around every nest tree.

The U.S. Fish and Wildlife Service, under the direction of Fred Robards, jumped into this project with both feet. They found a 65-foot surplus military steel-hulled boat, and converted it to the mother ship. They put two skiffs on deck. Fred and his boyhood friend and fellow law enforcement officer, Sid Morgan, started finding and marking bald eagle nests in 1968.

Fred and Sid learned that they could become very adept at finding the nests from the sea. They filled out a nest data card for each nest, with descriptive information about the tree and nest condition. Two skiffs could each cover roughly 20 miles of shoreline a day. That first year, they found over 300 nests. Unfortunately, the following winter, all of the nest data cards were stolen from Fred's office. So in the summer of 1969 they had to resurvey all of those nests and work on the new set of shorelines as well. The mystery of the stolen data cards was solved a few years later. A mentally ill man confessed to authorities that he had entered an office in the Juneau Federal Building and took a stack of cards because they were communist records and needed to be destroyed.

By early May of 1975, I had finished my graduate school requirements and was able to head directly to Juneau. The M/V SURFBIRD was ready to go. They welcomed me on board and the vessel was soon gliding out of Juneau. Just motoring through the inland waters, lined with forested mountains and teaming with marine mammals was thrilling. The previous winter must have produced copious amounts of snowfall because some of the beaches above the high tide line still had snow drifts. Four of us, Fred, Sid, myself and Andy, the skipper, would be working in a 40-mile long fjord called Tenakee Inlet, which was a full day of running from Juneau.

The next morning we climbed over the side of SURFBIRD into aluminum skiffs. Fred and I zoomed off to a point where the map showed we were to start. Fred slowed the skiff down to an idle and began paralleling the coastline at the optimal distance for our search, usually around 100 yards offshore. A pair of binoculars, hung by a strap around my neck, was my survey tool.

Ever since I was a kid, I have been fascinated with binoculars. They are truly magical. There is no other way to describe them. They have the amazing ability to transport me to a new place in space, seven times closer to the object I am looking at. Here, the binoculars could bring the trees up close for us to see whether a dark mass was actually an organized pile of sticks carefully placed there by an eagle. When we found a nest, Fred dropped me off on the beach to scamper up into the woods, find the nest tree, and nail a sign onto it. This was wonderful work, if it could even be called work – being out on the water, searching for bald eagle nests and exploring forests.

During that first week, I couldn't spot a nest before Fred. However, I was confident I could learn, and I was determined to become as good as Fred. He knew how to select specific trees to scrutinize. I began to realize that the eagles pick trees with large limb structures to hold their heavy nests. Trees with deformed tops, or broken tops often provide these types of limbs. If the tree was large with a normal top, then I should look lower down in the tree for large limbs and a dark mass. By the end of the trip, I had found a few nests before Fred.

After two field seasons with the project, I summarized the nine years of data cards and wrote a report. I listed Fred as the senior author because he was responsible for designing and implementing the work. It was titled, "Observations from 2,760 bald eagle nests in Southeast Alaska". I sent a draft of the report to Sig Olson, the U.S. Forest Service biologist largely responsible for their cooperation on this project. Sig was good at drawing sketches and had a keen sense of humor. He returned the report to Fred and me with a sketch drawn on the front cover. It showed a tree with an eagle nest in it. Standing on the nest, was a biologist looking intently through a pair of binoculars. There was a note under the drawing that read "Fred, I couldn't help but imagine your observations from eagle nests." That was my first real government report.

The author nails an eagle nest tree sign onto a large spruce tree.

We reported that the average nest diameter was 3.6 feet, which represented a tree that was about 400 years old. The average distance of the nest from the shoreline was 40 yards. That meant that when we located an average nest tree, we were protecting an average of 5.7 acres of forest around that tree. This preservation of land was what drove me to work as hard as I could to find every nest. Each nest was a treasure, not so much because it was a nest, but because it protected 5.7 acres of ancient trees from being destroyed.

I became highly skilled at finding nests. The experience was like that of a hunter who needs to bring home meat for his family. The hunter can read tracks, partial tracks, hints of tracks and has instincts for where tracks should be. At first glance, the forest looks like thousands of trees, side by side and stacked one behind the other. Initially, the task of looking at every gap in the trees from every angle seemed impossible. But it indeed could be learned. Some nests were obvious when pointed out to the new student. Others were hidden in the fabric of the trees so intricately that the student observer wonders what led the driver to move the skiff ever so slightly so as to look into a dark recess in the forest at a particular moment. Binoculars were used to confirm the nests by the presence of sticks. I was proud of my prowess.

A few years later Fred retired and I became the bald eagle specialist. I pointed out to the U.S. Forest Service that our agreement would only protect ten percent of the shoreline habitat. In the long term I felt that amount of protection would be inadequate. If the nest was destroyed by natural causes, we were not assured a replacement tree would be available within the buffer zone. We also were unable to protect the zone after the nest was gone. I further argued that we had no provision for intermediate perching trees between the nest buffer zones. The U.S. Forest Service accepted these arguments and a provision was put into the Memorandum of Understanding between the agencies to protect the buffer zone even after the nest was lost. Another provision stated that a tree or group of trees, if necessary for wind firmness, would be left in every 100 yards of shoreline. The upshot of these changes was that we started to notice that the new clear-cuts were not taking every tree to the shoreline. Because it was a hassle for foresters to lay out timber sales along the shore and abide by the new provisions of the bald eagle agreement, the shorelines in logged areas began to have a narrow fringe of trees – which was definitely minimal, but was also a great improvement over previous clear-cut landscapes throughout Southeast Alaska.

A recent huge land exchange between the federal government and the Alaska indigenous peoples had placed more than 500,000 acres of forested coastal land into private ownership. By 1980, the Native corporations were moving rapidly to log their newly acquired lands. They were keen on removing the old growth forests to make money, and to begin the regeneration process. The big, valuable logs were sent to Japan. I tried to work with them to help protect their bald eagles, having our agreement with the U.S. Forest Service as an example. They were unwilling to negotiate. By law, the nests on their land could not be destroyed, so we had the daunting task of surveying all of their lands for eagle nests. There was a notable exception. The village of Kasaan invited me to help them find all of their eagle nests. The village chief drove the skiff. Their professional forester was along as well. They proudly pointed out to me the largest of their cedar trees and exclaimed that this one or that one would surely make a beautiful canoe. And too, there was the village of Angoon, the only village to choose not to log their lands. There was no need to survey their lands.

Years later, in 1997, the U.S. Forest Service adopted a policy of a no harvest zone within 1,000 feet of shorelines. This was a wonderful evolution in forest management and I felt pride in the part the eagle project had played in bringing this about. I had hoped this type of change would eventually transpire and our difficult task of finding and managing the eagle nests would no longer be necessary.

Chapter 3 - Radio-Tagging Bald Eagles
1979 - 1983

There was a very special eagle which spent its summers in Seymour Canal on Admiralty Island. Seymour Canal is an area that is very remote, so not many people saw her in summer. We called her Blondie. She could have been a male eagle, we never knew for sure. She was not known to have successfully mated with another eagle. I suppose the other eagles might have rejected her because of her feather color. But to us, she was beautiful. Every feather on her body and wings was outlined with a broad white border. Her appearance was angelic. The other eagles didn't harass her, but she was always alone on the nesting grounds of Admiralty Island. In the fall she migrated 130 miles north to the Chilkat River and joined approximately 3,000 other bald eagles feeding on the last salmon run in the northern panhandle region.

Blondie at Winning Cove in Seymour Canal.
Photo by Gordon Fisch.

When we travelled to the Chilkat River for our annual eagle count, we always hoped to see Blondie. More often than not, she would be there, perched on the far side of the river. Occasionally, we found her next to the road near the village of Klukwan and we would get another close-up view of her.

The eagles congregated along the Chilkat River late into the fall and early winter because of a unique run of chum salmon. The salmon had adapted to a hydrological phenomenon. This part of the river did not freeze during the winter. Upwelling of warm water from the Tsirku River kept a three mile stretch of the Chilkat River ice free. The salmon adapted to this warmer water and spawn there in November and

December, long after the other runs had finished. The eagles learned to take advantage of the late fall fish supply. It was the largest concentration of bald eagles in the world.

A battle was raging in Haines between the Tree Cutters and the Tree Huggers. The local saw mill needed wood from the local forests. The Tree Huggers felt the fishery resources and bald eagle phenomenon was were too important to risk harming from extensive resource extraction. The community was highly polarized. The geology of the warm water upwelling had not been studied, nor had much scientific research addressed the bald eagle concentration. In the late 1970's the National Audubon Society and others became concerned that the river valley needed protection to ensure the perpetuation of the eagle concentration and the fish run. They hired Erv Boeker, a retired golden eagle biologist from Colorado, to head the studies. The U.S. Fish and Wildlife Service was a cooperator, and as such, I was in charge of the aerial counts and the capture and radio-tagging of eagles for migration studies.

Blondie at Chilkat River.

Erv was a joy to work with. Everyone seemed to love him. He was a real father figure to the community of Haines. Over the four year period of his study, he slowly warmed the community to the idea of increased protection for the eagles. As a wildlife pilot himself with thousands of hours of flight experience, he appreciated our airplane, N754, as a premiere wildlife survey platform. Pilot status for me would not happen for a few more years. Bruce Conant, who later became my supervisor when I was hired as a pilot for the U.S. Fish and Wildlife Service, would fly N754 from Juneau to Haines with me on board. The eighty mile flight was straight north from Juneau, up Lynn Canal – part of the longest fjord in the world and known for its fierce north winds when the weather turned clear. We needed good weather for our surveys, so many a time Bruce and I would have a 45 knot headwind over Lynn Canal. The sea would be smoking below us, the tops of the waves being blown off. We knew that the eagle concentration area up the Chilkat River valley would be nearly calm, as those winds almost always bypassed it.

We landed at Haines to pick up Erv. We covered all four river valleys in the Haines area as we documented the size of the eagle population. Erv used two tally counters. In one hand he counted eagles by tens and in the other he counted by ones. The eagles were so thick that Erv counted the eagles in the trees while I counted the eagles on the river bars. Erv would tell me, "Jack, that Bruce is a darn good pilot." Erv knew airplanes. He was a navy pilot in World War II. Following the war, he flew thousands of hours for the U.S. Fish and Wildlife Service in the American west. In the early years of the whooping crane recovery project he was responsible for following the few remaining birds during their migrations from breeding areas in Alberta, Canada, to their winter habitats along the Gulf Coast of Texas.

Capturing animals has been a part of human endeavor since humans evolved in Africa. Usually early man was interested in obtaining meat, so capturing without harming was not a priority. But for us, safe handling during capture and releasing birds unharmed were a necessity. Wildlife biologists often tap into those basic capture instincts. For me, the capture and handling was exciting and challenging. Always there was a responsibility to treat the animals as humanely as possible.

Fred Robards paved the way for my bald eagle capture efforts. In the early 1960's he was tasked with live trapping bald eagles for a DDT study. He captured dozens of eagles at Chilkat River and transported them 200 miles south to Petersburg, where they were kept at an Experimental Fur Farm and held for up to 6 months. Known quantities of DDT were mixed with their food in order to determine how DDT was incorporated into their tissues.

Fred tried many methods of capture before settling on what he called the "power snare". It was made of 3/16 inch spring steel wire. When sprung, it would close a nylon noose around the eagle's foot in an instant, without harming the eagles. He picked natural perches on the river bar to set his snares. The perch couldn't be solid like a stump, because he used the motion that the bird transferred to the perch upon landing, to jiggle a lead weight loose from its precarious mount. Tied to the weight was a 12 inch length of monofilament line. That line pulled a nail out of eyelets causing the release of the power snare. Later, I enhanced this technique by fabricating fake perches out of natural pieces of wood. I cut through the wood and installed a hinge. The horizontal portion of the perch attracted the eagle to land upon it, and the weight of the eagle caused it pivot at the hinge and release the power snare. I enhanced this technique by fabricating fake perches out of natural pieces of wood. I cut through the wood and installed a hinge. The horizontal portion of the perch attracted the eagle to land upon it, and the weight of the eagle caused it to pivot at the hinge and release the power snare. Roughly one third of the time that a snare was sprung, the cord would successfully ensnare a talon, and the bird was caught.

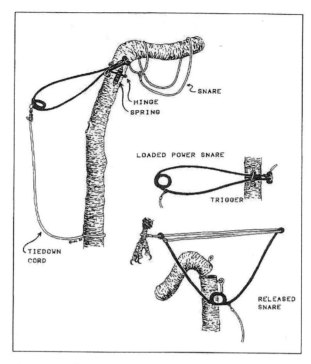

SNARE

HINGE
SPRING

LOADED POWER SNARE

TRIGGER

TIEDOWN
CORD

RELEASED
SNARE

Drawing by Laurie Craig.

We set about half a dozen snares out on the river bar. Because there were so many eagles – often over 500 within our view of the river – any object on the river bar that was suitable as a perch site was likely to be used by an eagle, sooner or later. We sat in the warm car overlooking our perches. Many hours were spent waiting in anticipation, expecting each eagle in flight to land on one of our beautiful perches.

As we waited, Erv told me stories of his near death experiences as a pilot. I was a fledgling pilot at the time – not yet a pilot for the U.S. Fish and Wildlife Service. These stories should have been sufficient fodder to discourage me from a career of flying, but that wasn't the case.

Erv told me about the time when he and several other pilots of fighter planes were practicing maneuvers over the Gulf of Mexico. The wing of another aircraft clipped Erv's tail. The other plane could still fly, but Erv's plane was descending to the ocean. Before crashing, he successfully ejected and spent six hours in the Gulf, worrying about sharks, before he was rescued.

In another incident, Erv was ferrying a military fighter plane from the east coast to the Midwest. En route, he became entangled in a bad thunder-storm. It was nighttime. He was flying on instruments and had inadvertently entered the severe storm. With turbulence so heavy and constant, he lost control of the airplane for over 30 minutes. By the time he was spit out of the storm, the windshield was broken by hail and the leading edges of the wings were completely bashed in. He regained control and was able to successfully land the plane.

While still in the military, Erv was at an airport standing in line for his ticket to board a commercial airline flight. He was in uniform, and military personnel had priority over civilians during the war. A woman near him was pleading with the ticket agent to help her get a seat on the flight that Erv was on. She told the agent there was an emergency in her family. Erv overheard the conversation from his position behind her. He offered his ticket to the lady, which she accepted. Later, he learned that the plane crashed during the flight, killing everyone on board.

After flying in the military, Erv had a job flying an aerial spray plane. Since the planes were loaded so heavily, their flights began at dawn and were terminated at 10:00am. The planes needed the cool morning air to have adequate performance for takeoff. One particular morning, Erv tried to get one more flight in before the heat of the day. He lifted off the runway, but the plane would not climb. Whenever he tried to climb out, the plane settled back down. Only ground effect was keeping it airborne. He knew that the outcome of this situation could end poorly, so he headed for a hay stack and purposely directed the plane into it. The plane hit the stack and then flipped over, coming to rest on its back. Erv was able to get out and away from the plane. He had gone just 50 yards when it exploded. He was uninjured.

One of Erv's assignments with the U.S. Fish and Wildlife Service was to haze geese off of fields, using small charges about the size of a hand grenade. Roughly four out of every one hundred bombs would be a dud and fail to explode. While flying one of these missions in a supercub, he grabbed a bomb, pulled the pin, and tossed it out the window. However, this time the bomb hit the door post and ricocheted into the rear of the plane. Erv knew it would blow the tail off of his plane, so he immediately dove towards the ground and leveled it off, just a few feet above the field. He waited for the explosion. It never came. That one was a dud.

A more amusing event involved the transport of a hawk, this time while flying his Cessna 180. Erv was alone at the controls. The hawk was in a cardboard box on the rear seat. He entered some turbulent air, and next thing he knew, the hawk was out of the box. It didn't much like being in the airplane. It flapped around and then landed on Erv's shoulder. Erv couldn't deal with the hawk while he was flying, so he let the hawk stay perched. Every time the plane bounced in the rough air, the hawk would sink its talons deeper into Erv's shoulder. This was how it went until he could get the plane to an airport and on the ground.

Erv's stories made our time pass quickly. As soon as we saw a bird caught in one of the snares, we jumped out of the car, ran out to it, folded its wings in, grabbed its legs and put a hood over its head to help calm the bird. We then outfitted the eagle with a backpack radio transmitter. A U.S. Fish and Wildlife Service metal band was placed on one leg. Once the eagle was released and the snare was reset, it would take another hour or two before eagles started to use that area again, giving us another chance at catching one. Between 1979 and 1982, we radio-tagged thirty-one eagles at the Council Grounds of Chilkat River.

Despite having a less than one in a hundred chance of capturing Blondie, it happened on October 21, 1981. Looking back, I wish she had not been caught – and having been caught, I really wish we had not put a radio transmitter on her.

26

We were incredulous when we saw her in one of our snares. It was exciting to hold her and to see her up close. She was beautiful. Every feather was slate grey with varying amounts of pure white etching on the edges. The regal Emperor Goose is graced with feathers that have a similar appearance. She was our Emperor Eagle. Each of us had our picture taken with her. We should have let her go without a radio. She was not like the rest of the eagles. Therefore, the tracking of her movements was not of scientific value. She could not be an unbiased representative of an adult bald eagle from the Chilkat River Council Grounds. These measured thoughts escaped me at the time and I was blinded by the excitement of the moment. I was young in my career and more prone to a mistake like this. We knew that she was probably not part of a mated pair. In the end, I had to discard her movement data when I analyzed the rest of my data. To this day, I deeply regret my inability to recognize this at the time of her capture. There was simply no scientific reason for her to be encumbered with a radio and I fear it shortened her life.

Blondie is captured at Chilkat River in 1981. Photo by Karen Bollinger.

The radios were designed to eventually fall off – cotton string held the backpack together at a strategic location. When the string rotted through, the harness would be shed instantly. The range of the radio signal was 20 to 80 miles. I tried to get *Alaska Airlines* to put an antenna on one of their jets for us, but they wanted no part of it. So every month during the winter, Bruce and I would take off from Juneau in N754 and climb to 9,000 feet. During the 5.5 hour flight we would make one big loop over southeast Alaska. It was boring up there droning away at 140 mph, except when we heard the pop . . . . pop . . . . pop . . . . pop of the radio signals through our headsets, which meant we had found an eagle. Each bird had its own frequency or its own signal pattern. We had a good chance of picking up the signal of an eagle if it was below, because eagles spend almost all day perched high in a tree. In March, we would extend the loop over all of British Columbia to the Olympic Peninsula in Washington.

We learned that all of the adults stayed in southeast Alaska, the great majority of them in the northern half, within 150 miles of the Chilkat River. The immature birds were wanderers. They were spread throughout southeast Alaska and some into northern British Columbia. A few made it to Washington State. Three eagles were radio-tagged near Fairbanks, Alaska and two near Whitehorse, Yukon Territory during the nesting season. None of those five came to the Chilkat River. None of our birds were found northward, along the Pacific Coast towards Cordova. The closest source of birds, the northern half of the panhandle, turned out to be the actual source.

After her capture, we never saw Blondie again. Two months later – around Christmas time – we did locate her radio signal from high altitude, at her old stomping grounds in Seymour Canal. Then in mid-January, someone in Canada found her dead at Quatsino Narrows on northern Vancouver Island. I was crushed. If I had a time machine, I would go back to that October day on the Chilkat River, and watch Blondie fly away without a backpack harness. I felt responsible. Of the other 14 adult eagles that we radio-tagged, only one was found dead. I believe our harness somehow contributed to, or caused, her death.

Collectively, the Haines people held a lot of sway with the state government in Juneau. They knew how to raise a fuss and often got their way. What scared them the most, though, was the federal government. They had little or no influence over the politicians in Washington, D.C. Therefore, when Senator Gary Hart from Colorado introduced legislation to help the Chilkat eagles by adding federal lands in the Chilkat River Valley to the Glacier Bay National Monument, the locals decided maybe it would be better to have more localized control and protection through the State of Alaska. And so they sprang into action. In June of 1982, the Alaska Chilkat Bald Eagle Preserve was created to protect and preserve the largest bald eagle concentration in the world. Governor Jay Hammond came to the Council Grounds for the announcement. The 48,000 designated acres encompassed most of the bottom lands of the Chilkat, Klehini and Tsirku Rivers. The efforts of Erv, myself and others led to the recognition and protection of this truly special place.

Chapter 4 - Translocating Bald Eagles from Alaska to New York
1980 - 1983

Alaska's bald eagles were called upon to help rescue, in a sense, our national bird in the continental United States. One hundred years ago, the state of New York had an estimated 70 pairs of bald eagles. By 1975, only one pair remained. The culprit was primarily the pesticide DDT. The lone nesting eagle laid an egg every year, and each year the egg failed to hatch. Too many chemicals were in the old bird. State biologists started helping her by climbing up into the nest just prior to incubation and placing a placebo egg, made of plaster, into her nest cup. If any eggs were present, those were removed. Then five weeks later they climbed into the nest again and replaced the placebo egg with a tiny eaglet from a captive breeding facility. The instant "hatch" worked, year after year. Although successful, this process for repopulating the state with eagles was too slow to assure success.

In 1980, New York requested permission from the U.S. Fish and Wildlife Service to translocate about 20 nestlings each year from one side of North America to the other – from Alaska to New York. The primary concern with this proposal was the mixing, or possible replacement, of genetic adaptations the eagles in New England may have developed with those from Alaska. Would the fitness of the New England eagle population be compromised? I shared this concern. At first, I thought the translocations were not worth the risk. But when I realized that the Endangered Species Act could only protect habitat where eagles were present, I decided that the sooner eagles began nesting in New England, the sooner those habitats would receive protection. New York received their permit.

Peter Nye was in charge of the New York Department of Environmental Conservation translocation project. He contacted me, asking what kind of logistics would be required to make this happen. I told him we could do everything on the Alaska end. They just needed to be able to climb the trees. I told him our trees were really big. He assured me they could handle it. I wondered if he had any idea what it might be like to climb some of our eagle nest trees. He wanted the eaglets to be about 7 weeks old, so I told him we should schedule for early July.

Peter arrived in Juneau the next summer aboard a chartered *King Air* with twin turbo-prop engines. Peter had made special wooden crates that would fit into the aircraft for the return flight to New York. Even after making it to Juneau, Peter still needed to get a permit from the Alaska Department of Fish and Game. Maybe the permit needed a public hearing and couldn't be accomplished ahead of time – I can't remember. Peter was on pins and needles worrying about this detail. It took several days before he got his final permit from the State of Alaska. We also needed to fly the preliminary nest survey by helicopter to determine which nests had young and how old the eaglets were. Peter and I scoured the shoreline of the capture area from the air, searching and finding the nests. Peter was well satisfied with the magnificent forest and the abundance of eagles. There was no way he could evaluate, from the helicopter, how easy or difficult a tree would be for climbing. It was impossible to look down through the forest canopy.

As our vessel, SURFBIRD, left the dock, Peter was chomping at the bit to get to the first nest. It took us five hours of running to reach the capture area. Once we got near the first nest tree, we lowered the skiff into the water, loaded it with climbing gear, a wooden crate and ourselves. As we approached the nest, the two adult eagles circled overhead, distressed by our presence. They whistled loudly their displeasure. The eagles didn't know that the situation was going to get a lot worse. With our preliminary survey we had purposefully picked nests with two young so that we could take just one of them and still allow the nest to be successful. Peter was the primary climber. All of us would go into the woods on this first one.

It was a *very* big tree – a full five feet in diameter. It was sixty feet to the first limb and the trunk tapered only slightly by that point. I think if it were me, I likely would have bypassed this tree and headed for another one. I told Peter as much. Peter was wired though, and he was absolutely determined to conquer this tree. His dream was on the verge of coming true. He had planned for, and been focused on this, for several years.

Peter methodically put on his harness and strapped the climbing spikes to his feet. I was surprised he didn't have a safety lanyard. Loggers generally use the safety lanyard around the tree so they can lean back from the tree and force their spikes to penetrate through the bark into solid wood beneath. A safety lanyard also keeps the climber in contact with the tree if his spikes were to slip out, or he lost his grip.

Peter apparently didn't use a lanyard. To start out, Peter sunk one of his spikes into the tree and then the other. Just two feet off the ground, he attempted to get finger holds on the bark. Sitka spruce trees are not like cottonwood trees, or other trees that have rigid irregularities in the bark. The bark of the large Sitka spruce is scaled. Peter fingered at the scales. The scales just flaked off from the tree. Because Peter's arms didn't even reach half way around the trunk, his fingers had to find something to give him at the very least, a little bit of a grip. After failing over and over to find a flake that would hold, his fingers finally settled on a flake that presented some resistance without popping off. Then he sunk his spikes another foot higher. Again, his fingertips tested the tenuous flakes. It took him nearly 15 minutes to climb the first fifteen feet. At that point he rested. We were silently staring up at him. We could tell he was trying to relax. A long, 165-foot climbing rope hung from his harness. He would use that rope later to lower the eaglet to us and then to rappel down to earth. He started to progress a little faster at this point. The trunk was getting slightly smaller and he was probably gaining confidence. We made sure his rope, laying on the ground, was free and untangled. Slowly, but steadily now, more and more of the rope was lifted skyward. He got past the first limb and then moved on to others.

30

The adult eagles continued to squawk. Sometimes they landed in a tree, but most of the time they were flying in circles. They never attack a climber. Eagles that nest on the ground in the Aleutian Islands, where there are no trees, are different. They will attack a ground predator or human predator. Fortunately, we knew these eagles would not attack, even though they sounded very upset. Peter had a nylon bag with him. The bottom of the bag was padded with foam. He gathered up one of the eaglets, put it in the bag and started lowering it to the ground. The weight of the eaglet helped the bag to slither around the limbs. When it reached the ground, we told Peter we had the bird. We let the eaglet out of the bag and onto the ground. It wouldn't attempt to escape. Eaglets innately know to stay in one place if they find themselves on the ground, before they are able to fly. Had we left the eaglet there, the adults would have continued to bring food to it on the ground.

Peter looped his rope around a limb at the nest. He lowered the other end to us. We held the two ends of the rope together and pulled out the slack. The rope, doubled on itself, barely touched the ground. He quickly rappelled down the doubled line. We carried the eaglet to the skiff, put it in the crate and called it a day – a very long day for Peter. He was one tough and determined guy. I was duly impressed.

A year later Peter would have a sobering event at one of these trees. I was watching from the ground. He was rappelling down from the nest as he had done many times before, and on this occasion showing off a little bit. He dropped rapidly 20 feet or so and then stopped his descent in an instant, bouncing up and down slightly as the rope acted a bit like a rubber band. He did this about four times, enjoying the easy and quick descent compared to the arduous ascent to the nest. When he was 35 feet from the ground he did another rapid drop and checked his descent at 16 feet from the ground, suddenly Peter's climbing rope broke. He fell unimpeded to the moss covered forest floor. Fortunately, he was uninjured, but all of us were in a mild state of shock – knowing that the rope could have broken while he was still far up in the tree. Had that happened, he might not be around today. He concluded that his nylon rope must have accidentally come in contact with gasoline, either in Alaska or in New York, which dissolved the core of the rope. I still have the remaining parts of that rope and use them for odd jobs around the house.

And so it went. Peter climbed the difficult trees while his assistant climbed the easier ones. I even climbed a couple of the easiest trees. Even so, this seemed to me to be a dangerous way to make a living. One time I was in a scary situation, seventy or eighty feet off of the ground, when my legs started to shake. The whole upper part of the tree was dead. Some of the limbs were not only dead, but rotten. At times, it was hard to determine if a limb might break unexpectedly. While trying to get out and around the three foot diameter nest, I became stuck, paralyzed – too scared to go up or to go down. I had to talk myself into relaxing. I knew that shaking would only make me grow weaker and put me in greater peril. The talking helped, because

I began to regain control and stopped shaking. I continued on and finally got to the point where my head was even with the top of the nest.

Two eaglets stared at me and backed away to the opposite side of the platform, hissing and occasionally flapping their big, dark wings. I secured myself to the tree. The eaglets had sharp, curled talons and were clearly willing to use them. I managed to grab the wingtip of one of the eaglets and pulled it towards me, using my other hand to pin the eaglet's body to the nest. I never wore gloves when handling eagles. I wanted to be able to have full use of my hands and to feel everything that was happening. I folded each wing into its body, still keeping it pinned down. Carefully, I reached underneath the frightened bird, feeling for its legs, just above the talons. Thus secured, I was able to place the eaglet in the nylon bag. After lowering it to the ground, I rappelled down. Peter had taught me how to rappel. Safely on the ground with time to relax my weary muscles, I began to feel the lice crawling around on my body. It was common, but very disconcerting. They were avian lice, and after an hour or so they would leave on their own accord, having figured out I was not a bird. Back at the boat we deloused the eaglets with powder.

The author with an eaglet for New York. Photo by Mike Jacobson.

By the end of five days, we had our allotment of 17 eaglets. The *SURFBIRD* was a floating zoo. The birds needed to be fed and the crates cleaned. We caught pink salmon with rod and reel to feed the babies. They wolfed down the chunks of fish with relish.

Seven-week old eaglets aboard *Surfbird*. Photo by Peter Nye.

It was late in the evening when we returned to Juneau. And it was midnight before the *King Air* was loaded with the precious cargo and took off for New York. I understand they landed in Canada to refuel along the way and had some serious explaining to do to the authorities about the live bald eagles they had on board. Transport of endangered species across international borders was illegal.

In the next three years, we gathered and sent off 72 more eaglets. After that time, the project continued, but I was no longer involved. I changed jobs to become a pilot biologist with Bruce Conant in the U.S. Fish and Wildlife Service waterfowl project. Mike Jacobson replaced me. During the next nine years Mike facilitated the Alaska end of the eaglet captures.

A grand total of 394 eagles left Alaska from 1981 to 1993. New York received 178 eaglets. The remainder were translocated to Missouri, Indiana, North Carolina and Tennessee. The programs were wildly successful. All of these states and their neighbors soon began to enjoy substantial populations of bald eagles. On June 28, 2007, the bald eagle was removed from the Federal List of Endangered and Threatened Wildlife and Plants. Their population in the contiguous states had climbed from an estimated 400 nesting pairs in 1967 to 10,000 pairs forty years later.

Chapter 5 - Fledgling Pilot
1984 - 1986

Some pilots live to fly. I was not one of those. I preferred driving a boat to flying an airplane. Becoming a pilot never crossed my mind until my late-twenties. Then I began to see it as an exciting challenge. I also thought there was a chance I might have the opportunity to fly in the Alaska Waterfowl Program, because the Waterfowl Supervisor, Jim King, was planning to retire soon. The assistant position would then need to be filled. My horizons would be greatly expanded if I were in a project that flew low level wildlife surveys all across the state of Alaska and parts of Canada.

I began taking flying lessons. My apprehensions about flying started to subside as I saw my training successes mount. It was gratifying to practice hard and study hard and pass the milestones of soloing and receiving my private pilot's license. One of the minimum requirements to fly for the U.S. Fish and Wildlife Service was 500 hours of pilot-in-command time, so I leased a Cessna 172 on wheels from another individual in Juneau. It was in this plane that I learned a sobering lessen. I had just 150 hours in my log book. A young couple asked me if I would fly them to Sitka to attend a music concert. It was mid-June, so we would have enough daylight to return to Juneau after the concert. It should be a one hour flight each way in good weather. We left Juneau at 5:00pm and had good weather all the way to Sitka. The concert ended at 9:30pm and we were in the air, on our way back to Juneau by 10:00pm. Less than 30 miles out of Sitka, rain began to pepper the windshield. The lowering ceiling forced me to fly lower, over the water but between the mountains. A direct and quick flight to Juneau was now out of the question. We were weaving our way through a narrow waterway, appropriately named Peril Strait, which divides Baranof and Chichagof islands. I had little piloting experience under my belt. I expected the conditions to improve at any time. Instead, they kept getting worse. The rain had now become heavy and was making it difficult to see, as it smeared on the windshield. I should have turned around earlier, but now I was committed to continuing because we were in danger of running out of daylight. I was scared. We were down to 400 feet above the water and our visibility was down to one mile at the most. This was a wheeled airplane, giving me no option for an emergency landing on the water. I forged on, wishing we were back at Sitka, landing on its nice long runway.

Finally, about 40 miles from Juneau the weather lifted and we were able to make it there as deep dusk was settling in around 11:30pm. After we wiggled out of the plane, the couple congratulated me on my success at getting them home. I was disappointed with myself and would not accept the praise. I told them I had performed poorly, that I should have turned around and returned to Sitka. That flight was part of a learning process that led me to develop a rule for myself. I would always keep track of the number of issues I was facing in flight. On this flight there were three issues. (1) the visibility was low, (2) daylight was disappearing, and (3) I was flying over water on wheels. From that point on, my rule was this: one issue is manageable, two issues means I need to be looking for a way to get out of the situation, three or more issues means I am in serious trouble. For the Sitka flight, consider each issue alone. Low visibility would not have presented a difficult situation if I had been on floats and I had plenty of daylight to work with. Impending darkness alone would not be a problem if the weather was excellent and a direct flight to Juneau was guaranteed. Flying on wheels would not have been a concern if the weather had been excellent and sufficient daylight was available. Now consider two issues at a time. Low visibility and impending darkness – there will be insufficient time to explore various options and turn back if necessary. Low visibility and flying on wheels – there is no option for landing on the water if needed. Two issues means I need to turn around. All three issues – means I was stupid and put us at risk.

I decided that I should continue to earn additional ratings, rationalizing that even if I didn't earn a pilot position with the U.S. Fish and Wildlife Service, I should be as qualified as possible, given the responsibility of having passengers' safety in my hands. I went on to receive my glider's license, instrument rating and float rating.

My timing was good. When Jim retired, I was ready to take the waterfowl pilot-wildlife biologist position under Bruce Conant. I had known Bruce for 13 years by then. He was the pilot I flew with as a fisheries technician during my college years. His confidence and poise in the cockpit were impressive to me. He had not acted conceited, but rather showed great care, diligence, and thoroughness. It would be an honor to fly with him and under his direction. I was also pretty sure he was instrumental in convincing Fred Robards to hire me for the bald eagle position out of college. We knew each other well and had mutual respect for each other.

I began my government flight training under the direction of Tom Belleau, check pilot for the Office of Aircraft Services. Right off the bat, Tom asked me how old I was. I told him I was 33. He said he generally considered age 30 to be the cutoff for starting a flying career. He gave me the impression he thought I was making a mistake. Tom was gruff, to put it mildly. Some of the pilots were annoyed by his antics and his angry outbursts. I saw his anger as a show. What was important, is that he had his ways of letting you know that he cared deeply about you and your safety and his responsibility to teach, and teach effectively.

I remember one instance when Tom was working with me on a flight. He reached across the cockpit with his left hand and pushed the big red button in front of me labelled "Fire". The bright red light came on and he said, "What does it mean when this light comes on?" I said, "It means there is a fire in the engine compartment." He glared at me and yelled in my ear, "NO. IT DOESN'T MEAN THERE IS A FIRE. . . . . IT MEANS THAT THIS RED LIGHT HAS COME ON". He was teaching me to not make quick judgements or take quick actions until I knew what was going on. Years later the red

Fuel Pressure light came on as I was taking off from the runway at Anchorage International Airport. I remembered my lesson, looked it my other gauges and saw that the fuel pressure gauge was reading normal. I asked the tower for clearance to land and had the mechanics check it out. They found that anticorrosion fluid had been sprayed behind the fire wall and the air flow on takeoff had caused excess fluid to move around and create a temporary short.

In April 1984, after just 14 hours of time with Tom Belleau as my instructor in the turbine beaver, I passed my check ride and became a U.S. Fish and Wildlife Service pilot. One month later I was thrown into the frying pan. Bruce and I were flying the statewide waterfowl population survey together. Initially, I was strictly an observer in the copilot's seat. My job was to observe how Bruce flew the plane and learn to identify the ducks and geese. Identifying duck species out to 220 yards from the plane while quickly passing by at 100 miles per hour is a skill that takes weeks, and in some cases years of practice. Just like finding eagle nests in the forest, identifying the ducks was a process, fueled by a desire to conquer the skill.

The ducks were rarely visible to the aerial observer like they appeared in field guides, where they were depicted with good lighting and a nice large side profile. From the air, they were most visible when they were close to the plane, which means a downward profile. When they presented a side profile, they were small and much further from the plane. Often the lighting was poor, such as sky glare on the water, and usually they were facing towards you or away from you. At first it seemed like I could only positively identify a few of the birds. Bruce would tell me the species he was seeing on his side of the plane. I would try to make the birds on my side into those species. Every so often I would get affirmation that I was correct. For example, I might see a male duck with some white on top of its head. Then it might happen to fly and I would see the brilliant white patches on the leading edge of each wing. The confirmation would give me 100 percent feedback that I was correct in thinking the duck was an American widgeon. This process took time to learn to interpret the most subtle indicators. I learned that red-necked grebes had long thin necks and green-winged teal were tiny dark ducks. The slinking, almost snakelike grey bird, was a red-throated loon. Still, there were always some birds that I would get a pretty good look at and not know what I had seen. But I got better.

After ten days, Bruce put me in the pilot's seat – first on flying transects with fewer birds. This added a whole new level of mental gymnastics, far more demanding than only observing and recording birds. We were required to fly straight lines, just as they appeared on our maps. Each hand had double duty. The left hand held the yoke for flying the plane, and held the map for navigating. The right hand held the tape recorder microphone and also manipulated the throttle. The brain had five duties – search for birds, identify and count birds, fly the plane at unwavering and correct altitude, navigate constantly and dictate the observations into a microphone. Precise navigation when flying at 100 feet required me to look at the map and note where the transect line crossed lakes and ponds and then relate that to what I could observe ahead of the plane. But interpreting the shallow view of the world from 100 feet was far more difficult than it was at a higher altitude. I would look ahead on the map for a lake that had a distinctive shape and try to find that lake in my view through the windscreen. The compass was my friend, but my best friend was a good landmark in the distance, such as a mountain or even a cloud.

When I first tried to do all of these tasks at the same time, I thought it was a ridiculous request and not humanly possible. I would be flying, focusing on the map and navigation, concentrating on keeping the proper distance from the trees and ground, when Bruce would look over at me and say, "Don't forget to look for birds." My brain was in full overload and I had to put the birds at a lower priority than hitting the trees. Over time, it became possible. The flying became instinctive. Navigating became tolerable. Observing and recording of birds became rewarding as I gained confidence and realized I was accurately identifying a large majority of the birds.

This survey took us to every major waterfowl breeding habitat in Alaska, except for the coastal plain north of the Brooks Range. Bruce and I flew the waterfowl population survey two more years together as I learned how to deal with challenging weather conditions and a mixture of landing and takeoff situations. I was now a bush pilot of sorts. In two ways, wildlife survey pilots had it easier than bush pilots. First, we generally didn't fly in the difficult winter months. Second, we weren't under outside pressure to maintain a schedule and rush to get people to their destinations as soon as possible. But in other ways, we faced greater challenges than bush pilots. Bush pilots have their well-trodden routes and territory that they become intimately familiar with and transit in all conditions. By contrast, it was common for me to fly in totally unfamiliar places, and at times in very challenging weather conditions. I eventually flew across all of the state of Alaska, but also as far as Siberia, Russia and Ontario, Canada. Another challenge for us was that most of our hours were spent at 100 feet above the ground, whereas bush pilots usually flew much higher. When flying in Canada with its array of towers and power lines, I could never relax at 100 feet. When flying in rugged terrain, such as the fjords of Alaska, I always had to be mentally ahead of the airplane at those low altitudes.

Chapter 6 - Prairie Canada
1987

I was, in a sense, a pilot without a project. The other three survey pilots in our U.S. Fish and Wildlife Service division were responsible for "operational surveys," meaning their surveys were flown every year to maintain long-term data sets. I didn't have any surveys of my own. I was asked to fill in wherever there was a need. That fit my personality, because I enjoyed change and new challenges. I have been accurately described as a "Jack of all trades, master of none."

By my fourth field season, 1987, my supervisors were ready to send me to Canada. They wanted me to fly the waterfowl survey in southern Manitoba, southeastern Saskatchewan, and Ontario. The plane was N727, a Cessna 185 on amphibious floats. I had 1200 hours total time, 500 of which was float plane or amphibious time.

The prairie country was all new to me. It was totally flat land. Tiny ponds were scattered almost everywhere and they provided rich nesting habitat for ducks. I was used to large landscape features in Alaska to keep track of my position, but these were not present in the prairie provinces. Large lakes were scarce and mountains were nonexistent. There were gravel roads every mile, east-west and north-south. Every gravel road looked like the last one. Small clusters of structures occasionally showed the location of a tiny town site. Sometimes a water tower would display the name of the village, which really helped when I was seriously perplexed as to my whereabouts.

My transect lines were co-located with the east-west gravel roads. I was to fly down the road at 100 feet above the ground. Farm houses were usually placed near the road, so we were often closer to people and habitation than general aviation aircraft were allowed. The U.S. Fish and Wildlife Service had a waiver for this. Sometimes a farmhouse would have a vertical radio antenna sticking up to a height that was close enough to my altitude to give me some concern. The people living in these homes were accustomed to the U.S. Fish and Wildlife Service airplane buzzing by their houses every spring. But on two occasions I saw vehicles ahead of me on the gravel road whose drivers must not have been familiar with our flights, because they drove their cars right off the road into the ditch. My plane was so low, that I am sure they thought I was attempting an emergency landing and they didn't want to be in my way.

The flight lines I was surveying were sometimes over 100 miles long. They were subdivided into segments, each 18 miles in length. It was relatively easy to find the beginning of a flight line and start flying down the road. But the data had to be separated by segment, so I needed to know when we had flown 18 miles – which of course consisted of 18 crossroads that all looked the same. I couldn't keep track of the miles in my head, and a tally whacker wasn't much help because it required me to remember to advance the counter at every crossroad. After two days of struggling to know where to call out the segment end points, I invented a solution.

It involved the Epson portable computer I had with me. In 1987, the Epson computer was an impressive little machine. It had a full keyboard, an LCD text screen (four lines by 20 characters), tape printer and a microcassette recorder for data storage. I wrote a simple computer program that kept track of our miles across the ground. This is how it functioned. When I started flying the first segment, I hit the space bar on the keyboard. The program assumed we had a ground speed of 100 mph and began to display our distance to the closest hundredth of a mile. After flying one mile we would be at the first crossroad. The computer would show a distance, such as 1.07, due to a headwind. If the computer was showing .94 miles, we had a tail wind. As we

crossed the road, I hit the space bar again and the program instantly rounded our distance to the nearest mile. It would know how long it took us to get there and it would recalculate our ground speed. Now the miles would just click off accurately for me. If at any time the displayed miles began to lose accuracy at a crossroad, I would hit the space bar again and the computer would recalculate our ground

Epson HX-20, a computer ahead of its time.

speed from the last time the space bar was hit. The Epson sat on the lap of my observer, Ernie, where we could both see the screen. Navigation became mindless, and I was happy as a clam at high tide. Ernie thought it was the greatest. He really liked knowing where we were.

Years later, in the late 1990's, when GPS became available with receivers that could send position data to a computer, I wrote a program that displayed a moving map in the cockpit. The transect lines were on the screen. The pilot could easily watch and keep himself flying along the transect. Segment transitions were as simple as looking at the screen. A GPS location was saved onto the computer whenever the observer made a voice recording with the microphone. The GPS locations and the voice recordings were linked together. From then on, all survey crews in North America used my program and the data was no longer just attached to a segment, but rather was attached to a specific location on the ground. This program, with its updates, is still in use by U.S. Fish and Wildlife Service today.

While I was flying in Manitoba that spring, wildfires broke out and there was a lot of smoke in the air, reducing visibility to only a few miles. In Alaska I was able to deal with some smoke and still fly. But this was not the case in the prairies. I was flying where antennas reached almost 1500 feet in altitude and their guy-wires stretched a quarter mile away from their base in four directions. Massive power lines also skipped across the landscape at 200 feet elevation. It would be dangerous to fly at 100 feet with 2 miles of visibility in smoke.

Two weeks later and two days lost to smoke, we finished the prairie habitat. For our next transects, we moved on to Ontario, which was similar to Alaska in that it was wild and undeveloped. It lacked mountains, but small lakes were everywhere. So were rocks. I would drop the plane a couple of hundred feet into a small cut in the rocks, hope to see a black duck, add power, and climb over the next rocky rise to descend again. And so it seemed to go, all day long.

Ducks were few and far between. On the third day I found myself 130 miles from O'Sullivan Lake, our home base, or any other place I could see on the map to spend the night. Wicked thunderstorms were all around me. Rather than struggle with dangerous winds, hail and lightning, I took a look at a nearby village called Lansdowne House. It was on a good-sized lake and there was a beach with a church on the hill above it. I decided to land. I taxied to the beach and secured the plane with an anchor. Ernie and I sat in the plane until the heavy rain stopped. Then we walked up the hill to the Catholic mission.

We cautiously entered through a large wooden door. There was a priest watching television. I recognized the cartoon from my childhood. It was an episode of the *Flintstones* and the priest was quite engrossed in it. He took notice of us and gave us a cordial welcome. He introduced himself as Father Maurice Quimet. He looked to be about 70 years old and had a thick French accent. He was clearly embarrassed that he was watching TV when we arrived. He quickly explained to us that the mission did not have TV until three months prior. I suppose he was just catching up with the rest of us, starting with the cartoons. He had been at the mission for almost 50 years. He told us how he used to travel several thousand miles every winter to be a minister for the native villages of northern Ontario. Prior to snow machines, introduced to the region in 1959, he travelled those miles by dog sled.

Father Quimet said we could spend the night with him and he appeared pleased to have someone to talk to, although he was melancholy about the situation at his mission. He was disappointed with his flock. The Indians (Ojibwa) had recently told him that they were going to move to a new town site 6 miles away, because the fishing would be better there and firewood would be more abundant. Father Quimet just couldn't understand why they would move. He had built a saw mill for them and now they were leaving. This was upsetting to him, after having dedicated his entire life to helping them.

We were still conversing with Father Quimet when the church door swung open and four young Indian boys burst in, all talking at once. The loudest was yelling, "He did it. He did it. He did it!" pointing his finger towards the lake. "He stole the cookies." This wasn't making much sense to me, but the boys motioned, indicating that they wanted Ernie and me to follow them. They led us down the hill to our plane. On the beach I saw several Ritz crackers on the ground. I looked at the plane and saw that the left rear window was broken. It was now clear that the "cookies" were the box of Ritz crackers, and one of the kids had broken our window to steal them.

We walked back up to the mission and told Father Quimet what had happened. His face took on a deep sadness. He was embarrassed, again. I could tell that he took this personally, as if his own child had been responsible. He apologized. He was a courageous man who had survived many decades of wilderness travel and devotion to his chosen people. It was all coming undone. I felt great sympathy for him. Ernie volunteered to sleep in the plane that night. That was a very nice offer and allowed me to get a good night's rest in the mission.

The next morning Ernie was in reasonably good spirits, but I am sure it must have been difficult sleeping in the copilot's seat. We returned to civilization that afternoon, and the rest of our survey went smoothly. The duct tape I had used to cover the window held up. There was a reason pilots called it "hundred mile an hour tape."

Chapter 7 - Russia Thaws
1991

Our historic first flight in Siberia at low level occurred in 1992. My involvement in the ground work for that event began the year before, in 1991. By then, the collapse of the Soviet Union had been underway for several years. The military had lost most of its clout. The government was in a state of chaos. The cold war was rapidly thawing and with that, the relationship between our countries was improving. The U.S. Fish and Wildlife Service saw an opportunity to finally conduct low altitude wildlife surveys in Siberia with our own aircraft. The first attempt in 1990 had failed. The military squashed it. So in 1991 the strategy shifted to one of starting modestly, by trying to do the surveys with Russian aircraft. A contingent of three American biologists was sent to the region to establish rapport with organizations, conduct surveys with Russian aircraft, and determine whether it appeared reasonable to subsequently attempt to bring our own aircraft across to Siberia.

Bill Eldridge and I, both from Alaska, were tapped for the challenge. Rich Maleki was selected from Cornell University. He was an expert on aerial surveys of arctic waterfowl. He was keen on getting an aerial census of pacific brant, white-fronted geese and emperor geese, and also banding geese if possible. Rich ended up being very disappointed with the outcome of his trip. Bill and I were less disappointed because we knew that we were seeking a much bigger prize. We had our sights on getting our own plane to Russia the following year. We were both in the middle of our careers as wildlife survey biologists in Alaska. Bill was particularly valuable because he was seasoned at working in foreign countries and had an innate instinct for measuring officials, identifying the key people, recognizing problems and coming up with solutions. He had conducted his graduate research in Chile. He had worked extensively in Mexico on cooperative government projects, often involving research students. He later would become involved with many different wildlife conservation efforts in various parts of Africa. He was a good choice as a biologist to send to Russia, to figure out if cooperative surveys with American aircraft were potentially feasible.

Bill was told to take a seasonal employee along as a helper. Bill refused. He called me instead, because I was one of two biologist/wildlife pilots flying the only single engine, Department of Interior, turbine aircraft in Alaska. A turbine powered plane was necessary because aviation fuel for piston aircraft was rarely available in Russia, while jet fuel was universally available. I had flown surveys throughout Alaska and many parts of Canada. I knew how to deal with weather challenges in remote and unpopulated areas. I could assess the feasibility of bringing our specially modified turbine Beaver to Russia. I told Bill to count me in.

We expected to fly waterfowl surveys with Russian helicopters out of Anadyr, paid for by the Russians. That idea would get stymied at every turn. We had learned only a month earlier that a Japanese contingent would be involved with the Russian biologists in Anadyr at the same time we were there. The Japanese wanted to photograph the banding of geese, since some of these species wintered in Japan after nesting in Siberia. They were enamored with Siberia, and of course were equally enamored with photography. They came with ample money and willingness to give it to the Russian field projects. The Russian biologists were really strapped for money and as a result, we frequently found ourselves having to take a back seat to the Japanese.

In that same year, 1991, *Alaska Airlines* opened the first commercial flights to Siberia from North America. The two Russian cities they serviced were Magadan at the north end of the Sea of Okhotsk, and Khabarovsk adjacent to China near the south end of the Sea of Okhotsk. On July 11, Bill and I and Rich boarded the *Alaska Airlines* non-stop flight to Magadan from Anchorage. Had this flight not been available, we would have been on a multiday flight in the other direction, all the way around the world through Europe and Moscow.

There was an air of excitement on board the plane. Even the captain was in a good mood. As we approached Magadan he announced on the intercom, "We will be landing in 15 minutes. I want to warn you that the landing will be much bumpier than you are accustomed to. It is not the pilot's fault. It is not even the copilot's fault. It is the asphalt."

Our ultimate destination was Anadyr, a small town approximately 1,000 miles northeast of Magadan, and 1,000 miles back towards Alaska. That flight would occur a few days later, after the Japanese contingent arrived. In the meantime we were each given a room in a hotel. One night at about 2:00am the phone rang in my room. I stumbled out of bed and answered it. A woman was on the other end yelling at me, ranting about something, obviously very upset with me. I couldn't understand any of her Russian barrage. She went on and on. I finally just hung up, a little bit scared because someone in Russia was so mad at me. I didn't know if she was a prostitute, upset that I was not responding, or maybe a woman who thought I was someone else. Nothing further came of that mysterious, intimidating phone call.

During the wait in Magadan I took the opportunity to walk the streets of the city. At a fairly large store front, I saw three baby carriages parked outside the store with babies in them and no mothers in sight. I thought how this would never occur in a large city in America. Little did I know that crime would soon explode in Russia in response to the new freedoms of Perestroika. Three years later, on a survey flight across Siberia, I would be fearful of anyone knowing that I had $18,000 U.S. cash with me to pay for fuel and other fees. People were being murdered in Russia for much less American money than that.

On these walks, I was dressed in drab clothes. In particular, I wore a brown wool sports jacket. It just so happened that I blended in with many of the Russian males in the city. Often I had people come up to me and talk to me in Russian. They seemed to be unable to comprehend that I couldn't talk to them in their native tongue. It is very likely that they had never met anyone in their lifetime that couldn't speak Russian. They were baffled by me.

Finally, on July 14 we boarded an Aeroflot jet from Magadan to Anadyr, a two-and-a-half hour journey. It reminded me more of a bus than an airplane. All manner of people boarded. Numerous folks had their feet propped up on boxes between the seats. There was no rule that items had to fit under the seat in front of you. Part way through the flight, a stewardess came through and served juice. It was a large glass pitcher with a few pieces of cooked fruit inside. The fruit gave the water a little bit of flavor. The whole atmosphere was very informal.

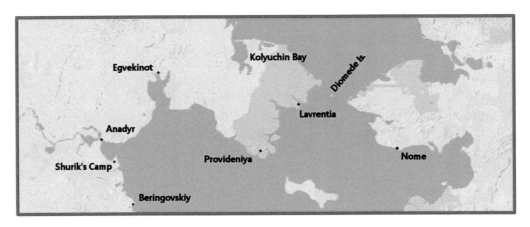

From the Anadyr airport, a small ferry took us across the three-mile-wide channel to the opposite shore, the town of Anadyr. This was a modest town of maybe 15,000 people, the administrative center and transportation hub of the Chukotka Region. The community sat right where the beautiful Anadyr River connects to a small bay. When we disembarked from the ferry we could see a man pulling a little gillnet onto the beach with a half dozen entangled pink salmon. The scene reminded me of Alaska.

What we saw and didn't see in the city was shocking. Large cement buildings lined the streets. There was little indication that people used them. There were no signs, no plants, no grass, not even trash. It was stark and mostly deserted. The sighting of a car was rare – a green military truck was more likely. People walked. We actually didn't see very many people, considering all of the large buildings. The experience was surreal, as if some disaster had befallen this city. Later, we would step inside a few stores and see almost nothing on the shelves. Where did people get food to eat? Clearly the breakup of the Soviet Union was having an adverse impact on eastern Siberia.

The author on a street in the city of Anadyr in 1991.

I would come to learn that what I was seeing in Anadyr was typical of many cities in Siberia. And we were to see more examples on our travels in the next few years.

At the height of Soviet power, the party leaders in Moscow developed a grand scheme. They would show how the mighty communist machine could tame the boundless Siberian expanse. Their investment in this project was huge, occurring over several decades from the mid 1950's through the 1970's. Many cities were built from scratch and often industries were born alongside the cities.

Clifford Gaddy and Fiona Hill 2003 (Senior Fellows, Brookings Institution) described this ambition as follows:

> "Cities were an important feature of the plans for a Siberian industrial utopia. Cities were developed in Siberia in tandem with industries to provide a fixed reserve of labor for factories, mines, and oil and gas fields. In many respects, however, the cities were not really cities. Rather than being genuine social and economic entities, they were physical collection points, repositories, and supply centers—utilitarian in the extreme. They were built to suit the needs of industry and the state, rather than the needs of people. Indeed, primary responsibility for planning and constructing city infrastructure fell to the Soviet economic ministry in charge of the enterprise

the city was designed to serve. Few responsibilities were assigned to the municipal governments."[1]

Anadyr was perhaps an extreme example. It was the center of the Chukotka National Region, but more importantly, it was tantalizingly close to capitalist America. Settling the Far East would also help deter aggression from foreign entities. Gaddy and Hill explain the disintegration of the plan:

> "By the 1980s the massive investments in Siberia and the Far East were offering extremely low returns. Many huge construction projects were left incomplete or postponed indefinitely. At first, the troubles were blamed on disproportional and incoherent planning, ineffective management, and poor coordination. But by the reformist era of the late 1980s under Mikhail Gorbachev, the problem was seen to be Siberia itself as well as the efforts to develop it. By 1989 the industrialization of Siberia was beginning to seem a monumental mistake. The Siberian enterprise was, in any case, brought to a screeching halt by the collapse of the Soviet Union."[2]

A reverse migration of people back to their homes of origin must have occurred before I arrived in Anadyr in 1991 and saw a mostly deserted city.

We were soon introduced to an extremely enthusiastic Russian biologist named Alexander (Shurik) Kondratyev. He was small and compact, extremely fit and trim. Also striking was his exuberant and joyous exclamations of happiness to be meeting American scientists. Bill and I did not consider ourselves distinguished American scientists, so the situation felt somewhat awkward. I didn't want Shurik to be disappointed should he ever learn that I was not a prominent research scientist at a famous university. Meeting us truly seemed to be a momentous event for him.

Shurik told us that he had trouble getting to Anadyr from his field camp to meet us. He was scheduled to have been picked up by a chartered fishing boat two days earlier, the boat never showed up. As a result, he started hiking across the tundra. He wasn't going to miss this incredible opportunity to be in Anadyr when the American scientists arrived. The distance was 60 miles, which he walked in 30 hours, swimming a few creeks along the way. It was mid-summer when darkness was never complete.

We thought we would be working out of Anadyr and its nearby airport, but we learned that different plans had been made for us. We were also told our Russian hosts had no money for helicopter time. Furthermore, we would be shipped out to Shurik's field camp for the duration of our trip. We knew it would be difficult to arrange and conduct aerial surveys from the field camp. Bill went into diplomatic

---

[1] Gaddy, C.G. and Hill F. September 2003. The Siberian Curse: Does Russia's Geography Doom Its Chances for Economic Reform?. Brookings Review.

discussion mode and convinced Shurik to talk to Dr. Andreev, the man who was responsible for setting up our biological mission. We had planned to visit the field camp for only a short stay.

We had also been given to understand that the camp had two cabins. As we would soon learn, it was a good thing Bill had insisted we bring a survival tent in our luggage.

The next day our hosts relented under Bill's pressure and successfully arranged for 16 hours of helicopter time. This was a very limited amount of time, but enough to get us into the air and evaluate the helicopter, the pilots, and the logistics of aerial work. The aerial survey effort would not happen until Dr. Andreev arrived four days later.

On July 16, we were flown by helicopter to the camp. The helicopter was very large. It had no problem carrying the three crew members, the nine of us and our gear. The crew included a navigator by the name of Victor Shlyaev. Bill and I were impressed with this young man from the moment we met him. We took every opportunity to ask him how aviation worked in Russia and what he thought of the idea of bringing one of our planes to Chukotka. He spoke good English and warmed quickly to the idea of an American plane. He also explained the potential obstacles. He said that he might be able to help us next year. He struck Bill and me as a very good contact, extremely interested in seeing that our efforts succeeded. We could work with people like Victor.

Once at Shurik's camp, we were struck by its disheveled state. One of the so called cabins was a tiny, beat up trailer. It could sleep only Shurik and his assistant, Andre. The other structure was simply a rusted metal shipping container, suitable only for storage of gear. Bill, Rich and I had no option but to cram into our two man survival tent. Fortunately for us, it had mosquito netting.

The Japanese had not brought a tent from home. They were given an old heavy canvas surplus military tent with no floor and no netting. I can only imagine the misery they must have been subjected to with the fierce mosquito population. In the evenings, when it was time to go to bed, the three of us gathered at the entrance to our tent. One person would quickly unzip the tent and immediately another person would dive in through the opening. Instantly, the zipper monitor would close the zipper. This was repeated for all three of us. Once inside, we went to work killing the 20 or so mosquitos that managed to sneak in with us.

The only communication available in the camp was a Single Sideband (SSB) radio. To use it, Shurik's assistant, Andre, went outside the trailer, sat on the hand crank electric generator machine and twirled the handles, like an upside down bike powered by his arms. All the while he would monitor the voltage meter in front of him. When Shurik, inside the trailer, keyed his microphone to talk, the radio needed a lot of electrical power. Andre would have to grind hard on the machine to keep the voltage up. In this way, contact was made sporadically with Anadyr. It was apparent we may not be able to arrange for our helicopter surveys from this place.

Shurik's "camp" and our waterfowl "survey aircraft".

The next two days were spent at the camp with no chance for aerial work. I was trying to make the most of this interesting experience, even if our aerial survey objectives were in jeopardy. Shurik was so pleased to have us. He seemed to feel very important and was excited to show us his study area. The weather was warm and sunny, and the air was full of mosquitoes. Shurik told us all about his waterfowl ecology and habitat use studies and guided us and the Japanese on a hike to see some of his geese. The tundra can be difficult to walk across with its tall tussocks. As fit and well adapted Shurik was to this environment, several of the Japanese men were equally and remarkably unfit. After a couple of hours, one of them began to stagger and falter. I suspected he may be diabetic and hypoglycemic. If so, we needed to get some sugar into him. A month later, Shoji Okinaga wrote about this incident in a letter to our colleague, Dr. Dirk Derksen:

> "All four of the Japanese crew who visited Anadyr River basin are very grateful to the Americans; Bill, Jack and Rich. We cannot thank them enough for their kindness especially about the two occurrences. First; our main objectives for this trip to the Anadyr lowlands were to take part in banding projects for the geese. But we could not carry this out because the goslings were too small to be caught in late July. Our mistake apparently came from lack of information about the ecology of Russian waterfowl. But Bill kindly invited us to an aerial survey of migratory waterfowl that inhabit the Anadyr River area. If it had not been for them, all we could have done was to eat, to sleep and to donate our blood to noisy mosquitoes! Thanks to them, we had a narrow escape from a no-yield trip. Second; on the next day after our arrival at the field camp, we took a short trip to observe a molting family of bean goose by foot. We succeeded in finding two flocks of white-fronted family and non-breeders of bean geese. But on our way home, two of our members became too tired to walk, and another person fell into

48

hypoglycemia with the symptom of strong sleep. Jack kindly came back to us to know what happened, and then Rich brought some sweets for us from our field camp. We appreciate their kindness which saved us from appearing on the Russian news station. Me? I was O.K. because I trained myself on the Yukon-Kuskokwim Delta in 1983. But the accident taught me that walking on open tundra consumes more energy than I expected. Please give my kindest regards to the members of the American aerial survey team."

On July 19, Dr. Andreev arrived at the camp along with his wife, Kira, and daughter Dasha. After considerable discussion we agreed that we must take advantage of the helicopter that brought them and fly a survey. Eleven people piled on board for the

Andre lying across the internal fuel tank searching for waterfowl.

survey flight; two pilots, three Americans, four Japanese and two Russians. Only the pilots wore seat belts. The rest of us bounced around as we pleased. The circular windows worked reasonably well. Andre draped himself over the huge internal fuel tank. I sat up front between the two pilots. I was responsible for directing the flight path. I used hand signals to indicate my wishes, since the pilot did not speak English. This was a reconnaissance effort, where our goal was to pick the best looking habitats, rivers, ponds and lakes, and maximize our chances of seeing waterfowl in the least amount of time. The survey was successful. The Japanese were busy filming the habitat. The pilot held the 100 foot altitude well, and the birds didn't seem unduly freaked out by the machine.

When fuel was getting low, the pilot indicated with hand signals that we would be heading to a refueling location. I nodded. Then things got interesting.

The pilot decided to either impress me, or intimidate me, or both. The terrain was gently undulating with occasional rises. The tundra vegetation was no higher than a foot or two above the ground. The pilot was almost scraping the tops of the grass with the landing gear, traveling at 140mph. We were hugging the ground with a mere three foot clearance. I was scared. It looked to me like one tiny mistake and we would clip the top of a rise. Several times the pilot turned his head to look at me.

I believe he was hoping to see fear or admiration. I was determined to show no sign of emotion whatsoever. I stoically looked ahead, trying to appear nonchalant. I pretended this was nothing special. As an airplane pilot and a glider pilot, I was capable of judging our height above the ground, and our clearance was no more than two or three feet for 15 miles. By any standards, this was unnecessary exposure to danger.

Emperor Goose and Black Brant.

We surveyed until 7:30 in the evening. At least we now had one day of survey data in the bank. It was not a total count of the coastal area between the Avtatuul River and Beringovskiy (150 miles to the south), but more of a reconnaissance. That day, we counted 19,000 greater scaup, 1600 white-fronted geese, 1400 emperor geese, 350 brant, 1000 common eiders, 500 northern pintails, 400 Eurasian wigeon, 3 white-tailed eagles, 130 sandhill cranes and 8 swans. The swans were tundra swans – the same species we have in Alaska. Shurik told us the whooper swan was rare but present here.

While we were flying, a private commercial fishing boat had arrived in camp. This boat was supposed to arrive the previous day to take us on a tour of the lower river. They had run aground on a sandbar and were forced to spend the night there until the tide refloated them. At least they had a gill net with them and were able to net some pink salmon for us. We were all happy to have fresh fish, and it tasted good.

The next morning, we were supposed to fly another survey. So we eagerly packed our gear and then sat on the riverbank to wait. Hours passed and still no helicopter showed up. Reluctantly, after lunch we climbed on board the fishing boat and headed down river to the coast. No sooner had we pushed away from shore when we heard the helicopter approaching. It was late in the day – already 2:30pm – but we abandoned the boat trip for the helicopter. We were only able to fly an abbreviated portion of the inland area and the helicopter had too little fuel to do a very good job of it.

Upon returning to camp, we noticed in the distance that another group was camping about 4 miles away. We were told that it was a reindeer herders' camp. With a spotting scope I could see their orange yurt, and what looked like fish drying on a wooden rack. I couldn't see the reindeer herd.

The following day the helicopter didn't show up in the morning as had been promised. My curiosity about the reindeer herders was strong. By early afternoon, I couldn't resist any longer. I headed off alone across the tundra to meet these people. I had no idea what kind of reception I would get. After trudging a couple of miles, I began to see the reindeer, spread out across the tundra. Not far from the near edge of the herd were two people sitting on a rise overlooking the deer. They were facing away from me. I altered course so that they would see me as I got closer. They remained seated while I approached them. One was a middle aged native man, the other a native woman, possibly his wife. She looked very much like an Alaskan Yup'ik Eskimo. They nodded, and I nodded. They turned their gaze back to the reindeer. Not knowing anything else to do, and being very certain they didn't speak English, I just sat down on the tundra next to them. We sat like that for about 10 minutes, without a word spoken. I reached into my pocket, pulled out a small tin with little candies inside, opened it and offered the tin to them. They each took a piece. Then we sat some more, in silence. After about 15 more minutes, the man and woman stood up, so I stood up. He pointed to the reindeer herders' camp and I nodded. We started walking together.

Chukchi couple offers to take me to their camp. Reindeer are in the background.

There were perhaps 2000 reindeer scattered over several miles of tundra. Reindeer sauntered out of our way as we passed through. They looked like caribou, but were smaller and most were very dark brown. I wondered how the herders could maintain control of these animals on the open tundra.

They led me on to the camp. Roughly a dozen people materialized. Some may have been in the yurt, others may have been out on the tundra. They were native Chukchi; women, men and children. At some distance stood two Caucasian teenagers and one Caucasian man. Four smaller tents accompanied the large yurt. A fire was burning. Over the fire, three poles formed a tripod from which a pot was suspended. Fish were hanging to dry on a rack was just outside the camp. Four smallish dogs showed mostly indifference to me, either lying down or just watching. A woman near the fire motioned towards a wooden box which had cups, squares of sugar, a container of tea bags and hardtack biscuits. I accepted a cup of tea and said thank you. She smiled. In the pot, reindeer meat was simmering. Presently I was offered a plate of rice with meat and broth. It was very tasty. I was the only one eating, but several of them were having tea with me. I offered them bubble gum which pleased them very much.

I told them that I came from Alaska. They didn't act as if they understood. Soon, though, a handsome woman, wearing large glasses, disappeared into the yurt and came back to the fire with a little pocket atlas. I found a map that showed our region of the world. It was tiny. I pointed to Juneau, and then I pointed to Anadyr, and then I drew a slow arc with my finger from Juneau to Anadyr. Those that could see chattered knowingly. It felt good to be able to show them that I came from a place not too far distant.

These were rugged looking people. They fit the landscape. They appeared comfortable, healthy and happy. I imagined they were probably regarded in fairly high esteem by society, because certainly native and Caucasians alike would cherish reindeer meat, especially when food in stores was mostly absent. Their skills and knowledge were critically important. I found myself puzzled by the white man and the two teenage boys. They kept their distance from me, and the natives. How and why were they associated with this camp and these reindeer, I wondered? They certainly were not in charge. They likely served under direction of the natives.

After receiving their hospitality, I decided to bring out a small present I had brought from Juneau. It was a simple gift that I thought might be very special to someone in Siberia. It was a solar powered calculator, costing only a few dollars in the United States but probably of incalculable value in eastern Siberia in 1991. I chose to give it to the woman with the glasses since she seemed likely to have had the most education. I pulled it out of my pack and handed it to her. The others gathered around to see it too. She pushed a few keys and said the first English words I had heard, "OK".

Solar powered calculator draws great excitement.

She was so appreciative. Everyone was smiling, sharing her happiness. After satisfying herself how well it worked, she went off again to the yurt. When she came back she was pleased to be able to extend a gift to me. It was a little plastic net needle, about 4 inches long, wrapped with light nylon fishing line. Tied to the end of the line was a nail that had been fashioned into a homemade fishing hook. This clearly was a jigging setup she used for ice fishing in the winter time. I was honored to receive it and I hoped my expression conveyed that.

Not far away, I was surprised to see an object that didn't belong in this scene. It was a huge military style track vehicle, like an armored tank. But there was no cannon. It presumably was designed to carry people and equipment. These reindeer herders apparently didn't move their camp using reindeer and sleds, as I had seen on television. I walked over to it. A Caucasian man, well-tanned, with a beard was standing next to it. I approached him. He seemed proud of his machine. I assumed he was the driver / captain of this monster. He climbed up into the driver's seat and started the engine to impress me with its deep rumble. After he had climbed back down, I decided to give him a present. I reached into my pocket and pulled out my Swiss army knife. I held it out for him to take. He turned his head slightly and opened his palms to me as if to say, "I don't know". I gestured my hand, with the knife in it, again, as if to say "Please, it is for you." He again relayed his reluctance and this time tapped his right hand against the sheathed knife on his belt, as if to say "I have a knife." I still wanted to give him my knife, so I reached out with the knife even farther. He shrugged, then began to unbuckle his belt. He slid his knife off of his belt, and my heart started to sink. He stepped toward me and handed me his herder's knife. I gave him my pocket knife. I felt quite overwhelmed by this exchange.

The boat from our camp, with the rest of our crew onboard, was approaching the river bank. I said good-bye (dos-ve-donya) to the reindeer people and boarded the

The machine used to transport the herders' camp.

boat. We headed downstream on our sightseeing tour to the coast. I told everyone about the reindeer camp and how happy the woman was to receive the calculator. I told them how the man had given me his knife.

Dr. Andreev provided me with the explanation of what I had done. He told me that in the Chukotka region, there is a custom. When one man gives his knife to another man, that man is obligated to give his own knife in return. I felt terrible. I had given him a pocket knife and he had given me his reindeer herder's knife, with its wooden handle and its homemade sheath. Dr. Andreev told me not to be too concerned, that this man will own the only Swiss army knife in the region, and that he could always get another herder's knife. I hoped he was right, but I feared he may be wrong.

On the return trip up the river from the coast, the boat engine quit. The prospect of spending the night on the tundra without gear seemed unpleasantly real. The crew opened up the engine room and discovered that the belt on the alternator had broken. In the meantime, we were drifting back downstream. They rummaged around and managed to find another belt, but it was too big. To my surprise, they decided the solution was to take a hack saw and cut off a corner of the engine, so that the alternator could be rotated enough to tighten the belt. There was a lot of metal to cut through and it took them close to an hour to accomplish the alteration of the engine. The plan worked and we finally got under way again. It was 12:45am by the time the boat nudged into the bank at our camp.

Two more days passed, and it became apparent that there would be no more helicopter surveys. Rich and I decided to walk to the reindeer camp. He wanted to meet the herders and take pictures. Their camp had been moved to within a mile of our camp. The reindeer cannot be held in one place for more than a couple of days. They want to keep advancing across the tundra, pushed by their constant instinct to move. We were well received, as I had been before.

After an hour of visiting, Rich and I started walking back to camp and had covered about a half mile when we heard a shout behind us. Turning to look, we saw one of the Caucasian teenage boys running our way. When he reached us, he began to talk in Russian, but we had no idea what he was saying. So I pulled out my pocket English/Russian dictionary. He opened it and found his word. I read the English word, "meat". It seemed that he was asking me if we wanted meat. I said "da". And I also said "malinki", which I thought meant "little bit". He didn't seem to understand me. I looked up the English word for "small". He then opened the book and found his word. Next to it was written in English "whole". I said "Nyet, Nyet". He then began looking for another word and showed it to me, "half". I decided I better accept this offer, and we turned back to their camp.

Our messenger passed along our agreement. People started moving, but very casually, imperceptibly. Rich and I didn't even realize that something was happening, it was so subtle. Then we began to see the plan. Everyone in camp, except the children, had quietly surrounded a group of about 200 reindeer and isolated them from the rest. The humans were evenly spaced apart in a large circle encompassing the deer. The deer were calm at first, but became agitated as the human circle slowly contracted in size. The clan leader entered the circle and made his way to the center. His presence repelled the deer from the center of the circle, and the humans on the perimeter kept them from leaving the circle.

The deer began to run, as one endless circular herd. Around and around they ran, 200 strong but unable to run away. The leader formed a small loop with his lariat. Later, I saw that the lariat was beautifully braided from leather strips. The slip knot was formed from a bone, a reindeer vertebrae, cleverly attached to the end of the braided line. He began swinging the loop and placing himself closer to the stream of running deer. Most of the deer had antlers, the biggest belonging to the large bulls. When he threw his loop, I am sure he had chosen a large bull from the frantic herd. The noose closed on the antler. The humans opened a gap in their circle and the rest of the deer ran off. One animal was left, defiantly straining at the lariat. The two Caucasian boys helped hold the animal until the leader could grab an antler with his left hand. In his right, he held the knife. He poised for the thrust – for just the right moment to present itself – when he would be sure of his mark. The motion was quick and the knife found the deer's heart through the rib cage. The animal struggled for only a few moments before it became weak and unsteady. It fell to the ground. It was dead.

The fatal thrust is made with a knife.

Two women approached the deer. The men backed away. Each woman held a large knife. One of them went to the head of the deer holding the blade of her knife in her right hand, the handle away from her. She bent over and positioned the handle close to the animal's head and solemnly swung it three times. I could tell it was a ritual of respect. Then one woman began skinning the front legs, the other the hind legs.

Within minutes, the hide was removed, even from the head. The carcass lay upon it. The body cavity was opened and the entrails removed. The small intestine was given special treatment. It was carefully laid out upon the tundra in a dozen adjacent rows, three feet long. The intestine looped back and forth. One swipe of the knife cut the loops off of one end of every row. Another swipe cut the loops off of the other end. What was left was a dozen segments of intestine, each three feet long. With her thumb and forefinger squeezed on a segment, she slid her fingers the length of the segment, purging its contents out onto the ground in one motion. This was done for all segments. Certainly these would be used for sausage casings.

The camp leader with his lariat. I surmised they were brother and sister.

Then the top rib cage was removed. Blood had pooled within the inside of the lower rib cage. Each of the organs was in turn washed in this basin of blood; the liver, the heart and the kidneys. The heart had been cut in half lengthwise to drain the blood. The wide tendon covering the long muscle next to the back bone was carefully removed. The woman held up the three foot long strap of tendon and made sewing motions with her other hand, indicating to Rich and I that sinew thread would be made from the tendon. Having grown up in the suburbs of Washington D.C. and marveling at the American plains Indians and their interrelationship with the buffalo, this was as close as I would ever get to such a scene in my lifetime. There was obvious respect for all parts of the animal. They indicated they would bring the half carcass to our camp, which they did. We thanked them. I felt humbled by their open sharing.

Later that day, we saw that the reindeer herders were moving. The tents were gone. The reindeer were getting closer to our camp, with the military vehicle in the rear. It had gear stacked high on the roof. The herd ambled by, not far from our camp. Some of them were even within a few yards of our tent. The herders' leader stopped to talk with Dr. Andreev for quite some time. I asked Andreev to ask the leader why they had the dogs, for I had not seen the dogs doing anything but hanging around the camp. The answer came back through Andreev. The dogs became critically important in August when the mushrooms emerge in the tundra. The reindeer consume the mushrooms and become crazed and unmanageable without the dogs.

The herd had completely moved past our camp and the two men were still talking. Presently one lone reindeer ran close by our camp, but it was running in the opposite direction from the herd. It was completely separated from all of the other reindeer and I was certain it should be a major concern to the leader. The leader seemed not to notice this reindeer and kept on with his conversation. I decided I needed to alert him to the errant reindeer, which I did through Andreev. The leader explained that this was a female. She had become separated from her calf in the confusion of the relocation of the herd. She would return the two miles to the previous location of the herd to look for her calf, and when she was unable to find it, she would catch up to the herd. Again I was amazed by the intimate knowledge these people possessed about the deer which were the lifeblood of their culture.

We had half of a reindeer to deal with. We would not be at the camp much longer and we thought the meat would spoil before Shurik and his assistant could eat it. That was when Shurik showed us his refrigerator. He and Andre had dug a hole into the bank of the river, under the tundra surface. The permanently frozen ground (permafrost) at the rear of the hole provided a perfect refrigerator.

The next day was our last day in camp. The *Aeroflot* helicopter picked us up and carried us to Anadyr. For two more days we tried without success to arrange another survey flight. We were told that tundra fires, medivacs, reindeer camps and too few flight crews prevented our flight. Even Victor Shlyaev, the navigator, whom we had befriended as a key contact for future efforts, couldn't make it happen.

Victor did invite us to his apartment. His family was vacationing in Moscow, so we were not able to meet them. That pleasure would have to wait until the following year. Even though our survey effort was a failure in 1991, it led to our historic flight in 1992, and repeated successes in 1993, 1994 and 1995.

Chapter 8 - The First Thousand Miles
1993

After the successful flights we made out of Anadyr in 1992 in our own aircraft (described in Chapter 1), Bill and I were again able to fly in 1993 with permission from the Russian military. We were also able to secure Victor Shlyaev as navigator. This was the true beginning of our efforts toward our objective, flying comprehensive and systematic surveys of the Arctic coastal zone and river deltas, focusing on numbers of eider ducks but counting mammals and other birds as well. Two of the eider species had exhibited serious declines in recent years in Alaska. These surveys would provide good estimates of wildlife population sizes across the eastern 2000 miles of Siberia. This year, 1993, we would fly the initial 1000 miles, from the east coast of Chukotka to the lowlands west of the Kolyma River.

We connected with Victor in Provideniya and immediately flew on to Anadyr. We were again unable to survey the intervening coastline, this time because of fog. At Anadyr we met our new Russian observer, Dr. Nikolai Poyarkov, an ornithologist who would serve with us the next two years. He turned out to be a perfect fit for our mission. His light weight meant our plane would perform better, and yet he was physically durable and tough mentally. Perhaps most importantly, Nikolai was a good companion, with a warm personality. He worked for the Moscow Ringing Center, the equivalent of our Bird Banding Lab. He proved to be an excellent student of aerial surveys, with keen eyesight and a genuine love of birds.

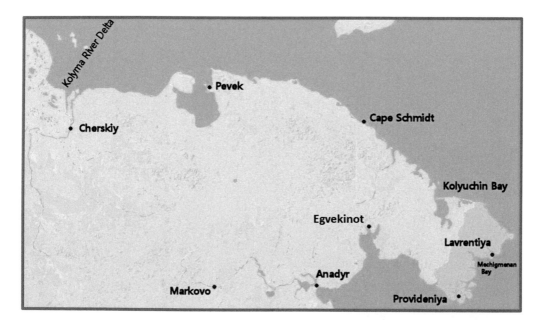

The survey began the next day. We flew to Egvekinot to refuel. From there it was more than 100 miles over fairly rugged mountains, 3000 feet in elevation, to Kolyuchin Bay. Much of Kolyuchin Bay was enshrouded in fog, as it had been the previous year. We surveyed a portion of the south end and then covered the large lagoon east of the bay. Victor was reporting our position every 30 minutes using the SSB radio. He was able to get weather information as well. He informed me that the wind had picked up to 30 knots at Lavrentiya, our intended destination for the night, and it was a crosswind. I decided we better terminate the survey and head for Egvekinot, or even Anadyr, because we had enough fuel. We started back across the mountains. Part way through, the weather became more and more threatening. The mountains were now in the clouds and it was darkening. The wind was tossing us around. Then I started seeing lightning ahead. I was not at all interested in flying through those mountains with thunder storms and lowering conditions. I made a turn to head for Provideniya. Victor got on the radio and asked for the weather at Provideniya. He learned that fog had moved in over the runway there. I was out of options. I was afraid of what we might face in the mountains and thunderstorms to the west. I decided to take my chances with the crosswind at Lavrentiya.

When we got to Lavrentiya, the wind had increased to 35 knots, at a 70 degree angle to the runway. That translated to a crosswind component of 33 knots, which was far more than the operator's manual stated as the maximum allowable crosswind of 15 knots for landing. The runway at Lavrentiya was gravel, not very wide, with some grass on the sides. I decided to attempt to land at about a 30 degree angle to the runway. This gave me very little distance to stop the plane, but I felt that with such a strong wind, my ground speed would be pretty slow (I later calculated it to be 25 knots). The 30 degree angle of my approach favorably changed the angle of the wind to my aircraft to 40 degrees. This gave me a manageable crosswind component (later determined to be 22 knots).

My agency training pilot, Tom Belleau, had explained this technique of landing at an angle to the runway at one of our ground schools. Tom had directed his lecture to the tail wheel pilots, but I absorbed it and thought to myself that I could use it for our amphibious aircraft as well. He told us that after touching down at an angle to the runway, you can initiate a sharp turn to align yourself with the runway. The centrifugal force of the turn makes the plane tip towards the wind, and the wind catching the plane and the wing, pushes the plane in the opposite direction. The forces are compensatory. I often tried to pass along to fellow pilots the merits of landing at an angle across the runway, but most of them were firmly stuck on their training to land on the center line and stay on the center line. This time, at Lavrentiya, it was a good strategy. My ground speed was so slow that the plane stopped just at the grass on the far side of the runway. All was well, and we were down.

The next morning the weather had moderated. It was 300 miles to the next stop at Cape Schmidt, and we had plenty of surveying to do en route. When we reached Kolyuchin Bay, the third time in two years, we were again hampered by fog and unable to complete coverage of the bay. We were able to bypass the fog and continue up the coast in good weather. The coast was straight, flanked by large lagoons and lakes. A zigzag series of transects allowed us to sample all of the coastal waterfowl habitat and still progress nicely towards our destination.

When we reached a point 50 miles from Cape Schmidt, Victor led us a few miles off of our bird surveying transect to the location of the Ben Eielson crash. Victor knew exactly where it was. Carl Ben Eielson is considered the father of aviation in Alaska. He is well known internationally as the pilot of the first plane to fly over the Arctic Ocean. His route was from Barrow, Alaska to Spitzbergen, Norway.

In October of 1929, an American fur trading ship was frozen in the ice off of Cape Schmidt with 16 tons of furs and 15 people on board. Eielson was contracted to fly the furs and the passengers back to Teller, Alaska. That was a distance of 450 miles, at a time of year when daylight was extremely limited. He and his mechanic had made one successful trip from the ship to Alaska. They were attempting to reach the ship again on November 9, but never made it. A massive search ensued, with the use of airplanes and dog sleds. It took 77 days to find the crash site. I am surprised it took so long since the site was just 10 miles inland from the coast. I learned later that Eielson's plane was recovered in 1991, probably because of the fall of the Soviet Union, and that is probably why Victor knew its exact location. Eielson Air Force Base, located just outside of Fairbanks, was named in honor of Ben Eielson in 1948.

Cape Schmidt on the coast of the Chukchi Sea. Ice hugs the shore.

We continued our surveying to Cape Schmidt. It was a dreary looking community from the air: gray, dirty and haphazard. We made history. We were the first foreign airplane to land there since World War II. After securing the plane, we walked into town but could not find any place to get dinner and had to settle for a pub. The best they could do for us was to sell us French wine and snickers bars. Victor told us that snickers bars were abundant everywhere in Siberia.

It started snowing that night, June 22nd. The next morning was cold. The propeller on N754 was gear driven from the Garrett engine. That meant it took a large amount of electricity to get the engine up to operating speed, especially when the gear oil was cold. Whenever the temperature was below 40 degrees, our policy was to preheat it. Here we had no means to preheat it. If the batteries could not get the propeller up to a fast enough rotation speed, the engine would get stuck at a low RPM. If the pilot tried to add more fuel, it would simply cause a rapid rise in the internal temperature of the engine to a critically high level and beyond. Exceeding the temperature limit would burn up the engine. This predicament was called a hung start. If we had a hung start, I would have to shut down the engine and let it cool down. At that point, I likely would not have enough battery power left to start the engine. We would be in a real bind without a way to recharge the batteries at Cape Schmidt.

I thought I could help avoid that scenario by having Bill hand turn the propeller up to about 30 RPM before I kicked in the starter. That would save the batteries from having to accelerate the propeller from a dead stop. I had never done this before, nor had I heard of anyone doing it. I asked Bill, and he agreed to do it. He was getting the propeller moving as fast as he could. Then I hit the start button. I expected that Bill would hear the starter engage and know that I was spooling up the engine. He didn't hear it and it scared him as he tried to catch the propeller while it was accelerating. Luckily, he realized soon enough to stop his efforts, before having his arm hit by the spinning propeller. He was very upset with me, and let me know in fierce fashion that I should have yelled out the window when I hit the starter. He was absolutely right, I shouldn't have assumed anything. He was uninjured and the engine started without reaching a critical temperature.

We were pleased with the good visibility and light winds along the coast to Pevek. The runway at Pevek was excellent. We landed to refuel and learned that we were the third foreign aircraft to land there since World War II. The airport was apparently abuzz when everyone learned that an American aircraft was approaching to land. Unfortunately, they were expecting a large passenger or cargo jet. I guess we were a considerable disappointment. We took off right away to finish surveying the habitats around Chaun Bay and returned to Pevek for the night.

The next morning Victor went for his weather briefing and medical check, as always. The medical checks were mandatory for all Russian crew members. Victor didn't explain to us the details of the medical checks. He did imply that the Russian officials wanted to know if the crewmember was under the influence of alcohol. I suspect that was the main reason for the medical exam. I was never required to have medical exams.

63

Victor received his weather briefing and relayed it to me. He explained to me that he didn't always trust the weather forecast. I told him it was the same in America. He explained that in Russia there was a saying, "They pulled it from the ceiling." I smiled and told him that we have almost the same saying in America. We say, "They pulled it out of thin air."

We lifted off the runway into another nice day. Pevek had felt refreshingly pleasant compared to Cape Schmidt. A large measure of pride was evident at Pevek. The folks that lived in this particular spot on the edge of the continent seem to enjoy a reasonable outlook on life. This was probably not the case 40 years earlier for the political and criminal prisoners that were used as workers in the nearby uranium mines.

Our next destination was the Kolyma River Delta. We were anxious to see it. It would be our first real exposure to one of the many grand rivers that flow north into the Arctic Ocean and drain vast regions of interior Siberia. We believed those river deltas would have the best chance of holding large numbers of eiders and other waterfowl, and we hoped we wouldn't be disappointed. Just before reaching the delta, we were given a rare treat. We sighted a pair of Siberian white cranes. We had not been certain we would even get a chance to see one. They were exceedingly rare, only numbering about 3,000 individuals in the wild. Almost all of them spent the winter in the Poyang Lake basin in China. They were pure white, with jet black wing tips. Their seven foot wing span and slow methodical strokes made them a beautiful bird to watch in flight. We were looking down on them as they floated across the tundra. Few of them had been documented on their Siberian breeding grounds. Nicholai was about to jump out of his skin.

Clockwise; Spectacled Eider, Steller's Eider, King Eider, Common Eider.

All of our observations and species identifications were made without the aid of binoculars or cameras. I was responsible for the sightings on my side of the plane and Bill counted on the right side. We each observed and recorded the birds we saw out to 200 meters (220 yards), making our survey swath 400 meters (1/4 mile in width). Our altitude above the ground was 100 feet. Most of the areas we surveyed were extensive in size and required that we sample the habitat with parallel lines. It would be like someone sampling a baseball field with a lawn mower, and crossing the field once every 25 feet. What we would see on our ¼ mile strip would then be expanded and apportioned to the entire area. We assumed that the birds we saw on our strips were representative of what we would have seen between our strips.

From Chaun Bay we headed for Cherskiy. Cherskiy was a small town located right on the Kolyma River, about 60 miles from the sea and just where the river begins to expand into its broad delta. The Sakha Region is the largest subnational governed area in the world, and is drained by four great rivers that flow north. The Kolyma River is one. The others are the Indigirka, Yana and Lena rivers. We would have to wait until the next year to study the other three rivers. We were keen to systematically evaluate the waterfowl of this area in the coming days.

In 1821, Ferdinand von Wrangel noted the effect of humans on the waterfowl of the Kolyma River delta:

> "The chase of the birds does not begin until they are molting and unable to fly, when a great number of the fishermen leave the rivers and go to their breeding areas. They employ trained dogs to pursue them, and kill great numbers with guns, arrows and sticks. This chase is much less productive than it was formerly. Twenty years ago several thousand geese were sometimes thus taken in a single day; whereas now it is called a good season when 1000 geese, 5000 ducks and 200 swans are killed at the mouth of the Kolyma River."

I wondered how these populations had been treated in the last 170 years since Wrangel was there. What was left? We would try to find out.

A crowd of interested people drawn to the floats of N754 at Cherskiy.

We landed at Cherskiy in beautiful weather. Our parked plane, perched high on top of two speed boat hulls, was again a curiosity. We would spend the next three nights at Cherskiy and fly every day in good weather. But the next morning I noticed that our left front tire was flat. We carried a spare inner tube for the front gear tire and one for the main gear tire. I had seen these front tires taken apart by our mechanics in Alaska and I figured I could do it myself. I had a small bag of tools, and we could borrow tools if necessary. I don't remember how we lifted the front gear off the ground. Maybe we borrowed a jack. There were a couple of *Aeroflot* mechanics that were watching the operation and they had offered to help. I wanted to do it myself, if I could. It went relatively smoothly. I had some tools setting on the top of the float. I noticed the two Russian mechanics had picked up my vice grip and were very carefully inspecting it – turning it this way and that way. I didn't say anything, but I am sure that it was the first vice grip they had ever seen. They were both very friendly, inviting us to share their sauna that evening and to have dinner at one of their apartments. We happily agreed.

The sauna was the first order of business that evening. It was located next to the airport on the beach by the river. Made from a shipping container, it could be slid across the beach on skids to adjust for changing water levels. In winter it probably could be skidded onto the ice. A fire was lit in the wood stove that heated rocks. While the sauna was getting up to temperature, boards were laid out across the gravel to the water's edge so that overheated bodies could run quickly into the river.

66

I was sure I wouldn't be using those boards, as leaping into a cold river was not something I wanted to do to prove I was tough.

The smoked fish had to be cut up. The vodka drinking had to start. Presently another man, not one of our mechanic friends, went out and returned with fresh branches he had cut from a tree or bush. Once the sauna was sufficiently hot, we stripped. There was a platform in the sauna. Each man in turn laid out on this platform, belly side down. Another man, with branches in hand, whacked hard at the prostrate man, starting on the back of the legs and moving up to the neck and back down. This was repeated over and over. I took my turn on the platform. The sensation was sharp, on the very edge of painful. It was just tolerable, kind of like tickling is just tolerable on the bottom of one's feet. The overall experience was strangely enjoyable though. Some of the men ran into the river. We dried off, dressed and felt nicely relaxed.

Dinner at the mechanic's house was filled with lighthearted conversation. Our hosts didn't speak much English, but Victor and Nicholai helped as needed. Vodka continued to flow, before dinner, during dinner and after dinner. Bill and I, Victor and Nicholai, all held back on the vodka. None of us was interested in getting drunk, certainly not as drunk as our Russian friends. They were beginning to behave as one would expect after four hours of imbibing.

Finally, we started to say good-bye and head for our hotel. Our host insisted that he take us for a ride. He was immensely proud of his little car. This was not something we wanted to do, for our own safety. But he was so adamant that we couldn't hurt his feelings, after all of the entertaining he had done for us. We climbed in, three of us. Victor was able to bow out. The ride started out well, but shortly we were on a small dirt road, which pleased us since there were no other cars. Then the road became littered with huge pot holes that might have been fine for a dune buggy – but not for this car. None of us had seat belts. Our drunken driver was going much too fast and we were being violently thrown around in the car. Even with our hands above our heads, we couldn't keep from banging into the ceiling. I was hoping we could get through this without a neck injury and without him flying off the road. Finally the ride came to a successful conclusion. It had been quite a night. Even though it was close to midnight, it was still light outside.

After three days of flying on the Kolyma River Delta and the Cape Krestovskiy area, northwest of the delta, we had flown 1200 miles of transects. Our strips had sampled 6.5 percent of the habitat. The habitat totaled over 6,000 square miles. We estimated the populations at 25,000 spectacled eiders, 12,000 Steller's eiders, 6,000 king eiders and 300 common eiders. We were now west of where the common eiders lived, but we were getting impressive numbers of the other three species of eiders, especially spectacled eiders. This was good news for us. Spectacled eiders were becoming very scarce in Alaska for some unknown reason. Folks back home would be excited, and we would have good reason to come back to Siberia next year and explore further west to the Lena River Delta.

Bill, Russian mechanic (car driver), author, Nicholai, other mechanic.

We would be leaving Cherskiy the next day and flying up a major tributary of the Kolyma River on our way back to Anadyr. We talked about the brutal history of the Kolyma forced-labor camps. The death rate for those exiled to this region of Siberia was 80 percent. I had read that 3 million people died in these camps in the northeastern area of Siberia. Victor told us that there were two unwritten rules among these people, even today. If anyone – stranger, friend or foe – comes to your door asking for shelter for the night, they will never be refused. And if a person sees someone break the law, no matter if it is minor or otherwise, the incident will never be reported to the authorities. I closed my eyes, and I imagined a man that has escaped from a Siberian labor camp, and I understood what Victor had told us.

In the morning, Victor escorted me up to the small, rustic control tower at the airport to pay my bills. Entering the room was like stepping off of a time machine. All of the equipment appeared to be at least forty years old. Several large radar screens were off to the side. They no longer functioned. Old radios were stacked here and there. Victor told me that the government could not afford to maintain the navigation aids in this region, so large aircraft, flying on instruments, could only land here when the weather was clear. An old vacuum cleaner was on the floor, next to a pipe that came vertically out of the floor and then bent to horizontal at waist height. I saw a worker write a note on a piece of paper and put it in a small round container. He stuck the container, with the note, into the pipe. Then he put the vacuum cleaner hose to the pipe and turned on the vacuum cleaner. Apparently the hose was attached to the blowing end rather than the sucking end, because the container shot out of view down the pipe. I looked at Victor, and he said that was how the top floor communicated with the floor below.

A man motioned for me to sit down opposite him at a small table. He showed me the bills, one by one, for all of the fueling, for each landing, for parking overnight, for security overnight and for every kilometer we had flown. I pulled out my pouch of U.S. currency and handed over more than $2,000. Victor had approved all of the paperwork. He was able to convince the man that the 30 cents per kilometer should be based on the kilometers from the airport to our farthest distance from the airport and return. The man never knew that we had flown many more kilometers, close to 1000 kilometers every day, going back and forth, back and forth, on one transect after another.

The six hundred mile trip to Anadyr was smooth, in good weather. We landed at Markovo to refuel. On the other side of the apron was a large dump truck at the rear of a cargo plane. The truck was full of skinned animal carcasses, presumably reindeer. They were being loaded into the plane. The carcasses were completely exposed. I couldn't help but remember our experience with the reindeer herders two years before. And I couldn't imagine seeing meat loaded in this way onto a plane at an airport in the United States.

For the most part, the survey had gone well this year. We hoped we could get one more good year to fully complete our coverage of eastern Siberia.

Chapter 9 - The Second Thousand Miles
1994

Based on our success in 1993, our goal for 1994 was to cover six times as much area. Such an effort would fully document the eiders in eastern Siberia. We didn't realize at the time that our eider numbers would be considered suspect by some of our colleagues back home. They were not prepared for our report of hundreds of thousands of spectacled eiders. The spectacled eiders had declined to a critical level in Alaska, and some biologists thought the same thing must be happening in Russia. Confounding this uncertainty was a perplexing issue with the spectacled eiders. There were no fall and winter counts to give an indication of the world's population, because nobody knew where they went during the non-breeding period. It was a strange mystery in biology. How could hundreds of thousands of birds remain hidden from human beings?

We left Nome on June 20, headed for Provideniya. This time the Bering Sea was full of white caps. The wind at the surface was probably 40 knots. If our engine failed, our chances for survival were slim. We had wanted to leave a week earlier, but N754 was not available. Its first priority was to the Breeding Pair Survey that Bruce Conant flew every year. In the span of 25 days and 100 flight hours, Bruce Conant and Debbie Groves surveyed annually all of the major waterfowl breeding habitats in the state of Alaska south of the Brooks Range. It was a marathon effort that required excellence in piloting, decision making, waterfowl identification, navigating and patience. My survey flights in Siberia were over tundra at 100 foot elevation. Bruce had to fly half of his survey over forested landscapes. That meant the plane was often within 20 feet of the tree tops for hours at a time.

Our starting date was a little late, but luckily the weather along the eastern Siberia coast had recently been cold and the season was a week to ten days late. We picked up Victor in Provideniya, thankful that he was again available and willing to lead us. The first day was a long day of flying for me. I started at Galena, in interior Alaska and ended at Anadyr, Russia. It was 8 hours of flying, and included clearing customs in Provideniya.

I was apprehensive during the customs process, because this time I was hiding something. This trip was going to be extensive, with much more fuel to buy and fees to pay. I was bringing $18,000 U.S. cash with me. Two weeks earlier, in Juneau, I had gone to my bank with a government check made out to me for $18,000. I said I wanted cash. The teller went to the manager who proceeded to tell me that because the amount was over ten thousand dollars, they were legally obligated to record the serial numbers of every bill and commented that it would take quite a while.

U.S. currency would be the only way I could pay my bills in Russia. I hid $9,000 in the airplane. I unscrewed an interior panel and taped a cardboard envelope, with the money, to the inside of the panel and reinstalled the panel. When the customs officials asked to count my money, I handed them $9,000. I didn't want anyone to know I had $18,000. I had read that foreigners were being murdered in Russia for that kind of money. Crime in Russia was exploding. Inflation of the ruble was astronomical. Rubles were worthless as a means of holding money. At the time of my first visit in 1991, we were given 6 rubles for every U.S. dollar. In 1994, the exchange rate per dollar was 4600 rubles.

Bill next to a homemade tundra buggy, powered by a wooden propeller.

The Russian customs officials were always suspicious of our amphibious floats. Questions had started the year before. The officials had just finished inspecting our plane and were walking away from the plane towards the terminal when Bill went to retrieve some of our food in one of the float compartments, which had covers that could be unscrewed. After they saw that the floats could be opened, the officials immediately returned to the plane and carefully searched each of the four compartments. Every time we cleared customs after that, they made sure to inspect the float compartments. The $9,000 hidden inside of an interior panel were not discovered. I knew I would have to hide receipts on the way back out of Russia because they would total more than $9,000. It was not the way I liked to operate, but I felt it was the best approach this time.

After waiting an extra day in Anadyr for the weather to improve, we headed to the arctic coast at Cherskiy, where we had ended our survey the year before. Our good friend, Nicolai was again part of our team this year. The weather was great. We spent four nights in Cherskiy working the broad plain between the Kolyma River and the Indigirka River. On our final morning, while we were preparing and loading the plane, Victor came walking hurriedly towards us. He had been dealing with airport personnel. He asked Bill, "Do you have three oranges I can have? It would be very helpful." Bill told him he could have three oranges. Victor headed back to the offices with the oranges. We never learned how exactly he used them, but I imagine they were a very effective bribe in Siberia.

The distance from Cherskiy to Chokurdakh, located on the Indigirka River, was 350 miles and we had transect lines to fly along the way. When we were a long distance from either town, flying at 100 feet above the ground, Victor remarked, "Captain Jack, we need to climb." He had been unable to reach anyone for our 30 minute position report. So I started circling to 1000 feet, and still no luck. I climbed to 2000 feet, and still we were unable to make contact. Fortunately at 3000 feet he was able to reach another aircraft and they relayed our position information. When we had difficulty like this making contact, it gave me an uneasy feeling knowing that an unnecessary search might be initiated. I was so thankful our plane had the HF radio. Without it, I doubt we could have successfully operated in Siberia.

It was satisfying to see healthy numbers of eiders, especially the two species that were classified as threatened in North America. Along the coast, between the Kolyma River Delta and the Indigirka River Delta, and not including those deltas, we estimated there were 55,000 spectacled eiders and 26,000 Steller's eiders. These birds were the primary reason we had travelled so far from America. We were not disappointed, and there would be much more to see in the coming days.

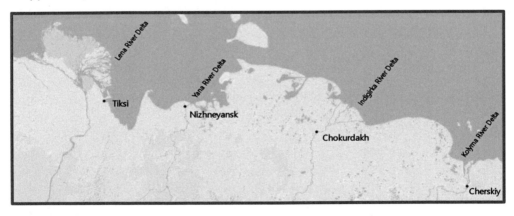

For scale, it is 800 miles direct from Cherskiy to Tiksi.

We continued on towards Chokurdakh in good weather. Chokurdakh was a small town of about 3,000 people, situated on the banks of the Indigirka River, 90 miles upstream from the East Siberian Sea. Downstream, the Indigirka River delta fanned out into a large wetland complex. It was considered a hot spot for spectacled eiders. We knew that this summer, two of our colleagues were there, conducting a study of the spectacled eiders in cooperation with Russian biologists. John Pearce and Dan Esler had arrived more than a month earlier and had been working out of a remote Russian weather station, called Tabor. Their objectives were to determine the distribution, abundance and nesting ecology of the spectacled eider on the Indigirka River Delta. We hoped that while we were working the delta, and were in the vicinity of the station, we would be able to land and see them. We had mail for them from America which we knew they would be anxious to receive. It would also be an amazing rendezvous of Americans here, at the northern edge of Siberia.

The runway at Chokurdakh was a mile long and adjacent to town. It was a good setup for the airplane. The hotel accommodations were another story. Bill, Victor, Nicholai

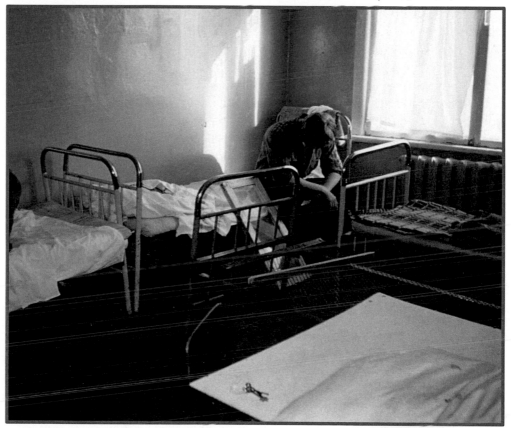

Bill after a long day, ends up putting the window pane under his mattress.

and I were put into one room. There were four pathetic beds and a small table with two chairs. The bathroom was at the end of the hall. No shower. And no sink. The toilet was extremely dirty. There was no toilet paper. Some magazine pages were lying near the toilet, probably intended to be used as toilet paper. Bill was disgusted by the deep sag in his bed. He found a small window pane in a wooden frame and slid it under his mattress. Since I was the pilot, the rest of the crew generally insisted that I take the best bed in hopes that I would sleep well. This courtesy did not extend

73

to tolerance of my snoring. One morning Bill informed me, "Jack, your snoring is going to have to stop."

That night, sleep was difficult to secure for me, I was worried all night about controlling my snoring. But from then on, I had no more difficulties sleeping and Bill told me he never heard me snoring again. A good night's sleep was also important for the observers, to avoid dozing off or contracting the "glazed stare" effect when they were looking out the window, but not really absorbing the sights due to exhaustion.

We were settling into our meager accommodations when a man in uniform knocked on the door. Victor invited him in and the two of them sat across from each other at the small table. They talked for 30 minutes while Bill and I wondered what was going on. Nicholai knew, but was silent. After the man left, we asked Victor for an explanation. He told us that this man came to confront us with the information that the Russian government believed we were illegally searching for mammoth tusks on the tundra and that they planned to follow us. Victor told him we were looking for ducks and geese to count, and they could follow us all they wanted, but they weren't going to see us finding and stealing mammoth tusks. He explained that we fly straight lines back and forth all day long and that they would just burn up a lot of fuel following us. As far as we know, we were never actually followed.

The weather held while we worked the Indigirka River Delta. On the second day, June 26, our survey lines took us close to the weather station where our Alaskan colleagues were located. I pulled off the survey and climbed to 500 feet to reconnoiter the situation. Nothing looked inviting for landing. The lake was littered with junk. It looked like a cemetery for old machinery and hunks of metal. I circled the lake many times without finding a path I could use through the treacherous metal. The likelihood of ripping open a float was far too great. The river was nearby, but there was a steady 25 knot wind blowing against the current. The combination of wind and current was creating two to three foot standing waves.

I could see John running across the tundra, waving his arms joyously. Dan was working his way back to the station as well. I worried that we would not be able to meet up with our fellow Americans. Finally, I saw a place that might work. In one stretch, the river made a slight curve, which deflected the current away from shore for several hundred yards. There, the waves were minimal. I knew I could land there, but I needed to be sure I could take off as well. If I couldn't get airborne before the curve, I would run full speed into the worst of the standing waves at the curve. After mulling it over and over in my mind as we circled, I decided there was probably just enough room for the takeoff. I came in and landed on the river.

As I taxied up to the shore, John and Dan grabbed and held the wing until I could get out on the float, open the float hatch and reach for the anchor. I knew they were both feeling a great sense of pride. I had felt that type of pride myself when I was at a field camp and saw another U.S. Fish and Wildlife Service pilot bring a plane into a tricky spot. I threw the anchor to Dan and he held us into the shore. The wind was strong. I jumped off the float and sunk the small anchor deep into the tundra. Then I took out a screw spike and screwed it into the tundra, twenty feet beyond the anchor, and tied a line from the anchor to the screw. Now I could feel confident the plane would stay put in the wind and current. Bill and I were greeted enthusiastically by John and Dan. We introduced them to Nicholai and Victor. The mail was retrieved from the plane and we all walked across the tundra to the station. We were invited to lunch and met the weather personnel. It was a happy reunion. Dan told us later that these weathermen would often get drunk and get into fights at this remote and lonely site. Fortunately this was a midday celebration without alcohol.

The takeoff went as planned. With four of us in the plane, I was glad to have the powerful Garrett engine. As soon as I was able to lift the right float clear of the water, I knew the left one would soon follow, especially with the strong head wind. The plane surged into the air just before getting to the standing waves. What a great sense of relief when the plane becomes air borne during a worrisome water takeoff. If the pilot's technique is wrong, if the yoke is pulled back in an anxious effort to get the plane into the air, the rear of the floats will be forced down into the water and the acceleration will be severely hampered. It takes restraint, which can be difficult when imminent danger is approaching the plane at 60 miles per hour.

Russian AN-2 aircraft, similar to the one used by John Pearse for waterfowl surveys on the Indigirka River Delta.

Our survey lines were a replication of transects that John had flown a week earlier. This was by design. John had used a Russian AN-2 biplane, which was far from ideal as a survey platform. He had to peer out of the small circular window at the rear of the aircraft. He had little or no visibility forward, and had to look to the side and to the rear. We saw 63% more spectacled eiders than did John, which is understandable. John had to fly at 250 feet altitude, while we were at 100 to 115 feet. We were able to compute and provide a correction factor for future surveys flown with an AN-2 aircraft.

We enjoyed several more productive days out of Chokurdakh. On June 28th we were ready to head farther west to the Yana River and then to the Lena River. As usual, while three of us prepared the airplane, Victor went off to have his medical checkup and weather briefing. Nicholai was cleaning the bugs off of the windshield. Bill was loading our gear into the cabin and setting up the computers. I was involved with the preflight inspection. A uniformed Russian official approached me. He was talking in Russian so I didn't know what he was saying. I said, "Nicholai, I need you over here." Nicholai came and talked briefly to the official. Then to me he said, "He says that he has come from Yakutsk and wants to inspect our airplane." So this man had travelled 800 miles to inspect our plane. Could this be related to the suspicion that we were collecting woolly mammoth tusks, or could this be even more ominous? I was concerned. I told Nicholai that we needed to wait for Victor to return.

When Victor walked up to the group of us, we told him what was happening. Victor and the official exchanged some words, and then Victor led him away from the plane, but still within earshot. Their discussion became more and more heated, becoming louder and louder until they were literally shouting into each other's face. I marveled at how these Russians could display such apparent anger without coming to blows. Then suddenly the uniformed man walked off.

"Victor, what happened?" Victor explained the heated intercourse, "This man told me he was here to inspect our plane for contraband. I told him that he could inspect our plane, but I reminded him that if he inspected our plane and found nothing improper, I could have him removed from his job." This statement was quite amazing to Bill and me. We would have expected that in Russia, an official would have nearly free reign to inspect property.

Russian official explaining to Nicholai that he wants to inspect our plane.

With the threat of investigation alleviated, we took off and headed for Nizhneyansk on the Yana River, a 300 mile flight. Flying across the tundra was never boring. Most of the route was at least 100 miles from the coast. We had not placed any transects in this vast inland area – not expecting to see eiders. Nonetheless, we were casually searching for waterfowl, mostly out of habit. Steller's eiders began to show up, sprinkled on various small ponds below us. It became more and more apparent that we should have planned to survey this area. It was decided that on the return trip home, after surveying the Lena River Delta, we would run a long, 130 mile, transect through this area and diligently count the Steller's eiders – so we could have a rough estimate of their total numbers. This was completely unexpected, to see Steller's eiders apparently nesting 100 miles from salt water.

Nizhneyansk was a small sea port situated 20 miles up the Yana River from the Laptev Sea. The airport was on the other side of the river from town. We had to board a ferry to cross the river. There would be no overnight security at this airport, and we would be unable to check on the plane ourselves. The ferry was a small boat capable of carrying a half dozen passengers. Passenger safety was a low priority. We had to walk a narrow plank from shore onto the bow of the boat. I was fairly athletic, but still, I scampered fast – in case the plank or the boat wobbled.

The town matched the ferry, as did our accommodations. Nizhneyansk was in decline at the time of our visit. Many buildings appeared unused. The streets were muddy. Everything was in a state of disrepair and degradation. The population in 1989 was 2,500. In 2002 it was 700 and in 2010 it was 400. We were just spending one night and would then head on to what we expected to be the granddaddy of deltas, the Lena River Delta. The Lena River, the largest river in Russia, splits the country in half. It originates near Lake Baikal in southern Siberia and empties into the Arctic Ocean. I had great anticipation and great expectation for the Lena delta.

Walking the plank to board the ferry at Nizhneyansk, on the Yana River.

The following day we finished our transects on the Yana River Delta and headed for Tiksi. For all the miles we had flown along the north coast of Siberia in the last two years, we had not seen any small native villages. In Alaska and Canada there were numerous native villages where the Inuit, Inupiat and Yup'ik people lived a mostly subsistence life style until recent decades. Many of them still lived in the villages, even if subsistence was less emphasized than it once was. I asked Victor why we weren't seeing villages here in Russia. He said that under communism they were gathered up and forced to live in towns – in the cement apartment buildings.

Tiksi was located at the southeast corner of the Lena River Delta. Its population was about 10,000 at the time we were there. It was the administrative center for this region – an important distinction which we now wished we hadn't overlooked in our planning. The runway was highly suitable and not far from town. After landing, Victor checked in with the authorities and learned that we would not be able to fly our low level surveys on the delta. We should have known that any activity on the delta required a prior request and prior authorization from the local government. This was a big blow to us. We had flown almost half way across Russia to the largest delta of the arctic coast, to be told we couldn't fly surveys there.

In the morning, Nicholai made contact with the government office and was able to arrange an afternoon meeting with the leader. The three of us, Bill, Nicholai and I walked to his office, armed with our progress report from 1993. That report had maps of the areas we had surveyed the previous year from Kolyuchin Bay to the Kolyma River. It had tables of the population estimates and numbers of birds seen. The leader gave us a reasonably warm welcome. He was of native ancestry and I soon got the distinct impression that we were dealing with some sovereign aboriginal rights. We had to put our case in Nicholai's hands, since the discussion was in Russian.

Nicholai showed the leader our report. We could see that Nicholai was explaining how we fly the transect lines at low level; how we count the birds we see; how we expand those numbers to estimate the total numbers of birds. He took twenty minutes to complete his presentation. Then the leader addressed Nicholai. He was like a chief. He clearly was the man with all of the authority. He would make the decision and it would be final. Nicholai turned to Bill and me to explain the situation. The leader had a concern. "His people tell him that there are very few caribou on the delta. His people say that the wolves have been responsible for killing the caribou. He wants to know if we could tell him how many caribou are on the delta, and how many wolves are there as well." Bill and I responded that we could keep track of all the caribou and wolves that we see. We could provide him with a report showing population estimates of all the animal species before we left Tiksi. The leader nodded his head and gave us his permission to fly.

That evening I made the biggest social and cultural blunder of all my trips to Siberia. We were in good spirits. All four of us were in the hotel room. We probably had had a few drinks. Everyone was happy that we were closing in on completion of our mission. We had secured permission to fly the Lena River Delta. We were joking and just plain feeling good. I made a comment, actually a gesture and a salutation. It was stupid, ignorant and inappropriate.

My father spent 23 months in Europe during World War II, and was in the Normandy invasion and the liberation of France. I should have known about the unimaginable loss of life in WWII. I knew that six million Jews had died at the hands of Germans. *That terrible piece of recent history* I had acquired. I had also read the Diary of Anne Frank. I knew that nearly five hundred thousand Americans had died. But as a lad, my friends and I would play around, and we would extend our arm out and shout "Heil Hitler." It was play. We would laugh and romp with each other, with no thought of war.

Here in Tiksi, in the middle of our gaiety, for some inexplicable reason, I extended my right arm and called out "Heil Hitler." Victor and Nicholai twisted to look at me. Directly at me. Directly into my eyes. Their faces were stone cold, grave – accusative. Silence. Staring silence. I waited. Then Victor, slowly and quietly, said, "Was that a joke?" I was stunned. "Yes, that was a joke." Then Victor addressed me, as a father would to his son, "There are two things in Russia that we never joke about – World War II and bread. Twenty five million people in Russia died in World War II. Millions of them died of starvation. There was no bread. We do not joke about this." I apologized to Victor and Nicholai. The party was over. It was time to go to bed.

At this point in the survey I realized we had an issue with the number of hours we were putting on the plane. By the time we reached Alaska, on the return trip, the plane would be at least 25 hours over the required 100 hour inspection period. I wouldn't be able to get the plane inspected in Russia. Only occasionally were we granted an exception, and even then the maximum extension was 10 hours. I didn't want to get into a lot of trouble back in Anchorage and I believed we were plenty safe going 30 hours over. So I started pulling circuit breakers until I found the one that made the Hobbs meter stop counting our hours. The only problem, that circuit breaker deactivated the oil pressure gauge. I had the oil pressure warning light as a backup. I felt safe enough pulling the circuit breaker whenever we were on the ground or we were at high elevation on cross country flight legs. I left the breaker engaged while we were low level on survey lines. The strategy worked.

As we flew our transects over the Lena delta, we noticed that the swans were flying away from our plane. Bill and I had never seen this in Alaska – not on the north slope or the Yukon Delta. Neither had we seen it anywhere else in Siberia. Clearly these swans were frightened by our aircraft. We could only conclude that they must have been harassed or maybe even shot at by Russian aircraft.

We saw 113 caribou and estimated 5,400 caribou for the entire Lena Delta. The density of caribou on the Lena Delta was one tenth the density of caribou on all other surveyed areas combined. Their population was severely decimated on the Lena Delta. I wondered if they had been harvested by people with access to helicopters. I kept my suspicions to myself. We did not see any wolves on the delta. We tallied and reported results to the local government as promised. The "chief" wasn't available at the time, so Nicholai was unable to see his response to our findings.

This was the most distant point on our survey. We were 102 degrees of longitude from my home base in Juneau, Alaska. That was nearly one third of the way around the globe at this latitude. The distance from the Lena Delta to home by way of Provideniya was 3,000 miles. We had completed our mission. We could now provide population estimates for areas which had never before been systematically surveyed. We estimated 146,000 spectacled eiders in eastern Siberia. We were flying at 100 mph and looking out from the plane to a distance of more than two football fields. We know we missed a significant number of ducks for a variety of reasons.

Therefore, the true number of spectacled eiders could have been close to 300,000. Why had the wintering grounds of these birds never been found? Many of our colleagues questioned our estimate when we presented it to them. They said something had to be amiss with what we had done. A very rough estimate of spectacled eiders in the 1970's was 200,000. The scientists said that the North American population had declined 96% since then. Surely the Russian population must have gone through some kind of similar decline.

King eiders were estimated to number 56,000; swans 32,000; and long-tailed ducks 124,000. Caribou numbered 334,000.

On our way back to Anadyr, we crossed the plain between the Yana and Indigirka rivers. This plain was larger than the state of Maryland. We ran one long, 130 mile transect, through the middle of it. We saw over two hundred Steller's eiders, which resulted in a rough estimate of 45,000 for this one area. None of the birds were in flocks, indicating they were there on breeding territories. We wanted to return the next year, 1995, and conduct a more complete survey of the Yana – Indigirka plain. This might be an exceptional area for Steller's eiders. In Alaska there was an estimated population of only 600 Steller's eiders, which was the entire North American component of the world population.

The successes of our three years of flying in Siberia hadn't gone unnoticed by our colleagues in Alaska.

Prior to 1993, virtually nothing was known of where spectacled eiders migrated to molt their flight feathers, or where they spent the winter. So in the summer of 1993, biologists implanted 14 satellite transmitters in spectacled eiders at the primary breeding grounds on the Yukon-Kuskokwim Delta. Four of the five radioed males were tracked by satellite to Mechigmenan Bay, Russia where they apparently molted during August. Mechigmenan Bay is located a mere 80 miles north of Provideniya, a place I was now very familiar with. Only one of those four transmitters remained functional until fall, and its last location was in the Bering Sea, 50 miles south of St. Lawrence Island on October 11, 1993. So the wintering grounds were still a mystery. Early in 1994, I was asked if I would make a flight to the Chukotsk Peninsula in August to find out how many spectacled eiders were using Mechigmenan Bay. The four transmitter locations in Mechigmenan Bay were intriguing. My observer would be Bill Larned. He was in charge of the effort to find molting and wintering spectacled eiders. I agreed to make that flight to Provideniya in August. Bill Larned was one of my fellow pilots in the Migratory Bird Management Program, and a much more experienced pilot than me, but I was one of the two pilots of N754, and I had the Russian experience.

The year prior, all breeding populations of the spectacled eider in North America were listed as threatened under the U.S. Endangered Species Act. Even though the molting and wintering grounds were still unknown, it was assumed that the decline must be caused by changes in those locations, and therefore the spectacled eiders in Siberia had probably undergone a similar decline. No recent population estimates or trend data were available from Russia when the decision to list them was made.

Victor met Bill Larned and me in Nome this time. With Victor on board, we were allowed to fly from Alaska to Siberia by way of the Diomede Islands. He could keep us from flying too close to the top secret radar installation just south of Cape Dezhnev. We all met at Nome on August 9 for our flight to Provideniya. Bill and I flew N754 into Nome that day, but the weather soon turned sour, with wind gusts to 33mph and over half an inch of rain. For the next 11 days the weather stayed lousy, with rain, fog and wind. An inch of rain fell on August 15. It wasn't until August 21 that the weather moderated enough for our departure. This twelve day wait for weather was my personal career maximum. I shouldn't complain, my supervisor, Bruce Conant, attempted a swan survey in Cordova during a month when the city drowned in 60 inches of rain.

We surveyed the entire coast from the Diomedes to Provideniya. We did indeed see the radar installation in the distance. It was not particularly impressive from a couple of miles away. It was strange to be in an American plane in proximity to this installation, and yet feel safe. The air raid drills in grade school still echoed in the back of my memory. Provideniya was becoming a familiar airport to me. The customs guys went through their ritual request to have me open the four hatch covers on the decks of the floats. The rest of the plane seemed to be of no concern to them. Their manual probably read, "N754 - Search the secret compartments in the long pointed aluminum things that hold the wheels."

We were greeted with good weather the next morning. In Nome, I had checked the weather maps the previous day and they showed several good days of weather in the forecast. So I was surprised when Victor returned from his medical checkup and weather briefing, and calmly told me the winds were predicted to be 50 knots that afternoon when we returned. I let out a yelp and told Victor, "We are not going anywhere today with that forecasted wind!" Victor looked a little puzzled and then realized he had made a mistake converting the wind speed to knots. In Russia the wind was always reported as meters per second. For me, Victor had to convert it to nautical miles per hour in his head. He corrected the afternoon winds to 12 knots. We flew north to Mechigmenan Bay and completed eleven transect lines. We saw 166 flocks totaling 37,397 birds. The next day we repeated the survey and expanded it by 4 lines and counted 41,209 birds. The largest flock contained 3400 birds. These large numbers of eiders in Mechigmenan Bay indicated that Russian birds must comingle with Alaska birds. It clearly was a critical area where a significant proportion of the spectacled eider population spent up to three months each year.

We saw 20 grey whales on the survey which was a good indication that the sea floor was probably rich with benthic fauna. We also saw 4 skiffs with outboard motors that were chasing either walrus or seals in an effort to harvest them. The town of Lorino, with approximately 1500 indigenous people, was located at the head of the bay. We did not see any other environmental threats to the bay. We expected to expand our efforts to document molting areas of the spectacled eider in Siberia the following summer.

Chapter 10 - Russia Refreezes
1995

Our earlier successes engaging Russian personnel in cooperative surveys started to erode rapidly in 1995. Victor was not allowed to be our navigator. Victor may have gotten cross-wise with the Chief Navigator, Akhmed Daraev. The excuse was that Victor hadn't taken a safety course which was previously offered to him. Our foreign affairs officer, Peter Ward, said that Akhmed's tone of voice made it clear to him that Victor would simply not be available. Instead, we would be assigned Pavel (Paul) Evsenko. He was from Magadan, far to the south. I managed to reach Victor by phone 7 days before our flight to Provideniya. He said he had no knowledge of our flight. He said he would try to be our navigator, but he held little hope for success.

Bill Eldridge and I met Paul upon our arrival in Provideniya on June 20. He was a diminutive man, with a square body and square head, cold in demeanor. He seemed to have little interest in this assignment. We were to find out that he was completely unfamiliar with the region we were about to travel through, including the terrain, the weather conditions and the airfields. He was a reluctant communicator on the radio. He seemed more interested in following rules than insuring safety. His body odor was foul and almost intolerable in the confined cabin of N754. It never improved on any of our flights over the next ten days.

This trip, our goal was to obtain more detailed information about two large inland areas. They were broad plains; one between the Kolyma River delta and the Indigirka River delta, the other between the Indigirka River delta and the Yana River delta. Together, they were larger than the state of West Virginia. The previous year we had not surveyed these areas because we did not expect that eiders would be 30 to 100 miles from the coast. This year we would fly a systematic sample of transects to obtain good population estimates.

We were disappointed to find far fewer Steller's eiders than we had expected. We carefully repeated the same long, 130 mile, transect on which we saw 205 Steller's eiders the year before. This time, we saw 16 Steller's eiders. The systematic survey did help us determine that the total Steller's eider estimate for all the areas we surveyed in eastern Siberian should be about 240,000. Just as with spectacled eiders, that number could be doubled for a reasonable actual number present.

To our great surprise, we saw 15 Siberian white cranes along the systematic transects of the interior areas. We now could estimate 1,852 Siberian white cranes for eastern Siberia. We had covered almost all of their breeding habitat and shown how they were distributed. I hoped their future would be better than what the whooping cranes of North America had endured. Whooping cranes were once estimated to number in the thousands but were pushed to the brink of extinction with only 15 adults alive in 1938. They now number over 300 wild birds.

We had a chance to land at the Tabor weather station again. This time the winds were light and I had no worries. Again, John and Dan were thrilled to see us. This year their primary goal was to capture spectacled eiders and surgically implant satellite transmitters. They succeeded in radio-tagging ten males. These males significantly helped Bill Larned find 227,000 spectacled eiders wintering in the Bering Sea the following winter.[2] The mystery of the wintering grounds of the spectacled

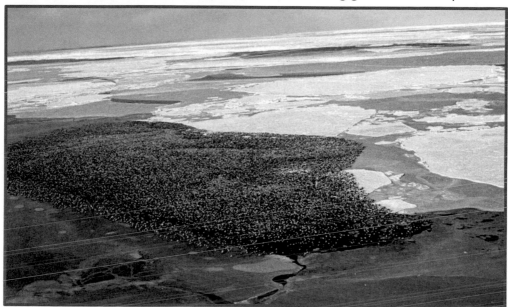

A flock of approximately 80,000 spectacled eiders wintering in the Bering Sea. Photo by Bill Larned.

eider had been solved at last. Remarkably, huge flocks of densely packed eiders were able to keep tiny oases of open water in the sea ice. The following winter of 1997, Bill found 363,000 spectacled eiders in the icy covered sea. This was an amazing match to our estimate of close to 300,000 in Siberia. Our Russian survey data for spectacled eiders was now finally accepted by everyone.

For three major breeding ground surveys, over a three year period, 1992 – 1994, our plane, N754 had performed admirably in Siberia. It had been designed and built for this work. N754 was a specially modified version of the most successful bush aircraft

---

[2] Petersen, M.R., W.W. Larned, and D.C. Douglas. 1999. At-sea distribution of spectacled eiders: A 120-year-old mystery resolved. The Auk 116(4): 1009-1020.

ever built, the de Havilland beaver. In 1966, Jerry Lawhorn, chief mechanic for the U.S. Fish and Wildlife Service in Anchorage, took the radial engine off of a standard beaver and attached a turbine engine. He added 9 inches length to the cabin. He eliminated the two front doors so that he could secure the new engine to the airframe without any support members in the pilot's field of view. He designed glass windows to the side, front and overhead of the pilot, giving visibility comparable to a helicopter. The pilot's eyes were just in front of the leading edge of the wing, so that in a steep angle of bank, the pilot could see the horizon to the side of the plane by looking through the side window or the glass roof of the cockpit. The engine was 60 percent more powerful than the standard engine, and yet it was much lighter. Therefore, Jerry had to mount the engine farther forward, giving the plane the appearance of a mosquito. This also put the air intake ahead of the water spray on water takeoffs and landings. I was incredibly fortunate to have been at the right place and the right time to reap the benefits of the genius and hard work that had gone into the design and construction of this marvelous airplane.

The turbine engine gulped more fuel than the standard engine. The reduced weight of the turbine and its extra power allowed Jerry to incorporate large additional fuel tanks. He put 167 gallons of fuel capacity in the leading edge of the wings, from the root to two thirds out the wing. The integral tanks strengthened the wings. The weight of fuel in the wings reduced the stresses of turbulence on the wings when in flight. The original floats were too small for the heavy plane. When the plane was fully loaded, the rear of the floats were severely under water. When the propeller was put into reverse in that situation, the rear of the floats dove even further under water and it appeared as if the plane was starting to sink, tail first. It probably would sink if the pilot was not careful. It wasn't until the floats were lengthened in the rear and also widened from bow to stern that she became a good float plane at all weights. The flight controls required only light pressures to operate. The yoke could be handled with three fingers of one hand. All of the warning lights were right in front of the pilot's vision in a row at the bottom of the windshield. There were warning lights for low fuel, low fuel pressure, low oil pressure, metal debris in the oil screen, etc. etc. Jerry had achieved his perfect goal, a superb wildlife survey aircraft that was in his words, "Biologist Proof."

Bill Larned had an ambitious plan for us to undertake in 1995. This was our second year of late summer surveys and he wanted to cover the entire northern coast from the Indigirka River delta to Provideniya, a distance of 1300 miles. Our route at times would take us 20 miles offshore. The radio transmitters placed on spectacled eiders by John Pearce and Dan Esler in June were showing the distribution of eiders along the coast as they began their migration. We would search those areas and count how many birds were at those locations. I had flown this area before, in 1993 and 1994.

This time it would be in late summer. We would be passing through Cape Schmidt, near the area where Ben Eielson crashed. In 1993 we had experienced snow at Cape Schmidt in late June. This time we would bring a portable generator to heat the engine prior to startup in the cold temperatures. I insisted that I would only undertake this trip if we secured Victor Shlyaev as our navigator.

Our Office of Foreign Affairs people, Steve Kohl and Peter Ward, worked hard communicating our demand to the Russian authorities, telling them that for safety reasons we must have Victor. Even Evgeni Syroechkovsky, our good friend that muscled through our first flight three years earlier, couldn't persuade the central flight administration people in Moscow. The answer was always the same, "Pavel will be the navigator." Since I would not fly the north coast of Siberia in the fall with Paul at my side, we had to truncate the survey to just a repeat of Mechigmenan Bay near Provideniya. This was a big disappointment.

Bill and I departed Nome for Provideniya on September 3rd. We were met there by Paul. We attempted the first survey the following day. As Paul and I crawled between the front seats into the cockpit, I was met with the familiar stench. It only took a couple of minutes for our first problem with Paul. The visibility to the north, our direction of flight was good. The ceiling was about 1500 feet, but south of the airport were ragged clouds and low conditions. We were cleared to takeoff to the south, and I planned to simply turn and head north before reaching the low conditions over the sea. Shortly after takeoff, on the climb out, and just before reaching the fog bank, I initiated a turn to the right. Paul began yelling at me, saying we must go straight and continue climbing. I yelled back at him that I was turning. He got even louder and more animated, motioning with his arm to go straight, demanding that I must follow instructions. I yelled back at him that I wasn't going to fly into the clouds. He became extremely upset. I made my turn just before reaching the fog and headed north. I don't know what kind of rules he was wanting to follow, but I wasn't going to fly into instrument conditions. We were off to a raucous start.

When we reached Mechigmenan Bay we began documenting the eider flocks by taking photographs for later analysis. The seas were choppy and the lighting poor. After several attempts, we decided the photography wouldn't work. We would go to Lavrentiya and refuel. Then we could return and conduct a visual count as we had done the previous year. When we landed at Lavrentiya, a town I had landed at two years earlier, we were met by Russian officials. They wanted to see our passports and visas. Then they motioned for Bill and I to follow them. Paul was to stay behind. The officers whisked us into a little room.

It was stark. The walls were bare. One clean desk and a couple of chairs were the only furniture. There was a lot of talking amongst themselves, in Russian. Bill and I began to feel uncomfortable. This was looking like something we had seen in the movies. After what seemed like an unnecessarily long period of time, one of them tried to explain to us in minimal English. Lavrentiya was not listed on our visa. This was a violation of Russian law. They did not have sufficient authority to deal with us in Lavrentiya. They told us we were to fly directly to Provideniya. There, we would be met by other Russian officials. Of course, Paul had been of no use to us confronting the authorities here in Lavrentiya.

Without completing a survey that day, we returned to Provideniya. A man dressed in a military uniform met us in the lobby of the terminal. He sat us down at a small table in the corner. He pulled out a few papers. Two sheets were for Bill and two sheets were for me. Everything was written in Russian. We had no idea what was written on these papers. The military official explained to us in broken English that we were being fined for our violation. The fines would be a week of Russian pay for each of us. He called it five Russian daily salaries. In U.S. dollars it would be $125 each. We were to pay that amount and we were to sign these papers. The money was not a problem, but signing papers which we couldn't read was scary. Bill and I agreed we would do it. We were later sternly chastised by our Foreign Affairs Office, telling us we should never sign anything in Russia. At the time, we didn't feel we had much choice. We had a 1.5 million dollar airplane sitting on the ramp that I am sure the Russians wouldn't hesitate to confiscate, and no Victor to advocate or intervene on our behalf.

Fortunately, the following day we were able to conduct a good survey of Mechigmenan Bay. We estimated 55,731 spectacled eiders, 35% more than we had seen the year before.

We didn't know at the time, but this would be our last survey in Russia.

Beyond U.S. Fish and Wildlife Service, there were other agencies which had developed cooperative studies between Alaska and Chukotka in the early 1990's. They too faced a changed Russia in 1995. On September 14, 1995, Dale Taylor, Natural Resource Coordinator for the Beringian Heritage International Park, wrote about the problems their fisheries project encountered at Provideniya that summer. In his notes, he observed:

> Scientific permits: Russian colleagues, Pavel Godkov and Chereshnev were arrested upon their arrival in Anadyr, en route to Provideniya and Markovo, because they did not have proper scientific permits. Their friends had to bail them out so they could begin the process of applying for the permits.

> Customs: Our scientific gear was a complete puzzle to customs. They finally approved all the gear for entry, except the collapsible rubber raft, motor, oars, and gasoline for the motor. This equipment was considered

commercial. The boating equipment was stored for us at a cost of $250 for five days, plus a duty cost of $426.

Transfer of money for helicopter support: A decision was made at the Alaska Science Center that money was to be transferred to Provideniya via wire. Carrying cash was ruled out. The original order to transfer money to Kompass Resources International was initiated in May 1995. Kompass transferred the money to Provideniya, but appropriate people were not present to sign for it. The money was sent back, then re-sent through France to Moscow. We were not able to confirm the location of the money. Airport manager, Ovchernko, required confirmation the money was in a bank in Russia before he would release the helicopter. Not being able to provide that confirmation, and with time running out on our visas, we returned to the United States. Now the problem is getting the money back from Russia, where ever it might be.

The following year, 1996, several biologists tried to organize a survey of Steller's sea eagles and osprey in the Sea of Okhotsk. I was asked to fly N754 on that mission, which I would have enjoyed. Eagle surveys were my favorite. However, approval from Russia was not granted. Our window of opportunity which had opened in 1991, closed in 1995. It may not open for another generation. This is sad.

I feel very fortunate that I had the opportunity to play an important role in cooperative efforts between our two countries. Fittingly enough, our mutual interest was in the wellbeing of the animals with which we all coexist on earth. Our project served as an example of what is possible. I learned that the Russian people are good people. They do not hate America. They opened their homes and hearts to me. Everywhere I travelled in Russia, I sensed a happiness, which I shared, that we were at last allowed to meet each other face to face, and connect as friends. Even as a child, hiding from potential Russian nuclear bombs, I think I knew deep down that these people from across the ocean were not so different from me and my family and my friends.

It is tragic that sometimes nations engage in wars to settle disputes. Seventy years ago a weapon was created that was so destructive, no nation has chosen to use it, due to the likelihood of mutual annihilation. The one exception was America, at a time when no other nation had it. Maybe that weapon prevented many deaths worldwide in the intervening years – we have no way of knowing. But as long as the weapon exists, its use is possible. Humans created that weapon and now our species must find a way to live with it, not die with it. It means we must keep our borders open and the interchange of people, ideas and commodities flowing. I do not want our children hiding under desks again.

When I was the age of these youngsters in Siberia, I feared Russia.
I hope our flights increased trust and respect between our countries.

Chapter 11 - A Computer Program for Aerial Surveys
1997 to 2017

Prior to the availability of Global Positioning System (GPS) capability for the general public, biologists conducting aerial surveys were unable to connect their sightings to locations on the ground. This was because the observations occurred too frequently to mark them on maps. Instead, they used tape recorders to document their sightings. Latitude and longitude coordinates were not recorded. Eagle observations were totaled by plot, and waterfowl observations were totaled by segment, usually 16 or 18 miles long.   Swans were an exception. Jim King had observers penciling in swan locations on massive rolls of maps, held on their laps.

I knew how valuable it would be to know the exact locations of every observation of eagles and waterfowl. It would allow us to relate the distribution of the birds to the distribution of their habitats. As soon as GPS navigation equipment became available which could communicate with a portable computer, I knew we had the raw materials for a system to capture the locations of every observation. I set about writing the software to do it. One of my fellow biologists, Mike Anthony, gave me the key idea. He casually said, "Why don't you use the computer to record the voice with short voice recordings (clips) for every observation?" I hadn't thought of that. A light bulb moment for me. The tape recorders could be thrown away. The computer

My moving map and voice recording software. Our position and track were continuously shown on the map as well as the plot we were surveying.

would record the observer's voice and simultaneously grab the current location of the airplane. I wrote a companion program for transcribing the recordings (clips), inputting the species name and the number of individuals seen, and combining that information with the latitude and longitude coordinates where they were recorded.

I also thought to myself that perhaps I could write the software for a moving map in the plane. If so, a detailed map would be continuously displayed on the screen, showing the plane's current location, the track of where it had been and where it was headed. The pilot could zoom in and zoom out. I would make it possible for the boundaries of eagle and swan plots to show on the screen, and straight transect lines and segment endpoints could be displayed as well. I wrote the software to make it happen. For many years the aviation world did not have moving maps, even as the world of boats and ships did have moving maps. I believe it must have been a liability issue. Software companies and their insurance agencies probably didn't want to take on the responsibility for the safety of passengers in airplanes. In our government aircraft, we could use my program. As of this writing, twenty years later, I am proud that my computer program is still in use by the U.S. Fish and Wildlife Service. I have upgraded the software several times to keep pace with the changing computer world.

Susan Savage talks into the computer on a bald eagle survey of Alaska Peninsula.

Had this technology been available in 1987, someone important to me would still be alive. The pilot of the *Piper Navaho* would have seen his location on a computer screen and avoided the collision into mountainous terrain. My neighbor, Glen Cave, found the wreckage of that accident. Then twelve years later, he attempted to fly into the Juneau airport in very low visibility and ceiling, lost visual contact with the ground and crashed, killing all four on board, including his wife. The moving map would have saved their lives as well. Maybe this program has saved someone's life. I can never know the answer to that question, but it feels good to have done something to give pilots and myself a better chance to avoid a terrible disaster.

Chapter 12 - Complete Shoreline Survey of Southeast Alaska
1997 - 2002

With this new technology, we could now preserve the locations of every observation. I realized that if we were to fly next to the entire shoreline of southeast Alaska, we would have a complete snap-shot of the distribution of birds and marine mammals for the whole region. We would know all of the locations where species occurred and where they were absent. Data would be available for any particular sub-region. If an oil spill or other disaster happened, the impact on each species could be predicted. Areas deserving of special protection could be evaluated. Any specific area could be surveyed in the future and changes in distribution and abundance could be determined.

In 1997, we set about accomplishing the task, flying at 100 feet altitude. The survey was comprehensive: every rock and islet sticking out of the water was included. Debbie Groves was my highly experienced observer. We flew the coast in winter as well as in summer, totaling 30,000 miles. The survey took five years to complete.

Flying coastal surveys for ducks, loons and seabirds in the fjord lands of Alaska was the most challenging of my flying responsibilities. I was flying well below the tree tops. The great majority of the birds were next to the shoreline, so I flew about 75 yards from the shore to give Debbie the best possible view of the harlequin, mergansers, goldeneyes, bufflehead, gulls and pigeon guillemots. I was recording birds on my side, towards the open water, to a distance of 225 yards.

We do not see all animals from the aircraft. Hence, there was a need to develop correction factors for each species by conducting concurrent boat surveys of portions of the shoreline. From a boat, it is possible to see almost all of the birds and to count them carefully and determine with certainty species identification. From the air we could not distinguish the three species of scoters reliably, the two species of goldeneye, the two species of mergansers and many of the gulls. Therefore, the boat surveys of sampled areas, both in summer and in winter, gave us the ability to correct the air data for total numbers of birds and mammals. This survey turned into a valuable data set that was made available to all land management and environmental agencies.

We wanted to continue this survey into the fjords and islands of coastal British Columbia, an equally intricate maze of intertidal and nearshore habitats. By the time there was money available for that effort, the U.S. Fish and Wildlife Service decided it was too risky to fly that low amongst the mountains and inlets. It did not happen.

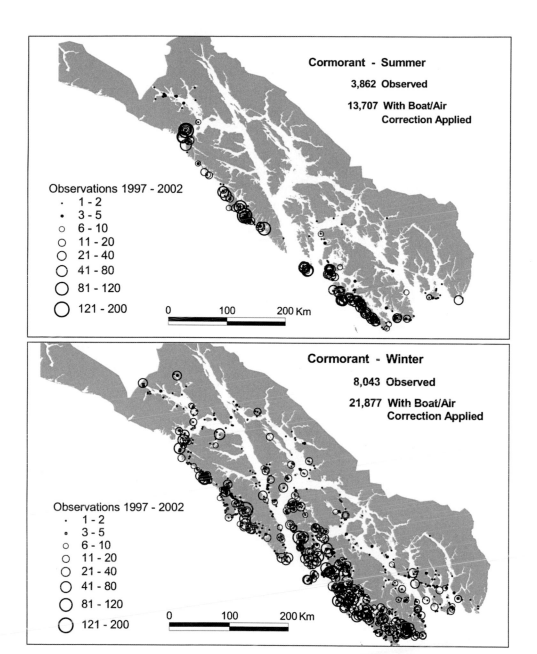

Pelagic cormorants in summer and winter: An example of our southeast Alaska shoreline survey data. Note how the summer distribution differs from the winter distribution.

Chapter 13 - Bald Eagle Surveys of the North Pacific Ocean
1977 - 2010

The first comprehensive bald eagle survey in Alaska conducted by Jim King and Fred Robards in 1967, focused on the southeastern panhandle. From that beginning, I developed a design for the entire North Pacific coast, from the Strait of Juan de Fuca to the Aleutian Islands. This 2,000 miles of the Pacific Rim actually encompasses a staggering 40,000 miles of intricate shoreline, and represents 7 percent of all saltwater shoreline in the world. Through the years we sampled 233 of 1848 possible plots. Each plot was 49 square nautical miles. The boundaries of any plot could be determined from the plot number and two simple mathematical equations. This meant that at any time in the future, any portion of the survey could be exactly replicated. This design serves as a baseline for measuring future broad scale changes in the eagle population. Over the period 1977 to 2010, I participated in the aerial survey of all 233 plots, either as pilot (10 surveys) or observer (10 surveys). For each survey, the average number of eagles per plot was expanded to the total number of plots within each region to estimate the total number of eagles. All regions combined led to a grand total of 58,000 adult bald eagles.

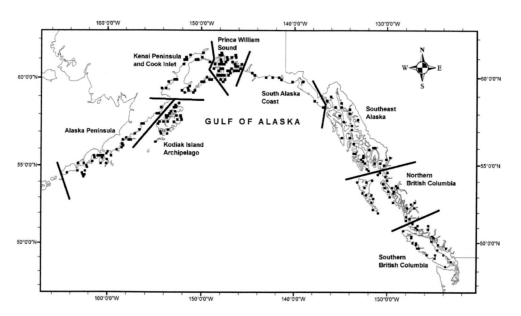

Locations of all 233 plots used to estimate the bald eagle population of the North Pacific Ocean.

The surveys were flown in April and May to coincide with the period when the adult eagles were incubating their eggs. This allowed us to see eagles on nests and obtain a measurement of productivity (nesting attempts). Most of the shoreline was cloaked with big evergreen forests. It takes practice to become good at spotting eagles and their nests in the trees. Radio telemetry studies have shown that about half of the adult eagles are not counted on an aerial survey because they are either located away from the shoreline, or are perching in a spot invisible to the observer, or are within sight of the observer but not seen by the observer.

Coastal eagle surveys were my favorite type of survey to fly. To me, the survey become an aerial dance. The plane moved in concert with the flow of the shoreline. Every turn was not perfect but I strived to be perfect on every turn. A perfect turn would put the observer in the best possible place for viewing and prepare the plane's position and trajectory precisely for the next turn. In the turn, altitude would be neither gained nor lost. Control movements would not be fast or jerky, but smooth and flowing. The plane floated beautifully, like a magic carpet. Eyes were constantly scanning. When approaching the head of a narrow inlet, I would climb to a height just above the trees, cross the inlet and enter a nice right hand turn over the trees at the head of the bay to give the observer a good view of the trees. The right wing was low, ideal for the observer. This positioning of the aircraft was much preferable to a steep left turn at the head of the inlet that would cause the right float to block the observer's view. Extremely narrow inlets were handled by entering the inlet at a higher altitude of 400 to 600 feet, flying beyond the head of the inlet, dropping the plane down to 150 feet, and then surveying the inlet on the way back out. My brain was continually thinking ahead of the plane.

Eagles were not always near the tops of trees. They could be on the beach or in the lower branches of a shoreline tree. They might be several hundred yards from the shore, especially on the steeper hillsides. Nests were found by focusing on the trees with the largest limb structures which were typically caused by a deformity or a broken top. It felt good to spot an eagle on a nest that was partially hidden in the canopy. Immature eagles, those less than 4 years of age, do not have the white head and tail. They are much more difficult to see among the trees. That is why we estimated the population of adult eagles, not total eagles. We had information about the immature eagles by analyzing the birds in flight. We made the assumption that all ages of eagles were equally visible when they were in flight and that all eagles were equally likely to be in flight. We could then use the ratio of immature eagles in flight to adult eagles in flight to estimate the percentage of immature eagles in the population.

Alaska Peninsula has no trees, yet bald eagles still find nest sites.

The most alluring coastline for me was the south side of the Alaska Peninsula. That was not just because it was treeless. It was the most challenging in terms of terrain, weather and remoteness. I never tired of surveying the rugged land of cliffs, tundra and pinnacles. It is the wildest place in Alaska, in my opinion. I surveyed it in the year 2000 and again in 2005. I vowed to return, if I could, to experience the beauty of the Peninsula from a boat and on foot. A few years later, after retiring from flying, I took my sailboat from Juneau to the Alaska Peninsula and fulfilled that promise. It was a trip that gave me some unexpected, as well as undesired, adventures. But that story comes later.

During one of my bald eagle surveys I almost crashed. The year was 1989. The Exxon Valdez oil tanker had run aground and unfortunately spewed 11 million gallons of oil into the sea. I was asked to fly a bald eagle population survey as part of the U.S. Fish and Wildlife Service response to the spill. My observer, Mike Jacobson, and I were returning to Cordova after completing our fifth day of flying in the Sound. The winds had dramatically increased in the Cordova area while we were out flying our plots.

There were two airports in the Cordova area. The main runway was 13 miles east of town on the Copper River Delta, a large, flat intertidal area – distant from the mountains and therefore free of turbulence. The other runway was next to town, tucked in the middle of 3,000 foot tall mountains. I was headed for the large airport at 13 mile.

I called Cordova Flight Service to report my position and announce that I was inbound for the airport. They informed me that the airport was closed. They would not tell me why it was closed. I had heard that U.S. Vice President Dan Quayle was going to arrive in Cordova to observe firsthand the disaster and the cleanup effort. So I had a pretty good idea that he was the reason. I then headed for the Eyak Lake runway near town, in the mountains – in the "cut", as it was called. It was windy. I guessed it was 30 knots. I found out later it was 30 knots with gusts to 60 knots. It was very turbulent on my approach to land. We repeatedly dropped 200 feet rapidly and then ballooned up several hundred feet. I fought the turbulence all the way down until we were close to touching down on the runway. The winds were bouncing us around to the extent that I felt there was too great of a chance that we might be smacked onto the runway hard. There didn't seem to be any need to take that chance and damage the landing gear or the plane for that matter. I initiated a go-around, adding power and climbing out for another try at it. I kept the landing gear down, as there was no need to raise it and then lower it again.

I climbed to 600 feet, still in very turbulent air. I maintained the standard pattern speed of 80 mph. The second approach was similar to the first one. I felt that once the plane was within a few feet of the runway, all I needed was 10 seconds of relative stability and I would have the plane on the ground, without hitting hard. I didn't get that cooperation from the wind. The plane continued to be buffeted heavily. I initiated another go-around.

Even though my training had taught me to use a pattern airspeed of 80 mph, I know now that I shouldn't have used that air speed in that kind of turbulence. More air speed would have given me more roll response. I was again at 600 feet above Eyak Lake on the downwind leg for another attempt at landing. Suddenly the plane rolled to the right – more than 90 degrees. We were closer to being upside down than right side up. I looked through the plexi-glass roof above my head and saw the lake. I applied full left aileron, full left rudder and added full power. The plane responded only a little bit. The right wing was pointing straight down at the lake. We were plummetting out of the sky. The plane was not in my control.

I had a distinct mental image of God holding the wingtips of my plane with his two huge hands, preventing the plane from righting. God wasn't letting go. We were rapidly approaching the lake. I told Mike to "hold on" – I thought for sure we were going to hit the water. I knew of nothing else I could do to avoid it. Just before we got to the lake, at less than 80 feet, the plane suddenly responded to the ailerons and rolled to level. The wind shear – wind rotor – whatever it was – had released its grasp on the plane just in time.

I climbed and headed out of the "gap", towards the tide flats. I learned later that the Flight Service Station at the 13 mile airport received four phone calls from concerned individuals asking them whether the turbine beaver was alright. They must have seen N754 fall from the sky and barely recover before hitting the lake. That explains the Flight Service response when I radioed them and asked how long the airport would be closed. They told me it would be about an hour and suggested I could declare an emergency and come in and land. I declined. As I circled and waited, I heard the radio transmissions from a flight of three National Guard helicopters report that they were taking off for Prince William Sound. They could save twenty minutes of flying time by flying through the "gap" rather than flying around the mountain, by way of the coast. Flight Service called me and asked for a pilot report of weather conditions in the "gap." I told them it was severe turbulence. The helicopters, one with the Vice President on board, changed course and flew out across the flats, away from the "gap". They avoided taking the Vice President through that turbulence.

Aerial view of an incubating adult in her nest on top of a sea stack. Harbor seals lounge nearby on the beach.

Chapter 14 - Annual Migration to California
1985 - 2002

The United States and Mexico protect and manage species of birds that migrate across their common border under provisions of the Migratory Bird Treaty Act. As such, American pilots and their planes have been responsible for monitoring wintering populations of waterfowl in Mexico since 1947. During my career, the plane used for the west coast surveys in Mexico was our turbine beaver, N754. In Mexico, they referred to our trusty plane as "Mosquito Grande." My supervisor, Bruce Conant, flew the Mexican surveys. It was my job to deliver N754 from Juneau to the Mexican border each December, so that it would be ready to start the Mexican survey in early January. The date of entry into Mexico had to be strictly adhered to, so the plane had to be stationed near the border ahead of time. Fifteen times I migrated south from Juneau with N754, a distance of 2000 miles as the mallard duck flies. Since these flights were usually in December, the rest of the avifauna had already flown south for the winter. I was a very late migrant.

Millions of birds spend their winters in Mexico. The coastal habitas they use are extremely important. These annual surveys provided valuable cooperation between our two countries and emphasized the mutual interests of both countries to protect those bird populations. Unfortunately, after I retired, the U.S. Fish and Wildlife Service was forced to terminate those winter monitoring flights because of safety and security concerns for the crew and the plane in a country with too many bad things happening.

December was the most difficult month of the year to ferry a plane south from Juneau. The weather along the coast was usually very bad, the days were very short and the amount of daylight was further reduced because the flight was made in a southeasterly direction, while the sun was moving towards the west. Still, I liked the long cross country flights because the challenges were many - and often new to me. Many of the rules governing flying in the lower 48 states were foreign to me as an Alaskan pilot. I landed the plane the best way I knew how, but it got me into minor trouble a few times. Two of these incidences were in northern Washington and two were in the dry region of southern California and Nevada.

On one of these trips, I was flying through southern British Columbia, headed for Bellingham Washington. That morning before departing Port Hardy,on the north end of Vancouver Island, I had arranged to clear U.S. customs at Bellingham. They were expecting me at a certain time. As I got closer to Bellingham I learned that their winds were out of the northeast at 40 knots, and 50 degrees to the runway. When I was five miles out, I asked the tower if I could overfly the airport and assess the situation. They gave me the okay. I noted the windsock was stretched out tight in the strong wind. I also noticed what appeared to be an old runway – aligned perfectly with the windsock and with the wind. There was a large yellow X painted on one end of the old runway, which meant that the runway was closed to the landing of an aircraft. The asphalt looked beat up, but I did not see any large rocks or boulders that would preclude my landing on it.

The tower asked what my intentions were. I was still thinking. It appeared to me that the safest procedure would be to land on the closed runway. I really did not want to land with a strong crosswind.

The tower called me again, "N754 what are your intentions?"

I hesitated another half minute and then asked the tower, "Can I land on that angled runway?"

They quickly answered, "No, that runway is closed, what are your intentions?"

"I am declaring an emergency. I will be landing on the closed runway."

"Roger."

The landing was easy, straight into the wind. The tower directed me where to park for customs. Paul, my coworker, and I entered the customs room and were met by two agents. They asked for our identification and other information to fill out their form. It took about ten minutes. Standing behind the agents were a man and a woman, dressed in full fire fighting gear – heavy fire retardent coat, pants and boots. They held their helmets by their sides. They waited patiently until we had cleared customs. Then one of them asked me, "What was your emergency." They had been placed on full alert and readiness for the emergency. I told them that I wanted to land into the wind, and so I had landed on the closed runway. They appeared to be quite disappointed with my answer.

The charming little town of Friday Harbor is situated in the middle of the San Juan Islands, about 100 miles north of Seattle. Best of all for a wandering pilot, the runway is right on the edge of town. In fact, residences are just a couple hundred yards from the end of runway 16. This close proximity is what got me into trouble on another flight from Juneau to Mexico.

Spending the night in a place where I could easily walk to a hotel seemed like a good idea. As I got closer to Friday Harbor the clouds became lower and lower. The base of the clouds was probably only 200 feet higher than the tops of the houses and small buildings in town. I knew where the runway was, just on the other side of town from me, but I couldn't see it. I skimmed right over the town expecting to see the runway within a few seconds. Sure enough, it came into sight. I had already prepared the plane for landing, with my gear extended and landing flaps deployed. I plopped it down on the runway. I felt somewhat disappointed with myself because this attemped landing would have been somewhat irresponsible if the runway hadn't been right where I expected it to be. I might have ended up on instruments, asking for help on the radio. Anyway, I was on the ground safely. What I didn't know was that two Federal Aviation Administration inspectors were on a boat in the harbor at the time I landed. They had watched me skim the tops of the houses and were not favorably impressed.

Several weeks later I received a call at home from someone in the Federal Aviation Administration. He asked me if I had landed at Friday Harbor on December 16. I acknowledged that I had. He then began to grill me about what the inspectors had seen, and telling me that they were filing a complaint against me. After a few sharp questions, I said, "It sounds like maybe I should have a lawyer." To which he replied, "You have that right." He said that I would be receiving a letter.

The letter said that my piloting previleges would be suspended if I was found guilty. It asked whether I would like to provide additional information. I wrote back and explained that the celing was very low, which made it necessary for me to fly that route and altitude on my approach to the airport. I drew my flight path on a map for them. Three months later I received another letter saying they had dropped the charges against me. In Alaska, there are numerous communities with the runway collocated with the town, so flying low over a town in order to land in foul weather is quite common. In fact, in one small town, the runway is the main road through town.

Flying east of the Cascade Mountains was usually my preferred path to southern California. It was a way to avoid the foggy Sacramento Valley and the massive sprawl of Los Angeles and its associated controlled airspaces. On this occasion, I was working my way south through Nevada. I definitely wanted to avoid Las Vegas, so I was futher to the east, over the great Lake Mead. I had always wanted to see this impoundment, the largest in the Unites States by volume.

The dark blue hues of the lake contrasted dramatically with its barren desert shoreline – strange to see so much water without any vegetation nearby. I could easily imagine a beautiful Colorado River meandering its way through a rugged canyon, now buried beneath the reservoir. There were no boats plying the water and the shores were all but uninhabited. It looked inviting to a float plane pilot. I felt like I could use a break to stretch my legs and relieve my bladder. The shoreline did not lend itself to beaching the plane. But then I noticed a small boat harbor with an inviting sandy beach next to it. In Alaska, float planes are often an accepted part of a boat harbor, and they may have their own dock or beaching area within the harbor. At the head of the harbor was a boat launching ramp, and next to the ramp was a sandy beach with a perfect gradient for N754. There were no boats to dodge; apparently people don't go boating here in the winter. I taxied right in, turned N754 around and backed her into the beach. It was a relief to hear the screaming engine wind down to a whisper as the three blades fanned the air and coasted to a stop. I wedged myself between the two front seats to the rear of the plane, kneeled on the floor and used my pee bottle.

As I climbed out of the rear door, I saw that a white SUV with police lights on its roof had driven onto the beach just behind the plane. "Bureau of Land Management" was visible on the door. As I stepped onto the right float, two uniformed men exited the car and approached me. The taller one said, "You better have one hell of an emergency. This is a swimming area."

This was not the greeting I was expecting in Nevada. Clearly I was in trouble with the law. I must have done something illegal. But his words echoed in my spinning brain, "emergency." This was an opening, if I could fill it. During the flight I had been contemplating the cover plate on the oil cooler. Stenciled on the plate were the words, "Remove above 50 degrees OT." OT stood for Outside Temperature. It was a cover that the mechanics put on in the winter and removed in the summer so that the oil would not cool too much in winter. It was definitely not an emergency, since we had never adhered strictly to those outside temperature conditions. This guy had given me a hint of how to get out of trouble and I latched onto it, "I do have an emergency. I am ferrying this plane south from Alaska. There is an oil cooler plate that has to be removed when the outside temperature is above 50 degrees. I landed because I need to remove that plate."

He may have wished he never mentioned the emergency thing. His shoulders even sagged a little bit, "Let me see your registration. Who does this aircraft belong to?"

I reentered the plane to get the papers, wondering to myself what he was going to think when he saw that this was a Department of Interior airplane, just like any of the Department of Interior aircraft he himself would fly in.

After reviewing the papers he began to lose his bravado, since I appeared to have an emergency of sorts and we both worked for the same department. He carefully wrote down information from the registration and then said, "How are you planning to get this airplane out of the harbor?"

From his tone of voice I concluded it must be illegal to taxi a float plane in this harbor. "I guess I will find someone with a skiff that can tow me out."

He was done being a jerk. "Just make sure you head straight out of here and slowly."

I got my little tool kit out of the plane. They were sitting in their car watching my every move. I unlatched the lower portion of the cowling. The oil cooler plate was revealed, but because I was standing on the float rather than on a ladder, I had to lean out over the water and use my arms to keep me from falling in. In this position I was unable to hold the wrench on each nut behind the plate while turning the screws with a screw driver. I could not remove the plate by myself while the plane was on the water. I pretended that I was working on the plate for the next five minutes while they continued to watch. Luckily they weren't close enough to see that I had removed nothing.

I latched the cowling back on, pretending that the job was done, quickly gathered my tools and sprang back into the plane. This had not been the relaxing break I had anticipated. The engine spooled up and I taxied out of that harbor, steering as straight a line as I could muster.

On another occasion I flew down the Sacramento Valley and was crossing the mountains just south of Bakersfield. My wife Molly and our two children, Jennifer and Kara were with me. The kids were 12 and 10 years old. This was a time when family members were allowed to accompany me if there was no additional cost to the government. As the plane jostled in the mountain turbulence, my daughters informed me through their headsets that they needed to go to the bathroom, badly.

The primary airport ahead of me was William J Fox Airport near Lancaster. The winds at General Fox were strong, 40 knots, and at about a 45 degree angle to the runway. The land was desert and flat, and the winds were steady. Turbulence would not be a problem. The runway was large, allowing for an angled landing into the strong wind. I landed and taxied slowly to the large apron area. Presently, a pickup truck and a fire truck headed out from the terminal to intercept me. I had no idea why they were doing this. The fire truck turned and stopped at right angles to me, just ten yards in front of me. Of course I had to stop. I hadn't asked for any of this attention.

Three men jumped out of the pickup. Before I knew it, those three guys had climbed up onto the left float of my plane, the windward side. The engine was still running and the propeller was whipping around at 1500 RPM. I was very concerned. I had no way of knowing what these guys would do next. One man was extended away from the float, hanging with both hands onto the wing strut. Then it dawned on me that they were trying to save me – keep me from flipping over. They had probably never seen a float plane on their desert runway before, at least not in a 40 knot wind. To them it must have looked like my plane was in eminent danger of being blown over. They were either very brave or very stupid or both. If they truly thought the plane

105

might flip over, why would they risk their life? The engine was still screaming. Their little amount of weight on the float was not going to hold it down. If the plane flipped, they would be tossed in who knows what direction, possibly into the spinning propeller. I shut down the engine.

They must have figured I had an emergency, to have landed in this wind. I pulled the window open and told the man closest to me, standing on my float, that my family needed to use the restroom. They took the news better than I expected and were kind enough to give Molly and the girls a ride to the terminal. Fifteen minutes later they returned. We got buckled in and I fired up the turbine. I turned on the radio and heard the tower say that a twin engine plane was disabled on the runway with a flat tire. The plane had apparently blown a tire while trying to land in the strong crosswind. Another small plane was flying in the pattern. The tower told him about the disabled craft and asked if he could stay aloft for a while, until the twin was removed. The pilot sounded like he was a student pilot, and he sounded like he was a Japanese national, because his accent was so thick I could barely understand him. The tower had to explain to him several times what was going on. They asked him if he had enough fuel. He answered hesitantly in his heavy accent, "I ... I ... I ... tiiiink so." I could see that things were getting complicated. I told the tower that I could takeoff from where I was waiting on the apron at the edge of the runway. Would they clear me? They were probably only too glad to get me out of there and they cleared me to go. It was an angled takeoff, just as it had been an angled landing.

Chapter 15 - Conservation Ethic

In 1927, Max Ehrmann wrote a beautiful poem entitled "Desiderata." My favorite line says: "You are a child of the universe, no less than the trees or the stars; you have a right to be here."

It assures me there is no guilt associated with being born among a species that is fouling its planet. We each had no control over what happened before we were born. But we do have control over how we live and treat our earth. Certainly, over-abundance of human beings is the root cause of our fears for the future of earth's precarious life forms. Humans have the ability to ruin their home in multiple ways; unrestrained burning of fossil fuels, environmental contamination and nuclear warfare. Earth has experienced and recovered from huge catastrophes in the past, including mega meteor impacts and massive volcanic activity. This time is different. The animals responsible for the desecration have the mental capacity to alter their behavior. Whether they will do that collectively, and soon enough is doubtful, but possible.

Humans, for the most part, have lost touch with the natural untamed world. Most live in cities. For them, the world is made of pavement, buildings, cars, buses, and an occasional grassy park. Food and clothing show up in stores. Waste disappears down the toilet. Oil and gas power their lives. Little serious thought is given to the sustainability of their life style.

Ideally, humans should number 7 million instead of 7 billion. They should live in moderate sized communities that are spaced far enough apart so that the natural habitats for plants and animals remain fully functional. We can probably never achieve that ideal, even though I happen to live in such a place. Juneau has 30,000 people and is surrounded by wilderness in the form of forests and marine waterways. We are able to shoot as many deer and catch as many fish as we need annually. We harvest mushrooms, berries, wild cucumbers and nettles, and grow other table items in our garden. Our house is heated with hydroelectric power. Nonetheless, we burn a lot of fossil fuel in our cars, and our boats, and our travel, just like everyone else.

Even in America, where we like to think our population is well educated and informed, we are unable to enact and sustain environmental protection policies. One administration makes headway, only to be undercut by another. Always there is the sacred economy. Our nation believes it must always grow. We must always have more; more pay, more cars, bigger houses, more roads, more trips. Almost everyone's retirement is tied in one way or another to the stock market. That means there will always be pressure to keep it growing. As national debt soars, more pressure is placed on growth to increase tax revenue. When will we wake up? Or will we die in our sleep? The container we are living in (called earth) is a closed system, vulnerable to our misguided actions.

Earth currently has the highest concentration of carbon dioxide that its atmosphere has experienced the past 800,000 years, and it may be the highest it has been in the last 20 million years. There is no question that we have greatly increased atmospheric carbon dioxide. It is irresponsible to hope that the current warming of our planet is a natural cycle, not the result of man's activities. Unfortunately, we have already set into motion unstoppable feedback systems; the loss of summer ice in the Arctic Ocean leads to more loss of ice. The thawing of huge expanses of permafrost across Canada, Alaska and Russia releases massive amounts of carbon dioxide and methane, which have been locked up in the frozen ground since the last ice age. The released carbon increases the global temperature, thawing more permafrost and releasing more carbon in an endless loop.

And then there is the acidification of the oceans, occurring in concert with and as a result of the ballooning abundance of carbon dioxide. How comfortable should we feel about having the most acidic ocean in the past 20 million years? What will happen to marine ecosystems? No one really knows the full extent of the impacts. Humans weren't around 20 million years ago to collect data. Again, is the gamble of ignoring greenhouse gases a responsible way to behave, to gamble with the future of the living world?

Humans are in the early stages of the sixth mass extinction of species on earth. Species are currently becoming extinct at a rate 1000 times higher than the natural rate. A plague is killing the life forms of our biosphere, and it is us.

For us to have *any* chance of saving our planet for future generations, scientific information which is published must be truthful and unbiased, including all publications for consumption by the general public. If bias creeps in, the two tribes of voters will fight over which science is correct. The messengers of the information, the media, must also be unbiased. If not, tribal warfare will prevail and lead to improper decisions, or no decisions at all.

In the latter stages of my career, I found myself in the midst of a scientific controversy. I was a whistleblower at my agency, pointing out that data had been analyzed incorrectly and conclusions were erroneous. I was accused of attempting to undermine the Endangered Species Program. They seemed determined to list the Kittlitz's murrelet as Endangered under the Endangered Species Act, regardless of how shaky the data was. I was told that they would not consider my arguments until I had published them. They said this work was not part of my job and I was to do it on my own time without pay. This I did. In the end, several of us were able to spur the government into looking at all of the data much more critically. They ultimately decided not to list the Kittlitz's murrelet as endangered.

Why would I, as a wildlife biologist, argue against listing a species and giving it greater protections? I knew if the species was listed, there would be court challenges, and I would likely be deposed to testify against my own agency. The credibility of the U.S. Fish and Wildlife Service was at stake. The strength of the Endangered Species Act could have been compromised.

I marvel at the natural world that has evolved through countless generations of life in the last several billion years. It is a fantastic interconnected web of relationships. In fact, we were an ordinary part of that web until a few thousand years ago. We must make a grand effort to not destroy it in the short time period we as humans are present.

We are incapable of predicting how billions of human beings will alter their globe over the coming centuries and millennia. We therefore must take the conservative approach of reducing our human abundance significantly and reducing our known impacts on air, water and land. These decisions must be made soon.

We have a right to be here, but not a right to knowingly ruin our spaceship.

Part Two

Personal Life

Chapter 16 - Childhood
1951 – 1969

According to my parents, they saw little indication their young son would amount to anything. I apparently sucked my thumb most of the time and stood around and watched what was going on. My father had meager success teaching me to catch a ball since my left thumb was always in my mouth. It remained shiny pink, even when I played in the dirt.

We lived in Portland Oregon until I was 7 years old. Ours was a regular middle-class American family. My mother took care of the household duties and my father worked as a fisheries biologist for the Oregon Fish Commission. My sister was almost four years older than I. Despite our difference in age, we were good friends. She taught me how to fish. She directed me to sit on the couch and told me not to peek over the back. My fishing pole was a stick with a string tied onto the end. Instead of a hook on the string, she had attached a rubber band. She would be hiding from my view on the other side of the couch. I threw the string over the couch and waited. Suddenly the string would jerk and my fishing pole would move furiously. I pulled the string over to my side of the couch and there, held by the rubber band, was my fish. Sometimes it was a penny, sometimes a piece of candy or maybe a pencil. Often it was nothing at all, for fishing is like that. I sent the line back over the side of my "boat" again and again.

I was supposed to also have a brother two years older than myself, but he was stillborn. My parent's genetics were such that they had the Rh Factor. The Rh Factor had only been known for 10 years before I was born, so it was a relatively new discovery and could not be prevented as is the case now. My mother's doctor expected me to die before birth, just as my brother had. So they took me several weeks early by cesarean section. The hospital was prepared to give me a blood transfusion at birth to try to save my life.

Fortunately for me, my blood type was the same as my mother's and the doctor did not have to perform an immediate transfusion. Apparently this doctor must have failed his class on genetics, because when he saw that my blood was not as he had expected, he told my mother that my father couldn't be the father. My mother responded "Then it must have been divine conception." Since I know I am not the product of divine conception, my father must have been heterozygous for the Rh Factor allele, which means 50% of his offspring would be like myself.

I should have had a younger sister, but she was also stillborn. I think this sadness must have taken a big toll on my parents, especially my mother. She struggled with mental problems later in life.

In 1958, my family moved across the country to Arlington, Virginia, a suburb of Washington, D.C. We lived on the northern edge of Arlington where I attended first grade. It was a white neighborhood. Many of the families had a parent working for the Federal Government. My father was one of them. On one side of us lived a Japanese family, the father a diplomat. On the other side, the father worked at the Pentagon. Three houses away was Mr. Oppenheim, a very intelligent man, who was not at liberty to discuss his government job.

Besides living amongst dignitaries, our close proximity to Washington D.C. endowed us with another, less desirable, circumstance. At the time, America and Russia were at the height of the Cold War. I was eleven years old when the Cuban Missile Crisis played out. It made a strong impression on me and it fostered fear.

At my school, there were frequent air raid drills. I remember one particular instance, probably during the Cuban Missile Crisis, when the school required all parents to determine how long it took their son or daughter to race home from school on foot. If their child took longer than fifteen minutes, he or she would be held at school should America come under attack. The day of the test, I remember running as hard as I could. My lungs were burning and my legs ached, but I wanted so badly to be allowed to run home. I made it in just under fifteen minutes.

What I didn't know then, was that my father was part of an emergency skeleton government. In the event of a Russian attack, he was to go immediately to a secret underground installation in the Appalachian Mountains. My father wouldn't have been with us even had I run home in time. My mother, my sister and I would have waited in the basement where water and food was stored. We would not have known what happened to my father. He was a good federal employee and would certainly have honored his allegiance to his nation. We knew nothing about his secret until years later.

My favorite books often had a theme of survival. Maybe this explains my quest for remote adventures later in life. I read many versions of *Swiss Family Robinson* and

Daniel Boone. I read *Robinson Crusoe*. I read about the Native American tribes of the east coast and of the central plains. Television shows were dominated by westerns during my childhood, such as "Wild, Wild West," "Bonanza," "Wagon Train," "Cheyenne," "Gunsmoke," "Maverick," "Rawhide," "The Rifleman," and "Kung Fu." I was a child that should have grown up in the woods or on a farm, not in a suburb.

I was lucky enough to have some open space near my house. It was the school yard across the street – a very large school yard. Probably six football fields could fit there. I spent most of my time on those grounds after school, playing basketball, football or baseball. The only woods near my house was a narrow fringe of forest that separated the school field from a string of houses. It was probably about 100 feet wide. Sometimes I would go into the trees when it had been raining or snowing and practice lighting fires in the wettest of conditions. Once the fire was giving off noticeable warmth and a nice wood smoke aroma, it was time to snuff it out before the smoke was noticed by anyone.

I was practicing survival. I made slings out of cord and leather. On the school yard, when no one was around, I practiced throwing rocks with the sling. I could throw a rock well over a hundred yards. One time I launched a rock over the fringe of trees and heard when it hit a house on the other side. I decided I better not do that again. I was glad I hadn't heard the shattering of a picture window.

Few adults jogged around on streets and school yards when I was a boy. But there was one man who did. My friends and I would jog with him once in a while. His name was John Glenn. We knew that he was the first American to orbit the earth a few years earlier. If he thought us kids were interfering with his runs, he didn't let on to it. He was always friendly, although not talkative while he was jogging. He lived on the opposite side of the junior high school from us. His drive to stay in good physical condition must have continued unabated for many more years because Glenn became the oldest person to fly in space at the age of 77 aboard the shuttle *Discovery* in 1998.

My sister, Shirley, knew him quite well. She was good friends with his daughter, Carolyn, who was known as Lyn to her friends and family. Shirley recalls when Col. Glenn picked her and Lyn up at a bowling alley. Some boys followed the car, which annoyed Col. Glenn. He turned into a cul-de-sac, hoping to cut them off. He jumped out of the car to confront them but the boys were just able to maneuver around him.

Another time, Shirley was picked up by a limousine at the Glenn's house and driven, along with Lyn and several other girls, to the Ringling Brothers Circus in Washington D.C. They had a police escort and Lyn was put under a spotlight and recognized to the audience. Carolyn Glenn was probably one of my sister's two friends that helped her to draft an affidavit for me to sign when I was in fifth grade. It said, "I, Jack Hodges, promise that I will never kiss a girl as long as I live." I was more than happy to sign it, thoroughly convinced it was true.

I was on the receiving end of a very fortunate consequence of living near Washington D.C. The solo trombonist for Pershing's Own Army Band, Keig Garvin, lived near us and attended our church. My parents decided I should play the trombone and they asked Keig if he would give me trombone lessons. He was somewhat reluctant at first, saying he normally didn't accept beginning students – he had all the serious students he could handle. For some reason he accepted me. Initially, I was not a dedicated student. I went to my half-hour lessen every week because my parents were paying for it and expected me to go. I practiced just enough to get by.

But then something remarkable happened, without me even realizing it. This amazing teacher slowly infused his knowledge into me, and even part of his character, I believe. He was a fabulous musician, known throughout the brass world, representing both *Conn* and *King* instrument manufacturers and gave clinics across the country. Keig Garvin was one of the best, if not the best, solo trombonist in the United States for many years.

He had expectations for me every week. He intertwined his criticism with enough humor to keep me engaged. For example, he might ask "How old are you?" I answered that I was 12. Then he would quip "Yup, just as I figured, you should be able to count to 4. There are four beats in that measure." When I would see him reach for his beautiful *Conn* trombone, I got excited. He was about to demonstrate something, or play a duet with me. As the instrument came to his mouth, his embouchure deftly settled in. The slide, gliding effortlessly by his relaxed wrist and fingers, went to the perfect locations. Beautiful velvet tones reached my ears. The sounds he produced were stunningly pure. I loved to play duets with him. When I left for college, he told me I was among his top four students. Music was a gift I continued to enjoy, but never pursued as a profession.

My closest friend in high school was Sandy. His grandparents lived on a farm just 35 miles west of Arlington. Every Sunday his family drove to the farm for dinner and to help with chores. I was often invited. Sandy and I would take his .22 rifle into the woods and plink at things. He was a good shot, better than I.

Sandy was extremely curious about a secret government installation that was nearby on a wooded ridge called Mount Weather. Several times we drove up there and walked near the high fence and tried to figure it out. There was a large area of mowed grass. An asphalt two-lane road curved around and seemingly disappeared. We couldn't quite tell, but we thought the road must lead into the mountain itself. From what we could see, we surmised that this place was a secret underground installation of some kind.

I had not the slightest inkling that my father would have been summoned to this place in the event of nuclear war. Six years later, on December 1, 1974, TWA Flight 514 crashed into the ridge next to Mount Weather while on its approach into Dulles International Airport. The Mount Weather installation became instantly exposed to the public and was unclassified after that. Once my father learned it was declassified, he told me how they had taken him there to see that facility years before and how he would have reported there directly in the event of war. I could never have guessed then, that I would someday travel to Russia, flying my own aircraft across thousands of miles of Russian landscape, just 100 feet above the ground.

Arlington was quite segregated when I was in school. Sandy and I attended a white high school that had only a couple of black students. The black high school was in the center part of Arlington. When our schools met on the athletic fields and on the basketball courts, it was white against black. I was not taught to be prejudiced, but prejudice was part of my environment. Adults around me talked with fear and trepidation about the misfortune that would befall a neighborhood if a black family moved there and bought a house. They worried that the "colored folk" would cause the value of their houses to plummet. If one black family moved in, they were likely to attract other black families. We, like most white families I knew, had a black woman clean our house once a week. Growing up, I never saw a white man collect garbage. In fact, I thought I would never see a white man collecting garbage. That was my perspective at the time.

My first real job was as a roofer. It was the summer after my senior year in high school. I had been on the gymnastics team the previous winter and was well muscled.

It wasn't easy to find a job and I was getting discouraged with my lack of success. One day, I walked past a roofing company and decided to inquire about the possibility of being hired for the summer. The owner looked me over and said he would try me out. He instructed me to show up at 7:30am the next morning.

When I arrived the following day, there were half a dozen workers moving about the yard and adjacent warehouse. I timidly entered through the outer gate and found the owner whom I had talked to the day before. He told me to help load that vehicle, pointing to a blue flatbed truck. Everyone in the yard, except me and the owner, was black. I started helping two black men throw bundles of shingles and rolls of tar paper onto the bed of the truck. When it was loaded, the three of us piled into the cab and headed out to some unknown destination. They joked with each other in their fascinating drawl, most of which I could understand, some of which I couldn't. They seemed not to even notice I was in the cab with them. I was a nonentity.

We arrived at a single level brick home in a suburban neighborhood. The job was to replace the shingle roof. First, we unloaded all of the bundles of shingles and rolls of paper from the truck and put them onto the lawn. Then the two roofers climbed up onto the roof and began ripping the old shingles off, using flat-edged shovels to pry off the shingles, nails and all. They pushed all of the mess over the edge of the roof onto the ground. I had to collect the rubble, haul it to the truck in a wheel barrow, and throw it onto the bed. The old roof was ripped off quickly. Within an hour, the roof was down to bare wood.

Then the workers came down to put on their carpenter belts. One man carried a box of roofing nails up the ladder and the other carried the first roll of tar paper. They rolled out the tar paper along the bottom edge of the roof and began tacking it down with roofing nails. Their motion was fluid, efficient and unbelievably fast. They walked across the roof, a handful of nails in their left hand, their roofing hammer in their right. Tap - whack - tap - whack - tap - whack, right across the roof. Mindlessly a nail was fed between the first two fingers of their left hand. The point of the nail was touched to the paper and a tap with the hammer temporarily secured it there, followed by one whack of the hammer to drive it home. The two men were nailing machines, beautiful to watch. Soon they told me to bring up more rolls of paper and in another 30 minutes the roof was covered with tar paper.

Next, the workers ran a tape measure along each side of the roof and used a nail to scrape a pointed mark on the paper every six inches. One man held the end of a long chalk line on a mark at one edge of the roof while the other held it taut on a mark at the other edge. The line was pulled like a rubber band and then allowed to snap down. A perfectly straight line was instantly marked with chalk the length of the roof. I had never seen a chalk line before. Parallel lines soon covered that side of the roof.

I was told to start carrying bundles of shingles up the ladder. They were to be placed near the top of the roof. Each bundle weighed 75 pounds. It wasn't difficult to put the bundle on my shoulder, but I felt quite top heavy climbing the ladder. My experience with ladders was rather limited. Stepping from the ladder to the roof was the trickiest part. The ladder was always extended at least three feet above the edge of the roof, so one hand could be on the ladder for stability as the critical step was taken. Each worker had their own bundle of shingles to work with.

It didn't take them long to go through the 29 shingles in a bundle. The shingle placement started at the bottom edge of the roof. The top of the shingle was aligned with the chalk line. Four nails were hammered into place with amazing speed, tap - whack - tap - whack - tap - whack - tap - whack. That day I carried 1,800 pounds of shingles up the ladder. My shoulder was raw from the edges of the bundled shingles scraping through my shirt. Facing the same task the following day, I brought a sponge from under our sink at home and put that on my shoulder, under my shirt. That got me through the second day and the additional 1,500 pounds of shingles I packed up to the roof.

At first I was scared to walk on a slanted roof, envisioning the risk of sliding off the roof. But it soon became mindless. The workers never let me get up on a slate roof though. Those were dangerous because the slate can break and send you sliding off the roof. Slate roofs are lifetime roofs, but occasionally they would need repair.

That first week, I was just a young white boy whom they were in charge of. The men would rarely talk to me and would eat their lunch apart from me. Then one day, when they were taking their morning break, I asked one of them if I could use his hammer and nail down a few shingles. He consented. I practiced their method of using the left hand to feed roofing nails between my index and middle fingers. They used a handful of nails, but I found I needed to start with just a few. All the nails in the hand must remain corralled while one was fed forward between the fingers. You can't have nails falling onto the roof.

I was awkward at the process, and very slow. I learned to tap the nail lightly in place, but was hesitant to send it home with a solid swing. The workers returned to the roof and I was back cleaning up messes and carrying shingles. No one expected me to pound nails, but I kept practicing whenever I had a chance. After another week I bought myself a roofing hammer and a carpenter belt to hold the nails. I continued to nail shingles at every opportunity, and I was getting better and better at it. I wasn't as fast, but I was beginning to feed nails between my fingers without even thinking about it.

With time, they began to approve of my work, and of course it was helpful to them. They could take longer breaks and still get more work done in a day. They started taking me along when they went to a store to get food for lunch. I enjoyed listening to their conversations and learning about their lives outside of work. I heard about a far different world than mine. Their wives or girlfriends were usually working as well and their many children looked after each other, and a grandparent or two was

117

probably also around. Some of the men in their families had been injured on construction jobs and couldn't work, and so they helped with the kids too. These were poor families. Owning a car was a big deal, any kind of car.

More and more responsibility was given to me, even having me drive the truck on some errands once in a while. I had respect for them and I think they were not displeased with the white boy.

The work was hard labor and sometimes dangerous. Several times I was on jobs where the men were reroofing flat roofs using hot tar. The process was one of mopping hot tar onto the old roof, with overlapping layers of tar paper sandwiched in. The top layer of tar was then protected with a layer of loose gravel. I carried the hot tar in buckets up to the roof, using a ladder of course. Nowadays the tar is pumped to the roof in a pipe.

One day I took off my shirt because the temperature was over 90 degrees. The sun was beating down, and the tar was really hot. A coworker looked at me and said, "You best put your shirt back on, kid. If you ever splash any of that tar, you'll wish you had it on." The tar in my buckets was roughly 400 degrees Fahrenheit. Everyone stayed well clear of the ladder while I was carrying the buckets. After a day of sweating profusely and working in thick tar fumes, a big surprise awaited me when I rinsed my face with water. My entire face felt like it was on fire. The intense stinging lasted fifteen minutes before subsiding.

I survived that summer without any serious injury. Just as important, I gained a measure of mutual respect with my black coworkers. It was a good experience to work with these men who were from a much different part of America than I. One white person and half a dozen black people moved a little closer to each other.

Chapter 17 - College
1969 - 1973

I knew that my father wanted to transfer from his job in Washington D.C. to one in Portland, Oregon. So I decided to attend Willamette University, a small liberal arts college in Salem, Oregon, about 45 miles south of Portland. I arrived in Oregon in late August 1969 to warm sunny weather and ripe blackberries growing along the roadsides. I was given a room in a freshman dormitory. My roommate was a strange fellow. He wore a suit and tie, everywhere. He showed up at the freshman softball game in his suit. Everyone called him Senator, because he said he would become one of Oregon's senators one day. He called his mother every day. After four months, he quit school to return to his mother.

The first weekend of school I saw notices advertising the freshman dance. They were having a live band. I decided to give it a try. I went to it by myself, arriving late enough to be assured the dance would be fully underway. I entered and found a place to stand next to one of the walls along with the other guys that were waiting to ask a girl to dance or were too shy to ask. I was among the latter. As girls arrived, they were approached quickly by the boys. By the time I had worked up enough nerve to walk towards one of the new arrivals, they would already be taken by someone else. I told myself that as soon as the next attractive girl showed up, I would move into action.

Shortly, two girls walked through the door. One had short dark hair. Her Mediterranean face was intriguing, but it was the girl she was with that really caught my eye. She was Asian or maybe Native American, with long black hair. I started to move quickly, but not quickly enough. A tall handsome guy was moving in ahead of me. I knew for sure he would ask the long haired girl. My shoulders sagged. I felt defeat again. He talked with them for a minute, and then the Mediterranean girl followed him onto the dance floor. I couldn't believe it, the girl with the long black hair was still standing there.

Don't hesitate now. Swiftly, I approached and asked if she wanted to dance. She said yes and we went onto the dance floor. After our first song and all the other songs that night, she made no move to leave, nor did I. When the dance ended, I walked her to her dorm, Lausanne Hall. Before saying good-night to Lisa outside on the sidewalk, I violated the promise I had made to Carolyn Glenn and my sister when I was eleven years old.

The next day she saw me in the commons. I was wearing glasses instead of my contact lenses, and I was wearing dorky Bermuda shorts. Lisa told me later that seeing me there was quite a letdown from the handsome guy she had danced with the night before. She decided to say hi to me anyway and from then on, we hardly missed an opportunity to be together. It was an exciting time, exploring a new world neither of us had known before.

Lisa was from Hawai'i. Both grandparents on her father's side were Chinese. On her mother's side, her grandmother was pure Hawai'ian and her grandfather was Chinese. Lisa was an only child. Her parents worked hard so that she could attend a private Episcopal school in Honolulu. She was surrounded by the Hawai'ian culture. Her Hawai'ian grandmother had eleven children, ten of them girls. Her ten aunts married Hawai'ian and Chinese men and created a lot of Hawai'ian cousins for Lisa. Only one aunt married a Haole (European descent) man, and they didn't have any children. Lisa's parents were extremely proud that they were able to send Lisa to a good mainland college, Willamette University. She meant everything to them, and a college education for her was their biggest dream. Their second biggest dream was for Lisa to marry a nice Chinese boy from Honolulu. Lisa falling in love with a Haole boy at college was not part of the plan.

During my freshman year, something grave was happening in my family back in Virginia. My sister's husband, Mike, was dying of cancer at the young age of 23. Shirley met Mike three years earlier during her sophomore year in college and fell deeply in love with him, similar to Lisa and me. Now he was being treated with experimental cancer fighting drugs at the John Hopkins Medical Center. It was horrible for him. He was one of those research specimens willing to suffer for the rest of us.

When I last saw him at Christmas break, he was occasionally having a good day and would even be able to play cards with us. But over the next 5 months it got worse and worse. I did not observe his dying process, because I was in school. It took a heavy toll on my sister. She loved him dearly and the anguish of seeing him wither in pain was crushing.

On May 19, 1970, I was passing through New York on my way to Glasgow, Scotland. I was part of a Willamette University choir and instrumental group that was heading to Europe for a six week tour. I played trombone. It was a wonderful opportunity for me to see Europe and bring beautiful music from America. I called home from New York. Mike had died the day before, but my parents decided not to tell me. They wanted to be sure I stayed with my University tour. In fact, they had protected me from all deaths in my family. I had never been to a memorial service for my grandparents, or anyone else, and I was going to miss Mike's service and burial. This would prove to influence my life later in ways I couldn't have imagined at the time.

Mike and Shirley before he became sick.

I learned of his death shortly after arriving in London. My grieving would have to be done alone. I was among friends, but none of them was in the emotional place I was in.

Another potentially life altering event happened that summer. On July 1st, The U.S. Selective Service conducted a random lottery to determine which young men, born in 1951, would be required to serve in the military. Our birthdate was our identifier. For those of us that were nineteen years old, this lottery would determine who went to Vietnam. Five hundred soldiers were dying in combat every month. It was almost considered a death sentence if your lottery number turned out to be low. Anyone whose birthdate had a lottery number under 100 was expected to be drafted. My number was 33. I was certainly going to be drafted.

I needed to think deeply about this situation. The war had become very unpopular during the previous few years. This was especially true among the younger generation. My father didn't express a dissatisfaction with the war, probably because he had served in World War II and felt our government was to be trusted and respected. My mother hated Lynden Johnson and didn't want her son drafted into this war. I tried to make sense of the war. As I understood it, we were in Vietnam to stop the spread of Communism. On one hand, that seemed like an important objective. But why was it taking so many years to win a war in this tiny country? We were a big powerful nation. We were told that gorilla warfare was different. The enemy was illusive and difficult to discern from the friendlies. On the other hand, why did we have to kill hundreds of thousands of people Insure that democracy prevailed over Communism? If our system was so good, wouldn't the people across the world migrate towards the better system? Maybe Communism would emerge as the best system, and eventually we would even want it ourselves. Why not just let countries make their own decisions? Why do we have to force ourselves on everyone else? I didn't want to fight in this war.

All of us young men were required to show up for the Selective Services' physical examination. I had a note from our family doctor stating my history of asthma. This was not a cooked up ailment for me. I was subject to serious asthma attacks under certain conditions. It was easily set off with grass pollen or cat dander or smoke, to name a few. My breathing was perfectly normal the day of the examination. At the end of the exam, each of us met individually with a military doctor. I showed him the note. He read it and then asked me to describe what it felt like to have asthma. Then he asked me, "Son, do you want to serve in the military?" I said, "No, not really."

He gave me the designation "4F", unfit for service. That designation began in the Civil War. If an inductee didn't have four front teeth suitable for ripping open the gun powder cartridge, they were 4f, disqualified.

A few years later, on more than one occasion, my asthma flared up badly during field operations, such as banding geese. We were working in tall grass, herding the geese and processing them. I covered my nose and mouth with a wet bandana in an effort to filter the pollen. Those nights were spent lying in my sleeping bag, in a tent, straining for every breath. I would have been a liability on the battle field. Nonetheless, I felt guilty that some other young man had to take my place in the military during the Vietnam War.

By the spring semester of my sophomore year, I realized I needed to attend a larger school, one that had a reputation in wildlife, the field I wanted to pursue as my career. Oregon State University was only 40 miles from Willamette University. They had a strong wildlife department. I decided I would transfer the following fall. I didn't tell Lisa about my plans, which upset her very much. We had become extremely close. It was scary for me to think that I might be getting locked into a path without an escape. Marriage was a decision that was so permanent, a lifelong commitment. I felt that some distance in the relationship might be good right then.

Near the end of spring, I was facing the one year anniversary of Mike's premature and heart rending death. I had no experience with grieving – no handbook, no role model, no one to share it with. On May 4, exactly 14 days before the anniversary of his death, I started a fast, which would end two weeks later on the anniversary date, May 18. I would honor his courageous fight by experiencing a tiny token of the suffering he endured.

Each day I ate just one slice of bread with butter on it, and an orange. I knew nothing about a condition called "survivor's guilt". That would be a term I would become familiar with much later in life. For now, this was the tribute I would give to Mike. It was not easy, but it was easier than I thought it would be. After several days, I started to get somewhat accustomed to the gnawing feeling in my stomach. Food was on my mind most of the time.

It was hard to concentrate in class, but I felt good about myself, like this was the right thing to do. I could have pride in myself even though no one, except my roommate, knew what I was doing. I got weaker as the days passed, and I had little energy to play basketball or other physical activities. I was surprised that I was able to stick with it. I looked forward to my bread and orange and focused on every bite with an appreciation I had not known before.

When summer break came in 1971, I was fortunate to obtain a temporary fisheries position with the U.S. Fish and Wildlife Service in Juneau, Alaska. It was a start of what would be a fulfilling career. Lisa was spending the summer with her parents in Hawai'i working for Dole Pineapple Company. We were in love and wrote letters constantly to each other. One of the letters I wrote to her that summer included a fantasy story about us. In it, she was rowing a small boat from Hawai'i to Juneau. Her plan was to show up at my doorstep in Juneau and surprise me. Simultaneously, I was paddling a canoe from Juneau to Hawai'i with the exact same intention. In the middle of the Pacific Ocean, when we were unknowingly close to each other, just a couple of miles apart, a terrible storm hit with frightening waves and lightning. I began to paddle into the wind to keep from capsizing and I came upon the tiny row boat with Lisa lying in the bottom. She was barely alive. We were together, and we were able to weather the storm in the row boat.

Sixteen years later, this fantasy story almost became a self-fulfilling prophecy.

In the fall, I began my junior year at Oregon State University. The prerequisite course list for Wildlife Biology was twice as long as the list for Zoology, so I decided to major in Zoology. This would allow me to take courses of my choosing in statistics. I much preferred math courses to biology courses. I knew how important statistics was to scientific research and I also knew that most biologists avoided math classes and were weak in math. I thought I would enjoy Statistics and believed the classes would help me compete for jobs in my future career as a Wildlife Biologist.

I filled my undergraduate schedule with as many statistical courses as I could fit in. Statistics begins with probability, so the first statistics course I signed up for was Introductory Probability. By the mid-term exam, it became clear just how well my plan was working out. I received a "D" on the exam. I had expected math courses to be easy but these concepts required some new thought processes. My professor was very smart. He told us if our grade on the final exam was better than our mid-term grade, he would completely ignore the mid-term grade. That was perfect motivation for a slacker like me. I came through on the final exam with an "A".

Lisa was only 40 miles away. We saw each other on weekends that fall quarter. Her parents were not pleased when she told them she wanted to transfer to Oregon State University. Her major was History, and Willamette would have served her well. They relented, and Lisa moved before winter quarter. She did not want to lose me. I was happy we were together and I began to realize that as scary as it was to commit my life to her, I could not imagine living without her.

We decided to plan our marriage for the Christmas break of the following year, our senior year. I visited Lisa and her family in Honolulu in late August, four months before our wedding date. Our plan was to tell her parents then.

It was a good thing we sat down with them shortly before our departure from Hawaii, rather than at the beginning of my visit. Lisa's father became very upset during the conversation. He started using harsh words against Lisa, even vulgar words. I told him that he could use any words he wanted against me, but he wasn't going to talk to Lisa like that. He jumped up out of his chair and said, "Do you want to fight?" I told him I didn't want to fight. Lisa's mother broke in and explained that Richard can become very excited when he is upset.

That was the end of the discussion. Lisa and I left Hawai'i the next day. On the flight home, we decided we would wait a month or so and then send them a letter inviting them to the wedding.

Lisa's parents attended our wedding and appeared to be happy during the ceremony and festivities.

I am sure it was hard for Richard to let his daughter go. He loved her deeply and always felt that she was his little girl. Unfortunately for him, his little girl would end up in Alaska.

Chapter 18 - It Happens
1987

Lisa and I moved into an apartment for married students at Oregon State University while I attended graduate school. My major professor was Dr. Scott Overton in the Department of Statistics. My minor professors were Dr. Howard White and Dr. Charles Meslow with the Oregon Cooperative Wildlife Research Unit. My love for math and statistics continued through my Masters Degree program to the detriment of my wildlife course work. I did not take an ornithology course while in college, and yet I ended up spending 34 years working with birds.

I was given a stipend by the U.S. Fish and Wildlife Service to analyze the first three years of data from their Scent Station Index to Predator Abundance. The data was collected in the 17 western states, amounting to 13,000 IBM data cards. Lisa helped me key punch those cards from hand written data sheets. I wrote the computer programs to collate the data. The computer on campus lived in a building of its own. I delivered the boxes of data cards along with my program to the computer center. Several hours later the result of my computer run was available, printed on large computer paper. More often than not, the result was an error in my program, which had to be found, corrected and the process started all over again. What took hours then, takes seconds now.

I graduated in 1975 with reasonably good grades. Lisa and I immediately moved to Juneau, Alaska as I had accepted the position as Fred Robards' assistant working with bald eagles.

By 1987, Lisa and I had lived in Juneau for 12 years and were well established. We had two beautiful daughters, Kara age 7 and Jennifer age 9. We owned a home and had already built two additions onto it. Lisa was working two days a week for a respected lawyer in town. She also volunteered at the Alaska State Museum as a docent and was finally using her history degree. She wrote a manual for all of the docents working there. Tourists assumed she was an Alaskan native. When Lisa went to stores, or other venues, the native women would approach her as if she were a relative.

After flying the waterfowl surveys in Manitoba, Saskatchewan and Ontario, I participated in waterfowl productivity surveys and banding activities throughout the summer. When September rolled around, I was part of a ten-member relay running team that was competing in the 110 mile Klondike Trail of '98 Relay from Skagway,

Alaska to Whitehorse, Yukon Territory. The race started at 8:00pm on Friday, September 18. I ran my 13 mile leg during the pitch blackness of a moonless night. Our relay team finished the race by early afternoon and Lisa was there in Whitehorse to cheer us on. She had come to Whitehorse from Juneau that morning by airplane. Our two daughters were left in Juneau, under the care of friends. Lisa attended the awards ceremony that night and the dance which followed. On Sunday I took her to the airport for the 4pm *Air North* flight back to Juneau where she would pick up the kids and have them ready for school on Monday. I would join her later. I was going to travel for an extra day with our friends, Kim and Ethel Smith, to do some recreational gold panning near Atlin, British Columbia.

The events that unfolded in the next few hours after leaving Lisa at the Whitehorse airport relate to Pope John Paul II and his travels in the region. Three years earlier, in 1984, he became the first Pope to set foot on Canadian soil. That year, he tried to visit the native community of Fort Simpson in northwestern Canada, but dense fog prevented his plane from landing there. He promised them that he would return someday to their community. He fulfilled that promise the day of Lisa's flight, September 20. This time the weather was good and his plane was able to land at the Fort Simpson airport. He spent five hours there. His speech to those gathered in his midst started with these words:

> "Dear Aboriginal Brothers and Sisters,
> I wish to tell you how happy I am to be with you, the native peoples of Canada, in this beautiful land of Denendeh. I have come first from across the ocean and now from the United States to be with you, and I know that many of you have also come from far away — from the frozen Arctic, from the prairies, from the forests, from all parts of this vast and beautiful country of Canada."

The small aviation service, *Air North*, was busy that day transporting some of the native peoples that Pope John Paul II was referring to — taking them to Fort Simpson to see the Pope. The airline was behind schedule. Lisa's plane was delayed for more than an hour.

The pilot was in a hurry to get to Juneau and had pressure to cut corners on his flight path in order to save time.

The next day Kim, Ethel and I were driving on the road to Skagway to catch the afternoon ferry to Juneau. We were talking about the various individual legs our team members had run. As we approached the summit, Kim turned on the radio. Soon, a news broadcast broke into the program. I heard the announcer say that a search was underway for a missing airplane. The *Air North* plane had left Whitehorse

127

at 5:00pm on Sunday to fly to Juneau. The pilot radioed 3 minutes out of Haines that he was cancelling IFR (Instrument Flight Rules, used to fly in clouds and at night) to fly visually. There had been no Emergency Locator Transmitter signal. Weather was still hampering the search.

I was sitting behind Kim and Ethel in the small pickup truck's jump seat. I knew that it was Lisa's plane. I knew she was gone. No ELT meant the plane hit hard, very hard. The terrain between Haines and Juneau is among the most rugged in the world – precipitous mountains and glaciers cover the entire distance. I stared down at the floor. Motionless. Catatonic. Frozen. A stream of drool flowed from my mouth, soaking my pants. I couldn't move.

When we reached the border and crossed into Alaska, Kim quietly asked if I wanted him to call Bruce. Bruce was my co-worker and a seasoned pilot. He would know the status of the search and the status of our daughters. I said yes. I stood against the truck – a cold, misty wind blew through me.

Kim walked slowly back from the pay phone, shaking his head. It was Lisa's plane, he said.

Once we arrived in Skagway, Kim and Ethel put me on a small plane to Juneau. I insisted on sitting in the copilot's seat. We flew alongside the mountains southward toward Juneau. I wanted to look at the terrain through the windshield on the pilot's side for any sign of a crash, but I couldn't focus on that. I mostly just stared straight ahead, deep in my own thoughts. In Juneau I was taken to the home of our friends, Bruce and Sue Conant, where my two daughters were. They knew that mommy had not picked them up as planned the day before and that her plane was missing. Maybe other people around me had hope, but I had no hope at all, and I was not going to pretend to the kids that I had hope. I am sure they saw the concern and pain in my face. I asked them to put on their coats and walk with me out onto the tide flats.

Darkness was fast approaching. It was cloudy and the air was heavy and damp. The tide was low. I knelt down on the wet sand, to meet their eyes with mine. I told them that everybody has a sad time in their life. That this is our very sad time. Their mother's plane has crashed. She will not be coming back to us. The girls could not comprehend the magnitude of what I had just said.

I couldn't either.

We sat at the dinner table with the Conants and our friends, Jim and Mary Lou King. I was unable to eat anything. For three days I couldn't eat. The kids and I were told that we would be sleeping at Conant's house that night. I couldn't sleep. At 2:00am,

I got up and drove 13 miles to town – to my office in the Federal Building. I knew I would be facing huge challenges. I would document it. In the office were high quality, hard bound field notebooks. I grabbed one and started to write.

> "Lisa always told me that she wanted to die before me. She really had a fear that I might die before her. It would have been really hard for her if I had. Lisa said that she disliked funerals and her own should be a very small affair. In no uncertain terms, she told me that I must not allow the kids to view her body as she was forced to do at funerals as a child."

Then I drove back to the Conant's house and climbed into bed for a few hours of sleep.

The next day, the weather had turned fair, good for a search effort of the mountainous terrain. One might think that I would beat the drums to make sure every possible means and method was being used in the search. I did not. I left it to the authorities. I knew that I was not fit to participate in the search, either mentally or physically.

By late morning, a telephone call came from Search Command. The crash site had been found. It was on the side of a hanging glacier, 17 miles southeast of Haines. No word on survivors.

Two hours later, my neighbor, Glenn Cave, drove up to Conant's house. He had been helping with the search, flying his plane for Civil Air Patrol. He said he was the one that found the wreckage. He told me there was no hope for survivors. It was confirmed now. I had expected, or had somehow known, that there would be no survivors. I stepped toward him and reached out for a hug. He stepped backward, away from me, as if I had the plague.

The kids and I returned to our house. I stared at the phone. It was time. It had to be done. I was the one that had to do it. Finally, I picked it up and called Hawai'i. Lisa's father was home. The words came from my mouth – words no father should ever have to hear, "Something very bad has happened to Lisa. Lisa died in an airplane accident." A period of silence followed. He said, "You are bringing her home, aren't you?" I hadn't thought about what I was going to do with Lisa. I said, "Yes". The decision was made. I had taken her to Alaska and now I would be taking her home. She would be buried at Diamond Head Memorial Park, alongside her grandparents.

The next day, two State Troopers came to my door. They told me that Lisa's body had been recovered. One of them had participated in the recovery. He said that she died instantly from a massive head injury. He gave me a bag with her purse and the clothes she had been wearing. Several days later, very early in the morning when no one was around, I discretely buried her clothes in a shallow hole at the Shrine of St. Terese, overlooking the waters of Lynn Canal.

To:

Mrs. Jan
Baura.

Me on a very sad day. My mom is missing she is lost they are looking for her but They mite noffide her I hope They do I am glad that my dad is save

From:
Karo
my mom is very spishol to me.

130

A week later, the girls and I were in Hawai'i. I had never been to a funeral service or a burial. Lisa's mother, Rosalind, was carrying a beautiful dress for Lisa to wear. It was their family's custom. She would dress Lisa, as was her responsibility. Sadly, the mortician told Rosalind that she could not see Lisa. I am sure he was protecting Rosalind from a horrific sight. He told her he would lay the dress across Lisa's body. From the mortuary we went to the burial site. Dirt was piled on a rug next to the grave. Artificial grass blanketed the near side of the grave. It was sunny and hot. The ocean was a deep blue. I had asked the Minister if I could play Taps on my trumpet. He told me that Taps was usually reserved for military burials, but if I wanted to, I could. The minister said some words, none of which I heard. Then it was my turn. I faced the ocean, away from the grave and those that were gathered near it. I slowly progressed through the mournful tones. It was a small tribute to Lisa, even if some may have thought it was inappropriate. Then everyone walked away, leaving me alone with Jennifer and Kara. The casket had been lowered, but not yet covered with dirt. I knelt down holding them to me and told them to remember this place, the two trees behind the grave, the sky, the ocean and the Diamond Head ridge. As we started to leave, a large cockroach ran across the artificial grass towards the hole where Lisa was. I ran to it, reached down, quickly grabbed it and heaved it as far as I could.

The three of us returned to Juneau. We needed to get back to our home and begin to let the loss settle in – to begin the grieving process, each in our own way. The kids needed to return to school and face the questions from their friends. I had a memorial service to plan. Our friends in Juneau were surrogate relatives because most of us did not have close relatives nearby. They needed a service to remember Lisa and to help them feel and share their combined loss.

A few weeks after the service was Halloween. That night as I was putting Jennifer to bed, she quietly asked me some questions. Her beautiful, innocent mind was trying to figure things out.

"Daddy, what is mommy doing right now?"

I said, "I don't know."

She continued, "Is it true that people come up out of their graves on Halloween?"

"No." I answered. My heart ached for her as she tried to deal with the thoughts in her head.

Then, "Daddy, how come the plane crashed?"

I tried to explain, "There is a right way to fly through the clouds. You fly from one radio station to another."

She interrupted, "Does the station stick up real high? Do you see it when you go by it?"

"No." I told her. "The station is near the ground and you follow the radio signals which you cannot see, but the needles on the instruments point to the station. This time, though, the pilot didn't obey the law. He broke the rules and tried to go down through the clouds his own way. Then he got scared and decided to go back. He began to climb up again and he started to turn the airplane around and then he ran into the mountain."

She asked, "Daddy, why did they let him be a pilot?"

I couldn't answer her.

I allowed my grieving process to play out untethered, unchecked. I didn't run from it, nor did I try to suppress it. The depth of my feelings and emotions was beyond anything I thought a human being was capable of. I knew that I would probably survive it because others had endured such tragedies. I was told that time would heal.

I didn't want to leave Lisa behind. I pictured us both walking down a path through the forest and suddenly she stops. I keep walking. When I turn to look back, I can see her standing there, but she isn't moving and I can't stop walking. I can't go back to her. She is getting further and further behind me. It is getting harder and harder to see her. I don't want to leave her behind. *"Please, don't just stand there. I can't stop."*

By early January, three and a half months after the crash, I entered a period of deep depression. My notes described it as:

Hopeless depression.
Gripping depression.
Severe depression.
Terrifying depression.

It is as if I have been placed in a hole in the ground. I can see the sky above me, but the top of the hole is too high for me to get out.

Then, in the grip of Alaska's winter and in the grip of consuming depression, I grabbed onto another man's story like it was a life raft and I was in a tempest.

132

Six months earlier, on August 27, one month before Lisa's accident, a man named Ed Gillet paddled his kayak into Kahului Harbor on the north shore of Maui, Hawai'i. He had been at sea in this tiny craft for 63 days. The last time he had seen land was on a sandy beach in California. He became the first person to paddle a kayak from California to Hawai'i.

I had never been in a sea kayak, but it looked like a great watercraft. It was the size of a canoe and was covered to keep the waves out. A plan began to creep into my head. I would paddle a kayak from Alaska to Hawai'i. I could do it. I had to do it. It seemed like the only plan of action that came close to matching my pain and sorrow. I felt I couldn't just walk on through life as if nothing had happened. There had to be a response – an epic response. I still knew nothing about something called "survivor's guilt". When I thought about the possibility of undertaking this odyssey, I felt a sense of relief from my anguish. Nothing else gave me relief. It became addictive. When I was suffering emotionally, I could work on my plan for this transoceanic kayak journey and it gave me a respite. The more I thought about it, the more I craved paddling the Pacific Ocean to Hawai'i.

I went to Seattle to look at kayaks. It is no surprise that I ended up buying the same kayak that Ed Gillet used to paddle to Hawai'i. It was a Tofino, made by Necky Kayaks. It was beautiful, gray, with red hatch covers. There were two cockpits, designed to be paddled by two people. Mr. Neckar was a very large man and he designed kayaks to fit himself comfortably, with high buoyancy and stability. The bow was bulbous, which would lift it over waves rather than diving through them. That would be a real benefit in the ocean.

I told my friend, Paul Shannon, who worked for the weather service in Juneau, that I was considering a *sailing trip* from Juneau to Hawai'i and asked him to advise me on the best time of year. He told me that I should wait until the Pacific high pressure system became well established in June. The winds would flow clockwise around the high pressure. There would be north winds along the North American coast and those would flow into the northeast trade winds, taking me to Hawai'i.

The distance from Juneau to Hawai'i is 2800 miles. But if I started the crossing from the north end of Vancouver Island, it would be 2530 miles. That was just 200 miles further than Ed Gillet's distance of 2330 miles, even though I would be starting the crossing 1000 miles north of his point of departure. I could paddle the inside waters from Juneau to Vancouver Island. Then, as I entered the open ocean and headed south from Vancouver Island, I would soon pick up the north winds. Pilot charts showed me the average wind speeds and directions for each month, across the Pacific.

I would design and build a sailing system for my kayak, unlike Ed Gillet, who used a parafoil kite to propel him with the trade winds. Unfortunately for him, he found that for most of his trip the winds were much lighter than he had expected and were too light for his kite. He had hoped to complete his trip in 40 days. He had packed food for 60 days. It took him 63, the last three without food.

I expected my crossing to take 55 days because of my option of sailing. The sail would allow me to take advantage of any wind that was behind me or 90 degrees to the side of me. I had less than six months to modify my kayak and prepare before the Pacific high settled in.

The first modification was to cut out the bulkhead between the rear and front cockpits, giving me room to lay flat for sleeping. I left one inch of the bulkhead intact all the way around the hull to retain rigidity and hull shape. I made a light weight floor board to raise my sleeping bag and sleeping pad one inch off of the kayak floor. This would keep me above a small amount of water inside the kayak.

The mast for the sail had to be very strong. I used fiber glass to install a two inch tube from the bottom of the hull to the deck, one foot in front of the cockpit opening. It served as my mast step. Sleeping comfort would have to be sacrificed for mast strength. The mast rested in this 15 inch tube. The mast itself was made from clear Sitka spruce, the wood of choice during the early years of aviation when wing spars were made of wood. It is the strongest wood for its weight. I cut a slot through my sleeping bag to accommodate the mast step. Each night, the sleeping bag would have to be slipped around the mast step and the open slot closed with Velcro. The mast would be inside my sleeping bag.

My sail was small and strong. I decided it should be six feet tall and three feet wide. A larger sail could cause the kayak to be blown over. This was not be a high speed craft anyway. Dependability was far more important than speed. The sail was a double sail, two identical triangles. It could be opened double wide for kayaking downwind or even quartering downwind. The sail could be rolled around the mast a few times for reefing. This was an easy way to reduce the sail area and lower the center of pressure of the sail. At the top of the sail I mounted a lightweight crab pot float. In the event of capsize, it would prevent the kayak from flipping all the way over.

I was thankful I had this project to work on. I could not concentrate on my U.S. Fish and Wildlife Service job. I could not focus on anything that didn't relate to the accident. Preparing for this expedition was the only thing that could mercifully pull my mind away from the constant anguish. It was the only thing that mattered. Of course my daughters mattered, but they did not moderate my grief. When I would attend a soccer game or other activity of theirs, I would silently cry, knowing how much Lisa would want to be there.

I needed to somehow rig a canopy over the cockpit, especially for sleeping, but also for protection from the sun or exceedingly foul weather. As I studied my mast, I realized that if I split the lower three feet of the mast with a lengthwise cut and

134

installed a bolt, I could swivel the upper portion of the mast down to the rear of the kayak and it would form a perfect ridge pole over the cockpit. I discovered the sail could be fashioned into a perfect canopy, either open in the front for paddling, or closed in the front for sleeping. When sleeping, the spray skirt was placed on the cockpit coaming. It was held up under the canopy by the shoulder straps and made a nice opening above my head for air. It was impervious to the rain, with the canopy overlapping the spray skirt.

I designed stainless steel fins on each side of the kayak, amidships. These would help reduce sideways drift when sailing, reduce the roll speed of the kayak and make the rudder more effective for steering. The rudder was a concern to me. It seemed to be the weakest link. I worried that it would get bent in heavy weather. I tried to think of a way to make it effective for steering but still have allowance for it to flex under severe pressure, instead of bending or breaking.

The expedition was becoming more real. My kayak modifications were working out, one by one. As the trip itself became more of a reality, I began to question whether I should follow through. What about my daughters? Wasn't I being selfish to place so much emphasis on myself? How unfair it would be to them if I died. How was I going to explain this trip to my parents? They would think I was crazy. What about the girls' grandparents in Hawai'i? They would think I was a terrible father. I imagined my family standing on the beach saying good-bye to me. In my vision, the kayak was perched on the edge of the beach, ready to go. I could see their tears and their fear.

I saw myself paddling away from them and wondering, "Why am I doing this? What am I getting myself into?"

Then I would come back to the present and realize that this goat, and my focus on it, was the only thing that gave me relief — that gave me purpose. Part of the recovery process for me involved re-evaluating life itself. How did I come to be on this earth? What makes life worth struggling for? Is a famous person any better off than a common person? How long do we have any influence on this earth after we die? Most people only know the name of one of their eight great grandparents, so aiming for being remembered after you die is not worth much in the grand scheme. But why be here if you don't do something special? Wouldn't it be worthwhile to add a milestone for the human race?

My kayak trip would do that.

The sail converted to a canopy for sleeping, or for paddling.

Modifications for a kayak journey from Alaska to Hawai'i. Sleeping area showing floor board and mast step. High quality compass - critical for transoceanic travel. Six foot by three foot sail for winds abeam. Wing on wing sail for downwind and quartering winds.

Chapter 19 - The Kayak Trip
1988

By May, I knew I wouldn't be kayaking to Hawai'i that summer. If I didn't have two little girls to think about, I am sure I would have done it, and I believe I would have had a high probability of success. I changed gears. I would do a long solo kayak trip. Until a few months earlier, I had never been in a kayak. My new plan was to leave from my house on the Mendenhall River, paddle to the outside coast, head south through 140 miles of open ocean, turn the corner at the south end of Baranof Island and paddle another 200 miles back home. This would allow me to experience the ocean in my kayak and test my modifications. I would sleep in the kayak, anchored offshore. That way I wouldn't have to move the kayak up the beach above high tide at night and back down the beach in the morning. It would also eliminate any worries about brown bears. My expedition to Hawai'i had to be shelved for now.

I left Juneau on July 6, 1988. Jennifer and Kara were in Hawai'i with their grandparents for the duration of my trip. I wheeled the kayak up the street from my house to a river access point. I was alone – no one to see me off. That felt right, since my journey through grief was a solo process. I floated down the river to saltwater. Finally I was on my way, headed across Auke Bay. Paddling the kayak was deeply satisfying. Each stroke was physical, silent, rewarding. The kayak glided forward, a graceful sea creature. Humans can't flap their arms and fly through the air, but they can thrust a paddle with their arms and fly across the water. I was making the first physical motions through a journey for mental survival.

My kayak was heavy with gear. I even had a wood stove which I erroneously thought would be helpful. My arms tired quickly, but I knew they would toughen up with time. I was finally on my way and enjoying every stroke. It was hard to believe my own power could move my new home.

I found a nice beach that evening where I could have a fire and cook dinner. After dinner it was time to prepare for my first night in the kayak. I laid out the small sleeping pad and slipped my sleeping bag around the mast step, by way of the slot I had sewn into it. I sat down in the cockpit and pulled my boots off, securing them on deck with the tops folded down. A few paddle strokes took me to where I could drop the anchor. My journal the next morning said that the kayak was "pretty cramped" for sleeping. I remember feeling the cold mast inside my sleeping bag, but it warmed up with my body heat in about 20 minutes. I could sleep on my back with the mast between my legs, but turning to sleep on my side required lifting myself to a partial upright position so that one of my legs could be moved to the other side of the mast. To return to sleeping on my back required the same series of moves in reverse.

Because I had not trained for paddling all day long, I was very depleted by the third day and felt sick, with a headache. But the following day my body seemed to start adjusting to the physical demands. My journal reads:

July 9 – (23 miles) – Up at 6:15am because the kayak was going dry on the beach. Gnats were terrible so I rearranged my gear as fast as I could and started straight for Pt. Adolphus, 16 miles diagonally across Icy Strait. Weather is calm, moderate rain. I ate an orange in the cockpit. 10:15am – Already have paddled 11 miles. Probably bucking a slight tide too. Had some really hard rain showers today. I used the canopy over the cockpit. It helps a lot in the downpours. I can open the front of the canopy and see just fine, and paddle too.

The first 100 miles, taking me to the open ocean, went well. I loved paddling the kayak. It was magical to use my own muscles to smoothly propel a heavily loaded boat through the water. It may have been slow, but the miles slid by. The experience was incredible. I could hear everything, smell everything, see everything and feel everything. To watch the bow of the kayak slice through one wave after another with zero wear and tear on the boat, zero hydrocarbons burned and nearly zero chance of engine failure, was truly gratifying. The engine ran well on bagels, peanut butter, oranges, fish, potatoes and candy bars. It was also mentally gratifying. I was learning how to kayak. I was testing my craft and my modifications. I needed this chance to spend hours on end thinking about life and death, and my place in the universe. There were no distractions. I may not have been on my way to Hawai'i yet, but I was taking a first big step. I was beginning to execute a response to Lisa's death which I had pledged to myself I would do.

On the seventh day, it was a thrill to finally experience the ocean swells in my kayak. The horizon went out of sight when the kayak was in the trough and come surging back when the kayak was on the crest. I floated like a duck. It seemed my vessel was designed for this. Indeed, the kayak was invented by the Aleut people to hunt and travel the most treacherous waters of the Pacific Ocean in the Aleutian Islands.

It was safer for me to stay quite a ways offshore, far away from potential breaking reefs. From my vantage point, the terrain slipped by so slowly that it appeared as if I wasn't moving at all. I knew how to read the water and watch for swells that lump higher than normal. Several years earlier, I had covered the entire outer coast of southeast Alaska by skiff, on a mission to find as many peregrine falcon nests as possible. I learned that the lumpers were a warning sign of a submerged rock. An area of water could look perfectly normal for five minutes or more and then suddenly a much larger swell hits the shallower area and it breaks. In a skiff, it may be possible to run from an unexpected breaker. In a kayak, there was no such possibility. I enjoyed the power and excitement of the waves, along with the intimidation that they brought.

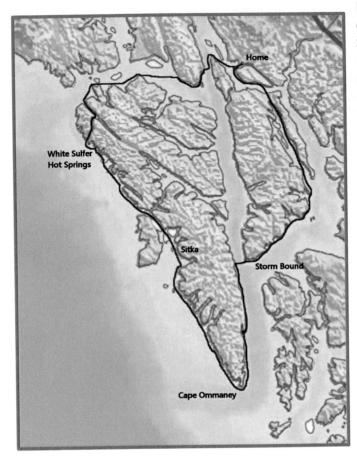

My goal for that first night on the ocean was White Sulphur Hot Springs. I made it there by late afternoon and sought out a nearby narrow channel that took me beyond the reach of the swells and brought me into Mirror Harbor. I quickly got to shore at the trailhead and hiked the two miles to the springs. The U.S. Forest Service cabin nearby was occupied by a young couple celebrating their honeymoon. They were from the lower 48 states. The Alaskan wilderness was new to them. He was Caucasian and she was Japanese. They reminded me of Lisa and myself, and I felt the sadness of the comparison.

My bath and soak in the hot springs was therapeutic. To have such a luxurious experience in the Alaska wilderness felt like cheating, but I enjoyed it anyway. The next morning I cast my lure in the tidal stream near Mirror Harbor and caught several fish. One was a nice silver salmon. I cut it in half and hiked back to the cabin to give half to Jay and Tamika as a wedding present. They were graciously pleased with the gift.

As I entered the ocean swells again, the sky was blue. The sun created twinkling diamonds on the ocean surface wavelets. The 15 knot northwest wind was a tailwind, perfect for testing my sail on the ocean. I opened it, wing on wing, gliding effortlessly along with the swells. It worked marvelously. In the next 6 hours I covered 18 miles without paddling a stroke. If I was headed for Hawai'i, I would easily cover 50 miles a day with such a wind.

It was gratifying to see my mast and sail perform. I tried sailing 90 degrees to the wind and found that as long as I was paddling, the sail would give me added power equal to having a second paddler on board. I am sure I could make 30 miles a day with a 90 degree cross wind.

The trip south along the coast went smoothly. By the time I reached Sitka, I had been on the water by myself for 10 days. I had a strange sensation when I entered a restaurant that evening. On the water, I had become accustomed to taking notice of every motion. It could be a seal diving, or a fish flipping, or a wave approaching. Most importantly I was watching all the swells on the ocean for any hint of unusual lumping, a sign of danger. As I entered the restaurant, I saw every motion in the room. I noticed everyone that was lifting a fork, reaching for a glass, shifting in their seat, or turning their head. I saw all of the waitresses moving around or wiping a table. The entire room seemed alive with motion, the majority of which my brain ordinarily would have ignored. It was sensory overload for a while.

My journal from the following days reads:

July 17 - (28 miles) – Spent last night with Kent and Bev Hall, just a mile and a half outside of Sitka. Had a nice talk about our philosophies of life and death. Good to find someone that wants to talk about these things that are important to me right now. They have a beautiful spot on a small island, 2.5 acres on a point.

Departed this morning at 6:30am under cloudy skies and calm. Light SE wind started at 7:30am which will fly the spinnaker as I head SW toward Biorka Island. I used the spinnaker off and on all the way to Goddard Hot Springs. I stopped and had lunch there. I planned on taking a hot bath but decided against it because there was too much activity with too many people. As I was leaving, a row boat and a Nautiraid double kayak showed up. The three had taken the Alaska ferry from Juneau to Angoon and had come around the south end of Baranof Island. They had been on the water for two weeks.

I left the hot springs at 2:30pm. The winds were very favorable. The spinnaker became too much to handle in Windy Passage. I got it down without mishap though. I figure my speed was up to at least 5 knots. I used my standard sail all the way until 8:30pm when I found a beautiful cove just south of Necker Bay.

July 18 - (22 miles) – Departed at 8:30am. Clear skies. West wind started by 9:30am. I put up the sail and started trolling. I caught a small silver salmon. I also had a big one on the line that spit the lure out after 5 minutes of fighting. The wind gave out in mid-afternoon. I had to do a lot of paddling. I had trouble finding a good enough anchorage that wouldn't require paddling several miles up into a bay. Finally I made it to the bay south of Byron Bay at 10:15pm. I snacked for dinner. In the rack by 11:00pm. At dusk I saw an eagle try to take a fish out of the mouth of a sea lion. He was not successful.

July 19 - (20 miles) – I had my fish for breakfast. It is another sunny day. No wind this morning. I saw a peregrine falcon being chased by a crow as I left the bay.

Paddled to Redfish Cape. Strong currents on my nose. In an eddy behind the cape, I saw salmon surfacing. I rigged up my pole and caught a pink salmon on the first cast.

The NW wind is starting to pick up now, which is a great help against this current. I'd hate to be fighting a SE wind and the current too. It sure is nice when the sail gives me shade from the sun.

The wind quit by noon. I stopped for lunch at 1:00pm. I cooked salmon and corn on the cob in a campfire. I should have let the corn cook longer in the coals. I started again at 2:45pm and made it to Eagle Rocks at 5:30pm. The currents there were spectacular. I had to really paddle to get by. A fishing boat came up next to me and tooted his horn to see if I was alright. There were unbelievable numbers of salmon from Redfish Bay to Larch Bay. I rounded Cape Ommaney at 6:30pm. I am bucking the tide up the coast to Port Alexander. Just south of Port Alexander it went from calm winds to 30 knot winds from the SW in about 30 seconds. Luckily I wasn't on the outside coast. It rained off and on all night.

July 20 – (12 miles) - I walked around Port Alexander until 11:00am waiting for the store to open, then I gave up and paddled out to the fish-buying scow in the bay. There wasn't much available, so I just bought Pepsi and some candy bars.

Departed at 11:30am and made it to the Marine Fisheries Research Station at Little Port Walter by 5:30pm. I was met by Bill Herd. He invited me to dinner and I took a shower. Also saw Bud Boddy who is the care taker. The bay is full of returning king salmon. Dinner was lasagna. They were very perplexed when I turned down their offer of a dry, warm bed for the night and I went down to the dock to sleep in my kayak.

July 21 – (9 miles) - In the morning it was raining buckets, so I just stayed in my sleeping bag, snug inside the kayak, until 11:00am when the rain slacked off. I got underway at 1:30pm. The wind was light, a head wind, but four foot seas from the north turned into six foot lumpy waves in the tide rips. It is disconcerting to see a point of land ahead with breakers extending clear out into the strait. There was no choice but to go through. The kayak did great. The herring were thick at Jerry Harbor, so I jigged and caught two of them.

July 22 – (30 miles) - Nice morning but the biting flies were bad. Slow start, then the wind really picked up from the south. Big seas with five and six foot waves in the tide rips. I took the sail down and used the parafoil kite. It works well as long as the wind is over 15 knots. It was a hard afternoon in four foot seas. In 13 hours I made 30 miles. Cloudy but no rain. I had picked out a spot on the map that I thought would be a good anchorage for the night, but after arriving, I saw that the bay is only accessible at real high water. So I continued on and found a spot on the other side of a high water island. I ate cold ham and bread for dinner, no time for a fire tonight.

During my trip, daily fires on the beach were very important. At the end of a long day of paddling, I would often be tired and wet. My mood might be gloomy as well, or very sad and lonely. After I had built a fire and it was burning well, my mental attitude would go through a transformation. Everything was cheerier. There was warmth and companionship in the fire. It seemed to have a life of its own. Most humans can sit for hours watching and attending to a fire. Every stick and log that is given to the fire, changes the fire. The flames dance. I came to think of the fire as life itself. Each stick is another human being. For life to continue, and for the fire to continue, it needs sticks to be added. Some sticks are small and do not burn for very long. Some babies die in childhood. Some logs burn a long time, but they too die eventually. Every stick and every human adds to the fire of life. The fire of life cannot exist without the logs, nor can it exist without new logs being added to replace the old logs that have burned and died away.

Memories of Lisa get blurry as she is left behind.

July 23 – (12 miles) - During the night a big east swell started to roll into where I was anchored. At 4:30am I had to get up. I decided I had to leave. With the lower half of

143

my body still in the sleeping bag, I started to paddle out of the tiny cove. I had to go through a thick bed of kelp. The four foot seas were steepening in the kelp. It was hard to paddle because the paddle blades wanted to slip right over top of the kelp. It got scary when a large wave threw kelp over the bow, pinning me there. The waves were breaking against a steep rocky shore about 40 feet away. I had to paddle forward enough so I could grab the bull kelp and tear it apart to free it from the bow. I struggled out of there and through the waves to another bay and found a pretty good little anchorage. I was able to get some more sleep.

I decided I could make the five mile crossing of Chatham Strait even with the 3 foot swell coming right at me. The clouds indicated a light northerly wind was blowing at my destination, the south tip of Admiralty Island. The crossing was good, but a strong northeast wind hit me near the point and I had to paddle the last 2 miles into a 30 knot headwind. I could only make the kayak creep slowly forward against the wind. I had paddled 5 hours non-stop. Misty rain this evening.

July 24 - (2 miles) – Stormy weather! Rain, Rain, Rain. Wind too. I got up this morning at 5:30am because the kayak was about to refloat. It had gone dry during the night. The wind would have banged it against the rocks as it was refloating. I made a fire under a big spruce tree and had pancakes. While sitting there, I saw a doe walk out of the woods and down the beach, right to where my kayak was anchored a few feet offshore. It was trying hard to figure out what my kayak was.

Got underway by 11:30am. Heavy rain still. I had only gone about two miles when the wind began to increase. I decided against trying to continue along the exposed shoreline. I hauled out on a small island and spent the day there in the storm. I put up a tarp under a rock face at the high tide line. This will be the sixth consecutive day of rain. Things are beginning to get very wet. My sleeping bag is all damp. I will sleep in the kayak on the beach tonight. I placed two large logs on the kayak to ensure that it doesn't blow away with me in it.

July 25 – (16 miles) - Today the storm is not so bad. The seas are still big and the wind is 15-20 knots. By dinner time, it was so rainy that I decided to keep paddling instead of stopping to fix dinner. By the time I found a place to spend the night, it was after dark. My sleeping bag was soaked. It was a cold and miserable night of shivering.

July 26 – (16 miles) - I had to get up at 4:30am because the kayak had gone dry near a creek. My feet and boots stunk so bad that I washed them both in dish soap. It didn't do any good. I put them back on, wet. I used three logs to slide my kayak down the beach and into the water. I am still hoping to get some good weather to dry my sleeping bag. It has been 8 days of rain. No such luck today. It is foggy and misty.
Just at the north end of Square Point, I hear the familiar whine of a turbine engine. I know that sound. It is coming from behind me. I have my canopy up and covering me and I can't see behind me. Then I turn the kayak so that I can look to the side, and there is N754 heading at me. I feel the emotion of seeing that trusty turbine beaver. Bruce circles me twice and I see Jake taking pictures of me. I cry. I learn later that my dad hadn't heard from me in two weeks and he had asked Bruce if he would try to find out how I was doing.

Tonight I thought I would try to sleep on shore, not in the kayak. I thought that if I kept a nice fire going all night, it would keep me warm. I didn't want to have another night of shivering like last night. But I couldn't find a suitable place. So I had to sleep in the kayak wearing two pairs of pants and a jacket inside of the sleeping bag. It was really difficult, almost impossible to move, but it kept me mostly warm.

July 27 – (18 miles) - Finally!!! A good day. The sun is trying to peak through the clouds and it is not raining. The wind is astern at 10 knots. Humpback whales are all around.

I forgot to mention yesterday that I had a big halibut on my hand line for a while. The line was tied to a float which I planned to throw overboard if I got a big one on. The halibut's head was jerking my arm up and down 15 inches, so I knew it was huge and I threw the float over, but the float was on the right side of the kayak and the halibut ran left. The float wouldn't go under the kayak easily enough and then the swivel broke. I didn't need one that big anyway. I am sure it was over 60 pounds.

A good tail wind in Seymour Canal. I had to double reef the sail after a while. A pleasure craft came by me and the guy yelled, "Hey, I saw you near Sitka, then at south Baranof and then at Port Alexander. You are making really good time. I thought you were a buoy near Sitka and almost ran aground following you!"

I decided to go all the way to Sandy Boyce's camp. He is operating a wilderness learning camp for a few weeks, about 15 students. I got there after dark at 10:30pm. It is inside of Faust Island.

July 28 - (4 miles) – I gave a talk to the students in the morning, then spent the day trying to catch a halibut for the students. No luck. It was a beautiful evening so I decided to leave the camp at 5:00pm. Not long afterward, I saw a huge halibut flopping around on the surface ahead of me. I know it was over 150 pounds. Too bad I didn't have a spear. I suspect it was chasing pink salmon.

I forgot to mention, yesterday evening at dusk, out of nowhere a humpback whale came up about 50 feet from me and blew. That got my adrenaline going for a few seconds. When I got about two hundred yards from there, it breached with a thunderous sound.

July 29 - (20 miles) – The tide was leaving the kayak dry so I got up about 5:30am. The wind was SE with intermittent moderate rain. I sailed and paddled up the canal at a good pace with the incoming tide as well. I was able to go all the way up the creek to the tram. I made it there just at high water. I saw three brown bears there that evening. Two of them seemed to be fighting or playing. They were standing up - pawing and mouthing each other.

July 30 - (30 miles) – Up at 5:30am. I wanted to make the outgoing tide in Oliver Inlet. I made it, but it was a raging river at the mouth. There were 3 foot standing waves. It was foolish of me not to wear my life jacket here. I came through alright. My arms feel really strong, hour after hour now. I called Bruce from Outer Point. I estimated my arrival time up the river to my back yard at 3:15pm. This was another 30 mile day. Friends were there to greet me and to give me a hug.

When the trip was over, it was a little sad. Yet, I knew my kayak and I would see many more miles together. It was a splendid craft – in my opinion, maybe the best water vessel ever built. After a 450 mile trip, how much had the Tofino depreciated? The bungie cords were slightly frayed and there were a few scratches on the bottom. That was it. I figured the only fossil fuel I used on the trip was the contents of one BIC lighter. What a feeling to have propelled myself over that much virgin country.

My grieving process was far from over, but this was a big first step. I spent several hundred hours thinking about things.

Clearly we cannot go backwards in time and change anything. Time leaves everything irretrievably behind. But we can change things going forward in time. We can make sure that we appreciate the time we have together with the ones we love. We never know how much future we may have with each of them. We can appreciate what we have, instead of blindly accepting our blessings as a right. A fish in the ocean cannot appreciate his good fortune by visualizing how much worse it would be to live in a goldfish bowl. But we do have the ability to mentally reposition ourselves in much worse conditions, and thereby recognize how fortunate we are. We turn on the faucet, and out comes clean water. We flip a switch, and the room is lighted. We pick up the phone, and call anyone in the world. We go to bed warm and dry. We reach for our food in the grocery store and put it in a basket. Someone even comes and takes away our garbage. These are not things that were guaranteed to us by the Universe. Life could be much worse. It is a waste of time wishing things were different. Nonetheless, it is important to mourn our losses.

Actually it is necessary.

Sail and mast stowed for headwinds.

Chapter 20 - I Meet Molly
1989

I met Molly 15 months after Lisa died. She was visiting her sister, Betsy, in Portland for the Christmas Holidays. Betsy was married to my step brother. I was also in Portland, visiting my father and step mother for the holidays. On Christmas Day, both extended families gathered at my parent's house. Molly had never been married. We were both single and six months apart in age. Molly and I suspect that Betsy was behind our chance meeting, but she has never owned up to it. When I arrived at the house, Molly was sitting on the couch wearing a pretty white silk sweater. I hadn't expected to see someone my age and I took special notice of her beauty, smile, and quiet demeanor. Suspiciously, she was also unaware that a single man her age was coming to the dinner. Molly says that what attracted her most to me that day was the fact that I willingly and playfully agreed to wear a stick-on earring on my ear.

After dinner, Molly was helping in the kitchen. I wanted to be working in the kitchen with Molly, but my dad insisted that he would be the one washing the dishes with Molly, leaving me unable to spend that time with her. I stewed while my dad, instead of me, was impressing Molly. Fortunately there was a card game that followed, a good family game called "Oh Hell." Molly and I both kept track of how Jennifer and Kara were faring and we subtly helped the girls. We also kept track of each other, as we tied for first place. I could see she was smart and tuned in.

We found ways to see one another other over the next several days before we each left had to depart for home. Then a few weeks later I visited Molly in Minnesota so we could get better acquainted. There I met Molly's friends and it was evident how much they loved her. I could see why. I liked how we seemed to operate at the same relaxed pace. We even had similar communication styles; often a smile was sufficient. It was becoming evident that we could have a great future together.

I longed for companionship – someone to share life with. I did not like being a single parent and being responsible for everything. A long distance phone relationship wasn't useful for any of us. In April, Molly came to Juneau. The mountains greeted her with pristine, glistening white grandeur, which was impressive to this Midwestern woman, and it didn't hurt our chances of keeping her with us in Alaska. Neither Molly nor I wanted a long courtship; the kids didn't need that uncertainty. We were married in July. Molly was willing to leave everything behind in Minnesota to move to Alaska and be my wife, and Jennifer's and Kara's mom. Now I could definitely surpass my dad with unlimited opportunities to wash dishes in the kitchen with Molly.

Nonetheless, it was very difficult for all of us to adapt to each other. I was still grieving. The girls were still grieving. Molly was grieving her separation from all of her friends and her career in Minnesota. Molly was not happy for the first few years in Juneau. It was difficult for her to fit in, largely because of our grieving. She still tucked the kids into bed every night, telling them she loved them. They struggled with letting go of their birth mom and accepting their new mom. Perhaps no one reassured them that letting Molly into their hearts wouldn't diminish their allegiance to Lisa. Molly and I struggled too. It would take many years for the real "us" to be fully revealed to each other.

Molly had always made friends easily, but now she was finding it hard. Juneau was a small town. She sometimes felt that people were remembering Lisa when they saw her rather than seeing her. Her underlying sadness didn't help as she tried to seek new friends. She found herself feeling very lonely.

We read books for couples and utilized three different marriage counselors, and never changed our goal of succeeding in our marriage. Somehow we persevered and made it through those tough times.

Chapter 21 - A Kayaking Family
1989 - 1994

Kayaking was a wonderful activity for our family. In Minnesota, Molly had loved to swim in the lakes. Kayaking in Alaska proved to be a great substitute. The first kayak adventure I took with Molly was a 60 mile trip from Juneau to Tenekee Hot Springs. I made sure we had good accommodations along the way.

The first night of the trip, a kind couple let us sleep on their commercial fishing boat anchored off of their wilderness home. The second night was at a friend's remote cabin on Wheeler Creek. This was a ploy to get Molly hooked, and it worked. She had no idea that her future would involve many nights spent sleeping in a kayak.

Once she had travelled by kayak on a few long trips, she no longer felt hemmed in by the mountains around Juneau and the lack of a road out of Juneau. It gave her a feeling of freedom, seeing the incredible water world around Juneau, and knowing that it was accessible to her by kayak.

We purchased a second large double kayak. It was a *Seascape* made by Northwest Kayaks. There was no center bulkhead. If the seats were removed, there was eleven feet of space to sleep. Believe it or not, Molly and I both slept together in this kayak, many nights in the wilderness, our feet together, but our heads ten feet apart – not very romantic for newlyweds. Molly never became a fan of the sleep-in-the-kayak mode of travel, but she tolerated it, for the most part. There were a few times when claustrophobia gripped her, and I heard about it loud and clear.

Paddling for Molly came naturally. She was very strong for her size and her love of swimming quickly translated into the paddling stroke. My strokes tended to be shallow and quick. Hers were deep and slow. When we paddled together, I had to adjust to her style.

I introduced the girls to kayaking shortly after Lisa died. Initially they were less than enthusiastic, complaining about the confinement, the weather, their desire to be with their friends, etc. etc. But as the first half hour turned into an hour and then into two hours, they began to realize they were stuck, without any escape. The antics of the sea gulls started to catch their attention. They tried draping their hands over the side into the water to watch the little wavelets form. They told me to stop paddling so they could see how fast they could paddle the kayak by themselves.

Molly and I took some short trips with the kids. They were becoming seasoned paddlers. When the four of us were paddling, Molly and Jennifer were in the Seascape, while Kara and I were in the Tofino. Kara was pretty small to add much paddling power, but Jennifer could help Molly significantly. It was soon time for the whole family to undertake long trips on the ocean.

Jennifer and Kara, content to sleep in Tofino's rear hatch.

I was determined that all of us would sleep in the kayaks, anchored out on the water. I used fiberglass to install a horizontal tube in the center of the Seascape. This tube accepted a PVC pipe that connected the two kayaks together for the night and made them into a catamaran. I fabricated two tent-like covers which spanned the cockpits

151

on each kayak, held up by the masts. The catamaran was extremely stable. The two girls adapted to the sleeping arrangement quickly.

Each night we stowed our gear in a pile on the beach and covered it with a tarp. We needed to unload quite a bit of stuff to make room in the kayaks for us in our sleeping bags. One morning we were methodically toting our gear down the beach from our overnight stash and packing it into the kayaks. Someone noticed a large brown bear sauntering towards us along the high tide line. Everyone quickly grabbed the remaining items from the top of the beach and threw them into the kayaks – forgetting about packing. We all jumped into the cockpits perched on top of the gear that had been haphazardly tossed in. The kayaks felt unstable, but the water was calm and we pushed ourselves away from shore just in time. Drifting in the shallow water, we watched the bear sniff all around the location where our gear had been stowed. Then we paddled down the shore half a mile, had breakfast and loaded the kayaks properly. Each night we took a chance that a bear would rummage through our gear, but we were careful to keep all of our food in the kayaks out on the water with us.

One of our trips was from Angoon to Hoonah, a distance of 100 miles. Our route took us to the 40 mile long Tenekee Inlet, oriented east and west. The weather was stunningly beautiful, clear, sunny, and calm, as we lounged at the east end of Tenekee Inlet, near the south shore. There seemed to be no need to rush into the 2½ mile crossing of the mouth of the inlet. I suggested we drift and rest while I tried to catch a fish.

After having no luck with the fishing, we started the crossing. The temperature was warm, so we were in light clothing and felt no need to have our spray skirts on. When we were halfway into the crossing, a blistering west wind hit us instantly. I am sure it was at least 35 knots. All of us dug in fiercely with our paddles. I told little Kara, "I need you to paddle as hard as you possibly can." Jennifer was digging in with all her strength. The waves were quickly building from our port side. Whitecaps were everywhere. We were making some headway, but it was slow. We couldn't take time to put on our spray skirts. If we did, under those conditions, it would have taken at least five minutes and we would have been blown out into Chatham Strait, which is 6 miles wide and over 100 miles long. We would have had no chance to make the windward shore. Only Kara was able to put on her spray skirt while I held our position.

Without spray skirts, in Molly's kayak, they were taking on water as periodic waves slopped into their cockpits. I told them to let the kayak roll with the waves, rather than keeping the kayak fully upright. They began to do this, and it worked. The waves slid under their kayak as it rode like a duck. Now it was just a matter of whether our strength would hold out and whether we could continue to gain ground. We inched forward towards the beckoning sandy beach that was just a half mile away now. The closer the beach became, the more motivated we were to get there. Every arm was aching, but no one gave up. We made it, staggered out of our kayaks, hugged each other all around, and laid down on the sunny beach. Together, it had been possible. These kayak trips were bonding experiences for our family and character building experiences for the two girls.

We later learned that the same west wind had caught four men in a skiff just 5 miles farther up the inlet from us. Their skiff was loaded with luggage and they were headed for the little town of Tenekee Springs, where three of them were to catch a float plane into town. Their skiff plunged into one of the oncoming waves and in a moment they were capsized. All four men stayed with the overturned skiff, holding on as best they could. As good fortune would have it, a purse seine boat saw them and rescued them after they had spent 45 minutes in the water. All were saved.

A few days later we found ourselves at the upper end of Tenekee Inlet. There was a portage there. On a good high tide it is possible to carry kayaks and gear a couple of hundred yards through the forest to a connection with Hoonah Sound. Without using the portage it would be a 95 mile trip to the other side. We had already paddled five miles in a steady rain to reach the portage. Then the clouds really opened up drenching us even more in a deluge.

The portage had to be completed at high tide. Everything was unloaded from the kayaks. The rain kept pelting us and our gear. Each kayak was carried by the four of us, Molly and I taking as much weight as we could and the two girls at the bow, with as much weight as they could handle. We completed the portage as the tide began its ebb. We settled into our cockpits, each of us in our own thoughts of cold and misery. The soaked seat cushions were chilly against our wet rain gear. It took a few minutes for our bottoms to heat up.

We could camp a short distance away, or we could paddle eight more miles in the pouring rain and reach a U.S. Forest Service cabin. It would be against a stiff headwind and relentless rain, but once there, we would be able to start a fire and be warm and dry. While the two kayaks were side by side, each of us with a hand gripping the other kayak, we made a family decision to go for it. The girls stuck with it, paddling steadily for another 3 hours. We pulled into the cabin site at 7pm after a 13 mile day of difficult kayaking plus an arduous portage in cold, soaking conditions. I was very proud of my family.

The kids find a way to be kids in the wilderness.

Using sails on our kayaks was important throughout our trips. I dreamed up the idea of an A-frame mast for Molly's kayak. It was made of lightweight aluminum tubing. The A-frame laid flat on the deck of the kayak until it was deployed. Deployment was accomplished by pulling the front stay which lifted the A-frame mast into place. Attached to the front stay was a very large blue sail we called the "bat-wing". It could be set with both wings on the same side, like a jib, or it could be set wing-on-wing, with a bat-wing open on each side. It was a lot of sail for a kayak. Many times I fretted about the safety of Molly and Jennifer as they sped ahead of me and Kara with the bat-wing full of wind. They were exhilarated to be fearlessly leaving us behind.

A number of years later, Molly and I were on a kayak trip with friends. We had kayaked to one of our favorite destinations, White Sulfur Hot Springs. The springs were literally perched at the top of the high tide line. There was a U.S. Forest Service cabin adjacent to the springs which could be reserved by the public. Our group of four couples had reserved the cabin for four nights. On this occasion the weather was so ideal that we decided to take a short overnight trip away from the cabin. We left a lot of our gear behind at the cabin because we were returning within a day or two. It happened that some folks off of a pleasure boat, or a fishing boat, came to soak in the hot springs while we were away on our little trip. They must have known we were travelling by kayak because of our gear, or maybe because of something we wrote in the cabin's logbook. They apparently spent the night in the vicinity, and of course we did not show up that night. The next day they became very concerned about us and radioed to the Coast Guard that a group of kayakers was missing. The Coast Guard radioed all boats in the area requesting any information about kayakers possibly in distress.

Jennifer and Kara were in high school at the time, and we had left them at home to fend for themselves. The Coast Guard called our house. Jennifer answered. They explained the situation carefully to her, hoping she had information about her parent's whereabouts. They were very sorry to be relaying this distressing report to her and her sister. Jennifer listened respectfully to the man on the phone until he was finished. Then she proceeded to tell him that the Coast Guard didn't need to worry about her parents. She told him her parents and their friends were fine. They would not get into trouble in their kayaks. That was the confidence our family trips had instilled in her.

Rain was usually our companion in the temperate rainforest.

Chapter 22 - The Waterbike Trip
1995

In the winter of 1994, I found myself on a beach in Mexico. In front of me, resting on the sand, was a unique pedal contraption. It had two narrow pontoons spaced about five feet apart. A strong molded plastic seat held them firm – parallel. I could see bicycle pedals extending from a drive unit which was similar in appearance to a lower unit of an outboard motor. A large propeller was attached. I began to see how it worked. The operator sat on the seat, rotated the pedals with his feet, which in turn rotated the propeller. It was an elegant marine equivalent to a bicycle. The seat was low, which inherently seemed wise for a watercraft. I really wanted to try it. At the time, I was on the Baja Peninsula, flying surveys to count Pacific brant. Pacific brant breed in Alaska, Canada and Siberia. Most of them spend the winter in Mexico. We were there to monitor the brant population. I was able to rent the Waterbike for two hours. It was a dream to pedal. The 16 inch propeller was extremely efficient. My legs made the 11 foot long catamaran glide through the water easily. I was hooked. I felt this Waterbike had great potential.

I was not an avid bicyclist. But I greatly admired those marvelous contraptions. Even though a bike cannot stand by itself, incredulously it becomes a stable vehicle when a human pedals It over a smooth surface. Bicycles transport people as if by magic. That simple apparatus seems to impossibly glide along and stay upright easily. It has been a gift to mankind, used ubiquitously around the world. The power of human legs is efficiently converted into fluid forward motion. Like binoculars, the bike holds a special place in human inventions.

This *Waterbike* I spied in Mexico might be able to combine the fluid power of pedaling with the limitless ocean. I had not given up on my commitment to kayak from Juneau to Hawai'i – even though at this point, eight years after Lisa's accident, I no longer felt that the 3,000 mile kayak trip was imperative to my survival. I had worked my way through the bulk of the grieving process. There was a serious problem though. I had truly believed I would kayak from Alaska to Hawai'i. That belief was what allowed me to survive the first year. I couldn't slip out from under that commitment. To abandon the quest would be cheating, plain and simple. You can't make a promise to someone, or yourself--- a promise that saves your life --- and then later say "Just kidding."

It seemed that it was less and less likely I was going to be able to make the trip happen. But an idea began to take shape. What if I were to pedal a *Waterbike* from Juneau to Seattle? It would be a big first step in my goal to power myself from Juneau to Hawai'i.

Molly was supportive. It couldn't have been easy for her to accept my fixation on reaching a conclusion to my grieving process, which led me to these singular undertakings. Even though she didn't understand my need for extended grieving, she gave me space and support for it. However, it did take a toll on our relationship for a significant number of years.

I contacted EcoSports, the maker of the *Waterbike* in Petaluma, California. They told me they were working on a design for a larger model that could accommodate two people, or alternatively could be a touring craft for one person. That sounded perfect for me. I travelled there to see their progress on the new model. Their prototype looked good. They said they were having trouble coming up with the money to produce the molds for the pontoons. I offered to lend them $15,000 for the molds, and they accepted it. I wanted this new model to get built soon. I told them about my plan to pedal it from Seattle to Alaska. I had decided to pedal from south to north. They thought that would provide them with great publicity.

Six months later, they informed me that the inventor had made a grave mistake when he designed the pontoons for their new craft. It was seriously deficient in buoyancy for two people. It had too little volume. It wasn't going to work. My $15,000 was used up, and there was nothing to show for it. I was very upset. I was determined to pedal a Waterbike to Alaska. I needed to make this trip. It was my opportunity to follow through with a significant portion of my Juneau to Hawai'i dream. At the very least, I would become the first person to pedal a watercraft from Seattle to Alaska.

They knew that they owed me $15,000 and were unable to pay me. They also knew that my trip would provide them with needed publicity. So they offered to make a special unit, a one of a kind *Waterbike* for me. The designer set to work on it. On each side of the craft he used two of the eight foot pontoons from the small model, placing them end to end and connecting them with a fiberglass coupling. That made the craft 17 feet long instead of the standard 11 feet. He built a special frame for the seat using stainless steel tubing. He also built a cantilevered platform behind the seat to hold my gear.

By April of 1995, I was anxious to get underway with my trip. I had to complete the trip before my field season started for the U.S. Fish and Wildlife Service in June. Unfortunately, the special *Waterbike* was not yet ready. So I had them ship one of their small, standard 11 foot models to Seattle to get me started on the trip. The large one would catch up to me in the San Juan Islands.

My father and stepmother, Marian, were at the dock in Shilshole Bay Marina to see me off. Marian, in her typical positive way, spoke last, "Be sure to have fun." The little *Waterbike* was loaded heavily with waterproof bags lashed to the seat. A sailboat was entering the marina as I was leaving. The couple in the cockpit saw my array of gear and called across the water to me, "Where are you headed?" I proudly remarked that I was headed to Alaska. They chastised me, saying "In that thing?"

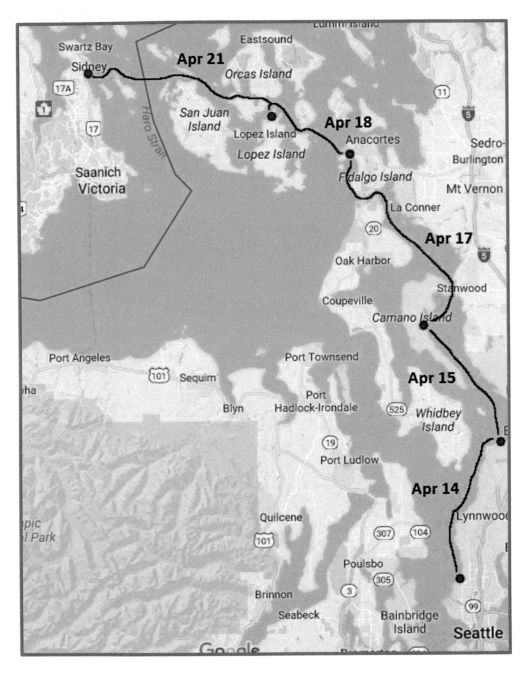

I pedaled north through a light chop. Conveniently, at lunch time, a nice public beach came into view. I stopped for a break. People were taking advantage of the dry weather to walk the beach. My *Waterbike* attracted attention. A young couple approached me and asked me how the bike performed, where I had learned about it, and whether it kept me dry in the waves. We were having a nice conversation. Then they asked me where I was pedaling to. I told them I was going to Alaska. Forthwith the conversation ceased. They quietly walked away. I think they probably felt they were talking to someone that was either lying or was stupidly naive. When this happened a third time, I decided to change my story. I began telling the curious people that I was headed for the San Juan Islands. That was true and the San Juans were only about a hundred miles away. Folks could believe that story and would continue to talk to me like I was a normal person.

The little *Waterbike* worked well for the first 90 miles to Lopez Island. It survived a powerful test when a strong west wind came up while I was exposed to the full extent of the Strait of Juan de Fuca. My journal reads:

"As I headed for Anacortes, the wind came up from the west and the waves got higher, about 4 feet. The waves reflected from a rocky shore causing confused and galloping seas. The bike was immersed in water a few times but always bobbed right back up. I was glad to have finally rounded the point and was headed into the bay south of Anacortes. I wondered if anyone was watching me from their beach front house. If they were, I expect they thought they were seeing a nut case out there".

The 17 foot long custom *Waterbike* arrived shortly after I reached Lopez Island. When I put it together, I liked its size and sleek appearance. But the fiberglass couplings that connected the two sets of pontoons together were very heavy, adding an extra 30 pounds. I wished I didn't have to expend the extra energy transporting the weight to Juneau. The EcoSports Company told me they only had an opportunity to test the new design in one and a half foot waves. They found that the front pontoons swayed around. So they attached a crossbar between them. That helped considerably and I ended up making another crossbar for the rear pontoons. After testing it out, I decided that it would probably get me to Alaska, if it didn't break apart in heavy seas. Unfortunately, I wouldn't know if it would hold together until I actually got out into the ocean.

Heading out from the San Juan Islands with the special Waterbike built for my trip to Alaska.

I cleared Canadian Customs at Sidney, on Vancouver Island. On the dock was a phone with a sign indicating new arrivals must call Customs. I picked it up and started talking to an agent. He had no idea what kind of watercraft I was travelling on. The conversation went like this.

"What is your full name?" – "John Ireland Hodges Jr."

"Are you an American citizen?" – "Yes."

"Are you the captain of the boat?" – "Yes."

"How many people are on board?" – "One."

"What is the length of the boat?" – "17 feet."

"What is the boat constructed of?" – "Plastic and fiberglass."

"What is your destination?" – "Juneau, Alaska."

"When and where do you expect to clear U.S. Customs?" – "Ketchikan in about a month."

"Okay, have a safe trip sir." – "Thank you."

A few days later, I had progressed a considerable distance along the east coast of Vancouver Island. I was disenchanted with the unbroken string of houses along the entire beach. For nearly one hundred miles it was one house next to another. I would eat my lunches while floating, because public beaches were rare. It was even more difficult to find a place to stop for the night and put up my one-man tent. Without public beaches or land, I couldn't build any fires and cook my dinner meals. It was a disappointing start for my trip through what I thought would be the wilds of British Columbia.

At Campbell River my route left the broad Strait of Georgia and entered the narrow waterway called Discovery Passage which led into the 70 mile long Johnstone Strait. Eleven miles north of Campbell River was the famous Seymour Narrows. Here the tidal currents can reach a phenomenal speed of 15 miles per hour.

I refer to my journal:

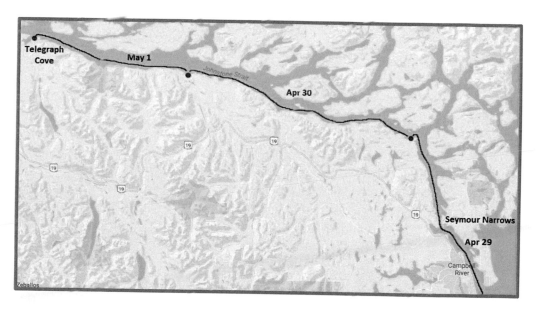

April 29 - This is another rainless day. I need to get to Seymour Narrows in time, before slack tide.

I went through the narrows about an hour before slack. Perfect. There were still whirlpools to make it exciting. In the middle of the narrows, a Canadian Coast Guard skiff came up to me and told me I wouldn't have wanted to be there an hour ago. I knew that. That is why I went through when I did.

I saw my first killer whale in the narrows. Actually it is my first whale. After clearing the narrows I spent the afternoon on the beach waiting for the flood tide to end. It was very pleasant. My ears seem to be reacting to the sun with red, itchy sores. I am trying to keep them covered all of the time now. Otherwise I am in good health.

I am finally getting into better settings. There are mountains to the water, fast streams, no more houses - side by side. I can stop anywhere now and have the beach to myself.

All through the late afternoon there was thunder and lightning. It was very ominous, with the tide rips roaring and the mountains booming. By 5:30pm it is raining very hard. As I consider camping around the next bend, I see my first black bear. I decide to go on. The wind is getting very strong and the rain is relentless. I round Chatham Point and there is a Coast Guard station. I spend 45 minutes standing in their boat house out of the torrential rain. Of course I am alone - there are no Coast Guard personnel to be seen. I then decide to go on to Rock Bay. I hope there is something there to tie up to and a place to put my tent.

I am very happy to see a recreational trailer park at Rock Bay, and a decent dock too. It is still raining hard as I stagger ashore. A man comes out of his trailer and asks me if I am okay. He said when he saw me coming in, he couldn't believe his eyes and he had to have another shot of vodka.

I tried using the orange sail as a partial rain fly over the tent. It worked pretty well. It allowed me to keep the screen open at the doorway.

April 30 - Up at 6:00am to catch the morning ebb tide. It is great. In the first three hours I make 18 miles. I'm going to milk it for all it's worth. These currents are amazing. I am beginning to learn how to play the whirlpools. I watch which way they are spinning and I head for the correct side and get catapulted ahead. When there are whirlpools on both sides of me, one is clockwise and the other is counter clockwise and I get catapulted through the middle of them.

The wind and rain started up again in the afternoon. Only one clap of thunder though. I stopped early at 5:30pm when I saw a good looking beach in a small cove. Stopping points are rare and I couldn't afford to get caught on a long straight stretch late at night.

May 1 - The tide came up to within 6 inches of my tent last night. I spent an hour awake from 2:00am to 3:00am making sure it wasn't going to reach the tent. I am on the water by 6:00am. Not so much current today as yesterday.

I found myself amongst a bunch of porpoises for about half an hour. They porpoise out of the water to breathe. Are they Grey Sided porpoises? I hope to make Sointula Bay today, but need to go 35 miles. The current is not so much of a help today.

The clear cuts here are massive. The concept of multiple use is nowhere evident. What a tragedy. I imagine Japan is happy about it though. They are so wise to grab these trees when they can.

Having said that, I just came upon a sign saying "Robson Bight, Michael Briggs Ecological Reserve." What a wonderful sight now to see the mountains rising to great heights fully clothed in forest.

A porpoise surfaced unexpectedly 20 feet to my right side. It gave me quite a start. The next thing I knew, it was swimming right under me, just four feet below the surface. As it went by me it turned on its side to look me over. It proceeded to do this repeatedly - about 7 more times. It surely must have been thinking that it had never seen a watercraft like this one. It was my temporary friend.

The weather has been good today, but the currents have not treated me well. I did make it to Telegraph Cove where Jeff was able to pick me up with his boat and take me to Sointula Bay. They fed me a tasty taco dinner and I get to stay in their beach cottage, which is wonderful. I am very tired tonight from my efforts to get here.

May 2 - A day off from pedaling. I bought groceries and also reorganized, including the equipment sent up to Jeff and his wife's place.

May 3 - Jeff took me in his boat back to Telegraph Cove. I departed at 9:20am. It is an absolutely beautiful morning – dead calm and partly cloudy. I made the eight mile crossing of Queen Charlotte Strait via a few small islands in the middle. A west wind started up 45 minutes before reaching the other side.

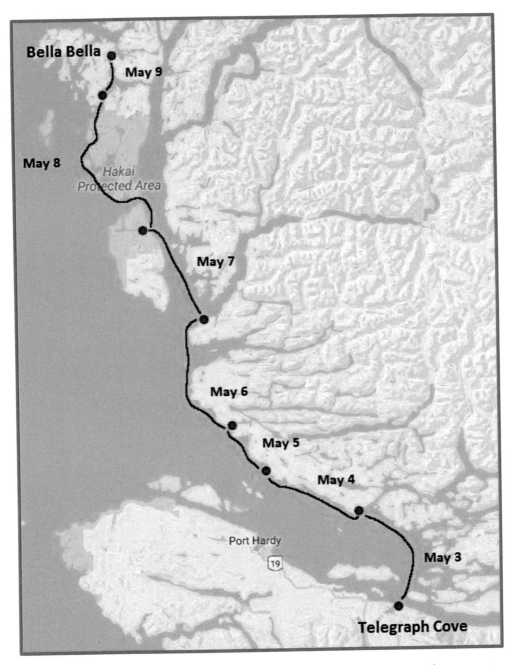

I made my first major mistake. When I stopped to get water, my thermorest seat cushion blew away. This is a very important item, as my rear end would get extremely sore without it. I tried for an hour to find it, but no luck. Because it is so important, I had brought along an extra one. I will have to take special precautions not to lose this one. A safety line is needed. I put on one of the new rudders. It is one inch longer and is made of thicker steel. I think I am going to like it. Also, I cut another ¼ inch off the right steering rod so it can finally be adjusted straight. Strong NW winds are predicted. The wind better not turn to the SE tonight or the waves will come right in

on the bike. I have lost track of the tides, but will start trying to keep my own records and figure them out.

May 4 - Up at 5:30am. The bike did fine overnight. The wind was westerly at 15 knots all day. It seems like I know of nothing other than head winds.

I cut the right steering rod for the third time. FINALLY, I can adjust it so the rudders are straight.

I passed by a fish farm. A fellow came over to me in a skiff. He couldn't believe his eyes. When I told him I was going to Juneau, he asked "where is that?" I guess that means I still have a looooooong way to go.

I stopped for the day at 4:30pm. The headwind is too strong so I can't afford to pass up a good spot. Now I have both new rudders on. I will leave one of the old rudders here on the beach. It is expensive to leave it, but I want to be as light as possible. One spare rudder is enough.

I called home by radio to extend my schedule to Bella Bella by one day. I feel much less alone after hearing Jennifer's and Molly's voices.

May 5 - Up at 3:00am because the tide is reaching the bike and I have to make miles before the wind picks up. I was able to break camp in the dark pretty well because I am used to the routine now. I hate to leave this nifty camp site. On the water by 4:05am.

After only one hour of pedaling I am frustrated by the intense headwind. I turn around thinking I should go back to the nice camp site and spend the day ashore. I could wait for the fishing boat there to pull anchor and then ask them for some fresh water, because I am almost out of water. But then I decide to stay where I am at until daylight and maybe it will not look so nasty.

Sure enough, at daylight I decide to press on. It seems to be getting better. I am down to my last half cup of water. The map shows a creek. When I get there, I find it is rushing out of a narrow passage. I taste it. It is salty. So I pedal furiously against the current for 150 yards and get into the saltwater lake - above. The stream seems to enter from the right side. I land there and get out to taste it. Even this is brackish. So now I must leave quickly before the tide drops any farther and the outflow in the narrows turns into a raging river.

I am glad to be out of there safely, but I am really thirsty and out of water. My mouth feels dry. Chap Stick on my lips no longer gives me a sense that they are okay. It is scary, the thought of not knowing how to stop the dehydration.

An hour later I see a float plane circle to land somewhere up ahead. He must be landing at a camp or near a boat. I go behind the islands and find the plane tied to a log raft and there is a tug boat working the logs. At last I can get some water. I ask them for 2 gallons of water. They say there is a stream around the corner. I ask them, "How far is it?" They just say "Around the corner. You wouldn't want the water out of our tanks." So I head on. My mouth is very dry. There must be 100 corners among these nooks and crannies. At every break in the shore, I look for a stream. I am getting quite worried. After 1.5 miles, I see greenish looking rocks. Upon closer inspection I find a meager stream of tannin water. My filter comes into good use and I again have water to drink.

The headwinds are 15 to 20 knots all day. Sometimes the seas are quite rough. The forecast for the foreseeable future is NW winds 25 to 35 knots. This is as far as I can go before tackling the biggest stretch of exposed ocean, around Burnett Bay and Cape Caution. I am disappointed that I may be stuck here for several days.

After a long search, I find a place to camp. Someone had made a little bed of several logs laid side by side on the rocks with cedar bows carefully placed on top. A stack of firewood was cut and split too. This is someone's special camp site, and I will settle in here for the night.

May 6 - Last night I slept on the bed of logs without a tent. Luckily the bugs weren't too bad. Up at 5:30am. Wind is light. So I pack up and get underway by 6:15am. The coast is shrouded with mist. But the winds are light and the swells are about 5 feet.

Out of the mist comes a 22 foot boat at about half speed. Upon seeing me it veers over towards me and as it goes by, a woman shouts, "Do you know where Allison Harbor is?" I shout back "No, but Burnett Bay is there." And I point to an imaginary place in the mist, south of the sandy bay that barely shows through the mist and has waves pounding onto it. They turn and start heading right at the beach. I wave my arms to try to get them to come back. They see me and turn around and come by me again. Apparently the driver didn't want to risk slowing the boat down or putting it into neutral. As they come by again the woman yells, "Is there any place nearby we can go to get off the water?" Now if you are in a boat on the water and want to get off of the water, you are probably scared. I told them that two miles further south along the coast was a long channel. So they motored off into the fog. I realized I was in much better shape than these folks. I wonder what their thoughts were, seeing a guy pedaling two yellow pontoons out there in the ocean swells and fog.

It turned out to be a very good day for rounding Cape Caution. Nonetheless, the swells lumped up to 8 feet and the kelp beds were everywhere, indicating the water depth was minimal. I am glad to be around and on my way.

May 7 - On the water by 6:20am. Very light winds but the coastal fog is drifting in. I crossed the mouth of River's Inlet in the fog, about 5 miles by compass.

Last night the water filter stopped working. It probably is clogged up. If cleaning the screen doesn't work I will have to send it home. I will have to boil all of my water from now on in that event.

I suppose I have been prone to this type of activity from an early age. I now remember vacationing with friends when I was about 12 years old. I would get up early each morning and row a skiff about 3 miles across the lake and have breakfast with the Irwin family. Terry Irwin, a cute girl about my age, was the family member I was trying to impress. She seemed to take little note of my prowess. As I write, I am out in the middle of Fritz Hugh Sound and a pod of killer whales has just surfaced about a half mile to my left. I am going to just stay still and let them go on by. I don't feel like having a close encounter of that kind.

I found a not so nice beach for the night. It turned out to be a pretty good camping spot once I got a fire going. A fire always makes me feel 100% better.

May 8 - I decide to head for the outside coast instead of taking Fritz Hugh Sound all the way. That should prove to be more interesting.

And it was. Just a wonderful maze of islands, which I was able to wander through. I had to go around a major point which turned out to be quite dramatic. I should have gone at least a half mile offshore but instead I went between a rock and the point. The swells were very powerful, like a whole subdivision coming at me and sweeping underneath me. There was a great amount of ricocheting of the swells off of the point and curling around the rock too. A tidal current, mixed in, made the waves jump everywhere. The entire surface of the water acted as though it didn't want to be part of the surface but instead wanted to be lifted into the air. It was total chaos. I managed to avoid the absolute worse area. The bike acted as though it was going to hold together in this huge washing machine, which made me grateful. I made about 30 miles today. I should be able to get to Bella Bella by midday tomorrow.

For the first time on the trip, the bugs are a problem tonight. Black flies. Yesterday I saw my first tour ship.

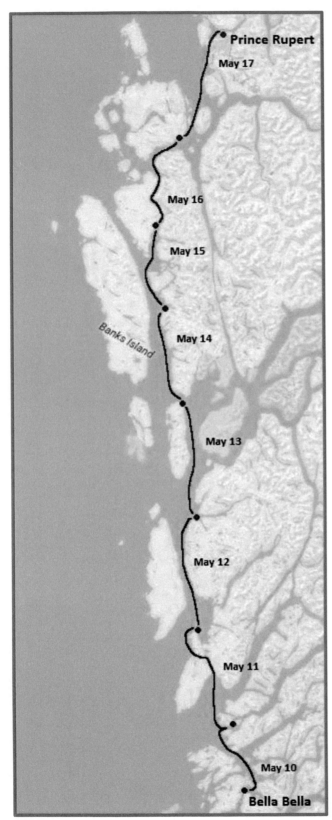

May 9 - I had an uneventful morning, arriving at Bella Bella at 12:30pm - enough time to go shopping and make phone calls. I had dinner at a bed and breakfast place, Alvina and Don. Stir fry. Very nice to have a change of diet. My meals are not very fancy.

I returned to the dock in time to see 3 kids on my Waterbike. One was rocking back and forth while standing on the cargo frame. They ran when I yelled at them. They had bent my cargo frame down three inches. I was perturbed at their lack of respect for personal property.

May 10 - On my way by 7:15am. It was raining very hard, and continued to rain hard until 1:00pm. I am not complaining. I had a tail wind most of the day, and it was great.

I had a quick meal at 5:00pm and then headed out across Milbank Sound. After about 2 miles of the 10 miles I had to go, the wind suddenly shifted to the northeast, blowing out of Finlayson Channel. I turned around and went the two miles back to a beach on a small island to spend the night. At the edge of the woods I noticed the ground was all torn up. The only thing that I could imagine that could have done that would be a bear digging up roots, but I was surprised that a bear would be on this little island. Closer inspection revealed something very different. Someone had recently cut and stolen a large spruce tree. The 4 foot diameter stump, just inside the woods, was freshly cut. Someone had carefully covered the whole top of the stump with moss, pulled from the forest floor. Apparently they were camouflaging the pale stump so it wouldn't be visible from an airplane. This is another case of lack of respect for laws and property. It is sad to see.

A weather front is predicted to hit this evening, another reason why I turned around and came back. This is the half way point of my trip, a significant event. It seems like I have travelled a very long time just to be half way, but it also feels good that every day from here on is like a day on the downhill side of the mountain.

May 11 - Off at 7:30am. The gale force winds didn't happen and they called off the warning. Winds are SW and very favorable. My aeronautical chart showed a way between two large islands (I don't know their names), but I began to get suspicious of my short cut when it became more and more apparent that no other boats were going that way. I would reach the narrows at high tide, so I figured there should be enough water for me to get through. When I got there the tide was just starting to drop. There was only a few inches of water between the boulders. I quickly dragged the bike across, hurrying because I didn't know if there would be more of these high spots. In the process, I broke the front wooden spreader bar. Once the bike was on the other side, I pedaled quickly until I saw swells breaking on the shore, indicating that this buckwater slough was going to reach the outside coast for sure. Then I took a half hour and lashed the spreader bar back together. I had an 8 mile crossing of Milbank Sound to make in the ocean swells so I hoped my repair would hold. It came through like a champ.

During one of my flights with N754 from Juneau to California, I had seen a dandy looking spot and had marked it on my chart. I was headed for that spot and knew that I could travel on, even though it was a little late in the day to be crossing Loredo Channel. I arrived at about 7:00pm. This is an outstanding place to stay. There is a great sandy beach on the protected side, then a narrow fringe of trees and easy access to the exposed side where there are acres of driftwood. What a wonderful feeling to land at such a welcome place. The feeling was soon tempered when I saw fresh wolf tracks in the sand. One was an adult, the other a younger one. I no sooner took a picture of the tracks, when I turned around and there was the little one, about 150 feet away. It stuck its tail between its legs and haltingly retreated another 200 feet. It kept looking at the narrow fringe of trees, probably for its mom. So I knelt in the grass and waited. After about 10 minutes, mom showed up. I took several pictures, then stood up and shouted. She just kind of looked at me as if to say what are you? Then she laid down. Then I walked out on the beach acting like I was a big bear. She started to lope off, showing the appropriate reaction I was looking for.

That evening there was a full moon and wolves were howling.

Wolf track in the sand.

May 12 - Steady rain this morning since about 5:00am. Got up at 7:00am and on my way by 8:15am. Very soggy. Rain quit by noon but a steady 10mph headwind makes pedaling tedious.

I saw 3 sandhill cranes fly over me, headed the wrong direction. They caught a little updraft and acted like they were going to turn and head north but then swerved to continue even further south. There is no place around here that would be suitable for cranes. They probably got separated from the main flock. I felt sorry for them because I know the feeling to be low on fuel, unable to find a good place to land, and not exactly sure which course of action to take.

May 13 – Today is Jennifer's 17th birthday. She is probably in the little town of Haines running track. Today it is crystal clear, bright sunlight, and relentless headwinds. At Ashdown Islands there was a skiff with two men. One old indigenous man and a younger fellow. They went by me and then into a bay up ahead. I was going to stop by and chat but then I heard a rifle shot. I assume they shot a sea lion because it was fairly close to a haul-out area. If it is illegal, I don't want to be a witness when they are the ones with the gun.

The tides are a problem now. They are very high at midnight which means the bike has to be stored very far above high tide line for the night. Then the tide is very low in the morning making it a problem getting the bike into the water. This morning I took the bike apart and reassembled it at the low tide line. That is too much hassle. I don't want to do that again.

I think the harlequin ducks really like Campania Island. They are abundant here. I bet they nest along the creeks of these barren mountains.

The northwest winds came up very strong in the early evening, so I had to stop for the night. I dragged the bike up a beach strewn with boulders. That is too difficult and too hard on the bike. I will need to do something different tomorrow night.

May 14 - Light rain in the morning but at least no headwind. Calm. Made good progress until early afternoon. I caught 6 little rockfish for dinner. The fillets are small so I wanted enough to fill the frying pan.

172

The northwest wind came up very strong in the afternoon and on into the night. I had to stop earlier than I wanted. I found a protected spot for the bike.

I am fortunate to find a nice beach for the night.

Dinner was excellent. The fish were great, breaded with Ritz cracker crumbs. A baked potato and sautéed onions made it my best dinner yet.

For the night I rigged up two lines to keep the bike in place offshore all night through the high tide. The stern line went to the anchor which was covered with three large rocks to keep it in place. Twenty feet of bungie cord was inserted in the line. The bow line went to a cedar tree branch and I suspended a 15 pound rock in the middle of the line to act as another spring. This will keep tension on the lines all night.

May 15 - Up at 2:30am to check the bike. All was okay. Up at 6:15am, just in time to keep the bike in the water as the tide continues to recede.

Sunny again today with a 10-15 mph headwind. I have forgotten what a tailwind feels like. The tops of my fingers are getting welts and sores. I have put tape on my fingers to protect them from the sun.
I have seen several tour ships now. To me they appear to be travelling at supersonic speed.

May 16 - The cold front is cold alright. Very cold, rainy, windy morning. The winds are from, you guessed it, the northwest. No matter how many turns I make through an untold number of channels, the wind is always in my face. At times today I am sure it got up to 30mph. The rain stopped by 2:00pm. It is becoming clear and sunny again.

My food is starting to get low. I ate my last candy bar this afternoon. Lunch tomorrow will have to be crackers and peanut butter, both almost gone too. I have several potatoes and one onion for tonight.

I saw a cabin in a small cove so I went in to check it out. The door was wide open. The cabin was nice but it didn't look like it had been kept up. The best thing for me was that there was an outhaul to run the bike out into the open water for overnight. No worries tonight. I cooked dinner on the beach then laid out my sleeping bag in the cabin.

May 17 - I thought I had only 17 miles to Prince Rupert and would make it there by mid-afternoon. Prince Rupert was off of my map and it turned out to be 30 miles. The winds were not too bad for the crossing from Porcher Island to Osland Island, thank goodness. Then they picked up to strong from the northwest. I arrived at Prince Rupert at 6:00pm, after a long hard afternoon. I am very weary. At times I got mad at the headwind and pedaled full speed for several hundred yards.

May 18 - I bought groceries. I bought 2 pairs of warm socks because my feet have been cold most of the time. I bought a pair of cotton gloves for protecting my hands from the sun.

A reporter for the Daily News drove me back to the dock and then interviewed me for an article.

Departed at 2:00pm. Strong 20mph headwind for the first 3 hours. I am convinced I could have made this trip from Port Hardy without a map. At every turn I would simply just face into the wind. I would have ended up in Prince Rupert. I am going to quit complaining about the wind and simply adjust to it. I will go slow and steady at a pace I can do all day without getting too tired.

The next four hours the wind was from my side – a west wind, which made a big improvement. I camped 2 miles south of Port Simpson. Stopped at 9:45pm.

May 19 - Up at 5:00am to try to make time before the west gets going. It was flat calm crossing the mouth of Portland Inlet. I am very fortunate to have had such conditions. The tidal currents were very impressive. This could have been one of the

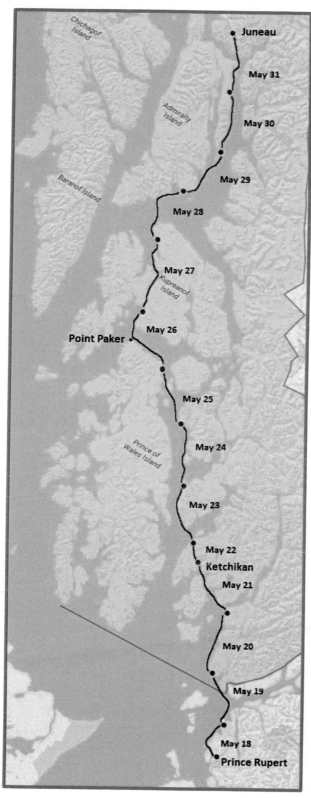

most treacherous crossings of the trip. I was across by 10:00am just before the west winds started up again. Sunny and clear.

12:00 noon – I just crossed the CANADA – USA border. I have pedaled from Seattle to Alaska. My right hand shook my left hand.

My body sometimes turns into a machine, a two piston engine. It just keeps cranking as long as I feed it fuel. When my arms don't want to pump any more, I tell them to get to work, that's what they were hired for.

I have been in the U.S. for just one hour and a skiff zooms up with a uniformed driver. I thought it might be customs on patrol. It turned out to be a trooper doing wildlife protection work. He checked my fishing license, which I believe is the first time in all my years of fishing, I have been checked.

I pedaled until 8:30pm. I found a very sheltered cove from the surge. My dinner was cold – canned salmon, crackers, a bagel and a cup cake.

May 20 - It is clear and sunny, north winds 10-15mph. Not a cloud in the sky. Up at 5:00am to beat the wind, but there are white caps by 10:00am. I stopped at 11:00am to rest

175

until 3:00pm. I drained some water out of the right rear pontoon, about half a gallon. The bike is still performing well mechanically.

Just as I got back out on the water, guess what, the wind died right down and then it switched to the south at 6mph. I can't believe it. It stayed light southerly until 7:00pm. At 8:30pm I stopped on a tiny little island about 25 miles south of Ketchikan. There is an eagle nest on the island with an incubating adult on it. I wonder how many people would notice a nest like this one. It is a nice evening. I will try to go to sleep early so I can get up early. I like these islets with no bears.

May 21 - Up at 4:40am, 3:40am Ketchikan time. I hoped to beat the northeast winds coming out of Behm Canal, but even at 6:00am in the morning they were blowing about 20mph with 3 foot seas and white caps. The second half of the crossing was not bad. It took 2 hours all together.

It feels good to be in my backyard, even though I have 250 miles to go. I saw devils club for the first time yesterday and I believe I saw salal for the last time yesterday. There apparently is little overlap of these two plants that often make travel through the woods extremely difficult.

After crossing Behm Canal the winds have become calm. Of course it is clear and sunny. Would I expect anything different in this temperate rain forest? As I was getting close to Ketchikan, a jet ski with two teenagers on it, came zooming right at me. The driver cut the power too late. They intended to scare me, but the jet ski actually hit my Waterbike, albeit just as it was coming to a stop. The kids laughed and then took off. That was a rude welcome to Alaska's first city.

May 22 - The News folks caught up with me at the dock. They were very impressed with my trip. The newspaper photographer said that for all the years he has been in Ketchikan and seen all kinds of people come through, such as kayakers - this is the most bazar. They videoed me too. I don't quite know what will come of all that.

I got away by 1:00pm. It is sunny and clear with 15mph north wind. I got to the end of Tongass Narrows and the winds were too strong to cross the north end of Behm Canal. I guess I will hope for them to die down overnight. I only made 8 miles.

May 23: Awake at 4:00am in hopes of making the crossing early, but the north wind was still strong. By 6:00am the winds died right down. I crossed Behm Canal in good shape. Then at 10:00am the north winds came up again, 25 knots. I took a two hour break. Three killer whales passed by me very close to the beach as they headed south. One was an extremely large male.

Except for a few day kayakers, I am the only human powered craft I have seen on the whole trip. I have seen no one else travelling by kayak or row boat.

176

It seems that every night I wake up once during the night because my knees are aching. They ache for about 10 minutes, then I go back to sleep. Of course it is sunny and clear again today. The gloves are helping my hands feel better.

May 24: Up at 5:00am to get across Ernest Sound early. I had a 10 mph north wind for the first half, then calm for the second half. Boy, the calm water feels so nice. I can stop to rest and I don't go backwards. It is also very peaceful. Hearing comments from the reporter in Ketchikan, I begin to see why people are leery of the Waterbike. To them I seem to be highly exposed, vulnerable and unprotected.

This is a very pleasant day even with the light headwinds. As I was rounding a corner, going through some islands, I saw an immature bald eagle fly from the beach. I noticed its crop was extended, indicating it had just gorged itself. So I looked at the beach with my monocular and saw a deer carcass. It was a fawn that had not been dead long. I am sure it died of thirst on that small island with no topography. The lack of rain is very unusual for this country.

May 25: It was flat calm all morning, very nice. I saw a flock of brant flying north, low over the water. I am sure this is very late for brant to be this far south. I bet the north winds have hampered them a lot too. I am sure they are appreciating the calm just as I am. Clear and sunny.

The northeast winds start up at 2:00pm. I stop at 5:30pm because I am extremely tired and the wind and tides are against me. I'll go to bed early tonight and get an early start tomorrow.

May 26 - I arrive at Point Baker at 4:30pm. The last time I was here was probably 17 years ago. The store then, as now, was built on floats at the dock. However, it had just burnt down and the locals were trying to figure out how to recover the cases of beer that must be on the ocean floor. This time, when I arrived, the store was out of commission again. They are repairing it after it received extensive damage last winter. It seems that on New Year's Eve they had a very high tide and a vertical dead head worked its way under the dock. Then when the tide went out during the night, the store settled on the dead head, which ripped it up real bad. The store owner said I could rummage around in there and select some items. I found 8 candy bars and a can of salmon. He gave me fresh water, and I left. I had expected to restock my food here. I would have to make due.

I started the crossing of Sumner Strait at 5:30am with a 25 knot tail wind. It was a very fast one hour crossing of the 5 nautical miles. Tide rips were interesting and put the pontoons awash several times. Once, my feet were awash as well.

I stopped at 8:30pm at the mouth of Rocky Pass even though it was very tempting to continue with the strong tail wind. I found a nice islet without bears. This is black bear country. I saw two today. It sure feels good when a nice haven like this is found for the night.

May 27 - Heavy rain this morning and strong southeast winds. The winds were 25-40 mph until 5:30pm. This was the perfect place to be on a stormy day, Rocky Pass. Rocky Pass is a 20 mile long passage of intricate windings through islands and rocks. I am very lucky to be here today. I made 34 miles today to Kake.

Just outside of Kake I saw a wheeled airplane fly by Kake. The weather was extremely foggy with intermittent heavy rain. It flew north. I would not want to have been flying in those conditions, even in a float plane. After a while I heard the sound of what I thought was the same plane coming back. I figured he had decided to land at Kake. But it didn't land. The sound quickly faded and then was gone. I wondered who was on board. Was there a 35 year old woman on the plane? Did she have two young daughters? Did she deserve better than to be flying in the fog in a wheeled airplane? It is Saturday evening. Maybe the pilot is trying really hard to get back to Juneau.

May 28: This is Sunday. I didn't get my groceries because the store in town is closed for Memorial Day weekend. The other store is 3 miles out of town and it doesn't open until noon. If it is also closed for Memorial Day weekend, I would be pedaling an extra 6 miles, and not get away until 3:00pm my time. I'll make do with what I have, which isn't much.

The 12 mile crossing from Kupreanof Island to Admiralty Island was going real well until 3 miles from Admiralty, when a doozy of a rain squall hit me. The seas got very rough.

I hope to catch fish to increase my food supply. I couldn't resupply at Point Baker and again at Kake. I didn't have any luck fishing this evening. I had 5 candy bars when I left Kake. I ate two on the long crossing. One of them I broke into little pieces and put them in with my dried banana chips. I usually have bread with peanut butter and honey, but I am out of bread. After tomorrow I will be out of peanut butter. I am dabbling the honey on the larger banana chips for desert. Tonight I had teriyaki rice. Then I cooked up tuna helper so I would have some leftovers for lunch tomorrow. I am out of powdered tang.

My Waterbike needs a shave. It is starting to sport a healthy green beard. I guess I can now say that I am on an extended trip. I called Molly this morning on the radio. It was good to hear her cheerful voice. She told me that Jennifer's 4x4 relay team won the state meet and that their time was within 1/100th of a second of the state record. As far as I am concerned, they tied the state record for the fastest 4 girls ever put together in Alaska. My chest is swelled out a little right now.

May 29 - At about noon today I was going along in light choppy water when I noticed just in front of me two areas where the water was smoothed in a circle apparently by currents. I hadn't seen or heard any whales all morning, but it looked to me like the pattern a whale leaves when it is swimming just under the surface. I figured it must be some weird currents and I passed over one of the circles and felt the current affect the drive unit. A few seconds later, the whale surfaced and blew just a few feet behind me.

I had a fish on the line but it got off. Later though, I managed to catch a 12 inch dolly varden. For dinner I put it in the pot with two packages of shrimp Top Ramen. It worked just great. Then I cooked the macaroni and cheese so I would have something to eat in the morning. It rained most of the day.

May 30 - Up at 6:15am. Slept late to recover a little. Off by 7:00am. Calm seas all day. I really need to catch some fish because of my limited food situation.

I caught a rock fish in the morning. Later I noticed a dolly varden not far in front of my waterbike flopping around on the surface. I quickly grabbed my fishing pole. Then right over my shoulder, an eagle swooped down and grabbed the dolly out of the water. It happen less than 50 feet in front of me. That's competition for a limited food supply. Later on I caught a nice big rock fish, so I have dinner. I used the last of my food, some dried mashed potatoes to go with the rock fish. I only ate half so that I have something left over for breakfast.

It was hard finding a good beach with adequate protection from the southeast. Finally I found one, but as I approached, I saw a large brown bear in the grass right where I wanted to camp. I pedaled up to the beach and shouted as loud as I could. On the fourth shout it finally ambled off into the woods. I decided I needed to camp there anyway. Good thing too, because in the evening the southeast winds came up very strong and I am glad I passed up the earlier spots and chose this one. I built a big fire to last through the night. I hope that does the trick - keeping the bear away.

May 31 - No bears during the night. But just after I got up and out of the tent in the morning, I was standing next to the tarp when I heard crashing sounds in the woods. Then out of the woods bursts a deer running at full speed. It was coming directly at me and only about 15 feet away. I shouted and put my arms up. It veered off and then ran straight down the beach and ran into the water. It swam a few seconds then turned and ran through the shallow water for 50 yards before exiting the water and running down the beach. My theory is that the deer was just inside the woods when I got out of the tent. It smelled my unbathed stench and just assumed the danger came from the woods and safety was to be found on the beach. It bolted for the beach and almost ran right over me.

I had left-over rock fish and mashed potatoes for breakfast. Today is a very good day for travelling, south winds 10-15mph and partly sunny. I should be able to make Juneau in good shape. My right foot blister and sore doesn't look very good, but it actually feels better than it did a couple of days ago.

I am pedaling up Gastineau Channel now. The sun is on the mountains, the wind is at my back. It is fitting that the sun is shining because that is how the majority of my trip has been. It is not fitting to have a tailwind. That suits me fine. I am very impressed by the beauty of the mountains that rise over Juneau. Nothing I have seen on this trip compares to this grandeur.

Just south of Douglas at Sandy Beach, photographer Skip Gray comes out in his kayak. EcoSports, the makers of the Waterbike, had arranged for him to photograph me. I was needing to hustle to make the bridge by 7:00pm, so I couldn't spend as much time with him as I would have liked.

I could see something white on the bridge from several miles out and thought maybe it related to me somehow. As I got close to the bridge I saw it was a large sign that said, "YOU DID IT JACK. 1000 MILES; SEATTLE TO JUNEAU". The outgoing current under the bridge was really strong. If it were stronger, I might not have been able to get through.

I landed at the ramp at Harris Harbor. There were about 40 people there to greet me. It felt good to see so many friends. I hugged Molly, then Kara and Jennifer, then Marion, then Dennis.

To all of them this moment was their contact with my trip, but to me, it was my last beach landing. And a happy one.

Jack Hodges is welcomed home Wednesday: 'It got really discouraging. ... Twenty days of head winds, it's just not fair.'

THE METTLE TO PEDAL 1,200 MILES

Jack Hodges completes his Seattle-to-Juneau water bike trip

By SUSAN PRICE
THE JUNEAU EMPIRE

When Jack Hodges stepped off the launch ramp in Seattle, he stepped into a world of head winds — a cumbersome obstacle if you're sailing or flying a small plane.

But when you're pedaling your way to Ju-

Harris Harbor at 7 p.m. Wednesday, after 44 days on his water bike. He was two days behind schedule, even though he had hit roughly 20 straight days of head winds.

The 20-year Juneau resident is thought to be the first person to do the Seattle-to-Juneau trip on the craft that is basically a seat 18 inches off the water straddling two 17-foot-long polyethylene pontoons. He uses foot ped-

He camped on beaches each night, but staye in motels and bed and breakfasts for a brea and a shower when he got to towns.

He arrived in one piece, minus a rudder that he took off when he bent it on a rock tha morning. He said his foot became infected when it blistered and he jammed it between some rocks, but it's doing better now. He solved the problem of the top of his hands bli

Making landfall at Juneau amongst friends and family.

Chapter 23 - The Sailing Trip
2001

Six years after my *Waterbike* trip from Seattle to Juneau, I met a man whose sailboat was moored near my boat in Juneau. His name was Andy and the year was 2001. He was probably fifteen years younger than I, fit and lean. Laughter came easy and often for him. His boat was neat and tidy. Whenever he saw me on the float, he gave me a quick and genuine greeting. Over the next few months, I learned that he had built his boat in Bellingham Washington and had sailed it many thousands of miles through the South Pacific Islands. He and his partner, Lisa, had also explored much of the coast of Alaska before arriving in Juneau. I did not meet Lisa because she was on the north slope of Alaska working at the oil fields, earning good money in anticipation of much more sailing and exploring with Andy.

Then one day while we were chatting on the dock, Andy mentioned that he would probably be leaving Juneau in a few months. He would take his boat back down to Bellingham, spruce it up some more, including solar panels, and then sail to Hawai'i. Nothing was definite yet. That was something I would come to learn about Andy, no plans were ever definite. He always left himself a lot of wiggle room for changing his mind. Lisa might be accompanying him for the crossing to Hawai'i, but that was not certain either. He might just do the crossing single handed.

Without a moment of hesitation, I said that I would gladly make the crossing with him, should he decide he wanted another hand on board. This was an opportunity for me to make that last leg of my journey to Hawai'i. I could experience the same ocean which I had planned to cross by kayak thirteen years earlier. We would be pushed by the wind, silent and intimate with the sea. Hopefully we would see a storm and I could imagine myself in the kayak. I would again be cheating on my promise to cross the Pacific Ocean by kayak, but this might be my only opportunity to make a surrogate trip. I hoped that Andy would decide he wanted me along. Molly agreed that Andy would be a reliable, knowledgeable sailor; an ideal teacher and companion.

A month later, Andy decided he would like me to help with the crossing. He said that he would prefer not to sail alone because that meant he would have to wake up every 30 minutes during the night to look for ships. I was excited. We would leave in September, even though that was during the Pacific hurricane season. Andy's boat was made of steel, with small, stout windows. It looked like a sailboat that could survive a hurricane, and Andy would be the ideal skipper to get boat and crew through a hurricane.

"Hey Jack. Everything is going well here in Bellingham. I should be ready to go in a couple more weeks." Andy's jovial voice sprang through the phone. It was the call I had been expecting. "How about you fly down here on September 11? We'll leave the next day, weather permitting."

This trip was really going to happen for me. By now I had researched hurricanes in the North Pacific Ocean. I had plotted on a chart, the path of every hurricane and tropical storm that had occurred in the past 30 years, roughly one every two years. Historical records gave me the locations by latitude, longitude, and date. These records showed me that the region where hurricanes and tropical storms occurred was fairly predictable. I figured we would be in that region about 7 days. The odds of us encountering a hurricane on this trip, according to my math, were about 1 in a hundred. That seemed to be an acceptable risk for me. Little did I know that a half dozen years later, on the other end of the North Pacific, I would be in a hurricane and captain of the boat.

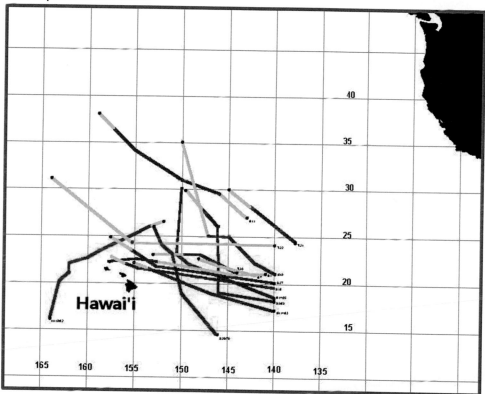

Thirty years of hurricanes(red), tropical storms(dark grey) and depressions(light grey).

When September 11 arrived, I was at the Juneau Airport by 5:00am. I checked in and was sitting alone waiting to board my flight. My good friend, Dennis, showed up to bid me farewell, just as he had promised. But the urgency of his approach was strange. His face was tense. He said, "Have you heard that a jet crashed into one of the World Trade Center towers in New York?" No, I hadn't heard. Just then the voice of an Alaska Airlines representative came on the loud speaker and informed us that the FAA had issued an urgent message. All planes in the U.S. had been grounded. All planes in the air were to land at the nearest airport. It was soon clear that I wouldn't be leaving Juneau that day.

My mind couldn't help but go back exactly 30 years earlier. It was September 4, 1971 and I was standing in the same Juneau airport waiting to board Flight 66 to Seattle. An Alaska Airlines representative announced that Flight 66 would be landing in 10 minutes. We were still standing there an hour later waiting for the plane. No one seemed particularly worried because air travel in Alaska was often delayed for various reasons. But then the announcer came on again and said that Alaska Airlines wanted everyone that was in the building waiting to meet a passenger on Flight 66 to go to the Customs Room. The rest of us continued to mill around, waiting. When some of those in the Customs Room began to emerge, the grim situation was transmitted by word of mouth. Flight 66 was missing. It had either been hi-jacked or it had crashed. Someone near me had a portable radio and they soon learned that it had crashed. At that time, this accident was the deadliest crash in U.S. history. All 111 people on board Flight 66 perished. Now again, I was directly affected by a tragic airline disaster.

My journal begins . . . . .

September 15 - I am on my way at last, after a four day delay. The plane was two hours late leaving Juneau because of fog in Ketchikan. I wanted us to take off and just skip Ketchikan. It is hard to believe I am actually going to be stepping onto a sailboat, bound for Hawai'i. I still don't know Andy's last name, but I expect I will learn it and a lot more about Andy soon.

The boat is called "Indefatigable". I asked Andy why he couldn't have just called it "Tireless." He didn't think that was funny. She is a 36 foot sloop, made of steel.

Andy and the author just before departure.

I am feeling a little bit of guilt. I know that some in my family will worry about me. So I start to think that this is kind of a selfish thing to do. But then again, we all have our own lives to live and sometimes we can do some things just for ourselves.

September 16 - We left Port Angeles at 7:00am in a very low overcast. The wind was nearly on our nose all morning but the tide was with us and we scooted along under power. The waves were quite choppy, about 4 feet. Andy showed me how to raise the mainsail, unfurl the roller reefing genoa, and raise the staysail. He explained how the harness would work and he suggested I wear the harness and be clipped in all the time while on the ocean. He made these harnesses for the trip. He did a real good job. He sewed them out of seat belt straps.

I learned that Andy gets most of his materials from the junkyard. He pays $.50 per pound. It seems like he can make anything. Almost everything on the boat he has made himself, and I mean made from scratch. He prides himself on making things that are better than store-bought and made from the scraps that others have tossed in the garbage. He says he has learned to live on the crumbs of our society, and it is a good life. Once he got past the embarrassment of being seen with his feet dangling out of a dumpster, he says it became easy enough.

It was windy and very cold all day. We ran the motor the whole way, 50 nautical miles. Neah Bay is the last outpost on the northwest corner of the continental U.S. It looks like it too, a small community not unlike what you would see in rural Alaska. We took on 10 gallons of fuel, what Andy had burned from Bellingham to here. I made

185

a final phone call to Molly. We anchored for the night in a misty drizzle. Andy said we should get a good night's sleep to be well rested for the morrow. The weather report still sounds good for our departure and the coming days as we head south.

September 17 - Day 1 - We took our time eating breakfast and making last minute adjustments to be sure everything was carefully stowed. After pulling the anchor, Andy took it off the bow and stowed it down below. We won't be needing it for the next 3 weeks.

We motored out of Neah Bay in mist and fog, but little wind. Another sailboat was just ahead of us. She headed down the coast and we headed for Hawai'i. After 3 hours we lost sight of her. We saw 3 tankers, a cruise ship and several fishing boats, but by mid-afternoon we seemed to be quite alone on the ocean. The fog lifted a little and we caught one last glimpse of the coast of Washington.

I took my first watch until noon. We set our clocks back one hour to be on standard time. That made my watch an extra hour longer. As we cross into the next time zone, Andy will add an hour to one of his watches.

Around 3pm we sailed right out from under the overcast into the clear blue and sun. It felt warm and pleasant. I happened to be looking forward. Not too far in front of us, out of the water came two porpoises simultaneously, each jumping toward the other. They crossed in mid-air as if they were jumping over a pole for a crowd at sea world.

My first watch at night started at 6pm and darkness came about 7pm. It was cloudy so it was very dark. All of a sudden a torpedo was streaking through the water right at the boat. It swerved and turned and then went under us. It was a porpoise turning the water into a fiery green color due to the phosphorescent glow.

September 18 - Day 2 - Andy turned the motor off at 5:30am. Now the sailing begins. It is so much more pleasant with the engine off. All of the rattling has stopped. A cold front is supposed to hit the Pacific Northwest on Thursday. We have another two days to get out of here ahead of it. At noon we have made 123 nautical miles since yesterday noon and we are abeam the mouth of the Columbia River. All is well. We are relaxed, well fed, and enjoying the placid sea.

The boat was sailing fast for my watch from 6pm to midnight. I eventually reefed the mainsail because we were hitting 6.5 knots. It is scarier sailing fast at night than during the day.

September 19 - Day 3 - I had trouble sleeping because the wind backed off and the sails were making loud banging noises as they flopped around.

We finally had to start the motor this morning so I had to steer for my whole watch. Steering requires constant attention. When we are sailing, the steering vane steers the boat. It uses a trim tab on the rudder that is constantly adjusting as the boat changes direction relative to the wind.

I saw two albatross on my morning watch. They are amazing fliers. They never flap their wings. They can cover amazing distances with very little effort. No porpoises today. We are well over 100 miles offshore and Andy was still able to get the weather on the VHF radio out of Coos Bay.

My arms and upper body are tired and sore. Not that I have been working much, but every time you move around on the boat it takes physical effort. The motion of the boat has to be constantly compensated for. After a week I am sure my body will have adjusted.

I learned that Andy's last name is Deering.

During my night watch I listened to the short wave radio and figured out that the storm information is given at 48 minutes after every hour. We can only receive it at night. During the day the signals are too poor. I also listened to various radio stations including the Mariner's game which they won. Sounded like it was their first game since the terrorist attack. It is somewhat reassuring to hear the radio. There was no mention of the remnants of hurricane Ivo off of the coast of Baja. It also appears we will out run the front expected to hit Oregon on Friday.

September 20 - Day 4 - My morning watch was characterized by a fitful wind. It was up and down, up and down, all morning. We must be in between two major air masses.

The afternoon has been perfect sailing conditions. We are doing 5.5 knots and the skies are clear. This is great. We are about 200 miles offshore and paralleling the coast. If we were closer to the coast the winds would probably be too strong for comfort, but if we get too far offshore we run the risk of getting into the middle of the pacific high pressure and be without wind. So we hope to thread our way in between.

September 21 - Day 5 - I slept better last night. Still five and a half hours doesn't leave me feeling well rested. I try to get another hour of sleep during my afternoon time off. My arms and shoulders ache from the unaccustomed crawling around and bracing. It is far more effort just to exist on a rocking, rolling boat than I ever imagined.

We haven't had any rain yet, and we really haven't had much blue sky either. It has mostly been thin clouds. Last night, on my watch, I wore all the clothes I could put on and I was still cold. Andy took a bath on deck today, but I am going to wait until tomorrow. It looks like a really cold operation.

This evening Andy and I were talking about how ideal the ocean conditions have been for our trip so far. We agreed that if you could expect it to be like this every time, it would be tempting to go up and down the coast frequently. Andy then told me about a couple they met in the Marquesas that had been beaten up making this trip and had been forced off the ocean twice along the coast. So they gave up trying and trucked their boat to San Diego. I told him that is exactly what happened to my cousin Carla and her husband about 6 years ago. Andy described their boat and that matched. Then he described them and it sounded like Carla and Casey. I said the boat's name had the word Rose in it, and Andy said "the Briar Rose". It turns out that Andy and Lisa met and got to know Carla and Casey. What a coincidence. We had a good laugh over that.

September 22 - Day 6 - Some firsts today. I saw my first shark. It was lazily swimming along the surface until we approached to within 30 feet and then it got startled and went down. I took my first bath, using buckets of saltwater. Andy allows about 2 cups of fresh water for rinsing the saltwater off. We put the fresh water inside of a tire inner tube to which he has attached a hose and nozzle. The inner tube is put above head level on the mast and you get a little sprinkling of fresh water. The bath felt good even if it is still a little cold. We are still 100 miles north of the latitude of San Francisco, but about 400 miles offshore.

About 10am this morning we made our turn to head direct for Hawai'i. Until now we have mostly been going south. Today the winds are light, the sea is gentle, and the sun is mostly shining. It is a day to relax. I feel tired, but I don't feel like sleeping. It is more of a physical tired.

It has been four days since we saw another boat. I have yet to see a jet fly over, although it has been cloudy most of the time. We haven't had a drop of rain.

Andy says we are going too slowly to fish for tuna. We have to be going at least 5 knots he says. The water is the deepest blue color you can imagine. It is unreal. Even in foggy gray conditions the water is blue. We are nowhere near the middle of this ocean and already I have the feeling that this part of the planet is incredibly huge and almost entirely void of human occupation.

September 23 - Day 7 - At about 5am this morning Andy spots a ship. This is the first vessel we have seen in many days. Andy was able to raise it on the VHF radio. It is a Norwegian ship. It is on its way from Japan to San Francisco. Andy asks him what we can expect for weather ahead. He says they have just come through a low pressure and a cold weather front. Their ship had a pretty rough ride he said. We can expect winds to 25 knots. He was very nice and said he would pass along a message when he gets to San Francisco if we want. So Andy gave him a number where Lisa will get the message. We told him to pass along that everything is fine and the location of where we are. This ship takes logs from British Columbia to Japan and then brings cars back to the U.S. They have 3,500 cars onboard.

A storm is brewing.

So now we have bad weather to look forward to. By late morning the signs are there. Gray clouds are coming in and the wind begins to really pick up. Andy decides to heave to for the storm. We roll up the genoa and put up the small staysail with one reef in it. We double reef the mainsail and tie the rudder hard over. Now we just go below and watch. The boat will take care of itself when we heave to.

The wind keeps building and the waves get nastier. Sure enough, we have a good steady 25 knots. The boat rides well, with the nose slightly into the waves and the wind heeling us over 20 degrees. It is uncomfortable, but not miserable. The waves lift us up like a fast elevator, then drop us back down. Then we lurch at a deep angle to leeward. Hold on. Cashews go flying, can opener sails out from behind the condiment rack, and everything in the forepeak becomes a conglomerate on the floor. I am feeling half seasick. I lose interest in eating and just want to lie down and close my eyes. Dinner for me was some of Molly's pickled halibut and Ritz crackers. Andy had a peanut butter sandwich.

Andy's watch started at midnight and I guess he had a terrible night. I was so tired that I slept through most of it. The wind died but the seas were horribly confused. Without the wind, the boat wobbled helplessly. When he tried to put up the sails to steady us, they would just flop and pound from side to side.

September 24 - Day 8 - Time for my watch at 6am. Andy is wasted. I am pretty well refreshed, but still a little seasick. The boat is still flopping every which way.

Soon the wind starts to pick up, and from a favorable direction. I hoist the genoa and kill the engine. Andy gets 3 hours of sleep as we ride the big swells fairly comfortably.

It is now 10am, the sun is out, we are on a heading towards Hawai'i, we are doing 4 knots, and all feels pretty good. I look over at the railing on the back of the cockpit near me and our spider has come out to check his web. I am surprised he is still with us. The web had to have been destroyed by the storm. He must have rebuilt it last night. The poor guy is going to be hurting for food. I haven't been pestered by any bugs out here.

Now it is early evening and we are getting hammered. We must have been in the eye of the storm today and now we are getting hit by the back side. The waves are huge. They approach us at great speed, looming over us, and it appears we are going to be squashed but at the last minute the boat rises up the wave and over the top. One wave though jumped up over the cockpit at the stern and landed on my head. Andy said it would have made a great photograph with the water perched over my head like a big green and white haystack. We of course were forced to heave to again. The moon is now half full so I have some light to see by. Too bad it sets right at midnight when Andy takes over on his watch.

I fear the spider is probably gone. I don't see how he could have survived the deluge of water on the stern during this last blow. Dinner tonight was a can of sardines that Andy and I shared, and crackers.

September 25 – Day 9 - I am hungry and the weather isn't too bad for the moment, so I make 3 soft boiled eggs and have them over bread, with tang to drink. By 10am a new band of scud approaches. Another front has hit us but this one is not so bad and we are able to sail through it and make progress on a southerly heading. By late afternoon signs of the frontal passage are clear. The barometer rises sharply. The skies begin to clear. The wind shifts 60 degrees to the right. We are out of this one, but the seas are still very rough and chaotic. Even though the wind is tame, the boat jumps and heaves quite violently. Andy is down below and says he is becoming weightless with every big wave and his stomach feels like it is going up into his throat.

Had I been in a kayak these past two days it would have been a miserable experience. The kayak would have fared better than the occupant. It would have bobbed on the wild waves like a duck. I probably would have spent the entire time lying inside, in a wet sleeping bag. If I still make the kayak trip to Hawai'i, it would be wise to test myself and the kayak in these ocean conditions beforehand.

September 26 – Day 10 - The seas have calmed, leaving just the large gentle westerly swells. The wind is variable and we are making headway at 5 knots. At that speed we can make 120 miles in a day.

But by 10am the winds have died and we are forced to start the engine. I hate to see us use too much fuel because we may need it to run away from a hurricane later. Andy says when we reach 30 degrees latitude we will be in the trade winds and we will have steady wind.

Hundreds of gray sided porpoises raced to play by our boat as we motored. They were with us for at least a half hour. The sun is pretty warm. I am wearing shorts for the first time. I took a bath too.

Porpoises befriending us and having fun.

My stomach is feeling better so my appetite has returned. The beef jerky is starting to mold so we have to eat it up. The apples taste good.

We are seeing much more garbage floating in this area. About each half hour we see something, like a coil of rope, or a piece of hose, or an oil bottle etc. We are motoring all day long because of the calm. We must be on the edge of the Pacific High Pressure area. It has been referred to as the toilet bowl. An incredible amount of floating garbage ends up here. Finally at 9pm we decide to stop the motor and drift for 6 hours. It will give us each time to get more sleep.

The sleep idea didn't work out as well as we had hoped. The boat wallowed so violently while drifting that the rudder would make loud banging noises no matter how well we tied it down. My thoughts kept centering on the importance of not damaging our rudder. Without a rudder we would go nowhere. And who is around to rescue us? In the last nine days we have seen only one vessel. The vastness of this part of the world, and the remoteness from any other human beings is humbling. I look at the boat and all seems comfortable and familiar. I look across the water to nothing but sky and clouds and realize that we are a satellite orbiting the globe at a very very slow speed. We are entirely dependent on this craft to keep us alive.

September 27 – Day 11 - I saw my first flying fish today. We should start seeing more and more of these. The water here is full of floating jelly fish that have little half moon sails they put up into the air to blow them around. Andy put the fish line out and immediately had a strike but it didn't get hooked. The fish must have been following our boat.

Six hours later we have a fish on the line. It is big. It is a dorado, about 20 pounds. It is spectacularly beautiful, bright golden color. Andy says it is too big for us to eat it all. So we let it go. Now we hope for a smaller one. We have just gotten south of the 35 degree parallel which is almost down to the latitude of Los Angeles. We are now 1400 miles from Hilo, Hawai'i.

Because the wind is against us we can't make headway for Hawaii so we are going southeast to try to reach the trade winds. Good thing we chose that direction. When we tuned into the weather we found out there was a low pressure area just northwest of us. We think it will miss us as it goes one way (NE) and we go another (SE).

September 28 – Day 12 - This morning dawned clear, but back behind us could be seen the disk of clouds from that low pressure system. Looks like we dodged a bullet. Winds are supposed to be 20 to 30 knots in there.

I found a little flying fish on the deck this morning. It is quite amazing to see a fish with wings. At 9am I spotted a ship on the horizon. It is the second vessel we have seen since getting out on the ocean. Andy talked with them on the radio. They are bound for the Panama Canal from Japan.

There is no way to describe how difficult it is to move around on the boat when it is acting like a bucking horse. My arms and shoulders still feel like I have been working out too much at the gym. The palms of my hands are sore from bracing against the railing for hours on end. My neck takes a beating too, trying all day long to keep my head straight when it wants to move around like a wobble head doll.

We were just boiling potatoes for dinner when Andy yells down from the cockpit, "Holy smokes we're dragging a huge net." Sure enough about 40 feet of seine net had hooked on a zinc somewhere on the bottom of the boat. We were able to pull most of it on deck but it was still snagged underneath. Little crabs started crawling off of the net onto the deck. We took all the sails down to stop the momentum of the boat. Then Andy stripped and jumped overboard. He dove down and pulled it loose. We didn't know what to do with this huge mass of net. We don't have room to carry it and we hate to leave it out there for someone else to get tangled in it. We had to throw it back into the water. The crabs were tossed too.

Dinner was excellent - boiled potatoes, canned venison and cabbage. After dinner Andy saw a jet flying over. I could try to call it with the aviation radio I had with me. I tried the radio yesterday, but the jet didn't answer. I called this one saying, "This is the sailing vessel Indy, calling the jetliner." He answered saying, "This is American 628. Who is this? Where are you?" I said, "We are on a sailboat and I wanted to test our radio in case we were to need it." He made no more response. I expect the airline pilot's nerves are still on edge after the horrific attacks of September 11. A response from one out of two aircraft means that we could call a jet if we needed to in an emergency.

September 29 – Day 13 - I guess Andy had to call to me 4 times this morning before I finally woke up. Usually I am one that wakes up with the slightest of ease. Either I am really tired or I have blocked out all noises. Waves bash against the hull. The pulleys on the mainsail squeak. The sheet on the genoa sail creaks. The rudder shudders. The dishes in the sink sometimes clank. The interior walls groan. Water gurgles in the sink drain. The whisker pole occasionally bongs against the mast. All this has to be tuned out.

Right at noon just after I got off of my 6 hour shift on watch, a fish hit the line. It was another dorado (mahi mahi). This one was a little smaller, maybe 15 pounds. So we harpooned it and Andy did a nice job of filleting it. The fresh meat is a welcome treat. We had it for lunch and will have it for dinner and for breakfast and lunch tomorrow I bet. Andy cut some thin strips, marinated them in some soy sauce and has put them out to dry. This is an experiment.

The winds have become more favorable today. After 4 days of having to head almost due south, we are now sailing only 20 degrees south of the course to Hawai'i. This has been a beautiful, relaxing day. With weather like this and fresh fish to eat, it at last seems like a fine place to be, rather than a place in the middle of nowhere to try to pass through and get beyond.

I think I am adjusting to this life now. The symptoms of seasickness are gone and I am not so tired and sore. I am able to read more now, which helps my watches go by faster. I have read four magazines and two books, "Ishmael" and "Medjugorje."

September 30 – Day 14 - The spider is still alive! He might not be feeling 100% though. He made a half-hearted effort to start a new web. He got one strand stretched from the railing to the steering vane post. When he was crawling back on this strand to the starting point, the wind started swinging him around pretty good. Maybe he got scared, because that's as far as he got with that web. Maybe he is running out of web material. We thought about putting one of the tiny crabs off of that net we brought aboard into his web for food, but there wasn't any web at that time.

The winds have turned back to the southwest again which forces us to steer south. When we do that, we make very little progress towards Hawai'i. Our wind regime has been totally contrary to what the pilot charts show we should be having in this part of the Pacific Ocean. Had I been in my kayak, I would be losing ground, since I would be unable to paddle very effectively against a constant headwind.
The excitement for today was the taking of my second bath of the trip. I'm all clean again. The salt water is 75 degrees but that is still cold when you pour buckets of it over your head while standing on the windy deck.

October 1 - Day 15 – We have 1200 miles to go. We are making good time right now, but the seas are fairly rough. We saw our third vessel of the trip, a cargo ship. We got the latest weather info from them. A gale is brewing NW of us and headed SE. We might come under its influence tomorrow. We hope to ease south of it. This morning we sailed past two glass balls, one small and one large.

I haven't worn shoes now for 5 days. My feet like it. At first I moved around on my bare feet like they were still encased in shoes. After 40 years in shoes, my toes had forgotten what they were made for. My bare feet seemed less secure than shoes. Then my toes began to learn to grip corners of the cockpit, to pick up a loose strand of rope, to curl over the edge of the lazarette hatch cover and to give me that feeling of being in touch with the boat.

We turned our watches back one hour to try to get the sun to rise and set at the right times.

October 2 – Day 16 - We seem to have finally reached the trade winds. They are blowing nice and steady. We made 120 miles in the last 24 hours. The sun is shining but it is still quite cool to be out in the wind with just shorts and a tee shirt. We have been on the ocean 16 days now. If the winds stay steady we should reach Hawai'i in about 9 days.

Andy asked what I would like for dinner. I said I would like barbequed ribs, mashed potatoes and corn on the cob and a chocolate milk shake. He came pretty close. We had canned venison, dried mashed potatoes, canned corn and a chocolate bar.

The moon is full now. The moonrise is spectacular. It rises through the horizon rapidly - orange, and large.

We no longer see albatross. Another flying fish landed on the deck last night. These fish are only about 4 inches long. I have seen a couple flying and it is amazing. They seem to float across the water like magic.

The strips of fish have now dried. They taste pretty good. It will make good snack food. Now that the weather is nice, I have been doing more reading. I have read four more books.

October 3 –Day 17 - My thoughts go to my family and friends. I wonder what everyone is doing. I wonder what changes will have occurred while I have been in this time warp. I realize that without my family and friends I am just so much seagull food. I try to help their lives to be better and they help mine, and so life unfolds.

I am anxious to complete this journey, but I know that I am still in the middle of a big ocean and patience is the only tactic that works out here. Getting impatient with the weather, or the damp salty clothes, or the stale tasting water or my shipmate will serve no purpose. I try to fit into Andy's style of living and he tries to accommodate me. We are getting along well. We both seem to know that courtesy towards one another is the only way to make this passage work. We are in close proximity to each other constantly, and there is almost no privacy. Andy took a gamble asking me to help with this trip. I am determined to make it as successful as I can.

October 4 – Day 18 - The ocean this morning is glassy, not a whisper of wind. We are forced to run the motor. The sea still undulates from multiple directions and the boat wallows around with unpredictable motions. Every moment of the day you have to be braced. You have to be braced by three points, which must be like a tripod. If your two feet and your hand-hold are in only one plane, you are destined to be flung from your position. You have to keep your three points of contact in a tripod shape.

The spider lives! On this beautiful calm morning I watched it rebuild its web. It doesn't take but about 30 minutes for him to complete it. He seems totally unaware that the nearest flying insect is 900 miles away. Before we reach Hawai'i I will have to bury him at sea. I can't knowingly contribute to the introduction of an exotic species into distant lands.

Right now the sea is as smooth as a baby's bottom, but the boat still lurches such that it is a struggle to write this. Without the sails up, there is nothing to stop the flop in the slop and chop.

I took a little piece of dried fish and placed it in the spider's web. He seemed to show no interest at all in it. After a length of time I jiggled the piece of fish with my fingernail. The spider rushed across the web and pounced on the scrap of fish. He carried it to the middle of his web but he doesn't seem to want to eat it.

Hundreds of porpoises showed up this afternoon. I guess we are the only entertainment around. They must be hard up for vessels because we are only doing 3.6 knots which can't be much fun for them. It is hard to believe we have only seen 3 ships in 18 days. Can you imagine being in a life raft for 18 days hoping for rescue and only see 3 ships, the closest of which still passed 1.5 miles away?

October 5 – Day 19 - Andy saw a ship early this morning. He tried to radio them but received no answer.

We had a ten minute heavy rain shower this morning. It was so nice to get the salt rinsed off of the deck and railings. That salt makes life a lot less enjoyable. It makes everything feel sticky and clammy.

It seems strange to me that we haven't seen one whale on the whole trip.

This afternoon Andy said "Shall we catch a fish for dinner?" I said sure. And two hours later we had another dorado on board. The hoochie just streams along the surface 40 feet behind the boat. No weights are used at all.

October 6 - Day 20 - I am fed up. I am really fed up. There is so much food here to eat and we are running out of time to eat it. We cooked up all of the meat from the 15 pound dorado and we have to eat it up in a day. Fish for dinner. Fish for midnight snack. Fish for breakfast. Fish for lunch. We have jars of nuts, candy, apples and crackers. I am so fed up. I can't eat any more.

We are in the trade winds. For a day we haven't had to touch the sails. The wind is straight behind us and Hawai'i is straight in front of us. The impression I have is that there is a long cable attached to our bow that stretches from Hawai'i and a winch is reeling us in. Only 760 miles to go. That seems pretty close. One week.

The radio isn't mentioning any tropical storms so we might be in good shape there too. Twice each day we listen intently to the radio at 48 minutes past the hour. They give the locations of the storms once each hour and only once. We strain to hear the voice fading in and out and write the coordinates down on a pad. Afterwards we compare our notes to see if we agree on the positions. Earlier in our voyage there was this clown that gave the weather information at the fastest talking speed you can imagine. There is no way we could possibly interpret what he said. We just wished we could grab that guy by the collar of his shirt and yank him out of his cozy little government office and put him on a little sailboat in the middle of the Pacific Ocean. Then we would see if he has any interest in where the storms are at, and can he make any sense out of his rapid-fire broadcast, the only source of information.

October 7 – Day 21 - The word that comes to mind now is monotonous. It seems like every hour is about the same as the last hour, and every watch is about the same as the last watch, and every day is about the same.

I worry that Andy is not getting enough sleep. Before the trade winds he seemed to stir whenever the boat moved in uncharacteristic ways, or when loud noises occurred. When we reached the warmer climate, he was too hot in his bunk. So he tried sleeping on the floor, which worked for a while, but then the rolling of the boat has been so relentless that he tried sleeping cross ways with a board between the seats. That doesn't seem to be working for him either. I am so tired when I retire to my bunk that I seem to be sleeping pretty well. If it is hot and stuffy I just think back to my childhood days of sleeping in Arlington, Virginia in the summer time. My bedroom had no air conditioning. That makes this seem almost like air conditioning.

October 8 Day 22 - Andy is still not doing a very good job of sleeping. He tried the floor again last night without much success. This morning he tried the bench seat and then finally ended up in his original cramped bunk, which he hasn't used for a few days. Through all of this I have continued to use my cramped bunk. It is not much more room than sleeping in the kayak. We each have a large, heavily stuffed pillow to use to wedge ourselves in at night to keep from being tossed around.

This is our 22nd day at sea. Rather than having the feeling that I am continuing to adapt to this way of life, this has now become my way of life.

It is afternoon now and I am relaxing, but I don't look forward to my 6pm to midnight watch. It gets dark about 7pm and I have so much trouble staying awake. I can read, but if I read I just go to sleep. I can eat, but I can only eat so much. I usually end up wedging myself in a corner and dozing for about 10 minutes, then get up and look around for ships and check the wind and sails, then get back in the corner all over again.

Andy just called me to help him lower the mainsail. A hole has worn through where the sail rubs on the spreader bar when we are sailing downwind. He has sticky backed sail material to affect a temporary patch. My job was to pull in the sheet on the boom as Andy let the sail down. The problem is that the sail comes down instantly but I can't pull the sheet in very fast because I have to hold onto something with one hand while I pull with the other. Also, the sheet runs through 3 blocks, so 6 feet of sheet has to be pulled to move the boom one foot. So the sail was down and I hadn't gotten much line in yet to get the boom under control. The boat rolled and the boom swung across the boat from one side to the other. I was focused on the line in my hand and didn't see what was happening. As it approached my head, I must have somehow seen it out of the corner of my eye, because I instinctively ducked a little, just as the metal boom whizzed by. I felt the wind from it as it passed within an inch or so of my head. If that had hit me I am sure I would have been knocked out and had a terrible wound. I suppose it could have even killed me. I need to be constantly alert for injury, as I am still a novice at sailing on the ocean.

We are now 500 miles from Oahu. We keep expecting to see some boat traffic, but not yet.

October 9 – Day 23 - Still we run before the wind, straight downwind on the trades. Frequent squalls hit us. They come from astern. I had a big one on my watch this morning. I saw it coming, so I double reefed the mainsail and left just a little of the head sail unfurled. We slowed way down to 4.5 knots but I knew the winds would come in the squall. The rain and wind came. Suddenly we were flying along at 7.5 knots which means we were surfing in front of the swells. The boat skidders and swerves around as if to say "It is hard for me to steer in this, Captain." The wind makes the top of the water look smoky. It looks a bit frightful. I climb down inside the cabin and close the door tight and let the rain pound and the wind howl. I hope we don't go any faster because then I would have to go out and try to reduce sail some more. In 30 minutes it is over. The seas are still riled up but it is time to put some of the sail area back up.

Every minute of the day the boat heaves, rolls and lurches. The ocean has all day long to try out various combinations of waves and angles and boat position and find one that does the unexpected, and really whollups us a good one. It might dump into the cockpit, or really put a gunwale under water and roll us on our ear. Never relax, the ocean isn't going to.

This evening we saw our fifth ship of the trip. This one did not respond to the radio either.

October 10 – Day 24 - If we were on a jet bound for Honolulu we would be about 40 minutes out and it would be time to fill out those little agriculture forms. We are still 3 days out.

Andy said at the start of the trip that we would keep the toilet shut off and we would use a bucket in the cockpit instead. That has been a challenge at times. As the boat rolls around, that bucket wants to slide, and anything perched on top of the bucket needs to move with it. Two arms are needed to brace during the whole affair. Therein lies the problem when it comes time to use the toilet paper. Please, no video cameras at this time.

I suppose that people may read this journal wonder what I have learned out here about the meaning of life. This has not been a journey that I have spent a great deal of time thinking about such philosophical issues. I know my religious beliefs are not exactly parallel to many of my friends and relatives. But I can say that in my mind, the true miracle is our birth, not our place in the universe after death. The fact that we exist as a thinking, functioning body, is beyond comprehension. We need to appreciate this gift of life and where we are at, as best we can. If we are in bad times, we can marvel at the feelings that accompany that, and work towards change. If we are in good times, we can marvel at those feelings, and try to enjoy them, because change will always come. The miracle is that we are here and we are capable of contemplating our existence.

October 11 - Day 25 - Another flying fish was on the deck this morning. About once every other day we find one on board. They are quite amazing fliers. I am sure I watched one fly at least 150 yards. The air temperature and water temperature are getting pretty warm. Most of the day is spent with just shorts on. Bathing would actually be enjoyable if it weren't being performed on a galloping boat. Try dumping a bucket of water over your head with your eyes closed while the boat is attempting to throw you overboard. We do this job on our knees and they get quite scraped during this type of activity when both hands are needed for the job.

We see a lot of jets at night now coming at us from Honolulu. I guess we must still be on course. We might even make it by tomorrow evening. Onions and cabbage are still good. We tried to have eggs for dinner last night but the yolks held together for only 3 of the remaining 18 eggs. Those 3 tasted okay though. One more night watch to stay awake for. Eating is the best anecdote against falling asleep on my watch. The best is the dried fish strips. I can bite off tiny little shreds and chew on them slowly and make the strip last a long time.

October 12 – Day 26 - Andy figured out a good way to keep himself awake on his watch last night. Remember those last 18 eggs? Well 3 of them were stuck to the carton so Andy left them in the carton and set the carton on the floor near the forepeak. Last night at about 4am he walked to the forepeak to get something. It was dark, and yup, he stepped on them. Rotten egg went squirting onto the wall, along the floorboards, and with the rolling of the boat, it managed to spread out quickly. He said it was a terrible bad smell and took him a long time to clean up. That sure did help him stay awake. Luckily I managed to sleep through it just 15 feet away. I had seen those eggs there in the carton on the floor and figured that was a dangerous set up, but I didn't want to question the captain.

It is noon, we are 35 miles out. We are sure now that we can see the mountains. We are almost there!

A navy ship passes by us. It is like the one Tamara (the daughter of my supervisor and friend, Bruce Conant) was on for a while, the one that goes real fast and has the big guns. A U.S. Coast Guard C130 flew out and back from shore at pretty low altitude. My guess is they are looking for a possible terrorist vessel which could threaten the navy ship.

At 5:30pm we sail gently into Kaneohe Bay on the northeast side of Oahu. The steep mountains form a green backdrop. Four radar domes are on our left, on what must be a military air base. Andy has brought the anchor up from down below. He reattaches it and we anchor close to a little marina called Hee'ia Kea.

We are at rest! We are at rest! We are at rest! The boat isn't heaving around anymore. I am still bracing myself but I don't need to. For the first time, I realize the deck of the boat slants a little bit outboard. With the constant motion of the boat for 26 days, I had no means to notice a slant to the deck. The spider has been missing for days, so I probably won't have to kill it.

We paddle the inflatable kayak to the marina to make phone calls to let Molly and Lisa know we have arrived. When I take my first steps on land, I find that my legs don't want to stay together. I can walk, but my legs stay spread apart. I am not staggering, but it might appear that way to an observer because my weight shifts awkwardly from one leg to the other. I keep telling my legs that they no longer need to steady me against a lurching deck.

The journey is over. It feels natural to be here. Unlike flying here and stepping off of a plane into a blast of heat and humidity, we came here so gradually that there is no shock. Land was supposed to be here and sure enough it was. I am glad we had no serious injuries or illness or storms or breakdowns. There were times when I was anxious, but not scared. There were times when I was bored from lack of activity or stimulus, but I never wished I wasn't there. It was the experience I was hoping for and I got it. Had I been travelling by kayak, I would only be about half way through the trip.

I had one more task. Andy and I were anchored on the north shore of Oahu at Kaneohe Bay. My daughter, Jennifer, was living in Honolulu and working as a software engineer. Lisa's grave site was twenty miles away, at the foot of Diamond Head crater. I rented a bicycle and Jennifer and I pedaled from Kaneohe Bay to Lisa's grave. This isn't the ending I had planned thirteen years earlier. I had planned to land my Tofino kayak on a sandy beach and walk to Diamond Head. It was meant to be the gesture that would truly let me move on and leave Lisa behind. I had fudged on my promise to do that. I now knew that this would have to suffice. I had followed through well enough to let that obligation go. It was over. I could live with myself.

200

Chapter 24 - The Hurricane
2008

Molly and I purchased a wonderful sailboat in 1997. We were walking the Juneau docks one day looking at boats and commenting on the features we liked. We were not thinking about purchasing a boat. That was, until we saw a sailboat named

"*SIERRA*" for sale. This boat was too ideal to pass up. We might never have another chance at a boat like this. It would give us the opportunity to sail, which was an aspect of kayaking we had grown to thoroughly love. The unique feature of this boat was that it had a large pilot house with 360 degrees of windows. No matter where we sat at the table, there was a view out the windows. It had an oil stove to keep the cabin warm and dry. We decided to buy it and for the last 20 years have never regretted that decision.

SIERRA has treated us with many adventures, but none as expansive as our trip across the southern coast of Alaska, from Juneau to Sand Point and return, a distance of 2,500 miles, round trip. We began the trip in late April of 2008. If one were to describe a theme for this coast, it would have to feature the massive mountains that rise precipitously from the water's edge and the many glaciers that spill from the mountains into the ocean. Two massive geological events have occurred on this coast in my lifetime.

We passed Mt. Fairweather during our first day on the open ocean. It rises to over 15,000 feet in a short distance of 12 miles from the coast. Near the base of Mt. Fairweather is Lituya Bay, recessed six miles into the mountains from the sea. As we passed, we could clearly see the telltale evidence of the largest known tsunami (wave) in recorded history, which occurred on July 9, 1958. Imagine, a 1700 foot tall wave obliterated the old growth forest on the north side of the bay to that elevation. The wave was the result of a large earthquake that triggered a 90 million ton rock slide on the opposite side of the bay. We could still see the scar on the side of the mountain.

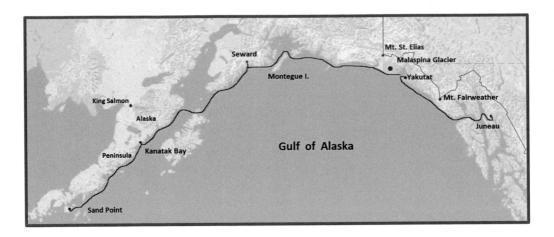

Our friends Connie and Peter met us in Yakutat for the leg to Seward. Soon we were passing the fourth highest peak in North America, Mt. St. Elias (18,000 feet). It is only 10 horizontal miles from salt water. The Malaspina Glacier showed us its rugged but low profile as it oozed towards the sea off of the right flank of Mt. St. Elias. This glacier, larger than the state of Rhode Island, had a forest of spruce and alder trees growing on it. As the glacier rubs the sides of mountains, it gathers sand and rocks on its surface. Over scores of years, vegetation begins to grow, leading to the creation of soil and eventually trees, some as high as 60 feet tall. In places, the ice underneath had broken apart or slid away, exposing the ice sheet under the forest. It was definitely strange to see a forest growing on ice.

Malaspina Glacier and its temporary forest. Photo by Ground Truth Trekking.

Our next amazing geological display was at Montague Island. On March 27, 1964 the second largest earthquake ever recorded in the world (magnitude 9.2) occurred not far north of Montague Island. The southwest end of the island was permanently uplifted 40 feet. All along the west side of Montague we could see the young vegetation where newly exposed land was sprouting trees.

For me, the climax of the sailing trip was reaching the Alaska Peninsula. During my pilot / biologist career, I had flown extensively throughout the Alaska Peninsula while conducting bald eagle surveys. I longed to experience this land intimately on the ground and in the beautiful bays and coves. The treeless expanses were abundant with wildlife. Hiking opportunities seemed endless. Viewing this tundra playground from the air had been tantalizing. There were caribou and brown bears to see, pristine streams and beaches to explore, and cozy harbors to anchor in.

On May 19, Molly and I and our friends John and Stephanie crossed Shelikof Strait from Afognak Island to the south side of the Alaska Peninsula, a 35 mile crossing, six hours for our boat. The high mountains on the far side of the strait were blanketed with pure white snow. The brilliant snow reached all the way to the shoreline, or so it seemed from our distance. I worried that the snow would interfere with our hiking plans. When we were half way across, we realized that the curvature of the earth had deceived us. The lower portion of the mountains, close to the beach were indeed snow free. The treeless landscape looked enticing and inviting.

No sooner had we reached the peninsula than we began to see brown bears and caribou. It was just as exciting as I had hoped it would be.

The author, Molly, John and Stephanie. Photo by Stephanie Hoag.

May 22 found us nearly a third of the way down the peninsula. I made my routine call for weather with my satellite phone and learned that a "gale" was approaching. We read in the *Coast Pilot* that the closest suitable anchorage to our position was Kanatak Bay. The bay was small, less than 2 miles in length and was protected from ocean swells at its mouth by a low elevation peninsula.

It felt good to be in there after passing through the narrow entrance. We anchored, and even went for a hike in the late afternoon before the gale was predicted to hit.

Shortly after returning to the boat at 5:00pm, the winds began to pick up considerably. I asked John to crank in the anchor. We would move to a position just behind the peninsula and anchor there, affording some protection from the wind and waves. We dropped the anchor and waited. The wind kept building in strength, probably up to around 40mph by 7:30pm. The anchor began to slip and drag across the bottom. I was disinclined to let out a lot of rope in an effort to help the anchor catch, knowing that if we continued to drag, it would be that much more difficult to retrieve the anchor. Our anchor winch was manual and very slow.

John cranks up the anchor in the storm before the hurricane hit.

I decided to raise the anchor and reset it. When John got the anchor up to the bow it was evident what the problem was. The anchor was totally fouled with huge kelp fronds. The anchor flukes had no chance to dig into mud or sand, or even wedge behind a rock. Kelp always grows on rock. As I contemplated anchoring again, the wind increased to at least 60 mph. I knew that we had very little chance of getting the anchor to hold in that wind, and if the wind continued to increase, working on deck would become not only difficult but could even be dangerous.

It was now 8:30pm. I decided our survival strategy would depend solely on our engine. I knew that if I put SIERRA into neutral, she would drift sideways to the wind, no matter how strong it became, especially if I turned the rudder into the wind. Broadside to the wind should be fine in this small bay and the hull and keel would slow our drift speed. I made a trial run. I drove the boat towards the peninsula at the mouth of the bay, the direction from which the wind bore down on us. As we approached the peninsula, the waves became smaller, although the surface of the water was in a frenzy from the wind. When the depth shallowed to less than 30 feet, I put the engine into neutral and turned SIERRA to the left so that the wind was hitting our starboard side. As we lost forward speed I turned the rudder hard over to the right, into the direction of the wind.

We waited to see how it would work. Sure enough, we stayed sideways to the wind. The boat heeled over exceedingly far from the wind clobbering the two masts, the house, and the hull. I told everyone not to worry about the boat blowing completely over, that we were a sailboat and it was designed to heal over sharply. We drifted for 8 minutes. Now we were farther from the protection of the peninsula and the waves were getting larger. I put the engine into gear to drive the boat back up to the lee side of the peninsula and started the drifting process all over again. This would be our strategy no matter how many hours it might take.

The wind continued to strengthen and gain power. As darkness approached, the wind reached a thunderous roar. By this time I believe the wind was easily over one hundred miles per hour. I have been in 90 mph winds twice while working aboard the M/V SURFBIRD and this wind seemed well in excess of that. I said to my shipmates, "If you are religious, this would be a good time to pray."

During the several minutes on each circuit when we were driving the boat towards the peninsula, the waves hit the side of the hull near the bow sending sheets of spray across the deck. It was only 15 feet from the bow to the wheelhouse, and yet in that short distance the spray was accelerated by the wind to such a speed that when it crashed into the cabin windows, I feared they might break.

I hoped upon hope that the mainsail and the missen sail would not blow loose from their ties and begin to flail in the hurricane. That would be total chaos and might even knock us over. I could not imagine how a person would be able to survive on deck if one of us had to leave the protection of the cabin. I don't believe it would have been possible. We were in a shell, battered mercilessly by wind and spray, but surviving as long as nothing went wrong – our engine kept running, the computer and GPS kept operating, the sails stayed secured, and the windows didn't blow out. This was no time for a fuel problem. That engine had to keep running. We got the survival suits out of storage and ready for use, and I reminded everyone where the Emergency Locater Beacon was mounted.

We began to relax a little bit because it appeared the strategy was working. Complete darkness would engulf us soon and we would no longer be able to see the peninsula and all navigation would be done using just the computer screen. I trained John on how to conduct the circuit. I knew it was going to be a long, difficult night for me. I wanted to try to get an hour of sleep before I took over for the night. In the fading light, John was able to handle the boat and I got 30 minutes of rest. Darkness fell. From my bunk I heard the engine surge and then idle back and then surge again. John was having trouble. He was reluctant to add as much power as I had instructed and thus the boat would not respond well in the maelstrom. On the computer screen he was heading in a different direction than he wanted to be heading. On top of that, the surface waves were creating a froth of air and water which made the depth sounder think we were in 2 feet of water and the shallow water alarm kept blaring. John was terrified, and he told me those words when I emerged from my bunk into the pilothouse. It was my turn already, and I knew I would be at the helm until daylight.

The closest town to us was King Salmon, 80 miles to the northwest. After the storm hit us, it had to pass over a mountain range before reaching King Salmon. Much of its power was diminished by the terrain, yet we found out later that King Salmon had experienced the highest two minute average wind ever recorded there, reaching 70 mph in spite of the degrading effects from the mountain range. The area where we were, Kanatak Bay and Wide Bay, is known by mariners and aviators of the Alaska Peninsula as having the most treacherous winds, much stronger than the neighboring coastline. This fits with my belief at the time that we were in winds well over 100 mph.

We were alone in the bay, facing a monster. I had recorded a track line on the computer during one of our early circuits. The track showed up on the computer map. Our current position was displayed with the symbol of a red cross. I could see when we had reached the end of our drift, the place where it was time to add power and drive back towards the small but wonderful peninsula that blocked what must be huge ocean swells on the other side.

Molly sat on the seat cushions behind me, propped up in the corner. She helped me stay awake. We both donned sleeping bags to give us warmth. The cabin was the coldest we had ever experienced, even though the trusty oil stove stayed lit. In the past, even when we had been in 50 knot winds with an outside temperature of 20 degrees, the cabin had never been this cold. Now the temperature was probably 35 degrees outside and 40 degrees inside.

The wind and pounding spray was unrelenting. The strategy continued to work. Our safety now depended on the computer and its GPS, the engine, the integrity of the boat, and the lashings holding the mainsail and missen sail in check – and Molly and I staying awake. The next six hours pitted my nerves and stamina against the onslaught. I wanted desperately to sleep. Each drifting session lasted eight minutes – a time to relax and know that the boat would handle itself. During these periods, I seemed to enter a dreamlike, semiconscious state. I was always fighting to keep deep sleep at bay, because if we drifted too far, we would run aground in the small bay. The night dragged on, minute by minute, circuit by circuit. It might have been monotonous had it not been so terrifying.

The darkness was black as ink, punctuated by the white spray flying at the windshield. Finally, a little after four in the morning a hint of light began to show behind the peninsula. Daylight was coming soon. If something had gone wrong at night and we were forced to put on survival suits, jump into the wind blown waves, and struggle to the safety of shore, the potential for loss of life would have been real. In daylight, abandoning ship would likely be survivable. Now I could have John take over driving the boat and I could try to get an hour or two of sleep. The winds had backed off a little bit.

By 8:00am we saw some breaks in the clouds. Everyone was tired of the repetitive circuits, surging forward and drifting back. We had been doing this for 12 hours. As the tide receded, I noticed something on the beach that was becoming exposed. It wasn't a rock, rather it was some sort of rusty manmade object. Each time I drove the boat towards the peninsula, the object showed more definition, becoming more exposed by the ebbing tide. Then I realized it was a large hydraulic winch with rusty cable wrapped on the drum. Almost certainly it was intentionally put there by someone that wanted to survive a storm. It would serve beautifully as an anchor. If we could tie a long line to it, we could finally rest.

The winds were not hurricane force any more, but still much too strong to attempt using my own anchor and risk getting it tangled in kelp again. I drove the boat as close to the winch as I dared, tantalized by its sheer weight and the security it could provide. The depth sounder showed just 5 feet of water under us and we were still 50 feet from the winch. I drifted back into deeper water. It seemed too risky to send John off in the rubber raft to try to row that distance.

I really liked the looks of that winch and badly wanted to tie to it. I knew John was ready to give it a try. He said emphatically, "I just want to stop moving."

I thought to myself, "What if I drive the boat up until it touches bottom?" We eased forward again, our bow into the wind. The rain had stopped, which made this operation seem more practical. John was in the raft ready to make a go for it. The boat slipped closer and closer to the winch until our bow was just 15 feet from it. We were lightly touching bottom. I told John to go for it. We had a line tied to him in case he couldn't get there. The three of us watched gratefully as he made it to shore and climbed out of the raft. I had 200 feet of gold line which was now pulled to shore by John. He tied his end to the rusty winch and returned to *SIERRA*. I eased the boat backwards off of the beach until the gold line stopped us. We were secure. The engine was shut down. Breakfast sounded good even though I was tired to the bone. Finally we were able to relax.

I wrote about our experience in the log book. I wrote that we had decided the name of this bay needed to be changed from Kanatak Bay to DidAttack Bay.

The little peninsula that saved us from the mighty Pacific Ocean during the hurricane.

Kanatak Bay. Note the winch near shore in the right foreground and *SIERRA* anchored to the left.

Two days later we spent a restful night in Agrapina Bay, 30 miles to the southwest. I was anchored at the head of the bay near the tidal flat. After breakfast, we were ready to move on, so I asked John to raise the anchor. When I saw the anchor come over the bow, I put *SIERRA* into gear and turned the wheel hard to starboard, knowing that shallow water was nearby. I noticed on the depth sounder that the bottom was coming up, but I wasn't too concerned since we were turning sharply towards deeper water and the bottom was mud anyway. Then I felt the boat slide onto the mud. This is the point at which my experience as a float plane pilot seriously interfered with my ability to be a good boat captain. When handling a float plane, I learned that floats will slide over mud. If I felt the plane slide onto mud, I gave the engine a big boost in power, sliding my plane across the mud. I could steer the plane into deep water again.

My pilot instincts kicked in and I quickly pushed the throttle forward to full power, certain SIERRA would slide across the mud back into deep water. But that didn't happen. She dug deep into the mud and became solidly stuck. I turned the engine off, not wanting to suck mud into the raw water intake. I knew I would not be able to back her off. The tide was half way through the ebb. The tide would drop another six feet, and we drew five and a half feet. *SIERRA* was going to lie on her side, something I had no experience with. The outcome was unknown. I had to inform my shipmates of my mistake. We had slid to a halt so smoothly that they did not even know we were aground. They wanted to know what was going to happen and what we should do.

I told them to start taping all of the openings – all of the air vents, the fuel tank vent, the hatch, the door and the stove pipe. We put the boom over to the starboard side, the side I wanted her to lean to, so that the engine exhaust pipe would not be under water. In twenty minutes she was already starting to list. We brought the raft alongside and put the gun in it along with survival gear – including our satellite phone. We got the survival suits out for the second time in two days and put them on deck. I closed the through-hull valves; one for the engine, two for the sinks and one for the toilet outlet. I found my reserve bilge pump which I kept for just such an emergency. Long wires connected the pump to a cigarette lighter plug, so the pump could be used anywhere in the boat. A long discharge hose would allow me to stick the hose out of any available window. If she started to take on a significant amount of water before she righted, I could use the pump to transfer water out of the boat.

She began to list heavily.

It was no easy task climbing out of the uphill side door with the boat at such an angle. It was somewhat like climbing out of a hole in the ceiling. The clinometer indicated she stopped listing at an angle of 44 degrees.

Photo by John Staub.

It was cold perched on deck for six hours in a light drizzle and 10 mph breeze. We watched with apprehension as the tide worked its way back up the hull. I worried that the side door would be partially under water before she started to right. We had taped all around the door to slow the influx of water if it got that high. When the incoming tide was just 4 inches below the bottom of the door, *SIERRA* started to right. It was a great relief. We were going to survive our second disaster in two days. The captain had saved the crew from the hurricane only to put them into another jeopardy. I was happy that nothing was damaged. We were on our way.

Chapter 25 - Fortuitous Life

Throughout our lives we each have good luck and bad luck. Is it fate? The poem *Desiderata* says "whether or not it is clear to you, no doubt the universe is unfolding as it should."

We had good luck on our long sailboat trip. Our engine could have failed during the hurricane, because shortly after our return to Juneau, *Sierra's* engine suffered a complete breakdown. Also, I discovered that the steering could have failed us at any time. The hydraulic cylinder that moves the rudder was shabbily mounted to a little piece of plywood, which had become very rotten in the moist environment of the stern. We would have been helpless without steering.

During my career, I was amazingly fortunate. Not only did I live and work in a world class marine wonderland, with its 15,000 miles of wilderness shoreline, I had a 65 foot vessel with which to travel and work from. We were managing the bald eagle population and their nests. We saved tens of thousands of acres of prime wildlife habitat from a fate of clearcutting. To those that care about pristine expanses, it was tax payer money well spent. We sent eagles to the lower forty eight states to help them recover from endangered species status.

Then, how fortuitous for me to be in the right place and the right time to pilot the best wildlife survey aircraft in the world for 24 years. And to take that plane to Siberia six times. I am proud that I never injured an airplane or an occupant. But I must recognize the helpful role that good luck played in that outcome. I didn't make all the right decisions and I was not totally immune to the pressures of getting the job done or getting home. Through my career, I helped in a significant way to collect valuable data on wildlife populations. Those data sets will always be available to educate mankind about the abundance and distribution of fauna in Alaska and Siberia before the onslaught of global warming. We didn't know what threats would dominate the future of the northlands, not even global warming, but we knew threats would come. The value of our baseline data will only increase through time.

As Lisa's life ended in a fateful crash, mine took a sharp deviation in course. I spent countless hours trying to figure out the meaning of life. My own mortality was brought into much clearer focus. It has been said that we have a difficult time comprehending our own death, our own end of life. This is true, but the process of trying to comprehend our non-existence does help bring urgency to appreciate each day. I decided I would try to make a small mark on the universe, to notch a small accomplishment for mankind. Now, when I see a globe of our earth in a library or in a museum, I like to look at the waterway from Seattle to Juneau, measure it between my index finger and my thumb, and say to myself, "I pedaled across that segment of earth using my own power."

Change will always occur, some good and some bad. It is our ability to adapt to those changes that allows us to navigate through life. Some call it accepting change. I prefer the notion of adapting to change. Adapting implies an active response, while accepting implies a passive response.

We live in a great period of human history. Medicine has given us much longer and healthier lives. Our earth is still vibrant and supportive of life. But our global habitat is changing rapidly, so I hope humans can adapt soon and have the self-control it will take to reverse the course of environmental degradation.

As I age, I find that I must adapt to my changing body. I have three artificial joints, which are fantastic gifts. But there are still the other 357 joints to deal with. My muscle strength has waned greatly. I never had a good memory, so that transition should be relatively seamless. Most of the hair on top of my head has disappeared, but interestingly enough, hair is erupting in other areas. My five year old granddaughter unwittingly has helped me adapt. She was sitting on my lap, looking up at me and said, "Grandpa, what's that beard?" Not knowing why she was asking, I stroked my beard and said, "Yes, grandpa has a beard." To which she replied, "No, the one in your nose."

My grandchildren will soon be hiking, boating, fishing and hunting with me. I hope that Alaska gives them an appreciation for the world we share with all of the other creatures and plants. They love the dried salmon I make for them. Their parents tell me that when all else fails, the dried salmon always works. It saves them on long airplane trips and long car trips and other meltdown scenarios. This makes me feel good. I tell Molly I need to catch ever more salmon to keep my grandchildren healthy.

Our house overlooks the Gastineau Channel, just west of the city of Juneau. Every day during the summer months I see the flight-seeing airplanes circle over the channel in preparation for landing near the tour ships to pick up a fresh batch of eager sightseers. The planes are de Havilland Otters that have been retrofitted with the same engine we had in N754, the Garrett TPE331. We began using that engine 40 years before they did. I hear that familiar sound, the steady hum-whine, and my attention is drawn to them. I smile to myself. For the moment, I am not retired, and the endless tundra is sliding under me again.

Appendix I - Example of Russian Authorizations

ГЕНЕРАЛЬНЫЙ ШТАБ
ВООРУЖЕННЫХ СИЛ
РОССИЙСКОЙ ФЕДЕРАЦИИ

24 " апреля 1993 г.
№ 312/5/137

ДИРЕКТОРУ ИНСТИТУТА ЭВОЛЮЦИОННОЙ
МОРФОЛОГИИ И ЭКОЛОГИИ ЖИВОТНЫХ
В.Е.Соколову

117071, Москва, Ленинский пр.,33
На № 4502/127 от 8.4.93 г.

Копия: НАЧАЛЬНИКУ ГЛАВНОГО ШТАБА ВВС
НАЧАЛЬНИКУ ГЛАВНОГО ШТАБА ВОЙСК ПВО
ГЕНЕРАЛЬНОМУ ДИРЕКТОРУ ЦДУ ГА"АЭРОТРАНС"
125836 Москва, Ленинградский пр.,37

    Генеральный штаб не имеет возражений относительно продолжения в июне-июле 1993 г. совместно с американской стороной исследовательских работ с целью оценки окружающей среды на Чукотском полуострове с использованием американского самолета ДНС-21, полеты которого будут производиться по маршруту: Ном, Провидения, Анадырь, Эгвекинот, мыс Шмидта, Певек, Черский, Марково, Анадырь, Провидения, Ном с посадками на аэродромах Провидения, Анадырь, мыс Шмидта, Певек, Черский и Марково.

    Вместе с тем, необходимо, чтобы запрос на выполнение полетов указанного самолета был произведен американской стороной установленным порядком, а вопрос обслуживания и обеспечения самолета и экипажа на аэродромах посадки был согласован Вами с органами гражданской авиации.

ЗАМЕСТИТЕЛЬ НАЧАЛЬНИКА ГЕНЕРАЛЬНОГО ШТАБА
генерал-полковник

В.Барынькин

Translation: Ministry of Defense letter to Air Force and Air Defense Department, Academy of Science and Aeroflot that they have no objection for flights in 1993.

General Staff
of the Armed Forces
of the Russian Federation

24 April 1993
#312/5/137

To the Director of the Institute of Evolutionary Morphology and Animal Ecology
V.E. Sokolov

117071 Moscow Leninsky pr. 33

Re: #4502/127 from 8 April 1993

CC: Chief of the General Staff of the Air Force
Chief of the General Staff of the Air Defense Forces
General Manager of the CDOS CA "Aerotrans"
125836 Moscow Leningradsky pr. 37

The General Staff has no objections to continuing the research aiming at environmental assessment of the Chukotka peninsula together with the American side using the American airplane ДHC-21 (DNS-21) in June-July 1993, with the flights on the route: Nome, Provideniya, Anadyr, Egvekinot, Cape Schmidt, Pevek, Cherskiy, Markovo, Anadyr, Provideniya, Nome, with landings at Provideniya, Anadyr, Cape Schmidt, Pevek, Cherskiy and Markovo aerodromes.

At the same time, it is necessary that the request for the flights of the above mentioned airplane will be made by the American side according to the established order, and the question of maintenance and service for the airplane and the crew on the aerodromes of landing will be agreed on by you with the civil aviation authorities.

Deputy Chief of the General Staff of the Armed Forces
general-colonel

V. Barynkin

Appendix II - Scientific Publications by the author

Cain SL, Hodges JI. 1989. A floating-fish snare for capturing Bald Eagles. Journal of Raptor Research 23(1):10-13.

Eldridge WD, Hodges JI, Syroechkovsky EV, Kretchmar EA. 1993. The Russian-American aerial waterfowl surveys in the North-Eastern Asia in 1992. Russian Journal of Ornithology 2(4): 457-460..

Hodges JI, King JG. 1979. Resurvey of the bald eagle breeding population in southeast Alaska. J. of Wildlife Management 43: 219-221.

Hodges JI. 1982. Bald eagle nesting studies in Seymour Canal, southeast Alaska. The Condor 84(1): 125-127

Hodges JI, King JG, Davies R. 1984. Bald eagle breeding population survey of coastal British Columbia. J. Wildlife Management 48: 993-998.

Hodges JI, Boeker EL, Hansen AJ. 1987. Movements of radio-tagged Bald Eagles, *Haliaeetus Leucocephalus*, in and from Southeastern Alaska. Canadian Field Naturalist 101(2): 136-140.

Hodges JI. 1993. Count – A simulation for learning to estimate wildlife numbers. Wildlife Society Bulletin 21(1): 96-97.

Hodges JI, King JG, Conant B, Hanson HA. 1996. Aerial surveys of waterbirds in Alaska 1957-94: population trends and observer variability. In: Hager M.C., McGrath D.S., technical editors. National Biological Service Information and Technical Report 4. 24p.

Hodges JI, Eldridge WD. 2001. Aerial surveys of eiders and other waterbirds on the eastern Arctic coast of Russia. Wildfowl 52: 127-142.

Hodges JI. 2004. Survey techniques for bald eagles in Alaska. In: Wright BA, Schempf PF, editors Bald Eagles in Alaska. Proceedings of a symposium Nov. 1990; Juneau, AK. Univ. of Alaska Southeast and Bald Eagle Research Institute. 245 – 250.

Hodges JI, Groves DJ, Conant BP. 2008. Distribution and abundance of waterbirds near shore in Southeast Alaska, 1997-2002. Northwestern Naturalist 89(2): 85-96.

Hodges JI. 2010. Bald eagle population surveys of the North Pacific Ocean, 1967-2010. Northwestern Naturalist 92: 7-12.

Hodges JI, Kirchhoff MD. 2012. Kittlitz's Murrelet *Brachyramphus brevirostris* population trend in Prince William Sound, Alaska: implications of species misidentification. Marine Ornithology 40: 117–120.

Jacobson MJ, Hodges JI. 1999. Population trend of adult bald eagles in southeast Alaska, 1967-97. J. Raptor Research 33: 295-298.

Kirchhoff MD, Lindell JR, Hodges JI. 2014. From critically endangered to least concern? – A revised population trend for the Kittlittz's Murrelet in Glacier Bay, Alaska. The Condor 116(1): 24-34.

Made in the USA
San Bernardino, CA
23 January 2018